Philosophy
and the
Passions

Literature and Philosophy

A. J. Cascardi, General Editor

This series publishes books in a wide range of subjects in philosophy and literature, including studies of the social and historical issues that relate these two fields. Drawing on the resources of the Anglo-American and Continental traditions, the series is open to philosophically informed scholarship covering the entire range of contemporary critical thought.

Already published:

Philosophy

and the

Passions

Toward a History *of* Human Nature

by Michel Meyer,
Université libre de Bruxelles

Translation, Preface, Introduction, and Bibliography
by Robert F. Barsky

The Pennsylvania State University Press
University Park, Pennsylvania

Cet ouvrage publié dans le cadre du programme d'aide à la publication
bénéficie du soutien du Ministère des Affaires Etrangères et du Service
Culturel de l'Ambassade de France représenté aux Etats-Unis.

This work, published as part of the program of aid for publication,
received support from the French Ministry of Foreign Affairs and the
Cultural Service of the French Embassy in the United States.

This book is a translation from the French edition, *Le Philosophe et les
passions: Esquisse d'une histoire de la nature humaine* (Paris: Hachette,
Librarie Générale Française, Livre de Poche, Biblio Essais, 1991).

Library of Congress Cataloging-in-Publication Data

Meyer, Michel
    [Le Philosophe et les passions. English]
    Philosophy and the Passions : toward a history of human nature / Michel
Meyer ; translation, preface, introduction, and bibliography by Robert F. Barsky.
       p.   cm.—(Literature and philosophy)
    Includes bibliographical references and index.
    ISBN 0-271-02031-8 (cloth : alk. paper)
    ISBN 0-271-02032-6 (pbk. : alk. paper)
    1. Emotions (Philosophy)
    I. Barsky, Robert F.   II. Title.   III. Series.

B105.E46 M4813 2000
128'.37   99–047157

Contents

Translator's Preface

I started this project in 1995 while still a fellow at the European Institute for the Study of Argumentation, Free University of Brussels, under the tutelage of Michel Meyer. I have worked sporadically on it since then, but it was on account of the encouragement and the support of Michel Meyer himself, and Sanford Thatcher, of Penn State Press, that it now stands before you.

One of the difficulties of translating a book like this is its sheer length; each page of the compact Livre de poche edition seemed to store an endless amount of clearly rendered, but quite complex philosophical ideas. I have made a faithful translation of the original, but I have also tried to make this book suitable for an American audience by changing some of the examples, smoothing out some of the stylistically exciting, but sometimes untranslatable French prose, and in certain cases, offering interpretations of problematic passages.

The reason for my having inserted a dose of interpretation into the task of translation relates to the French context for which the original text was written, an issue that is of great significance for readers who are sensitive to the strange (mis)appropriations that have been made of (sometimes dubious) translations of French philosophers or theorists who have been so significant for the American literary, philosophical, and cultural scene, notably Baudrillard, Cixous, Derrida, Deleuze, Foucault, Guattari, Kristeva, and Lyotard (this is in fact one small part of the problem brought to the fore by Sokal's Hoax).[1] Meyer's text is much closer to traditional philosophy, both in style and in influence, so it poses no significant problems in this regard; nevertheless, it does read as though it was written for some audience other than an American academic one. This fact came through clearly in the assessment by one of the project's

---

1. See *Impostures intellectuelles,* and the many debates (described in Barsky, "Intellectuals on the Couch") that have raged subsequent to the publication of Alain Sokal's hoax in the journal *Social Text.*

original reviewers, who wondered if in my earlier translation I wasn't "perhaps trying too hard to be faithful to the flavor of the original, which has a certain French arrogance and off-handedness about it that might not come across too well to an American audience." This "flavor" is indeed present in the French text, although the exact qualities to which this reviewer is referring would be hard to pinpoint. Furthermore, many issues which appear at the very center of postmodern texts, such as those relating to the "situatedness" of the author, the status of the "subject," the slippery signifier, the complex sign / signified relationship, and the like, aren't at issue here. Ideas are presented, clearly and convincingly, and historical texts are mentioned and interpreted specifically as regards the central discussions of this book. Implicit, and sometimes explicit, however, is Meyer's condemnation of sloppy philosophical reasoning which is rampant, partly on account of what he takes to be the oft-misguided task that philosophers have set for themselves, and partly, perhaps, on account of their avoidance of the domain of "questioning." More on this in the introduction.

The reviewer may also have had some difficulties with the examples given in the text, which often place men in the forefront of significant actions described. I would think about this problem as I'd work through the translation, or as I'd place my coffee cup down on the "Jupiler" Beer coaster I brought from Brussels when I moved back to North America which bears the slogan: "Mannen weten warrom": "Les hommes savent pourquoi." The book, like the coaster, needs a little bit of cultural translation to ensure that the audience focuses on the broader questions relating to passion, rather than the problem of gender discrimination (although given the ambition of Meyer's project many of his ideas could be fruitfully used for work in this and many other domains). I will offer a brief overview of these questions, and I'll also offer some general observations about Michel Meyer's broad corpus of work, in the introduction that follows.

I would like to thank Michel Meyer, who proposed and then followed this project to the very end, and who has consistently supported my work while making invaluable suggestions about the translation. François Laville, whom I've never met but for whom I have the greatest respect, went through the entire translation and checked it against the original; I am very grateful indeed for the many suggestions and corrections he made. Ramen Gakhal, Katie McInnis, and Nancy Ray were financed by our wonderful University of Western Ontario work study program to track down translations and to trace texts relating to the introduction. I am also grateful to Penn State Press's copy editor, Andrew

Lewis, for his careful, meticulous work. Ray Dearin, who has written the biographical chapter for a forthcoming book (with Alan Gross) on Chaim Perelman, has generously offered invaluable information for the introduction, as have two of Perelman's former students, my teacher Marc Angenot and my colleague Alain Goldschläger. Michael Holquist has given me the welcome occasion of spending a semester as a Visiting Fellow at Yale University, which has allowed for passions and dialogue appropriate to the completion of this project.

Funding for this project was provided by Les Fonds national de la Belgique, the Social Sciences and Humanities Research Council of Canada, the French Consulate in Washington, D.C., the University of Western Ontario, and Penn State Press. I wish to thank Yzabelle Martineau, and I passionately dedicate this translation to my sons, Benjamin and Tristan, who have put up with and responded to my interminable questions, while creating the pleasures of a bilingual household.

Robert F. Barsky
Brussels, Montreal, London (Ontario), New Haven (Connecticut),
1995–2000

Translator's Introduction

L'Institut de Philosophie, the Centre de Philosophie du Droit, and the European Institute for the Study of Argumentation (EISA) are housed in an old, rather Gothic-looking building located at 143 Buyl Street, Brussels. Although situated beside the campus of the Université libre de Bruxelles (ULB, the Free University of Brussels), of which it is part, this edifice stands strangely alone, several hundred meters from another building, right on campus, which houses the rest of the philosophy department.

Inside one can often find Michel Meyer, editor of the *Revue internationale de philosophie*, founder of the journal *Argumentation*, director of the *Institut de Philosophie* as well as the EISA, and the scholar who succeeded Chaim Perelman in the role of Professor of Philosophy and Rhetoric subsequent to the latter's death in 1984. Meyer is a well-known figure in European philosophical circles and is in fact one of the most famous and significant of contemporary philosophers; nevertheless, and despite the fact that a range of his work is available in English, Meyer remains little known to the English-speaking world outside certain philosophical circles. This is unfortunate given current debates within the domain of philosophy, and surprising given the breadth of his project, which touches on a range of fields including philosophy, history, rhetoric, law, and literature.[1] The purpose of this introduction is to offer a general introduction to the context from which Meyer arises and to which he contributes, a sense of his overriding hypotheses, an overview of his approach to the domain of literature and philosophy, and a sense of the legacy he inherited from the venerable Chaim Perelman.

---

1. The other candidate I would propose is Marc Angenot, who like Meyer, was a student of Chaim Perelman at ULB, in Brussels. To this end, see the volume of essays and translations I have edited for the journal *SubStance,* no. 92 (Fall 2000).

Perelman's Legacy

Michel Meyer had large shoes to fill when he assumed the role of Perelman's disciple-turned-inheritor, on account of the latter's intellectual legacy, and also because of his great personal achievements, which have led to his being considered one of this century's great humanists. It's worth pausing for a moment to consider this relationship, especially in Europe where inheriting the Chair occupied by one's mentor carries a deep significance, and suggests a certain heritage that must be taken into account in later work.

Born in 1912 in Warsaw, Perelman first studied rhetoric in gymnasium, where he developed an interest in the formal study of the law, which he pursued at the Université libre de Bruxelles in 1944.[2] He wrote his dissertation on the work of the logician Gottlob Frege, who was interested in the analysis of the reasoning of mathematics. His legal background led to some of the work for which he is best known, notably his studies of formal justice, the idea that beings of one and the same essential category must be treated in the same way, of practical reasoning, and, of course, the *new rhetoric*.[3] The latter work grew out of his and L. Olbrechts-Tyteca's interest in informal reasoning and the ways that different authors use arguments to reason about values. This led them to Aristotle's work on analytical reasoning (which focuses on syllogisms and other modes of deductive reasoning) found in the first and second *Analytics,* and moreover, to the neglected area of *dialectical reasoning,* described in *Rhetoric,* the *Topics,* and *Sophistical Refutations.* Here Aristotle departed from Socrates "by suggesting that dialectical reasoning is concerned with opinions." This is a significant departure, says Perelman, because "dialectical reasoning, from Aristotle's frame of reference, had as its primary goal to defend your opinions, to attack the opinions of others, and to persuade an audience. Arguments constituted the core of his theory of dialectic. Topics are developed through reason or logos." And in his *Rhetoric,* he affirmed the idea that a speaker may impose his own authority (ethos) or arouse the emotions of the audience (pathos). But he is quick to point out in his *Topics* and in the *Rhetoric* that "dialectical reasoning is a justifiable means of persuasion."[4] This rediscovery of a

2. See Perelman's "Address Delivered at Ohio State University, November 16, 1982," in *Practical Reasoning in Human Affairs: Studies in Honor of Chaim Perelman,* edited by James L. Golden and Joseph Pilotta (Dordrecht: D. Reidel, 1986).

3. See Chaim Perelman and L. Olbrechts-Tyteca, *The New Rhetoric: A Treatise on Argumentation,* trans. John Wilkinson and Purcell Weaver (Notre Dame, Ind.: University of Notre Dame Press, 1969).

4. Perelman, "Address," p. 6.

whole neglected area of study, originally elaborated during the era of classical Greece, is not unlike what we find in Meyer's work, as we'll see further on. But it's not only the scope of Perelman's project, and the institutions that he founded, that stand as backdrops to Meyer's work. There was as well the mythical personal attributes of Chaim Perelman, who was known for his great humanist achievements within and beyond the ivory tower.[5]

Chaim Perelman, honored laureate of the International Academy of Humanism, is said to have changed his first name to Chaim from Charles or Henri in a period when being a Jewish intellectual could be fatal. Indeed, it was suggested to me during my stay in Brussels that Perelman made this change in 1940, to irk the Nazis during World War II, to call attention to his Jewishness, and to demonstrate his fearlessness in the face of oppression. The idea was that Chaim, unlike, say, David or Sydney, was as in-your-face a Jewish name as Perelman could find. At first glance this seems unlikely, given that although his first *essai, De la Justice,* appeared in 1945, all of his publications, including the ones he wrote as an undergraduate student at the Free University of Brussels (the first when he was nineteen years old, in 1931) are published either as "Ch." or as "Chaim" Perelman. Moreover, Ray Dearin has reported to me that all of the memoirs he has seen from the Belgian resistance members refer to him as either Chaim or his nom de guerre "Dumont," never Henri or, for that matter, Charles.

The second possibility is recorded in an interview between David Frank and Perelman's daughter Noemi, who apparently reported that Chaim's given name was Henri, but after the war he adopted the name Chaim to honor Chaim Weizman, the first president of Israel. According to Dearin, the latter part of this account is verified by Mieczyslaw Maneli, a close friend of Perelman's; again, however, Perelman was signing his articles "Chaim" long before the birth of the Jewish state, which perhaps means that he had already signed works with his Jewish name, and now in honor of the newly founded Israel would use it permanently. One way or another, he most certainly was known as Charles to many persons, even if one of his other given names was Henri. I recount this not to recall oft-contradictory rumors, but simply to call attention to a small example of the stories, true and untrue, that circulate around the figure of Perelman and which make up the legacy Meyer inherited.

5. I owe a special debt of thanks to the generous and forthcoming Ray Dearin, to Marc Angenot, who taught me about Meyer and Perelman long before I'd ever heard their names, and to Alain Goldschläger, who provided me valuable information about the Université libre de Bruxelles, and about the Belgian resistance.

Another example: I learned in Brussels that Chaim Perelman registered Jewish students in Catholic schools to save them from the Nazis (who, incidentally, had tremendous co-operation from the Belgians, notably the Flemish Belgians, who proved to be remarkably obedient to the orders to round up Jews). Dearin offers a similar version, confirming that Chaim Perelman's wife ran a school for Jewish children and looked for safe homes, generally Catholic homes, in which to hide them, and that Chaim participated in this effort (which apparently led to the saving of several thousand Jewish children). Indeed, many professors and administrators at the Free University of Brussels were part of "Perelman's List," saved from certain death by the Perelmans and other members of the Belgian resistance. In short, it's not clear what precise role Perelman played in these events, or how his given name played into his overall objectives in this period, but what is not in doubt is that Chaim Perelman, along with his wife Fela, were active members of the resistance movement, and that Chaim continued his humanist work after the defeat of the Nazis in 1945.

The fact that Perelman first worked on issues of justice while living in a context of Nazi occupation must have played a significant role in forming his approach, which is on the one hand deeply rooted in traditional rhetoric, logic, and philosophy, and on the other, very much applicable to contemporary issues of justice. As Perelman himself stated: "It is instructive to observe here that during the German occupation and at the end of the war, I had to stay home for good reasons. At this juncture, I decided to write a book on justice,"[6] which lead to the essay "De la justice" (1946) and the book *Logique Juridique* (1976).[7] Ray Dearin comments on Perelman's decision, and on Einstein's 1940 reiteration of "one of the cardinal tenets of the wisdom received from rationalism and positivism," that it was futile to argue about ultimate values:

> Four years later, when all Europe groaned under the weight of such ideas as they had been effectively translated into public policies, it was time to form an underground resistance in the name of other—more humane—values, and to wait for civilisation to marshal its own counterattack in defence of these values. It was time also, thought Chaim Perelman, to re-examine a

6. Perelman, "Address," p. 3.
7. The reader is referred to *Logique Juridique,* 2d ed. (Paris: Dalloz, 1979). "De la Justice" can be found in *Justice et Raison,* 2d ed. (Brussels: Editions de l'ULB, 1972). For Perelman's earlier work on related issues, see *Traité de l'Argumentation,* 4th ed. (Brussels: Editions de L'ULB, 1983).

concept that epitomised the confusion surrounding the problem of finding rationality in a world gone berserk—the concept of *justice*.... He therefore undertook to discover whether or not an analysis of an enigmatic value like justice could yield a rational basis of making value judgements, as well as whether any incidental light could be cast on the enterprise of philosophical reasoning.[8]

Chaim Perelman has come to be well known for this work on justice, rhetoric, and argumentation. Founder of the so-called new rhetoric, which, adopted from the tradition of the classical rhetoricians such as Demosthenes, Thucydides, and Pericles, has provided the tools to encourage contemporary jurists to reflect on their work while also providing the basis for philosophical reflections about law. His sense was that rhetoric needed to be rethought because it had become the study of style at the expense of significant issues of rationality, and he found in Aristotle's three oratorical forms, the forensic, the deliberative, and the epideictic, a way of advancing his own approach. He felt that a theory of argumentation was needed that would allow values to be assessed in a rational manner, as is generally the case for the assessment of facts and policies. Indeed, Perelman's concern for rationality is a relevant background for the present text, since it speaks to the relationship, discussed at length by Meyer, between reason and the passions: "If the application of means to ends is the sole object of rational investigation and the ends themselves are the results of irrational choices, which reasoning does not allow us to decide, then our highly qualitative technological civilization will be put in the service of irrationally uncontrollable passions, desires, and aspirations."[9]

Perelman's work on argumentation involved the study of how ideas are received, which led him to suggest that the "idea of the audience" of traditional rhetoric (ibid., 6) must be considered when assessing the success of a given demonstration, an idea which flew in the face of the largely accepted premise that demonstrations are assumed to be true or false regardless of whether an audience agrees with them. In other words, according to Perelman, speaker and audience had to share a frame of reference. He studied the nature of the audience, particular or universal, and drew up some postulations about how to open an

8. Ray D. Dearin, "Justice and Justification," in Golden and Pilotta, *Practical Reasoning in Human Affairs*, p. 156.

9. Chaim Perelman, *Justice, Law and Argument: Essays on Moral and Legal Reasoning*, introduction by Harold J. Berman (Dordrecht: D. Reidel, 1980).

argument before different types of audiences. Then, of course, he discusses the techniques of argumentation employed by the speaker, of
which he isolated quasi-logical arguments, the arguments based on the
structure of reality, and arguments establishing the structure of reality.
So for Perelman, the speaker presents to a specific audience and must
therefore rely on practical reasoning and persuasion. Traces of this
approach to rhetoric, and of Perelman's work on the Cartesian theory of
knowledge, are present in Meyer's work through the link between problematology, questioning, and rhetoric that he establishes with reference
to the current crisis in philosophy.

> The old models of thought, the old values have given way to the
> conceptualisation of their own collapse. They have been radi-
> cally problematized and this in itself was supposed to be a suffi-
> cient solution, at least for nihilism. In all cases that we have
> considered, what is problematic is seen as something negative,
> to be dissolved if it cannot be solved; and this is true for logical
> empiricism as well. Problematicity is associated with the crisis,
> with a rupture and a fragmentation of what has constituted a
> whole previously. In this historical context, rhetoric has re-
> emerged. When values are controversial, and experienced as
> such, it cannot be otherwise. This only proves that rhetoric is the
> adequate method for treating what is problematic. Rhetoric has
> an intrinsic relation with questioning, a relation that has never
> been fully perceived in all its consequences; and we shall have
> to ask ourselves why it has been the case.[10]

This leads us directly from Perelman, and the studies that have followed
his revival of rhetoric, into the project that Meyer has carried forth in his
own work, which tackles the issue of how questioning has been "dis-
graced," and why even in Perelman's work, it is "a mere subsidiary and
limited technique."[11]

Meyer's Problematological Projects

Meyer is best known for this work on *problematology,* the study of
questioning, and for his study of the passions. His work in the domain

---

10. Michel Meyer, "Problematicity and Rhetoric," in Golden and Pilotta, *Practical Reasoning
and Human Affairs,* p. 130.
   11. Ibid., p. 134.

of problematology, fully articulated in his book *Of Problematology*,[12] is, like his work on rhetoric and the passions, well known in France, where he is published in very popular Livre de Poche editions, which generally run to tens of thousands of copies each. Meyer proposes by this problematological approach literally to re-view the tradition of radical questioning, which dates back to the earliest philosophical texts but which has, for some reason, disappeared, with the consequence that "philosophical attention has been directed to language and discourse" (1).

In Meyer's opinion, the effect of this neglect of questioning by philosophers has been grave, as is clear from certain postmodern philosophical work: "In so changing, philosophy has ended up renouncing itself, so to speak, in favor of superficial topics, exhibiting a lack of rigor which has made possible the most esoteric word games" (2). Meyer's work is all the more viable right now on account of the current debates, which suggest that philosophy lacks not only a central set of texts, but is even in search of some stable common ground for debate and discovery. This philosophical fragmentation, which Meyer calls a "contradiction in terms," and the fact that Meyer's work speaks strongly toward current issues in the "basics"—history, reading, writing, and rhetoric—means that he may very well be the emerging figure for a new approach to American philosophy.

All of Meyer's writings have strong historical biases, which makes them useful for those interested in situating issues in question within an appropriate philosophical tradition. As such, problematology is described in terms of the history of questioning and problematizing, although for Meyer the originality of the problematological approach is a consequence of the fact that the Greeks weren't able to "conceive of" questioning. Meyer also holds that the present status of philosophy is a product of the fact that radical questioning, like our innermost passions, has been repressed, which he considers an attack upon the very force of philosophical work, and upon fundamental human tendencies as well. Meyer described this paradox as follows: "A swift survey of history should suffice to convince us that questioning has never been the central theme of philosophy. Yet philosophy would never have developed nor been able to survive without resorting to questioning in practice. This is how questioning, by failing to thematize itself, was displaced and directed towards objectives outside itself" (6).

This is a very radical proposal, for it demands that we cast a new look

12. *Of Problematology: Philosophy, Science and Language,* trans. David Jamison, with the collaboration of Alan Hart (Chicago: University of Chicago Press, 1995).

on the history of philosophical practices, and that we consider the debil-
itating effect that the autonomization of answers as propositions has
had, notably, the subordination of the idea of resolution to what Meyer
calls the *propositional model* of reason, which Meyer considers a
"betrayal" of philosophy. Meyer's work is an ambitious project that
emerges in the face of this "betrayal," and it responds to "the need to
restore to [philosophy] a principle and remove its ontologization, realizing that its deepest reality is not only in questioning, but in *radical*
questioning, if we want it not to be altered into some kind of occult
answer" (9). David Jamison, who has done more than anyone to help
bring Meyer's work to the Anglo-American world, through his translation
(with Alan Hart) of *Of Problematology,* and his articles (with James
Golden) in *La Revue internationale de la philosophie,* and *Questioning
Exchange,* gives some indication of how this project looks:

> Meyer has constructed a theory of problematology which
> focuses on the interrogativity of the mind. His abiding concern
> in all his major writings with the phenomenon of questioning is
> consistent, he feels, with the developing interest in this subject
> by students of logic, philosophy, psychology and anthropology.
> With some of these scholars he has come to believe that ques-
> tioning is "the fundamental reality of the human mind, to which
> all other intellectual powers are connected." It is, in short, "the
> basic principle of thought itself, the philosophical project *par
> excellence.*"[13]

The work that remains to be done is, according to Meyer, vast, and this
is because the philosophical project has been inappropriately cast for
thousands of years, because "by constantly posing questions in a non-
problematological way, philosophy has not questioned questioning, but
has instead turned elsewhere, placing itself in competition with science,
which, by the way, it has nonetheless made possible" (12). His solution is
dramatic; he calls for a return to the idea, begun but not pursued since
Socrates and Plato, that interrogativity is the highest value of thought
(indeed, say Golden and Jamison, in "Meyer's Theory of Problematology,"
Meyer believes that in the dialogues, Plato "gradually but perceptibly
moved toward the belief that questions held a subordinate position to

---

13. James L. Golden and David L. Jamison, "Meyer's Theory of Problematology," *Questioning
Exchange* 2 (1988): 149.

that of answers" [151]). To prove such a thing, Meyer must review the history of philosophical work on dialectics, questioning, rationality, meaning, logos, and scientific knowledge, and then propose a new approach:

> It is time we restored philosophy to its natural function, which is metaphysical, thanks to problematological conception, if we want to arrive at an understanding of how thought takes root and grows. It is high time to abandon the sterile philosophical arguments which have ... been part of the Kantian heritage. Both positivism and ontological metaphysics, renewed by a difference bearing the same name (i.e., the ontological difference), reflect a contradiction as insurmountable as it is inadequate, especially between science and philosophy. Both conceptions depend upon the propositional model, a self-justificatory model, because insofar as it *only* admits justification, as in positivism, it destroys itself as philosophy. Or else this model functions as the straw man for the metaphysics of the ontological difference, because it still functions on the level of ontologization but accepts no model of *rationality* other than justification in its assertive meaning, which it precisely rejects, thus plunging into irrationality as its only alternative. (*Of Problematology*, 19)

A tall task for philosophy, a whole critique and reorientation of philosophy which runs from Socrates, Plato, and Aristotle to Descartes, Locke, and Kant, then all the way to Heidegger, Wittgenstein, and Foucault. Nothing if not ambitious.

Literature and Philosophy

The series into which this volume fits speaks to the overlap between literature and philosophy, and the implications of the present text and Meyer's overall project for such work are powerful indeed.[14] Literature plays a prominent role in much of Meyer's writing, sometimes as an example of the questioning process, and sometimes as the locus for a systematic analysis of how questioning can work. Although we are

14. This area of study remains remarkably unexplored. Some indications of where one could go in this regard can be found in the special issue of the *Revue international de Philosophie* devoted to questioning, notably Jean-Pierre Cometti's "Alternatives et questions dans la littérature romanesque" and Susan J. Wolfson's "Questioning 'the romantic ideology': Wordsworth."

accustomed to the tacit philosophic norm which privileges answers, literature is not, because it has as part of its very nature a questioning that can reject or refute propositions.

The most extended discussion of Meyer's work on literature appears in his book *Meaning and Reading: A Philosophical Essay on Language and Literature*. The question that begins this book sounds oddly formalist: "How does language work and how does it affect literariness?" (1). Meyer quickly moves to familiar ground, however, first by proposing that he will consider literature from a philosophical standpoint, and then by suggesting that "the question is here the essential notion to be taken into account and the answer must then count questions, hence answers, as the grounding notion in the theory to be constructed" (2). Given their specificity, literary texts serve both to foreground and to illustrate Meyer's problematological approach:

> Literary texts, on the one hand, are characterised by their auto-nomization [*sic*] from the problems they treat, leading to a rhetoricalization of these problems to which no literal ready-made substitute can correspond. Ideology is the cause of such treatment. An ideology must be able to answer all questions with which it is confronted. This is clearly impossible. The questions it must deal with are treated as rhetorical with respect to the available or derivable "answers" of the ideology in question. This, in turn, implies that one needs a *medium* (or mediator) that transforms a non-rhetorical or real question into a rhetorical one. The expression of the rhetorical problem can then have a literal counterpart in the ideology. This process of mediatization is called *fiction*. (5)

This description concerning the particularity and role of fiction is surprisingly radical and political, if only in its implications. This is true of the present text on passions as well, for passions and problematology speak to the uncertain, searching, and *passionate* quality of human nature, something that is of concern to ruling institutions, which work to consolidate and legitimize their own power and control in the face of questions. To the degree that literature fictionalizes the questions that challenge the ideological system, it is unproblematological, it treats questions as though they were not questions: "Fiction takes up questions confronting the ideology and rhetoricalizes them via another but derived problematic issue that is solved in a literary text and that argumentatively suggests an *a priori* ideological 'answer' to the original question challenging the ideology" (6).

On the other hand, and this is where things get more exciting, fiction can be a space, indeed a unique space,[15] in which questioning can occur: "Fiction, through an act of *poeisis,* creates this environment that would not have existed otherwise. The question of the questions referred to in fiction arises, hence the need for an interpretation. When these questions are specified, such a need is narrowed down to a progressive reading of the text which is sufficient to enable the reader to grasp the resolution of the questions, as in detective stories" (6). According to this reading, it's not fiction that is unproblematological, but rather *literary criticism*, something that is indeed evident to most people who have ever read theories applied to literature. This approach helps us to clarify the adage, variously mentioned but most famously associated with the formalists, that suggests that literature cannot be paraphrased or, in Meyer's sense, reformulated:

> The questions dealt with in each constituent answer of a text refer to a unified problematic: each answer is in reality a guiding principle for discovering a non-literal answer associated with the text as a whole, i.e. with textuality. The questions raised by literary texts are formalised. They are not literally expressed, and literal readings only limit the range of possible non-literal answers to the questions of interpretation. What remains problematic, inherent in the very nature of literary textuality, is what does not lend itself to a literal reformulation; no substitutive translation of the text could render it totally transparent in all its meanings or readings. (7)

A Meyer-inspired approach to literary criticism would produce some powerful readings, and a number of passages in this text provide some clue of what a problematological criticism might look like. For example, his suggestion that texts, particularly literary texts, "do not say what they mean even when they express what they answer" speaks to the problem of providing provisional answers to what are fundamentally irresolvable questions. What texts *mean,* therefore, is a question and not an answer,

15. Marc Angenot, whose link to Michel Meyer runs back to Chaim Perelman and the Université libre de Bruxelles, also tackles the provocative questions of what literature knows and what literature can *do* in his article "Que peut la littérature," which I've translated for *SubStance,* no. 92 (Fall 2000).

and they express their meaning "without saying it and this leaves room, even at the level of minimal rhetoricity, for multiple readings, though we must recognise that, when the problem is clearly stipulated, various meanings are factored out. Nevertheless, nothing will prove that the real questions are the avowed ones" (7).

The implications here are significant for how we come to talk about literature; if the meaning of a text is not related to our capacity to rewrite it, and if questions are considered in terms of other questions rather than as catalysts for the production of necessarily insufficient propositions, then the problem of literary analysis is recast and the works of authors take on different and more open-ended meanings. This applies to literature, and indeed all texts, in a general sense; but certain literary texts are likely to be more problematological than others by their very nature, which makes for a distinction in Meyer's sense between types of literature on problematological grounds:

> The case of popular novels is interesting too. They do not seem to involve what I call *second-level* reading (or interpretation). Popular novels are generally associated with what is called "escapist" or even "bad" literature, possibly on the grounds that the unfolding of the resolution coincides with that of the problematic as if the two were one and the same. The problematic is blatantly and explicitly put forth, rendering any second-level reading superfluous. Once read, these books seem transparent. The problems they present are not put rhetorically. No reflexive process constitutive of the second-level reading, called interpretation, need take place for the reader to be able to grasp what is meant by the book. The process of understanding the problematic is reduced to a mere *progressive* reading and ends with the final line of the text: then you have understood the book. (83–84)

By this criteria, one could assess the value of literary texts from a problematological perspective, and even suggest that although all texts are to some degree problematological, certain fiction can, despite its capacity for radical questioning, remain at the first, literal level, and hence certain fictional texts simply don't raise further questions about their own nature. From this standpoint, more significant literature consists of texts that move the reader beyond this point, "for texts requiring a second-level reading to be grasped *as a whole,* the regressive procedure characteristic of such a reading must be involved, i.e., the *hermeneutical circle*

or [a] to-and-fro movement." For such a case to occur, the reader must be
led to retrace his or her steps, that is, "something in the text renders a
progressive reading of the story insufficient for the reader to comprehend the text." In this case, "the literary text remains problematic
because the problems involved in the textuality of the text are not all
explicitly stated; instead, many are merely implied. On the other hand,
the problems that are explicitly presented to be explicitly solved in the
text do not raise the question of the meaning of the text, which is
entirely unfolded in order to present such a resolution" (84).

To sum up: "Literature," says Meyer,

> suppresses the problem of the real world that gave birth to it by
> fictionalising the problem: fiction is the solution to some ideo-
> logical quandary met within the real world. When reality is
> negated, fiction necessarily ensues. When the real problem is
> fictionalised, it is translated and transfigured. Since the literary
> solution evades the *real* problem, its solution must be *fictional*
> though it is indirectly related to and deals with reality. Thus, even
> when it is meant to distance itself from ideology, fiction always
> has a bearing upon reality and can thereby address readers over
> a gap of centuries. (128)

So in the end, literature, unlike other genres of discourse, doesn't appear
as a *solution,* because "its displacing function guarantees its autonomy
with respect to the problem from which it originated. Nonetheless,
the literary solution is the problematological expression of a certain relationship to reality" (ibid.).

The approach proposed in *Meaning and Reading* is articulated for
the most part as regards other theories of literature—those of Bakhtin,
Barthes, Booth, Chatman, de Man, Dubois, Eco, Frye, Gadamer, Hirsch,
Iser, Jauss, Lukács, Rifaterre, Scholes, and Shlovski—and is set up in terms
of philosophical discussions of meaning and texts by Frege, Granger,
and Ricoeur, with implicit references to classical Greek philosophy.
The literary examples are, with the exception of Don Quixote, mostly
modern texts, including Joyce, Musil, and Proust. Given the nature of literature published within the last century, with its rejuvenated levels of
questioning, which derives in part from our having lost the anchor
that was provided by God and State, this is unsurprising. Each literary
theory has a corpus to which it best applies: Bakhtin to Dostoevsky and
carnivalesque literature, formalism to structured poems, Barthes-style
reader response to the *nouveau roman,* Marxist literary criticism to

realist novels, and so forth. As is apparent in this text and in *Rhetoric, Language, and Reason,* Meyer is best when it comes to questioning modern fiction, as we shall see.

Rhetoric, Language, and Reason contains articles and chapters from some of the aforementioned books by Michel Meyer, and in its scope is perhaps the best overview of Meyer's projects. It is also an especially valuable text for those interested in an application of Meyer's work to modern fiction, for a simple reason: "The increased anonymity, i.e., depersonalisation, that we find in modern narratives ('who speaks?') embodied in Joyce's *Ulysses* or Robert Musil's *Man Without Qualities,* finds its natural consequence in the literary question of literary thematization, thereby rendering the logic of modern writing more auto-referential than ever." This is true on account of a shift in the very nature of fiction, which has tended toward what he calls the "metafictional," and as a consequence, fiction has come to express "problematicity more and more, through enigmatic modes of writing" (42).

For Meyer, modernist questioning refers to "the question of the Self, or the Self as question," because, in a line of thinking that will sound familiar to postmodern literary theorists, "traditionally, the Self, or the I, has been conceived of as the unity of experience, that which synthesises the diversity of sensations into a homogenous reality. The fragmentation of reality refers back to the correlative fragmentation of the Self as a pole of unification." What is unique here is the upshot, which brings us not to postmodern relativism or the death of the subject, but back instead to the problematological approach: "The puzzle of existence mirrors the increased absurdity of the real as being a discontinuous bundle of experiences. The Self reflects the question that the whole is now for himself, including himself as a mere part of it" (42). The example Meyer gives is a "classic" of the Meyer corpus, since it encapsulates in but a few lines some of the arguments that run through Meyer's texts. It comes from Franz Kafka's 1920 short story "The Test," which depicts a character who is in search of employment, and who, while out for drinks at a tavern one evening, meets an important servant of the house where he'd like to work:

> "Why do you want to run away? Sit down and have a drink! I'll pay." So I sat down. He asked me several things, but I could not answer, indeed I didn't even understand his questions. So I said: "Perhaps you are sorry now that you have invited me, so I'd better go," and I was about to get up. But he stretched his hand out over the table and pressed me down. "Stay," he said, "that was

only a test. He who does not answer the questions has passed the test." (Quoted in Meyer, *Rhetoric, Language, and Reason,* 42)

Meyer offers a range of possible readings, including a "traditional" one, which would suggest that the scene is quite simply "absurd," and a "deconstructivist" reading, which "will be structuralist in spirit in the sense that it will consider the text as a code for textuality itself, a secret language referring to language itself, a signifier indirectly signifying itself through its very semiological function" (42–43). Such a reading suggests that the servant who is unable to enter the house where he'd like to work is like the modern reader who cannot comprehend the (modern) text, so "the reader will only have access to the meaning of modern fiction if he understands that there is no longer a meaning to find," which suggests, of course, that the question itself is meaningless. For Meyer, this deconstructivist reading turns the text into a simple "allegory of fiction by fiction," and that "such an interpretation is a denial of any possible interpretation and that it, therefore, defeats itself, because it nonetheless serves as an interpretation." In short, it doesn't go beyond the traditional reading that the scene is an example of absurdity.

To go beyond both the "traditional" and the deconstructivist is the only way to avoid this contradiction and get at the real essence of the text: "The question of meaning, if we accept that it is allegorically raised in Kafka's text, does not lead to the meaninglessness of the text but to the idea of meaning as a question posed by the text itself. Meaning is still an answer, but in modern fiction, an answer becomes questionable. The question of meaning has to remain without answer, but this is already an answer. In fact, the answer is the question itself: the meaning of fictional texts now imposes itself as the affirmation of their problematicity" (43). The text, like other modern texts, doesn't yield up a single answer, the text remains abstract and enigmatic, and the stability of the text is jeopardized. And yet although there is no overarching subject of the text, there is nevertheless a discernible subject: us.

Passion and the Philosopher

This leads us to the present text, in some ways a further study of the problematological approach from another, related angle, and in others a broad summary and evaluation of how passion has been considered by philosophers since Aristotle. I would emphasize a few points here, to help guide the reading. First, none of the previous discussions are left behind in the present text because, consistent with all of Meyer's work, there is an overall project which demands that certain areas receive careful study, areas which happen to include the domain of literature and the problem of passion and its relationship to rationality. Second, I would once again suggest that the implications of this book are surprisingly radical, since they speak to basic human impulses, the way that we come to know things about the world, and the complex and often paradoxical relationship between our passions and our quest for knowledge, a relationship which seems sometimes to be a harmonious and mutual effort, and at others to be a struggle of opposites that wish to impose norms and interpretations based on vastly different criteria.

The subject of the passions is of interest in light of the previous discussion because they, like powerful literary texts, are troubling, worrisome, even frightening. This is where Meyer's writing turns downright exciting and speaks in direct and specific ways to some of the most topical issues of contemporary philosophy and criticism:

> Passion must be seen as something other than some extreme emotion or the underlying foundation of sociability. It is above all a form of sensitivity, before being amorality or, worse, immorality. It is the sign of the contingency in man, that is to say, what he wishes to master. By being the place where temporality and the reversion of all truth into its contrary converge, passion upsets, destabilises and disorients by reproducing the uncertainty of the world and the course of events. It is in fact *the other* in us, without which we would not exist, but with which it is difficult and dangerous to be. Passion is the word for all risks, as well as the one for infinite promises. There is a moral choice implied in passion on account of the fact that it opens up contradictory choices, alternatives. If passion and morality have always been closely associated, it must not be forgotten that *pathos* was originally this sensible, unreflexive consciousness which plunges us into the stream of life, and which pushes us to flee from dangers as much as to seek pleasure.

It is this contradictory quality of the passions, the endless paradoxes that are created in our consideration of them and our relationship with them either through reasons or the senses, that guides Meyer's readings of philosophical work on passion: "Passion is as much that which attaches us to the world as that which can save us from its dangers by warning us of their existence. Passion swallows us up in an ever present reversibility of existence, by changing its course and, thereby, it confronts us with the chasms and the illusions of life. Both a signal of alarm and the danger itself: it is the alternative which refers to all possible existential alternatives."

So the passions are the representatives in the human being of excess and deviance, they are the uncontrolled elements of our (flawed?) human nature; these are claims which relate to as vast a project as one could imagine. To address such a complex area of study, and to assess the relationship between specifically "human" nature and "nature," critical issues for philosophy and theology for millenniums, Meyer characteristically follows a historical pathway. He offers a tapestry, a survey of the history of the philosophical approach to passions in the works of, for example, Aristotle, Saint Augustine, Descartes, Freud, Hobbes, Hume, Kant, Locke, Machiavelli, Mandeville, Marx, Nietzsche, Plato, de Rougemont, Rousseau, Saint Thomas, Smith, Socrates, Spinoza, and Wittgenstein. In so doing, he offers a reading of each philosopher, useful even for those interested in their respective general approaches; but he goes further still, indicating flaws or gaps in their respective reasoning, the contradictions and paradoxes of their approaches, and as such provides a look at how the reasoning mind can operate on the process of reasoning, which is laid bare in each of the texts discussed.

As might be expected, this present text also offers a Raymond Williams–style keyword reading of passion, a study of how the term has been employed, and interpreted, since the dawn of classical philosophy. In so doing he offers a history of ideas, complete with the fundamental breaks that have occurred, specifically regarding the understanding of the passions, at particular moments of history. The ruptures, the consequence of the rise of Christianity, the views of the Stoics, the revolt of the romantics, the peculiarities of the modern era, are all described and assessed as regards the problem of the passions.

Along the way, Meyer's problematological and historical approach forces us to confront our own preconceptions, and self-satisfaction, concerning the society within which we live, for

> there is no society which allows for the freedom of unregulated passions. There is no more arbitrary exchange of goods in a barter system than there is unregulated economic exchange under capitalism, not to mention the accession to power (the exchange of positions and of functions), which is also always codified: evidently, *total* liberty has had no other reality than an illusory one. Even liberated passions have found their antidote in theorisation. Montesquieu against Machiavelli, Marx against

Smith, and probably Freud against himself. Even our society has its own methods of controlling passions. There is a democratic legislation of the election and of the eligibility for all citizens who can thereby express an individual's will to power with regards to others, as in the case of others with regards to him. The pursuit of material interest itself abides by restrictions, even when there is liberalisation, since economic activity obeys rules of concurrence assumed just (fair). Affective and sexual relations don't escape socialisation either, even if they are no longer expressed through the negotiation of parental alliances or by the mere, but always castigated, exercise of violence. This remains the danger related to all passion, since power, pleasure and the expression of the "great Ego" reinforce one another in each person, over and above the equivalence of words which we have underlined and that illustrate their substitutability.

Hence the refusal by all authorities, legal, governmental, theological, to allow for a free reign of passions, for they, like the questioning previously described, and the literary texts when assessed in a properly problematological fashion, pose significant threats, even though they are clearly part of us, part of our most intimate nature, the source, indeed of our very drives. And so the questions come back, typically, and with a vengeance. Does passion tear people apart because it blinds them, or on the contrary, does passion permit us to become truly aware of our own nature?

Robert F. Barsky
Brussels, Montreal, London (Ontario), New Haven (Connecticut),
1995–2000

Preliminary Note

Passion has always been opposed to reason, the soul to the body, nature to human nature, and instinct to intelligence. But is there really an essence of man, or is there just a history?

This is the question that we have followed throughout the centuries, questioning the great philosophical movements as to their moral, political, and metaphysical vision of man. The theory of the passions offers a privileged viewpoint from which to view the enigmas of occidental thought.

The question that remains at the end of this journey is whether there exists something we can call a humanity of man and how reason, which would define it, is possible.

Introduction

A book about the passions and the way that they are conceived may seem for some people a frivolous, or even an impossible enterprise. Isn't passion by definition that which eludes rational discourse? Nevertheless, the subject is a topical one. Numerous contemporaries see in passion an alternative to a dull and overly regulated daily life. A possibly fanciful anti-dote to a mass society from which each person thinks himself capable of escaping, passion has become the secret hope that many of us harbor.

This is to recall how much the theme under consideration herein is serious and topical; but to limit ourselves to this observation would be to do an injustice to a long tradition, descended from the Greeks, which has steadily concerned itself with the passions. Philosophers of course, but curiously perhaps, doctors, psychologists, and sociologists have spo-ken of them, even if in many cases they have thereby associated passions with the worst kinds of dissoluteness, as much in terms of individual life as of existence in society. From political science to biology, the passions have traversed all of the scholastic and disciplinary barriers, which only goes to show that human beings exercise them thoroughly. Passion is this unique but enigmatic locus wherein people meet animals, and human nature encounters nature. A hybrid being, passion stems as much from the sensible[1] appetite and the representation that it provokes, as from

1. See page 30, note 3.

the urges and the emotions that we feel from it. But passion is also what is most individual about the individual; it crystallizes the conflicts that people have with themselves, and therefore with others. Vices and virtues are "pre-recorded" passions, responses that either favor or bridle senti-ments inspired by passion. The unbridled taste for gambling, for amorous pleasure, or else the greed or lust for power (which today one would refer to as "sport," "liberal moral standards," or "materialism") are no more than passion, or derive from it. The wisdom to which philosophical thinking lays claim is perhaps this impossible quest, which consists of pretending to put an end to the passions or, at least, restricting them.

In short, philosophers don't like the passions, which they gladly oppose to reason. For Kant, "It is easy to see that passions do the greatest damage to freedom, because they are consistent with the calmest reflec-tion, so that they need not be thoughtless, like affects, and consequently stormy and transitory, but tend to get themselves rooted and can co-exist even with subtle reasoning."[2] He needs to conclude that "passion is a *disease* that abhors all remedies; so that it is far worse than any such tran-sitory mental agitation, that at least stirs up the resolution to be better."[3] Kant hereby joins an old tradition which afterwards links passion and folly (especially in Esquirol), for which the origin is rather situated in some stoic radicalism, which sees in passion an upsetting of the spirit, anti-reason *par excellence*.

It is hereby clear what importance the *history* of thought takes in this matter, despite its apparent unrelatedness.

But the philosophical attitude raises of course another question: what would we be if not for our passions? Don't we live from our loves as from our pains, our joys as from our sorrows, our regrets of the time that passes as from our hopes for that which lies before us? If passion can be destructive, isn't wisdom equally so? Finally, reason without passion is but the ruin of the soul.

From here arises the problem of knowing what passion is. Is it always an obsession that absorbs us entirely to ultimately deprive us, or isn't it in most cases a simple emotion, admittedly a tad powerful, but not to the point of crystallizing itself in the form of a devouring hydra? It is clear from Aristotle[4] that calm, like shame, are both passions, proof that passions don't imply the most extreme experiences of our being. For Descartes, they are the movements of the soul that emanate from the

---

2. Immanuel Kant, *Anthropology from a Pragmatic Point of View,* sec. 80, trans. Mary J. Gregor (The Hague: Martin Nijhoff, 1974), p. 133.

3. Ibid.

4. *The Art of Rhetorics,* bk. 2, and M. Meyer, *Aristote ou la rhétorique des passions* (Paris: Petite Bibliothèque Rivages, 1989).

body, unlike innate ideas. They are the involuntary perceptions that affect us. This is the place from which consciousness loses introspective self-control as though in the process of becoming thoughtful with regard to that which swallows up and stifles it; it comes to resemble the unconscious through its commerce with the object that invades and single-handedly retains it. Depending upon whether consciousness resists or succumbs, this reaction is either deemed pleasurable or painful. We thereby either approach or retreat from the objects of pain and pleasure, and will want to either reproduce these sensations or repress them. If it is not as yet a question of the unconscious, as far as Descartes was concerned, consciousness delivered to the *pathos* is no less of a troubled area. Consciousness finds itself submitted to multiple variations imposed by the body, which it cannot, despite reason, neutralize through the indifference of a thought exclusively relinquished to the immutable necessity of mathematical truth.

Descartes and Freud, Aristotle and St. Thomas, Cicero and St. Augustine: depending upon the author and the point of view, passions vary in number from fourteen, to eleven, to four or six. . . . Philosophy appears from this perspective to be governed only by arbitrary criteria, and it thereby rejects any logic of passions other than that which justifies one kind of reduction or another.

In fact, there is a rationality in the reflections concerning passions, and it is the object of this work to retrace the pathways thereof, as though to reactualize them through the action of pursuing them.

How are these matters presented? For the Greeks, passions were above all political, in the broad sense of the term: they permeated life in the City, that is, the relations that men who live among one another have among themselves. The issue is to negotiate the differences and the *différends* in the effort to reach a common *Good;* hence the role played by the passions in Aristotle's *Rhetoric.* In order to convince one's audience of something, it is necessary to move them and, as a result, it is necessary to know their passions, that is, the tendencies, tastes, desires, beliefs, and dispositions that characterize them. The seat of the individual *avant la lettre,* the passions are the signs of differences, of the diversity of human beings, that must be accounted for in order to make it possible for us to live together. It is through the passions that oppositions are manifested because they express these oppositions and thereby help to communicate differences of opinion. In short, passion is what would come to be called, several centuries later, self-consciousness, because it expresses a reaction to the other, an image of the self as seen by the other, a reflexivity, a spectacle, an observing consciousness of the passions. But this remains at the level of sociopolitical relations between individuals. Unregulated passions lead to the individual being banished, whereas later on, Christianity will see herein a question of personal salvation.

In the meantime the vision of the human being and his or her soul transformed in the course of changes within society. The fourteen passions of Aristotle became for St. Augustine three cardinal sins, all intermingled within the original sin, from which they emerged. Adam thought he could become the equal of God, and by biting into the apple, he condemned human nature to the Fall. A sin of the flesh, but also a sin of arrogance and, of course, a sin of declaring his mastery over the fruits of Eden, as though humanity were the owner thereof, when in fact God alone had granted the permission to live therein. The great passions, sources of all others, will thenceforth be power or vanity, sensual pleasure, and luxury. The good Christian will be he who takes a vow of humility, poverty, and chastity.

The entire vision of humanity is hereby altered, affecting the whole of the occidental world. But from 1500 to 1900, the period that separates Machiavelli from Freud, the three principal passions will slowly become if not rehabilitated, at least partly legitimized, thereby draining human nature of all of the content that had been defined by Christianity. This is the source of contemporary nihilism. But hereby arose the possibility, renewed during our own times, of harmonizing passion and reason by reconsidering both.

St. Augustine, more concerned with the City of God than with the City of Man, condemned vanity, the search for pleasure, and the accumulation of material goods, without really theorizing them. With Machiavelli and Hobbes, we witness the first reversal: the *libido dominandi* asserts itself. There is a rationality to political passion, which can assert a new legitimacy. Two centuries later, economic passion too becomes "normal," and the opprobrium associated thereto ever since the Thomistical condemnation of the interest-bearing loan disappeared in its wake. It became legitimate to wish to enrich oneself and to accumulate, since this contributes to the collective well-being, composed of the sum of individual wealth. This is the thesis of Adam Smith, who rehabilitates material passion in the form of interest. Foucault spoke of work, life, and language as the matrix of the humanities. Biology, hence the reproduction of the species (sexuality) which instinctively gives rise to representation of the instincts (the unconscious) and thereby engenders passion, is one of the great orientations of the nineteenth century. Freud arrives at the end of this evolution, and for what concerns us, provides a theoretical status to carnal passion.

The belt is thereby buckled. The passions, or all that is henceforth named as such, will all be able to speak for themselves. They can modify themselves and be substituted one for the other. Note the interchangeable quality of the following concepts: pleasure, possession, and will to power can be applied just as well to those we love as to those things of which we dispose or to the positions that we occupy. In order to combat the Augustinian tradition and bring forth a positive outlook on the cardinal passions, it was necessary to isolate them, and invite criticism for having substantiated for them some primary passion, like sexuality (Freud), the will to power and vanity (Hobbes), or interest (Smith). In fact, passion is defined precisely by the study of equivalencies, of substitutes that satisfy them in part, while expressing, and displacing them at the same time. We will return to this. For the moment, note that there is no society which allows the free exercise of unregulated passions. There is no more arbitrary exchange of goods in a barter system than there is unregulated economic exchange under capitalism, not to mention the accession to power (the exchange of positions and of functions), which is also always codified: evidently, *total* liberty has had no other reality than an illusory one. Even liberated passions have found their antidote in theorization. Montesquieu against Machiavelli, Marx against Smith, and probably Freud against himself. Even our society has its own methods of controlling passions. There is a democratic legislation of the election and of the eligibility for all citizens who can thereby express an individual's will to power with regard to others, as in the case of others with regard to him. The pursuit of material interest itself abides by restrictions, even when there is liberalization, since economic activity obeys rules of concurrence assumed just (fair). Affective and sexual relations don't escape socialization either, even if they are no longer expressed through the negotiation of parental alliances or by the mere, but always castigated, exercise of violence. This remains the danger related to all passion, since power, pleasure, and the expression of the "great Me" reinforce one another in each person, over and above the equivalence of the words that we have underlined and which illustrate their substitutability.

More important, passion must be seen as something other than some extreme emotion or the underlying foundation of sociability. It is above all a form of sensitivity, before being amorality or, worse, immorality. It is the sign of the contingent in human beings, that is to say, that which they wish to master. By being the place where temporality and the reversion of all truth into its contrary converge, passion upsets, destabilizes, and disorients by reproducing the uncertainty of the world and the course of events. It is in fact *the other* in us, without whom we would not exist, but with whom it is difficult and dangerous to be. "Passion" is the word for all risks, as well as the one for infinite promises. There is a moral choice implied in passion on account of the fact that it opens up contradictory choices, alternatives. If passion and morality have always been closely associated, it must not be forgotten that *pathos* was originally this sensitive, unreflexive consciousness which plunges us into the stream of life, and which pushes us to flee from dangers as much as to seek pleasure. Passion is as much that which attaches us to the world as that which can save us from its dangers by warning us of their existence. Passion swallows us up in an ever present reversibility of existence, by changing its course and, thereby, confronting us with the chasms and the illusions of life. Both a signal of alarm and the danger itself, it is the alternative which refers to all possible existential alternatives.

But to have a passion, in the original sense of the word *pathos,* simply means that the soul has suffered a movement, which is its expression of the exterior impression. Although the difference between the mere *pathos* and the overwhelming passion may well be long and sometimes, for good or for bad, insurmountable, it is nonetheless the case that these two states of the soul are of the same nature. There is a straight line running from the small pleasures of love to the absorbing difficulties of obsessive ideas and concern about living, right up to the passion for gain. How is one to trace it, and thereby establish a frontier between the passions, which devour us, and the passing emotions, which are closer to daily moods than to the torrents which carry them away? Perhaps we must follow Kant, who distinguishes between the *affects* and *passions?* "The inclination that the subject's reason overcomes but with great effort, or not at all, is passion. On the other hand, the sentiment of pleasure or displeasure that we court in the present state and which, in the subject, does not leave place for reflection (representation of reason from where one recognizes that one must deliver oneself from, or reject, this sentiment) is emotion (Affect)."[5]

Such a distinction is of course the mark of Kant's concern for ethics and goes beyond simple description. The asexualized neutrality of emotion cuts it off from passion in the name of the opprobrium cast upon it, which leads passion to be considered as autonomous. While emotion constitutes a normal state of the psychic life, passion expresses the pathological aspect. However, by saying this, one loses the trace of the passionate, its origin; one risks being unable to explain passion and to see it as a separate entity.

5. Kant, *Anthropology,* sec. 73.

If this vision is in many respects belated, nevertheless all theories of the passions present constant elements that have marked them throughout their long history. Below the *logos* and the universal, it is the individual, the fluctuating and therefore sensitive self. But if by the same token, passion poses problems for the *logos* which reflects upon it, the simple fact that this reflection is itself possible indicates that passion is simultaneously sensitive and *intellectualizable*. It is therefore the point of convergence of the sensitive and reflexive consciousness. It carries us in the world; and through it, the world takes us in. A sign of our individuality, it is at the same time the seat of our identity: we are what we feel and experience. Passion that submerges us will efface everything else from our preoccupations. If it is a state of fusion that unites our being and our desires into a single force, as has been proposed ever since the romantic period, if it gives us this sentiment of finally existing, then it is also, by virtue of its singularizing character, that which differentiates us the most from others. The logic of the passions in a human community is a logic of identity and difference. It forms the rationality of the passions from Plato to present day. The passions bring us together, and unify us just as they provoke our demise. Passion, in the end, is the alternative itself, and since Aristotle, it has been defined by contraries because it frees us from the repetitiveness of our daily existence and from the observance of those rules which have been since the dawn of humanity upheld by moralists. Whatever can be inverted, the alternative, reversibility, is marked with the sign of time. The temporal anchoring of humanity makes it such that whatever can be acquired can also be lost, and that which appeared impossible finally imposes itself as inescapable. Passion, in what it expresses of our problematicity, our contingency, reveals the almost metaphysical strongpoint of what must with reservation be referred to as "the human condition." It creates the necessity of a destiny where there had been but apparent liberty. It can elevate us just as it can put us down. And as such, over and above that which is often moralizing in discourses about the passions, there is an aesthetic dimension within them which can lead human beings to the sublime, whether that sublimity be one of horror or of greatness.

At the end of the journey, passion emerges as the fundamental crossroads of aesthetics and politics, where the most essential questions that have been posed since time immemorial finally meet.

1

From the Passion of Discourse to the Discourse of the Passions

How Did the Passions Come to Speak for Themselves?

According to Plato, we are trapped by our passions in the Cave of our own illusions. Appearance is mistaken for reality because the sensations that jostle around inside us have much more power over us than does any intellectual reality. This reality is less palpable and further from daily concerns. It is the product of a learning process and of a conquest over the obvious facts of the everyday which most people would be reluctant to renounce or fight over.

> "Next," I said, "here's a situation which you can use as an analogy for the human condition—for our education or lack of it. Imagine people living in a cavernous cell down under the ground; at the far end of the cave, a long way off, there's an entrance open to the outside world. They've been there since childhood, with their legs and necks tied up in a way which keeps them in one place and allows them to only look straight ahead, but not turn their heads. There's a firelight burning a long way further up the cave behind them, and up the slope between the fire and the prisoners there's a road, beside which you should imagine a wall has been built—like the partition which

conjurors place between themselves and their audience and above which they show their tricks."

"All right," he said.

"Imagine also that there are people on the other side of this wall who are carrying all sorts of artefacts. These artefacts, human statuettes, and animal models carved in stone and wood and all kinds of materials stick out over the wall; and as you'd expect, some of the people talk as they carry these objects along, while others were silent."

"This is a very strange picture you're painting," he said, "with strange prisoners."

"They're no different from us," I said. "I mean, in the first place, do you think they'd see anything of themselves and one another except the shadows cast by the fire onto the cave wall directly opposite them?"

"Of course not," he said. "They're forced to spend their lives without moving their heads."

"And what about the objects which were being carried along? Won't they only see their shadows as well?"

"Naturally."

"Now suppose they were able to talk to one another: don't you think they'd assume that their words applied to what they saw passing by in front of them?"

"They couldn't think otherwise."

"And what if sound echoed off the prison wall opposite them? When any of the passers-by spoke, don't you think they'd be bound to assume that the sound came from a passing shadow?"

"I'm absolutely certain of it," he said.

"All in all then," I said, "the shadows of artefacts would constitute the only reality people in this situation would recognise."

"That's absolutely inevitable," he agreed.

"What do you think would happen, then," I asked, "if they were set free from their bonds and cured of their insanity? What would it be like if they found that happening to them? Imagine that one of them has been set free and is suddenly made to stand up, to turn his head and walk, and to look towards the firelight. It hurts him to do all this and he's too dazzled to be capable of making out the objects whose shadows he'd formerly been look-ing at. And suppose someone tells him what he's been looking at. And suppose someone tells him that he's now closer to real-ity and is seeing more accurately, because of the greater reality of the things in front of his eyes—what do you imagine his reaction would be? And what do you think he'd say if he were shown any of the passing objects and had to respond to being asked what it was? Don't you think he'd be bewildered and would think that there was more reality in what he'd been seeing before than what he is being shown now?"

"Far more," he said.

"And if he were forced to look at the actual firelight, don't you think it would hurt his eyes? Don't you think he'd turn away and run back to the things he could make out, and would take the truth of the matter to be that these things are clearer than what he is being shown?"

"Yes," he agreed.

"And imagine him being dragged forcibly away from there up the rough, steep slope," I went on, "without being released until he's been pulled out into the sunlight. Wouldn't this treatment cause him pain and distress? And once he's reached the sunlight, he wouldn't be able to see a single one of the things which are currently taken to be real, would he, because his eyes would be overwhelmed by the sun's beams?"

"No, he wouldn't," he answered, "not straight away."

"He wouldn't be able to see things up on the surface of the earth, I suppose, until he'd got used to his situation. At first, it would be shadows that he could most easily make out, then he'd move on to the reflections of people and so on in water, and later he'd be able to see the actual things themselves. Next, he'd feast his eyes on the heavenly bodies and the heavens themselves, which would be easier at night: he'd look at the light of the stars and the moon, rather than at the sun and sunlight during daytime."

"Of course."

"And at last, I imagine, he'd be able to discern and feast his eyes on the sun—not the displaced image of the sun in water or elsewhere, but the sun on its own, in its proper place."

"Yes, he'd inevitably come to that," he said.

"After that, he'd start to think about the sun and he'd deduce that it is the source of the seasons and the yearly cycle, that the whole of the visible realm is its domain, and that in a sense is its responsibility."

"Yes, that would be obviously the next point he'd come to," he agreed.

"Now, if he recalled the cell where he'd originally lived and what passed for knowledge there and his former fellow prisoners, don't you think he'd feel happy about his own altered circumstances, and sorry for them?"

"Definitely."

"Suppose that the prisoners used to assign prestige and credit to one another, in the sense that they rewarded speed at recognising the shadows as they passed, and the ability to remember which ones normally come earlier and later and at the same time as which other ones, and expertise at using this as a basis for guessing which ones would arrive next. Do you think our former prisoner would covet these honours and would envy the people who had status and power there, or would he prefer, as Homer describes it, "being a slave labouring for someone else—someone without property," and would put up with anything at all, in fact, rather than share their beliefs and their life?"

"Yes, I think he would go through anything rather than live that way," he said.[1]

This myth, which Plato recounts in *The Republic,* illustrates very well humanity's bond with the sensible. What is misleading is that it is easier to consider the sensible as *reality* than it is to doubt it, just as it is often more enjoyable to consider that our desires are norms rather than sacrificing them in order to look to somewhere that would be hypothetically truer or more just.

And yet the argument is clear: that which we believe to be true is not true; it is but a farrago of shadows which dance before our eyes in which we *wish* to believe, and which we rarely consider necessary to question. Plato sets up an opposition between this universe of appearances and a more authentic world, which he would call *intelligible.* The *sensible* deludes us; it is filled with contradictions and marked by time, which passes and which destroys all things. How could the sensible be true if afterward it ceases to be?

Passion is indeed the name of this interweaving in the sensible, as it is the name of the belief which absorbs that which it captures. Passion is this blinding, and it is the sensations that promise to, or truly do, nourish and sustain it.

Passion is not reflected upon by those over whom it exerts its power,

1. Plato *Republic* 514a–516e, trans. Robin Waterfield (New York: Oxford University Press, 1993).

since they would thereby become conscious of it and by the same token be released from its yoke. Just like the prisoners of the Cave, they would have understood the nature of their chains and through this understanding be released from them and able to walk toward the light. From this comes Plato's famous thesis concerning goodness: nothing is voluntarily evil.[2] We impose pain without realizing it. From the moment that we know what must be done, the necessity of the action is revealed. One might object that some individuals commit evil acts knowing full well their case. In reality, they think that they are pursing their own interests, whatever is *good for them*. They err by dissociating that which is convenient for short-term interests, and that which is good in itself, in the long term, and which is also good for others with whom they must live. This ignorance stems from their passions and desires, in the clutches of which they remain. According to Plato, we try to achieve goodness as soon as we discover what is good. Moral virtue is a question of knowledge, and knowledge of what must be done is equivalent to wanting to achieve the corresponding ends. If we become conscious of our passions, we rise above them and cease to be subject to their powers. It could be that we succumb again to some temptation or another, like the child who knows that too much chocolate will hurt him but partakes nonetheless, but Plato sees therein the proof of a lack of discernment rather than lack of will. The child does not really know the degree to which his desire is dangerous; if he really did know, how could he believe for a moment that to eat this "last piece" of cake is not as bad as all that? The desire that haunts him is not *understood* as it should be, which shows that to be enslaved by this desire is the same thing as not recognizing the true nature of that which enslaves us. This creates an apparent necessity, which we don't permit ourselves to resist because we don't really understand that it is only apparent.

In short, to speak of the passions as Plato does, it is necessary to be above the obstacle which they constitute. It is in the domain of reason that we can expatiate upon the subject of passion. But this raises a fundamental question: to whom does this idea of passion apply if there are only those who know nothing about it and those who are above it? Aren't ordinary people and philosophers alike strangers to passions whether or not they have them? Aren't they all plunged into the same indifference? What sense is there in talking about what some people don't care about and others no longer have to worry about?

2. Plato *Protagoras* 345e. A thesis which will be reaffirmed right to the end. See *Laws* 860d–e, for example.

The Philosopher and the Ordinary Person; or,
How One Becomes a Philosopher

Passion is that which allows us to reflect upon the life of those persons who by their own desires are denied the ability to devote themselves to rational discourse because they are preoccupied by sensual pleasures. One might just as well say that the very concept of passion already expresses the point of view of the philosopher and falls into the domain of reason, in order to designate that which is exterior to the domain of reason. Surely we can affirm that passion reflects how philosophy thinks about the ordinary person, but the concept of passion remains, for all of that, just as paradoxical. This is a consequence of the fact that the concept of passion installs in the order of reflection that which by its very nature is supposed to escape it. Hence the appeal to myth, which allows Plato to mask the discrepancy that a literal account would have revealed. The philosopher who describes people in terms of their being "prisoners in a cave of illusions" betrays them, since it is unlikely that people perceive themselves in this manner.

In short, the paradox is as follows. If philosophy reproduces through reflection that which human beings thoughtlessly are, it is useless because such knowledge is given to all of us, naturally. On the other hand, if it adds something by resorting to rational discourse—the least that we can expect of it—it cannot really be considered an adequate reflection of our being, which it claims to do, because it goes beyond or above it. It does not express us as we really are, that is, it does not express our unthinking reality. On the contrary, it affirms by a secondary discourse what ordinary persons, all of us, do not reflect but simply live. Philosophy has gone beyond the limits of its own ambition by adopting as characteristic a quite surprising viewpoint. It situates itself beyond that which it is supposed to describe. Here, the mission of the philosopher becomes impossible, whereas in the first possibility described, it was simply useless.

If philosophy describes our nature, then we, being what we are, would ignore all of that which is deemed "philosophy" except whatever we practice intuitively—common sense—as though the passions that most often animate us were acting in the place of our reason. Philosophy abolishes itself by its own actions; it is an immanent truth. The second discourse, which brings this to light, shows itself to be superfluous unless we admit that it can say more about ordinary people than ordinary people can perceive on their own. Wouldn't there be, therefore, a schism between what we as philosophers say about human beings and the manner in which we as human beings say about ourselves? It is in this very separation that we can take up the perennial misunderstanding that separates philosophers from nonphilosophers. The latter group poses questions to which the first responds by resorting to utterances that seem incomprehensible. "You speak about us," they say, "but most of the time we cannot recognize ourselves in what you are saying." Between a philosophy that is superfluous to the reality it describes (if it effectively captures the truth of its own object) and a philosophy deemed impossible if it wishes to reflect upon that which is admittedly thoughtless, then thought finds itself plunged into the center of the paradox; that of its own making, which is also that of its function.

We find in this dilemma what is best referred to as the paradox of Menon, the dialogue in which Plato asks himself if one can become virtuous. The paradox is the following (80d–e): if I know what I'm looking for, there is no use in looking for it. It is this kind of philosophy that is useless, it is the one everybody knows. What good is it in terms of being a reasoned activity if everyone already knows that which it is trying to establish? But if I am unaware of what I'm looking for, I cannot find it because I have no idea what I'm looking for. It is the kind of philosophy that goes beyond ordinary human beings, whom it is supposed to reflect upon and describe by going beyond them: but to say what?

The Platonic revolution coincides with the establishment of Western philosophy in that it takes up this very dilemma. What does it mean to think in a world where we are absorbed by the life of passions more than by spiritual reflection?

Plato's solution involves the idea of passion. Without it, the paradox of Menon would be irresolvable in his eyes. The passions plunge us into the illusion that surrounds desire; but by knowing this we have a tendency to go beyond them. We know what we are looking for, and because we are under the spell of the passions, we have not yet been able to find it. It is true that the major objection to this argument consists of our saying that if we know that we have passions, we don't have to acquire reason, since we cannot be conscious of the passions except through reason, which unmasks them for what they really are. On the other hand, if we don't know that we have been victims of our passions as long as we don't perceive them for what they are in reality, how can we even have the idea of liberating ourselves from them? Passion is at once something of which we cannot become conscious, since it is a creator of illusions, and something which we must recognize as being a source of trickery. Isn't this contradictory?

Plato's reply rests on the distinction between philosophy and nonphilosophy, the latter being the mode of thought for ordinary persons, or more precisely, of each person in his or her material and corporal life.

Philosophy is the stage at which passions are discovered, thus of the body that must be overcome, while life (which is centered upon our daily desires, nutrition, the quest for money, the sex drive, and so forth) makes us believe that the representations arising out of these activities are the truth of our existence, a purely sensible truth.

How therefore does one become a philosopher? Plato says that:

> It looks as though a sort of narrow path will bring us out on to the trail, because so long as we use the body as well as reason in our search and our soul is tainted with that sort of blemish, we will never fully attain to what we want—namely, the truth. The body presents us with innumerable distractions, because of the necessity of looking after it; and again, if any illnesses assail it, they too hamper us in our pursuit of truth. The body fills us with emotions of love, desire, and fear, with all kinds of fantasy and nonsense, so that in very truth it really doesn't give us a chance, as they say, ever to think of anything at all. In fact, wars and strife and battles are all due simply to the body and its desires. All wars take place because of the acquisition of property, and property we are compelled to acquire simply because of the body—we are slaves in its service; and so, for all these reasons, we have no time for philosophy. And, lastly, even if we do get some time off from looking after it, and turn to some investigation, it keeps on turning up everywhere in our search, and causes disturbance and confusion, and thoroughly dumbfounds us, so that because of it we cannot catch a glimpse of truth; it really is proved to us that if we are ever going to have pure knowledge of anything, we must get rid of the body and survey things in themselves by means of the soul herself alone; then it seems, we shall have our heart's desire, that of which we claim to be lovers, even wisdom—when we die, as the argument indicates, but not so long as we live. For it is not possible to have pure knowledge of anything so long as we are with the body, then one of two things must be true: either it is nowhere possible to acquire knowledge, or only after death—for then, but not till then, the soul will be independent, free from the body. So long as we are alive, it seems likely that we shall come nearest to having knowledge if we do our utmost to have no contact or association with the body except in so far as is absolutely necessary, and do not infect ourselves with its nature, but purify ourselves of it, until God himself gives us final release; and if we are thus purified and

freed from the foolishness of the body, we shall probably be in the company of the pure, and through our very selves come to have knowledge of all that is unsullied—that is, I suppose, of truth; for it is, perhaps, not lawful for the impure to attain to that which is pure.[3]

As long as I have not become a philosopher, I cannot imagine myself being ensnared by passion. To become a philosopher is to make this discovery and then to act accordingly with regard to having a body and the sensible desires that characterize it. This separation between one who is a philosopher and one who is not seems to be a gap that cannot be bridged, unless we admit that all human beings are potentially philosophers to the degree that they can liberate themselves from their bodies, educate themselves by reminding themselves of truths that are buried in their souls before birth, and which have been obscured subsequently by immersion in the sensible world. The recollection of these innate truths is the solution that Plato suggests to the paradox of Menon: I look for truth that the passions have overshadowed. On account of the passions, I am unaware: it is therefore useful to search, but I know what I am looking for, since I know the nature of the obstacle that stands before me, and therefore I am able to overcome it. Reason, Logos, is at heart an anti-body, always already there, of which it is necessary to retake possession in the struggle against the sensible.

Men According to Reason and Passion

Passion is a necessary condition for philosophy, and, therefore, for reason and rational discourse about human beings. As a consequence, there are three possibilities. There are those who are prisoners of the sensible, but who don't even doubt that they are. That is the majority: they occupy themselves by accumulating goods and by satisfying their immediate needs. After that there are those who, knowing this, are above it: they have reason and have overcome the sentiments inspired by passion. They are called philosophers, because they have the wisdom not to follow things other than those which reason dictates. Between the two, one finds those who know they must overcome the obstacle of the passions, or those who chose not to resist out of weakness, like the child who gives in to the chocolate despite the danger that it poses. This intermediate class, between the working masses and contemplative person Plato

3. Plato *Phaedo* 66b–67a, trans. R. S. Bluck (New York: Bobbs-Merrill, 1955).

sees as *Guardians,* those who serve the City. They can go in the direction of the masses and render themselves indistinct, if they are lacking in the courage needed to refuse the call of the passions. Or else they can follow the imperatives of reason and use them to straddle the masses.

In the tripartite nature of this description one might have recognized the ideal City, where according to Plato's description in *Republic,* equilibrium is guaranteed through the harmony of the three orders. These are similar to those of the ancien régime, unless by this we are referring to a proper division of Indo-European societies, as has been suggested by Dumézil. For Plato, the motivation seems to come out of a real philosophical imperative. It is important for him to understand why not everyone is capable of rationality, of evaluating whether that which confronts them is good or bad and under which conditions. The universality of Platonism consists of saying that, first, each person has a soul and a body; second, each person has the potential of becoming wise; and third, that each person is nevertheless enclosed in a sensible world which is his or her obstacle and within which most people prefer to keep themselves, since it is easier, without knowing, or perhaps even knowing, and it is there that the meaning of this intermediate position of which the Guardians are the representatives. But to affirm that a human being has a soul and a body, to explain the possibility of reason, the difficulty of its installation therein, and the exercise that could be done to this end, implies that each one of us is potentially one of the masses, a guardian, or a philosopher. Education, the teacher, will reveal to us the function that our soul is most likely to be predisposed to play. All souls have these three dimensions in them, intrinsically. Plato takes the example of the desire to drink:

> "Now, do we know of cases where thirsty people are unwilling to drink?"
>
> "Certainly," he said. "It's a common occurrence."
>
> "What would be the explanation for these cases?" I asked.
>
> "Don't we have to say that their mind contains a part which is telling them to drink and a part which is telling them not to drink, and that this is a different part and overcomes the part which is telling them to drink?"
>
> "I think so," he said.
>
> "And so those occasions when thirst and so on are countermanded occur thanks to rationality, whereas the pulls and impulses occur thanks to afflictions and diseased states, don't they?"

"I suppose so."

"So wouldn't it be irrational of us to expect that these are two separate parts," I said, "one of which we can describe as rational and the other as irrational and desirous. The first is responsible for the mind's capacity to think rationally, and the second—which is an ally of certain satisfactions and pleasures—for its capacity to feel lust, hunger and thirst and in general to be stirred by desire."[4]

Clearly, Plato opposes in the soul itself desire, which comes from the body—and which he assimilates to a malevolent or pathological affection, since it gnaws away at us—and the *logos*. The soul is not purely rational; it has a lustful part, the *concupiscible,* as he says. Such a viewpoint poses problems, for although I can understand the nature of a desire such as hunger, thirst, or sexual desire, I cannot really grasp what these same desires could be when they are considered afflictions of the *soul*. That passions are bodily is an acceptable notion; but that they are as much a part of the soul as bodily movements or, worse still, diseases, renders the whole question rather enigmatic. If they are part of the soul, they are judgments, representations of sensible impulses. Here, we think of Freud. Notice the relationship that exists between the Platonic model of the soul and that which Freud puts forth twenty-five centuries later: there are instincts and their unconscious representations, the censorship of the Ego, which for Plato evokes the intermediate and guardian part of the soul, and the Superego, which has responsibility for needs. Be that as it may, the idea of passions as corporal affections of the soul poses a serious problem which Plato does not attempt to resolve; on the contrary, he introduces this notion as a means of rendering philosophy possible by establishing an opposition between body and soul.

We still have to set out the domain and the role of the third element, which will not be any easier. Plato writes: "'Let's have these, then,' I said, 'as two distinct aspects of our minds. What about the passionate part, however, which is responsible for the mind's capacity for passion? Is it a third part, or might it be interchangeable with one of the other two'?"[5] Irascibility is a *sui generis* part of the soul, which helps us resist sensible impulses without helping us gain knowledge about the intelligible, from whence comes its status as simple guardian of passions. But isn't irascibility itself a passion which identifies itself with the movement that

4. Plato *Republic* 439c–d.
5. Ibid., 439e.

makes us angry? Isn't it that which gives us courage and determination to demonstrate both temperance and will?

All of this renders this third element quite mysterious. Plato is fully aware of the problem: "It's not all that uncommon to find a person's desires compelling him to go against this reason, and to see him cursing himself and venting his passion on the source of the compulsion within him. It's as if there were two warring factions, with passion fighting on the side of reason. But I'm sure you wouldn't claim that you had ever, in yourself or in anyone else, met a case of passion sided with the desires against the rational mind, when the rational mind prohibits resistance."[6] Here is the problem: if I *know* that something causes harm, how could I give into it since nobody voluntarily opts for harm?

From this point, weakness is impossible, and only ignorance is conceivable. And yet, Plato suggests that one can inflict harm and have remorse for it because reason is too weak, even despite the light that it sheds upon the act—and the necessity of abstaining therefrom.

Henceforth the *thumos,* the irascible, can either line up alongside of desires—we are too weak to oppose them—or it can ally itself with reason as a means of getting them to submit. But isn't it because reason is too weak that the irascible reinforces the violence of passions? And if reason gets stronger, wouldn't it suffice to dominate passions without a go-between? In this sense, take the person who feels he or she has been wronged. "Under these circumstances, your passion boils and rages, and fights for what you regard as right. Then hunger, cold, and other sufferings make you stand firm and conquer them, and only success or death can stop it fighting the good fight, unless it is recalled by your rational mind and calmed down, as a dog is by a shepherd."[7] And he becomes like a sheep dog:

> "That's a very good simile," he said. "And in fact, the part we've got the auxiliaries to play in our community is just like that of dogs, with their masters being the rulers, who are, as it were, the shepherds of the community."
>
> "Yes, you've got it," I said. "That's exactly what I mean. But there's something else here too, and I wonder if you've noticed it as well.'
>
> "What is it?"
>
> "That we're getting the opposite impression of the passionate

6. Ibid., 440b.
7. Ibid., 440c.

part from what we did before. Previously we were thinking that it was an aspect of the desirous part, but now that seems to be way off the mark, and we're saying that when there's mental conflict, it is far more likely to fight alongside reason."[8]

Would there be a freedom or a will which, according to Plato, would make us oscillate between the good and the evil, known one to the other beforehand? One might think so. But the very nature of the irascible leads to the question:

> "Is it different from the rational part, then, or is it a version of it, in which case there are two, not three, mental categories— the rational and the desirous? Or will the analogy with the community hold good? Three classes constituted the community— the one which works for a living, the auxiliaries, and the policy makers—so there is in the mind as well a third part, the passionate part, which is an auxiliary of the rational part, unless it is corrupted by bad upbringing?"
>
> "It must be a third part," he said.
>
> "Yes,' I said, "if we find that it's distinct from the rational part as it is from the desirous part."
>
> "But that's easy," he said. "Just look at children. It's evident that from the moment of their birth they have a copious supply of passion, but I'm not convinced that some of them ever acquire reason, and it takes quite a time for most of them to do so."[9]

This is why Plato is able to compare the soul to a cart drawn by two horses, which evokes the irascible and the concupiscible, driven by a coachman who represents reason. It is sufficient that the two horses align their efforts in the same direction for the coachman to find himself swept away. One horse that obeys, on the other hand, could reorient the "desirous horse," the symbol of the concupiscible.

Morality and Politics

After all, passions are bodily. Hence we won't be surprised to see them situated in particular parts of the body. "To have a heart," "hard-headed," are as much categorizations that remain for us from this conception, of

8. Ibid., 440e.
9. Ibid., 440c–441b.

which the *Timaeus* (70a–71b) by Plato is a good description. What is
described here is a tradition that, from Galen to Descartes, will impact
upon the entire tradition of Western thought. There is a physiology of
passions, linked to the humors, to movements of the body, internal or
from the outside, which is perpetuated to this very day.[10] The medical-
ization of passions leads later on to our seeing in the excess of passions
the organic source of what came to be known as diseases of the soul. At
the point where the body betrays the mind we find the overflowing of
passion: if the Other of reason, which it cannot utter even as it tries to do
so, is for Foucault, madness, it is more generally and more fundamentally
because madness emanates from passion. Therein, the mind ceases to be
itself, as though by an organic excess which can be cured following the
examples of disturbances which come in principle from the body.

But in the tripartite form of the soul there is more than a simple
description of the workings of our mental structures. Virtue, linked to
knowledge like evil to the ignorance of ends to be pursued, is the result
of the harmonized relationship of the three levels. The struggle against
the passions postulates reason as supreme, that is, the domination of inferior functions by that which has integrated the three moments within it
as stages of an education oriented toward contemplative wisdom. It is a
curious paradox that this consists of highlighting contemplation, and
then justifying this by and for political mastery over the City. From here
comes the crucial role of the *Guardians* who must assist the wise men.
What must be noted here is the close link between Plato's virtue, politics, and the division of the soul. The intellectual has wisdom resulting
from knowledge and which is the source of his legitimacy as the leader
of the City. The three notions go together: "Isn't it the combination of
culture and exercise which will make them attuned to each other? The
two combined provide fine discussions, and studies to stretch and educate the rational part, and music and rhythm to relax, calm, and soothe
the passionate part."[11] Only reason can speak about passion, since it is a
concept relating to reflection. Knowledge of passion, and the overcoming of passion into wisdom, is a fact of reason which affirms itself to be
the first, overriding, and superior principle.

If justice is the rational harmony of three functions, injustice is disharmony, that is, a passionate unruliness, a sickness of the soul which takes
possession of the social body and divides it up by upsetting its natural
divisions.

10. Cf. J. D. Vincent, *La Biologie des passions* (Paris: Jacob, 1986).
11. Plato *Republic* 441e.

> Isn't it bound to involve these three factors being in conflict, intruding into one another's work, and exchanging roles, and one part rebelling against the mind as a whole in an improper attempt to usurp the ruler—improper because its natural function is to be dominated unless it belongs to the ruling class? Our position, I'm sure, will be that it is disruption and disorder of the three parts along these lines that constitutes not only immorality, but also lack of discipline, cowardice, and stupidity—in a word, badness of any kind.[12]

Its harmony upset, the parts of the City enter into conflict with one another; the sense of *moderation,* the equal proportion, is crushed, and *hybris,* the sense of *immoderation,* takes its place and conflicts erupt. The ideal order gets corrupted little by little, like the soul, which finds itself submerged by the passions. The political constitutions degenerate into *timocracy,* in which the Guardians seize power for themselves, *oligarchy,* and *democracy*.

This division, which produces rivalry in the ruling class and a situation wherein Guardians mistakenly consider themselves wise men, creates an atmosphere of progressive decadence, characterized by the arrival on the scene of the lowest forms of passion. In the place of honor comes the desire for monetary gain, of which *oligarchy* is the manifestation. A small number of persons carry off the goods of the City for their own profit. The struggle continues and wins over those who, feeling dispossessed, break rank and rise up against the rulers, demanding equality in a free expression of passion It is the dominion of the appetite, of license, of an overall right to anarchy. Tyranny is inexorably waiting at the end of the road. From a desire for military honor we now have a desire for profit, and this desire for profit leads to the onset of a gangrene of the social body through passions (license), with the strongest claiming power (without right) and imposing his own passions upon everyone.

Education aims to inculcate virtue into the global chain of means and ends, a virtue which is the *telos* of a practice. The effect of a rupture is to suppress the view of principles, the Good, and each function of the soul or of the City establishes itself without regard for others: this is the source of the inevitable conflict which rises up between the parts of the soul, as between the corresponding social classes.

12. Ibid., 444b.

The Fundamental Ambiguity of the
Platonic Theory of the Passions

The reader will no doubt have already realized that passion, for Plato, is at once the name of a problem, to which reason is the solution, and also that which, by its own nature, opposes itself to all resolution, since it impedes our ability to see that there is a problem because it instills itself as a kind of blindness. By passion, we become aware that it is necessary to go beyond ourselves, but on account of passion, we cannot imagine that there is a place beyond ourselves that can be sought out. The paradox is a product of the fact that passion is both reflexive and the unreflected part of sensible life; an irresolvable contradiction.

Torn between these two poles, Plato does not cut the Gordian knot that he himself has tied. In the second hypothesis, concerning blindness, education does not aim to teach each person how to gain access to reason. Universalism doesn't have any meaning. There are those who know, those who ignore but ignore that they ignore, and those who know without being like the first group, who know that they know. Education aims to help each one achieve his or her proper ends to the degree of each person's own ability. Virtue is hereby that of the specialist who manages to successfully execute his or her own task. We are not elevated in society through teaching, which is the notion of education that we have imagined exists throughout this century; on the contrary, we learn through education to remain in our preassigned places. The harmonious unity of the soul reaches its goal in the organized division of work. But how do we become wise if we cannot acquire that which we had previously ignored? This is the impossibility harbored by the paradox of Menon: recollection doesn't resolve anything, since if I know that which I must remember, it proves that I have not forgotten it; and if I ignore that which should be recalled to memory, I cannot use the procedure of recollection. In short, the thesis of uselessness or impossibility is redirected by recollection, which was supposed to resolve it. We cannot acquire knowledge; we have it or we don't, and we can know that we don't have it (if we know that we have it, we know and fall back into the first case described). There lie the fixed situations which correspond to as many social situations, destined as well to remain stable according to a law of harmony of the whole.

Plato also defends the idea that the recollection of the true and the good is possible, that each person can have access to the light and leave the Cave of the sensible. It is possible to learn about that which one doesn't know, and even if Plato is not entirely clear on this point, he does admit in principle recollection as a "conversion of the soul" to the truth that it buries and ignores. All human beings are equal; they are no longer slaves, each is potentially a sage. *The Republic* does not really express this opinion, but *The Menon*, with the episode that describes the slave who recalls the truths that are dormant within him, seems to go in this other direction. Passions are not unmitigated and they can indeed be overcome. Education must fulfill this mission.

The ambiguous status of passion remains nevertheless intact. Passion is that which impedes our ability to gain access to Goodness as it does to Truth, while all the while being that which permits and renders useful the act of finding Goodness in that which it identifies as being the obstacle that must be overcome. Passion is the difficulty and that which impedes our ability to see it, surmountable in the first case, unimaginable in the second. The irascible is that part of the soul which reproduces the dilemma: courage, the power of the will (in an intellectual universe where there is no will, for to know what is good binds us to accomplish it), the irascible is either reason or passion, and at the same time different from both. The irascible part of the soul serves to explain that those who know what is harmful are nevertheless unable to forbid it to themselves. Passion creates in them a need from which they seem unable to escape because their "wills" are too weak, even if their lucidity is whole.

Plato seems to oscillate between a two-stage and a three-stage model. Passion that is unconscious, and which is overcome when it becomes conscious: this is the bipartite model. But to know this passion could be considered as implying simply our consciousness of the problem, without signifying that we are thereby rid of it. So either we give in or we resist: this is the dilemma which the intermediary faculty poses, and socially, it explains the existence of a class of Guardians in the City who can follow reason or rebel against it. Christianity and indeed Aristotle as well are both torn apart by this ambiguity of passion for reason: what is the knowledge of passion, having overcome it or having become conscious of what must be overcome? There are those who think that the discovery of passion saves you from it because it is unmasked; and there are those who think that to recognize the difficulty does not change it, it remains present. Ignorance of the problem, becoming aware of the problem, and its eventual resolution through reason are the three stages into which the process can be divided.

The Response That History Gives to the Paradox of Passion: Christianity as the Extension of Platonism

If human beings are bound within the sensible, and if this is the definition of passion, then they are necessarily condemned to commit harmful actions without realizing it, because they are not even aware of their own confusion. This natural state is both innocent and sinful. Conversion is based upon the existence of a master who is able to communicate truth. All Christianity is the product of this conception, and one understands therein the importance of Platonism in the emergence of the Christian conception of humanity. The ambiguity of original sin is nonetheless inevitable as well, since human beings are born guilty of Adam's sin, which they must atone for even as completely innocent babies; this sin is not really theirs. But that which they do not know, indeed cannot know, *we* know it for them: it is an inescapable kind of *over-determination* which weighs heavily upon their shoulders.

Passions are identified with sins, or radical evil, which necessitates for those who seek deliverance a conversion of the soul, a liberating and spiritual asceticism. All are condemned in advance, because since they are human they are also the descendants of Adam; and yet there does exist the possibility of being redeemed by the priest. Protestantism rejects this privilege; only God is endowed with the capacity to accord grace and salvation of the soul. But here as well, the contradictory character of passion is revealed through analysis. The innocent one is in reality a guilty one, and the priest is the one who knows this. He knows about original sin, this radical evil which sets off human history. He can proceed with the conversion and initiate salvation. Innocence is but an ignorance of the wrong, it is thus false innocence, despite the fact that prior to committing the original sin, Adam seemed to be exempt from all sin. Perhaps this only applies to him?

Note that Protestantism dissociates itself from Catholicism in that for the former all must be considered *a priori* guilty, from where emanates the uselessness of the priest, who cannot affect the human condition even if it is he who knows of the error, whereas the ordinary person remains in a state of blessed innocence. For Protestantism, all recognize that they are stained by the original sin and, restraining the passions, do not need to have their existence revealed; nor can they be pardoned in the course of confession, since these passions make up the human condition.

What must be recognized about all of these ideas is their source in Plato. For him, passion being that which impedes us from doing good, as though by virtue of a forgetfulness which passion perpetuates, since nobody could be evil without knowing it, passion absolves us even though it also represents malevolence. Yet passion being that which pushes humanity straightaway toward evil, a true state of innocence or ignorance is excluded. This is where condemnation of those trapped in the Cave comes from. And at the same time, Plato, like Christians, thinks that there is an original state where desire is innocent and ignorant of itself, protected from good and evil.

An alternative possibility to this untenable duality will nonetheless appear. We owe its existence to Aristotle, who will propose an original, if not contemporary, resolution to the problem of the passions which History will downplay, favoring instead Plato's view.

2

Passion as a
New Relationship with Being

Being and *Logos*

If it were possible to characterize the work of Aristotle with a single word, then the choice would have to be *ontologization,* a somewhat barbaric word that signifies the systematic reflection about what *is*. What *is* nature? What *is* language or reason? What *is* science? and so forth. It is certain that we already came across these questions in Plato's work, since, by putting them into the mouth of Socrates, he thereby placed his interlocutor in a difficult position. We must recognize, with Pascal, that "we cannot begin to define the being without falling in this absurdity because we cannot define a word without starting with this one, Is, whether we express it or imply it. Therefore to define being, you must say Is, and then employ the word defined in this definition."[1]

Socrates had the upper hand in these matters, since he was able to stitch together the answers offered up by those persons he was questioning. Since all answers are both improperly expressed and circular, then other answers would be just as valuable: but how do we know which ones? Socrates, who is always consistent in these matters, thinks that these questions cannot be resolved. So why ask them? To demonstrate that they cannot be resolved and, by the same token, to unmask as

---

1. Pascal, *Opuscules* (Paris: Gallimard, 1954), p. 580.

unduly pretentious those who pretend to know the answers to them. But Socrates seems to be attempting to undermine the social legitimacy of those who occupy important positions in society on account of the knowledge that they claim to possess. If for example the judge is shown to be incapable of defining justice, under which guise is he undertaking to exercise his functions as judge?[2]

Plato thought that if such questions were posed, they had to have answers. They are too important to just assign them a simple critical function. Plato tries to go beyond Socrates' "I know that I know nothing." Still, since all of the answers are equivalent, there is no way to decide among them short of embarking upon a bid for power; eventually, a contradiction will appear in them which will render illusory the resolution they suggest. As such, one can imagine that Socrates didn't write anything because he didn't believe that any answer would be possible which did not redirect the initial question, and keep it open, that is, forever unresolvable. But to believe this is already to answer. Even Socrates appears to be trapped to some degree in his own game. For Plato, things are clear; Socratic questions have one solution: it is enough to simply read them properly to discover the conditions to which they are directed.

What does Plato suggest? Quite simply that when we ask "what is X?," we are putting the accent not on X, which could effectively be all and anything, but on the fact that X *is* something. We are looking for the *being* of X; and this *being* of X will be uttered in the answer. As such, justice will be this or that, and the answer will stipulate what the being of justice is. Socrates could have been in agreement with this particular point; he would simply answer that X does not have a fixed and unique being which can be determined *a priori,* a determination in the name of which we would reject this answer, accept this other one, and exclude the others. But Plato goes even further, which is the basis of his originality as regards Socrates (if indeed it is possible to separate them, given that Socrates left no written texts behind); Plato's idea is that being is characterized by certain properties which are indispensable if an answer is to see the light of day. Without them, a multiplicity of assertions will exist and combat with each other without ever permitting the confirmation of one or another. This is what Plato means by the term *sensible*:[3] a universe of fluctuating, contradictory opinions (*doxa*) without any necessity; in short, what we have here is an unreliable, even dangerous

2. On these and related questions, see Meyer's *Of Problematology.*
3. [I'm using the same term the author used in French, "le sensible." *Trans.*]

universe, if we are to judge by all of these sophists who, being the good speakers that they were, were able to flatter the appetites of the People and thereby led them to their downfall with the defeat of Athens, which signaled its eventual and irreversible decline.

In fact, being must be defined in another fashion; in order to have a single answer, it is necessary that that which *is* cannot be otherwise. If John is bald, he cannot be hairy, he *must* be what he is. The being of John is that which makes him John; nothing else is relevant. Exclusivity is hereby affirmed, the alternative is excluded, and by the same token, we are certain not to fall back on questions which express other alternatives, which is what the dialectic of Socrates shows. With all answers having an equally undecidable status, the question remains. If we do come up with an answer, the question disappears; it abolishes itself in the answer which excludes all alternatives.

As long as there remain two answers, *a fortiori* more, the question does not have a solution, since it has several without having a single one, and the problem of knowing what could truly resolve it is perpetuated in the face of this multiplicity. Plato defines the being of X as that which makes it such that (= X) is indeed X and not something else: this is a principle of identity, of noncontradiction, but also, of it being sufficient to say that it is X that is in question here and not Y or Z, and the reason to say as well that it is X, and only X. As such, to say that the individual named John *is,* that is to say, if he is, he is necessarily himself. He cannot not be that which he is. Although this is formal, thanks to this Plato can set forth a *logos* which is not indefinitely problematic. He even defined it by excluding the problematic in the interest of necessity, because it is said that a thing, or a property, is necessary when the contrary is impossible. And to condemn the introduction of this contradictoriness which would reopen the *logos,* reason, to the alternative or the possible, in short, to the problematic, there exists the absolute requirement of noncontradiction: for instance, John is large, therefore, he is not "not large" or small.

Necessity thereby becomes the essential property of *logos,* of reason and its discourse. One speaks as well of *apodicticity,* from the Greek *apodeixis,* a term which signifies *demonstration.* Indeed, what is more constraining in its conclusion than a mathematical demonstration?

But we cannot reduce discursivity to the necessity of scientific and logical *logos,* as though everything else doesn't exist, under the pretext that we would thereby rehabilitate the uncertainty of sensible messages. There is a discourse on contingency, on non-logic, which must fall inside the domain of reason. This is clear with the idea of passion, which has a hybrid status. Passion is a rational concept for naming that which is not, which makes passion at once the absolute un-thought of human existence and also its abusive rationalization. A philosophical systematic, wherein one considers being in all of its forms, cannot avoid the multiplicity of that which is, and that which is includes the sensible. Is it possible to speak about this without falling into the Socratic impossibility with its unanswerable questions? This is indeed the Aristotelian challenge: upholding the primacy of apodicticity without ignoring whatever escapes it. This is the only way to secure a global view of the world of humanity.

Aristotle's New Conception of Being

The multiplicity of being leads to a multiplicity of ways by which to categorize or describe this being. Being is multiple, and according to Aristotle there are ten categories which permit us to grasp this multiplicity. But to affirm that being is multiple is quite obviously contradictory, to the degree that one speaks of being as a unity in itself, underlying multiplicity, which by the same token destroys the thesis put forward here. So much the better, according to those who stand up for *apodicticity* of the *logos,* since behind the notion of an exploded and dispersed being, one recovers its necessary unity. But the contradiction remains. Plato did not wish to know anything other than the necessity. This was of course just as contradictory, since the multiplicity of essences, although all necessary, is not in itself an essence and if it is, we find ourselves sent off into infinity. Aristotle's solution, which consists of his desire to articulate the unity of what is upon the different forms which could be, is thus an act of lucidity. What remains for him is to take on the contradiction that underwrites this short sentence: "Being is multiple." Aristotle's solution to this dilemma is brilliant and will have consequences for occidental thought that we have still not worked through even today, despite the aporias which accompany it.

He will, in effect, invent the *proposition*. Being is one as subject, and many as predicate: there is no more contradiction, since being is one and multiple according to different perspectives. If I say that "Socrates is bald," Socrates is necessarily himself, he cannot be not Socrates. It is the necessity of *logos* which is hereby assured. But he is bald, which is a contingent or accidental property, since Socrates could still have hair. Thus, the theory of Ideas has been replaced by the theory of the proposition, or propositionalism.

The norm of *logos,* apodicticity, is not only saved, but consolidated, even as it leaves a place, through predication, for multiplicity. In fact, categories such as quality (such as baldness) or location (such as being in Paris) have no autonomy, since they always refer back to the subject to which they are ascribed: *Who* is bald? *What* is found in Paris? In short, it is always necessary to recall the attribute to the thing of which it is an attribute. Being may well be multiple; substance has an essential unifying role in that it incarnates the norm of *logos*.

> The term "being" is used in several senses. In one sense, it signifies whatness and at-this; in another, it signifies a quality or a quantity or one of the others which are predicted in this way. Although "being" is used in so many senses, it is evident that of these the primary sense is whatness, and used in this sense it signifies a substance. For when we state that this one has some quality we say that it is good or bad but not that it is three cubits long or a man; but when we state what it is, we say that it is a man or a god but not white or hot or three cubits long. The others are called "beings" in view of the fact that they are quantities of being which is spoken of in this primary sense, or qualities of it, or affections of it, or something else of this kind. Because of this, one might even raise the problem whether walking, being healthy, sitting and others of this kind are beings or not beings; for by nature each of these does not exist by itself and cannot be separated from a substance but rather, if anything, it is that which walks or that which sits or that which is healthy that is a being. These latter appear to be beings to a higher degree, because there is something definite in each of them, namely, the underlying subject; and this is the substance and the individual, which is indicated in the corresponding predication, for we do not use the terms "the good" and "that which sits" without including the substance. It is clear, then, that each of the others exists because substances exist. Thus, being in the primary sense, not in a qualified sense but without qualification, would be a substance.[4]

In fact, if we speak of quality, for example, it is always in order to refer to something which *is* whatever the quality *in question* affirms: What is Socrates? A bald human being.

---

4. Aristotle *Metaphysics* 1028a10–33, trans. Hippocrates G. Apostle (Bloomington: Indiana University Press, 1966).

It is true that being remains multiple in spite of everything. This does not pose any problems for particular propositions, since a (logical) subject is different from its attributes; but when we consider being itself, the contradiction appears: being is one, as being, but it does not exist outside what is. It is this or that, and it never detaches itself from particular realities. Beings, not Being. The unity of being is impossible, since it fragments by virtue of the fact of the multiplicity of categories that expresses it. Aristotle, conscious of the problem, comes down on the side of the norm of *logos* as set out by Plato: necessity is on the side of the subject, thus "the inquiry or perplexity concerning what being is, in early times and now and always is just this: what is a substance?"[5]

If Aristotle thinks he is right, it is surely because of the reductive character of the propositional subject. This subject swallows up all possible alternatives, all multiplicity: Is Socrates bald or hairy? Young or old? One or the other, necessarily. Socrates cannot not be what he is, Socrates. By nature, if he is bald, he cannot be not-bald; if he is young, then his being old is necessarily excluded. The unity of the subject demands that of the proposition. The principle of noncontradiction, according to Aristotle, is the supreme principle of the *logos*: it is easily comprehended, since this principle stipulates that the alternative, the question of "A or not A," conceals in fact only *one* proposition: either A or not-A. The other is impossible, and if it is possible, it is not possible that it be the case except in another time frame. Socrates will be old after having been young. But each time, one and only one proposition will prevail.

Let's ask one simple question. Did Aristotle really resolve the problem of necessity by the primacy of substance, of the propositional subject? In order to discover that this is not the case, only the following form of reasoning will suffice. What is Socrates? Someone who is bald, or young, or Greek, or whatever. What he is, is that. But is he necessarily what he is? He is necessarily Socrates, that is sure. But he is not necessarily bald or young. Socrates cannot not be anyone other than Socrates, but to be Socrates comes back to seeing him associated with a series of contingent predicates. How can necessity be identified with contingency, and conversely, how can contingency be reduced to necessity?

Here again we witness the genius of Aristotle. To think about being, necessity, seems to be impossible. And yet, thanks to the principle of noncontradiction, the alternative is excluded *a priori;* thus we know that one proposition is necessarily true, and that its contradiction is necessarily false. We don't need a general theory of being for this, that is, an ontology; and this permits us to go beyond the impossibility of taking

5. Ibid., 1028b3.

sides on the contradiction implied by "being (one) is multiple." We make statements about particular beings: *Am* I young or old, at the moment when I speak to you? No ontology is needed to answer this question, but simply a good sense of observation. In short, Socrates is not necessarily bald, but he is necessarily bald or not bald. For the norm of *logos* to be saved, apodictically, it is necessary that logic, "science," speak out, since it alone has the wherewithal to generate propositions that are necessarily true in a systematic fashion in the place of ontological philosophy. The success of science or of its necessity, its institution, is the result of the failure of all ontology.

The consequence of such an answer is fundamental as well. That which achieves the essence of *logos* is scientific and logical discourse; in it we find the founding norm, and not in ontology, which speaks of a being that is as much necessary as multiple (that is both too much and not enough). Thus is born the rivalry between, and the contradiction of, science and metaphysics. And we know which will emerge the victor in terms of ability to offer a description of the world. But it is ontology that established the norm which was transferred to science, which could not itself have founded the norm even though it incarnates it. In many respects we have not escaped from this philosophical ping-pong game related to propositionalism.

We will leave aside this debate, since it has been the subject of other work.[6] What is important here is that the debate itself signifies the presence of an unsolvable difficulty. The abandonment of ontology and to move toward science are answers to the impossibility of thinking about propositional unity: this unity puts into place a formal necessity which only observation or logic can actualize. This is to say how much the very notion of necessity, an original norm of the *logos,* causes difficulties. But it is also in this very space that we have always had pathos.

We hope that the reader has been willing to accompany us to the land of necessity, since all theories of passion have been inscribed as replies to this concept, or more precisely to this problematic, which has defined reason ever since attempts have been made to conceptualize it.

The Rehabilitation of That Which Is Probable and That Which Is Contingent

Plato saw in the passions the place where the probable, the sensible, and the contingent are incarnated in humanity. His dialectic was aimed at freeing us from them: questions and answers are but the pretext for

6. Cf. M. Meyer, *Science et métaphysique chez Kant* (Paris: PUF, 1988).

recalling the truths that are buried within the soul. But Aristotle finds a strange incompatibility in this concept. Those who are caught within the gears of their own passions do not even put into doubt whether they should be questioning themselves. Only other individuals can make them realize it, from where this dialectical aspect typical of discovering knowledge comes. Isn't it absurd to render this accidental, even as we pretend to do away with all contingency? Isn't it true that objective truth flows from questions that some individual or another in one circumstance or another wishes to pose? And aren't these questions arrived at from perspectives that we would today consider subjective?

Aristotle's solution is clear: it is imperative that we separate the dialectic, as an interrogative process, from the science that is supposed to be its result. Science is apodictic, but dialectics cannot be. As to the role of the passions, there is nothing to deny, but something to recognize: they are part of dialectic, science does not have to treat them. It is possible to speak of their role and, moreover, to do so in a positive fashion. Notice that Aristotle split into two parts that which Plato amalgamated under the banner of the *dialectic,* calling them the dialectic, which he referred to as rhetoric or argumentation, and logic, therefore science, which he considered the discourse concerning that which is necessary.[7] The syllogistic thus found its Euclid, as did the rhetorical; Plato saved himself from studying both of them by combining them, like water and fire, under the single term, dialectic.

By the same token, it is clear that passion is no longer considered as necessarily opposed to reason, since the two domains have nothing whatever to do with each other. To make an accurate syllogism is not to take a stand against one's desires. What brings us to the proper conclusions flows from formal rules. Passions come under the dialectic, and we should therefore not be surprised to discover that they are treated in the work by Aristotle that is devoted to rhetoric. In themselves, passions are neither good nor bad; they represent types of audiences, and so doing, they implicate particular kinds of arguments. We don't convince people who are possessed by hatred in the same way as those who are possessed by rage. The commonplace and the arguments that must be put forward as pertinent are in those two examples different. It is necessary to know the passions of men in order to persuade them. Aristotle thus restored the passions, but not only from the technical rhetorical point of view, which Plato would have done too as a means of denouncing them as a whole.

---

7. Aristotle *Nicomachean Ethics* 1139b18, trans. Hippocrates G. Apostle (Dordrecht: D. Reidel, 1975).

How Far Could Aristotle Go in Rehabilitating the Sensible?

This is the question: it is necessary that what Plato responded to through the absolute apodicticity of *logos,* Aristotle satisfy as well, since this is the definition of reason: the discourse of necessity and the necessity of this discourse, which together make an absolute based upon itself. The absolute has always been nothing other than that: a reality that through its institution excludes all that is not itself, and which proves by the same token its unique necessity. And what could be more necessary as a discourse than that which wishes to recognize only necessity, and which makes it its very object? Reason, as hereby defined, could claim to be a perfect substitution for myth as a general and exclusive system for the explanation of the world.

The Platonic dialectic is in danger from the word go. I am looking to understand what X is, says Plato, that is, its essence, its Idea. Since I don't ask myself about Y or Z, this means that I think that I can already distinguish X from Y or Z, and that therefore I know that X is not Y or Z, and that I know what it is so that I will not confuse it with the others. It is as though I already knew the answer even before posing the question. This really is paradoxical, since if I am wondering about X, I do so in the hope of discovering what X is. And to ask myself about it, I must know what it is. How is it possible to reconcile the fact that I don't know what I know already without having the sense that this is contradictory? Plato's solution is that the sensible that is already given is not the same as the intelligible which lies dormant at the base of my soul; and which is awoken through Socratic questioning. Obviously, the dialectic, that which must join the intelligible to the sensible, which utters what it *is,* presupposes that the intelligible is itself different, otherwise contact with the sensible would be sufficient. Our point of departure is the sensible which evokes its own essence, and the dialectic in its supreme state would not have any business therein except in terms of essences and their logical combinations. This explains Plato's fascination with mathematics.

It is clear that the identification of the sensible X with its being, as a means of resolving difference (X is nothing other than its being, what it is, while all the while being something else, as sensible manifestation) poses some real problems—even when recognized after the fact. This is because the sensible is, for Plato, problematic; this signifies that we cannot derive any *logos* from it, that alternatives, changes, or variations that lead to contrariness, instability, in short, are inevitable. Plato does not wish to entrench *logos,* which is apodictic and therefore exclusive and adversary to all alternatives, in such a point of departure. If Socrates could not extricate a positivity, a way of answering, a *logos,* that would allow him to tirelessly preclude his returning to the problematic point of departure of his interventions, it is because of his fascination for that which poses problems and from which no solution can flow, just as long as questioning remains the measure of the *logos*.

Yet in his dialectic, Plato departs from the sensible and arrives in the end at the intelligible. Unless one believes in the magical revelation of Ideas which make themselves known to us at each instant. In short, no matter how problematic it is, there is no other starting point than the sensible. As such, all dialectic which flows from it becomes problematic. This is an unacceptable resolution. Wasn't Socrates posthumously correct? Plato separates the sensible from the intelligible, in his dialectic, while at once entrenching one in the other with the sensible as a point of entry, in opposition to the real order. My point of departure is the sensible, namely, a particular man, in order to obtain an Idea of Man in general; but it is this Idea which is primary because it is because man is Man that I am able to recognize in this particular being a copy of the Idea. This is what dictates that X *is* X; it is its *being,* and therefore its foundation. We therefore have two distinct orders of things; the analysis, that which departs from the sensible data and moves to what is primary, which is only primary for another order, which is the intelligible, where one considers what it is *in itself* and not for us. This second order is *synthesis,* which evokes the axioms and theorems of geometry. From the axioms, theorems are derived, which is the synthetic order. But often one does not discover axioms except after the fact, that is, after having discovered theorems. This is the order of analysis, which reproduces the intellectual pathway, but not necessarily the order of things, which we reestablish afterward when we expose causes and consequences independently of the manner by which we were able to find them. Take an example from daily life in order to illustrate this distinction between analysis and synthesis, which are also called *ratio cognoscendi* and *ratio essendi* (Descartes)—reason of knowing and reason of being. I see drops of water on my windowpane, and I deduce analytically that it is raining. And yet, it is obvious that it is because the rain is falling that drops of water are dripping down the window. This is the order that reproduces the series of real causes. That which analytically speaking comes last, the conclusion that it is raining, becomes through synthesis first. The order of things, of what is, finds itself reversed with regard to the order of discovery through sensible evidence.

And then comes the third moment: the rain is made of drops of rain. We identify in being that which was separated from it.

All of this is well and good, says Aristotle, but if the point of departure is the sensible, then we already have the Idea, in order to differentiate, categorize, and identify: there is no miracle in our rediscovery of the identity introduced at the beginning, but since the identity is problematic, the conclusion remains so as well. The only method of proceeding, in order to avoid the vicious circle, is to separate the dialectical and problematizing analysis from the synthesis, which is a sure thing, since it simply replicates the order of things. It is from here that emerges the scission of logic from science, which together with rhetoric, poetics, and dialectics belongs to the domain of the probable, the contestable.

The sensible, and the discursivity of which is it an object, is one thing, and that which is intelligible is another. The two movements, analysis and synthesis, are hereby divided up. But doesn't the intelligible offer intelligibility to the sensible? If the two orders of things were but one, we would already dispose of everything even before embarking upon the process of interrogation, which would render the whole questioning useless; but by dividing them, we establish an insoluble division between them. It is necessary to have a duality in order to give any meaning to the act of interrogating oneself about the sensible. The intelligible is therefore the difference which makes it useful to undertake this interrogation in the first place, since it is the result which will explain the sensible. Identity, which ensures that one is "in" the other, confirms that it is possible to arrive at one if we begin with the other. Yet Aristotle seems to preclude this possibility by a radical division. On the one hand, there is a sensible level, where that which is imposed upon us in the first instance is obviously not an essence or a substance, but rather a sensation, the particular. On the other, there is the universal, which comes first when we are speaking of the particular, but only in terms of its being, since it applies to a particular case with regard to something general, which it naturally includes logically. If all men are mortal, then necessarily, since I am a particular man, I am mortal; this is in the order of things; it is the general which determines my particularity.

The whole problem is to move from the particularity, which takes precedence in us, to the universal, which takes precedence in itself. Aristotle must make this link; here he finds himself in the same conundrum as Plato, who dissociated, first, an ascending dialectic toward the intelligible by beginning with the sensible, and second, an inverted dialectic, which falls back down again, with the whole forming but a single movement. But how can that which is different turn out to be the same? Aristotle separates the two movements so that it will be useful to question the sensible order as a means of understanding it. But it is also necessary to find it again, since it is necessary to explain it. But isn't to go beyond immediate reality in order to fix ourselves to the real, that is, to find what is even more real, necessarily paradoxical? Aristotle cannot escape this impossibility, and indeed he confronts it in his own terms. Instead of saying that the sensible "participates" (*metexis*) with the intelligible, he sees therein a logical relationship and he separates it from the cognitive relationship, that of knowledge, which is the inverse of all logic, which is itself rooted *in the first instance* in the sensible. As for the problem of radical scission, Aristotle finds the solution by saying that the universal is in *power* in the particular which is given to us. If we reestablish the logical and ontological order, then the universal, which comes last in the order of human knowledge, comes first in *act,* in that which truly *is* as the natural chain of things. In short, that which is last in power is first in act, thanks to the well-known dualism of the act and power, of form and matter, thanks to the dynamism characteristic of substance, which is both dual and unique. Since it is this universal substance which is both in power and in act afterward in a different ordering, that of reality itself, *Aristotle hereby reestablished the bridge between the two methods which he had previously isolated from one another*. By the same token he has everything and nothing, just like Plato. Anybody who has read Aristotle knows that logical order, with its universal premises and its particular conclusions ("All men are mortal, Socrates is a man, Socrates is mortal"), constitutes an autonomous perspective. The dialectical order is entrenched in particular facts, and it stays that way; even its apparently universal truths are but probable. We can not assimilate that which is problematic to that which is apodictic; the two are opposed to each other, just like death is to the life that it supplants.

Let us imagine a few more consequences than those which we've already considered in the hypothesis, whereby the analysis and the synthesis, discovery, and truth remain without a footbridge, deprived of a unity that would encompass them. What knowledge aims at is the *being* of things, if not it would exclude truth and would destroy itself. The course that the human being must follow, with his or her own point of departure, which is the sensible, cannot therefore be anything other than already intelligible. On the other hand, *to speak* of the *being* of things, from a specific order and logic, is still to *speak;* it only makes sense for a *logos*. To act as though this could be constituted by specific means, and then unraveled through a linkage which is uttered but which does not depend upon any discourse, since it reproduces the imbrication of things as they are, would be illusory or contradictory. And yet, we would answer, Aristotle did indeed isolate logical order, with its universal premises (better known in themselves) from the dialectical order, in which we have at our disposal only the probable. All *logos* is propositional, dialectical or not, and the necessity—even if illusory—is no less linked to that of the propositional subject, which, like Socrates, cannot not be himself, in this case, Socrates.

But in order to explain the acquisition of knowledge, it is necessary to uphold the division between the elaboration of truths, which we uncover, and the natural or intrinsic agency of these truths. It is necessary to ignore this synthetic ordering, the internal structure of truths, so that it will remain useful to look for them; but since the moment that this structure of truth is found, these two orders of things adhere to each other, then they must *also* identify themselves *a priori*. We will have understood that this is where we find a supplementary variation on the paradox of Menon: I know what I am looking for, which is what *is,* and what the knowledge of substance gives me, which renders all questions about this substance superfluous, but since it is what I am looking for, I must also ignore it, whence comes the difference of predicates and subject, which nonetheless express what the subject is, as well, the identity. As such, says Aristotle, "The inquiry or perplexity concerning what being is, in early times and always, is just this: what is substance?"[8] From now on, there can be no more of the oft-repeated distinction between the order of knowledge, in which we begin from that which is primary for us—the sensible—and the synthetic order, where there is something else that is *in itself* primary, by its very nature. This synthetic order is contained in the order of knowledge in power especially like the conclusion which afterwards must be reversed (in its synthetic order) in order to take its place in its initial role. We have here the impression that by defending *as well* the unity of the whole analytico-synthetic process, Aristotle rediscovers the unity of nature, of which the actualization of substantial virtuality is as much an act of nature as is our own knowledge of it through our soul. In fact, the separation between the virtual and the actual, the actual for nature and the virtual for itself, is eliminated in the identity of the substance, as though the "realization" of what occurs in nature for us was in fact always in it. But it is also as though the result swallows the process that leads to this result even as it continues to disassociate itself from it, thus annulling it and preserving it at the same time. As such, the substance must be "better known by itself," just as the premises of a process of logical reasoning must be more *known* than its conclusion.

8. Aristotle *Metaphysics* 1028a.

But to support this idea is to introduce into the synthetic order some analytical considerations that don't belong there. We have not left the realm of reductive assimilation even after having cried out about the heterogeneity of nature.

Note that since this amounts to an attempt to reconcile the unreconcilable, all of this remains paradoxical. Two distinct procedures are reunited at a single reductive dimension, that of the proposition, with being, the subject or the substance, which *is* both the act and the power, and which integrates *in itself* the order of knowledge which actualizes its being as such. Have we resolved that which we should have resolved, the acquisition of knowledge as a part of the actualization of the order of things, as though this rendered indisputable the knowledge we took from it?

The two orders of things are there as a means of showing that we ignore that which we are looking for; and the bringing together of the two of them, in order to account for the fact that what we are looking for is indeed that same thing as that which we were trying to find: and all of this leads us to suppress the difference that we had originally set out. In short, substance plays this very role. By virtue of the apodicticity that it imposes upon the proposition, the substance, the essence, evacuates all possible problematicity, which thereby becomes purely rhetorical. A rhetorical question is the interrogative form of a proposition, of an anterior knowledge. But all propositions, even dialectical ones, have a subject. This subject is what is out of the question, since the question always applies to the subject. We don't say "bald or not bald?" but ask whether *Socrates* is bald or not. The category expresses the alternative, and in Greek, categories are interrogative pronouns. As for the substance, it does not have a contrary because its apodicticity forbids it. What could be the contrary of Socrates? In short, the possibility of having a contradictory, upon which rests the dialectical or rhetorical analysis, is picked up again and then comes up against a further interdiction on account of the very nature of the proposition. What are contingent predicates good for? They indicate what the subject *is,* and they are useless, since we already know the subject beforehand. The complete proposition, with its dual structure, becomes superfluous. Without the knowledge of the substance, we don't know what the predicates apply to, and with this knowledge, they appear to be redundant. In other words, the subject is expected to resolve all questions (about itself), but these are questions which cannot be asked, since it is anterior to them. And the subject cannot answer the questions, since the subject exceeds any predication made about it even though such a predication characterizes the subject. Don't we hereby eliminate the propositional difference between the subject and the predicate, thus propositionality itself, which seems to be incomprehensible, even though it had earlier been deemed essential? Plato didn't do much better with his dialectic, and if there hadn't been the Aristotelian logic to support the emerging propositionalism, it could not have survived, with the propositional difference which reflects an identity but which all the while was just as much an irreducible difference.

The Being of Passion

And passion in all of this?

Once rehabilitated, with its rhetoric which tries to account for its various forms, it is quickly reabsorbed into the identity of substance, which is and cannot not be. Originally, the word *pathos* signifies affection or the quality of substance. Aristotle, in *Metaphysics* 1002b15, writes that "'affection' *[pathos]* means a quality in virtue of which a thing can be altered; for examples, whiteness and blackness, sweetness and bitterness, heaviness and lightness, and all others of this sort are affections." Such a definition of the word *pathos* follows if we consider that predication is at once a human action and the potential institution of what is necessary, substance, being, for which actualization will bring about the predicative moment as the moment of the substance itself, an affirmation of its identity. We ourselves cannot "make the difference." The knowledge that we have of essential things is determined by the *nature* of things, and falls inside our nature, which it thereby constitutes. The natural is necessary, and the *pathos* is nothing else than the impression that we have of what is essential ("This woman I love is essential for me"), which corresponds only to a particular fact: passion, as a sensible relation, is an illusion which is unveiled as soon as the nature (of things) is taken into account. *Pathos* is thereby absorbed, and what remains is only the necessity of that which is, which cannot not be. In this sense, passion is the myth that must be effaced along with the primacy of the sensible; it is a kind of obstacle but also a kind of strainer that, once it has brought us to the domain of nonhuman reality of nature, simply disappears. As such, passion is always a threat if it does not lead to its own suppression in the order of universal necessity. The term 'being' is used in several senses, as we pointed out previously in our account of the various senses of terms. In one sense, it signifies whatness and a *this;* in another, it signifies a quality or a quantity or one of the others which are predicated in this way.

Although 'being' is used in many senses, it is evident that of these the primary sense is whatness, and used in this sense it signifies a substance.[9]

This text is interesting, if not key, for several reasons. If *pathos* is to survive, it is necessarily opposed to nature, to the essential, to the durable; it is the alternative, the change, the alteration, which cannot be absorbed into the substance. It is also the human order of things in that the spirit, instead of achieving its own nature in identifying with Nature, persists in its most deceitful specificity: a wandering quality with regard to a destiny that is defined through necessity, by that which *must* be. In short, it is maximal alteration, that which escapes the substantial realm and indeed thwarts it at the point where it becomes a misfortune, a tragedy that leads to destruction. We find here the traditional meaning of *passion:* that which affects the human being when he or she loses sight of what is generic and essential. Passion in this sense is that which diverts individuals from their true nature and, by the same token, from what makes them individual and contingent. As a consequence it represents the most serious danger.

With this particular view of passion, we have an ethical correspondent, an ethic of *logos,* of necessity, and thus of knowledge, which necessarily affirms itself as the sole source of all necessity, an end in itself. We find here a point of intersection between Aristotle and Plato. The natural ethic is that which makes *logos* conform to a sense of necessity by imposing a universal end, *the Good,* as being immanent to the human being. This is opposed to the other ethic, which Aristotle would also advocate, which describes us as being free in our choice of ends, plunged into contingency and each time assigning to ourselves particular objectives which we are led to continuously redefine.

We observe that at the same time that passion is reabsorbed within a unique order there is an impassioned refusal on the part of Aristotle to abolish the distinction of the analytic (with its taking into account of the sensible) and the synthetic, which is linked to ontology. Thanks to this division *pathos* can gain a positive expression. Here, we are led into the other ethic, an ethic of *pathos,* which aims at governing passions without the pretension of suppressing them. This would be a vain endeavor. There are therefore two approaches, one which resolves duality in a generalized apodicticity, and the other which perpetuates it and thereby maintains *pathos.*

Passion, in the way that we usually understand it, does not remain irreducible except to the degree that the human order cannot be reduced to

9. Ibid., 1028a10–15.

the nature of beings. This is in fact its difference, that which renders it specifically human. A *pathos* which is not absorbed into substantiality (although substantiality affects pathos): such is the human being, who does not melt entirely into nature or cosmos.

On the other hand, the ethic of *logos* sees itself as a natural ethic: passions are artificial, contingent, as regards that which is substantial and which is itself the object of the *logos* which makes up our own nature. By contrast, the ethic of *pathos* opposes the artificial to the natural: we are beings that are made for a political life; passions must be regulated therein, but they can nevertheless find therein an outlet for expression. What is conventional, constructed, and deliberate is the way we conceive just regulation, the just negotiation of our passions.

The paradox of passion, reduced or irreducible, reduced and irreducible at the same time, pushes Aristotle to maintain two incompatible ethics. The paradox of passion is that the *pathos* is both the sign of a distinct human order and the illusion of this difference.

And that such a tension exists is explained by a double requirement which cannot be assumed in its totality. On the one hand, human beings and their passions are part of nature, with all that it imposes upon them. On the other, we are naturally different from all other beings in nature. We draw from a universal *logos,* as does all substance, and we also escape it. Rooted in the sensible, we cannot straightaway have access to the intelligible even though, on account of the universality of the intelligible, intelligibility remains immanent to the human.

From Passion to Action

Pathos seems to have to both sacrifice itself to the essential and maintain itself. Isn't this the fate of passions in general, that they are necessary and natural like sensible desires, yet the philosopher nevertheless tries continuously to conquer them, or at least to "rationalize" them as a means of dominating them? Passion is the movement experienced by the subject, it is the actualization of that which it was in power and therefore naturally: *pathos* necessarily belongs to the subject itself; it is the subject's own becoming, what it *is* (or has become). Nature reabsorbs *pathos* as an inevitable process of actualization of that which was naturally in power.

But what of human beings, in this case? Not all of the human being emanates from a single nature; we escape it to some degree through what we might call our degree of liberty or contingency. A plant naturally follows its preordained destiny, but humanity is subject to many detours from which we can choose one. Our end, our hopes, are not already there, given *a priori* to each[10] and to all as intermediate stages toward a given end. If this were the case, there would be nothing to look for, since everything would be preprogrammed and biologically regulated. This is clearly not the case.[11] Humanity, says Aristotle, is in search of goodness, happiness, and this requires effort. For Plato, ignorance is disastrous; for Aristotle, it's weakness of the will. But maybe giving in to temptation rather than resisting it; it is not to know, it is already to affirm indirectly and potentially a belief; in short, to support a rational trajectory of what fits or doesn't fit? Be this as it may, if all natural things possess within themselves their own principles of development, then we, who do not have specific ends built in, must look for them. We can make mistakes as we do so, but in any event they are exterior to us. The *pathos* does not disappear in the natural course of things as by an autonomous actualization of substance. We human beings, by our irreducible quality, our difference, affirms *pathos* as *our* particular difference: this is passion. Not passion in the sense of excess and overflowing, but as that which sends us to the action of which it is the complement or the opposite. From the natural we move to the artificial, to the putting into effect. We, and not nature, thereby become the *agents*. We *act* to realize our goals, they aren't realized by themselves according to some naturally preordained course.

We are passionate beings because we naturally are more so, than we are beings in nature. We must act, whereas a purely natural being has only to be. Our goals exist outside ourselves, and between these ends and our desires we need a kind of mediation, quite literally, a *means*. There would be no distinction between means and ends if we naturally attained our ends, but since this is not the case, we must choose the first in order to arrive at the second. The split between the means and the ends is the fact of being a being which is compelled to act, and to represent the ends to ourselves in order to discover what it is that we must do in order to achieve them. The verb *to need* indicates the *ethical* component which flows from the deliberation and from the "right choice." We, being not simply natural beings, are necessarily *ethical* beings; we ask ourselves questions about what we must do, whereas a plant inexorably realizes its own destiny as . . . a plant. Because we have no destiny firmly anchored in ourselves like a unavoidable necessity to which we cannot but obey, without posing any questions about what is incumbent upon

10. Aristotle *Nicomachean Ethics* 1136b5–10.
11. Ibid., 1032a, or 1095a15–20.

us to do, we find ourselves in the depths of the alternative; the possibility of being other, with all of the debates that flow from it, since nothing is necessary in these matters.

Passion, which is pure difference for a substance which cannot absorb passion in *logos,* is first, beyond discourse; second, the expression of difference which grants people their individuality (and there we can speak about it); and third, a threat for the substantiality of the human being, that is, that which negates his or her possibility to be other, at the point of becoming a necessity, a drug, an illusion, since only nature possesses necessity[12] as an internal principle. Tragedy, with all of its excess (hubris), is inevitable: passion has become destiny which prevails, a fatal passion.

Passion as Relationship with Others

People affirm their individuality through the passions. Each is him- or herself other from the Other, and in this sense, everyone is identical. This is not a contradiction, if we consider that everyone expresses passions differently, even if everyone has them. Some people are easily enraged, others more generous, and still others jealous. Passion is thus the mirror of the human being, but also his source of division. Luckily, passions reflect as much the compatibility among people as the dissonance between them. In any event, it is necessary to understand human passions, rather than denying them, in order to achieve a social equilibrium, that is, a kind of common denominator between us which allows us to live together. The regulation of passions rests upon our knowledge thereof.

We are far from the notion of morality, of History or politics as it has been described for the last two centuries. The Enlightenment thinkers, specifically Kant, took as a point of departure a human nature, the seat of universal reason that is found in each human being simply because he or she is a human being. Morals consist of reducing to this ideal of universality all the differences between people, their singular individualities, for the reason that they can be opposed to what we consider as human nature. The universalist perspective is ambiguous, since it is difficult without controversy or rhetoric—as Aristotle demonstrated—to determine

12. "Nature in the primary and main sense is the substance of things which have a principle motion in themselves qua what they are; for the matter is called 'a nature' by the fact that it is receptive of nature in the primary and main sense, and generations and growth are called so by the fact that they are motions from the point of view of nature in that sense. And the principle of motion in things existing in nature is also this nature somehow present in those objects, either potentially or actually." Aristotle *Metaphysics* 1015a12–15.

just what human nature is, that absolute universal in the name of which one must renounce one's interests and individual passions. This is an ideal which has fuzzy edges, from which Aristotle prefers not to start as if it were a clear idea, but rather at which he thinks that we ought to arrive, just as we can arrive at a conclusion after a debate filled with contradiction and dissension. Aristotle is in this sense closer to our own sensibility than is Kant: people of today feel that they are individuals above all, and not undifferentiated representatives of a human nature. They have their own desires, and they are in search of material advantages, and if they are ready to discuss them with others, so that they can arrive at a social or political compatibility, they are not ready to consider their ends, or *themselves,* unessential or, even worse, subject to *a priori*-condemnation, in the name of some absolute imperative that goes beyond them and of which it is difficult to name the precise content. Solidarity yes, ascetic renunciation, no. Kant took as a founding principle the notion of the universal as a means of integrating differences afterward as they arose, and if necessary by assuming that they disappear. Aristotle begins with the assumption that people are all different, that they must live together, and in order to do so, they must not only tolerate their differences but also take them into account in order to rise up to a common Good which will authorize life among other persons in society. Friendship in this sense becomes a fundamental virtue. Its effect is to bring people together by virtue of a common viewpoint and common sentiments, which makes them either put aside or admit to their differences.

In this way, the passions reflect inter-human relations. They (allow us to) indicate to others that we are responding to them. These are the responses to his presence, to what he thinks of me and how he treats me. I reflect upon his image of me, and I indicate to him what I think about it. A fusion is set up by passion between the consciousness of the other and that of the self, and at the same time, it reestablishes a difference between individuals in this case as a means of reinforcing and confirming the identity of reciprocal images. I am happy. I like him, or I don't. I get angry at the other, or else I despise him. I feel that I must help him, be indifferent to him, envy him, hate him, or whatever. In each case I come out in favor of an identity or a difference between the other and myself to abolish it afterward, or else to maintain or reinforce it. If we wish to get along, it is necessary that we negotiate these differences to come to some kind of identification; this is true for two persons just as it is for all free citizens who live in the City who must carry on in a manner that makes living there acceptable for the majority. From here emerges the idea that is elucidated in *Rhétorique des Passions*,[13] that citizens, having abandoned violence as a means of acceding to the ends which they would like to have considered common and freely accepted, have recourse to rhetoric, a way to convince their fellows that the policies that they would defend are desirable for the whole City. "Our passions are the only orators who always convince: being, as it were, nature's artistry, they obey infallible laws, and the simplest man, enthused by passion, is more persuasive than the most eloquent without it."[14]

So would passion be a kind of basic social consciousness inherent in all persons? Probably, but one should use the notion of consciousness with prudence, since we're speaking of pre-Cartesian and pre-Lockean philosophy. For the Greeks, the central concern was not the individual as such, but being. The standard, the measure, is found in everything that is,—the *cosmos,* nature—what the Greek philosopher is looking for is a *logos* that expresses its necessity. As for human beings, we wish to penetrate the secrets of the universe of things, the nature of all that is, in order to understand ourselves, we who also *are,* in order to learn how we must live and think, how the City must function, always with the same necessity, that of the *logos* that is modeled upon natural apodicticity.

Having made these qualifications, it is useful to characterize the passions in terms of consciousness, since they make up a part of our actual concepts and help us to think. Passion in this sense is a form of consciousness. It is the consciousness that I have of the consciousness of the other, and by the same token, it is an *image* of our relationships which I interiorize, a difference which unites us—or drives us apart.

I am taken in by the relation which I reflect upon, even as I integrate the two terms of this relationship into a single consciousness that itself asserts a kind of identity. The other in me, as an image of myself to which I react, is indeed the essence of passion in the Aristotelian *rhetoric of passions.* By them, I indicate to the other what I think of him and I make him understand how I evaluate, and how I reflect upon, his attitude with respect to myself. At once a mark of restored equilibrium and a sign of unbalance, passion is as much the spectacle of a human relation as the act of living it. All of Aristotle's poetics are built upon this ambivalence. Tragedy, for example, plunges us into an action which seems to us convincing, "as though we were there," by a specular imitation in which all actions participate. And there is no action without passion, from which

13. Meyer, *Aristote ou la Rhétorique des Passions.*

14. Duc de la Rochefoucauld, *The Maxims of the Duc de la Rochefoucauld,* trans. Constantine Fitzgibbon, vol. 8 (London: Millington, 1974), p. 32.

comes the fiction constructed upon the passions (in the Greek sense of the term) which those actions represent.

To know what separates people, it is necessary to have a minimum of identity between them which will permit them to *figure out* their differences, which explains why there won't exist only differences between people, not even in hatred or disdain. Since passion is for Aristotle that which I put up with from the other and to which I respond in order to provide a sense of what I think (about his or her attitude to me, about what he or she *is*), we understand why Aristotle includes among other passions (which he describes in the second book of *Rhetoric*), calm or embarrassment, two "passions" which we might hesitate to describe as such. A calm person is rarely impassioned, in the modern, postromantic sense of the term. For Aristotle to include calm, embarrassment, or impudence in his list of fourteen passions is perfectly consistent with the rest of his project. As such, being calm is a passion in that it responds to an action of the other, which we endure and which demands that a certain equilibrium be established or reestablished. Besides, the rhetorical strength of calm is important, just as anger is. We can rouse and orient the listener by adopting a calming attitude, just as through anger we hope to have the opposite influence.

The Chain of Passions, or Dis-equilibrium in the City

Passion is an intersubjective relationship. But what exactly does it signify? A disequilibrium, a problem which is posed in human relations? Or the contrary, does it aim to reestablish an equilibrium that is endangered beforehand, like anger which we show toward someone so that he or she will change in our view, unless it is a letting-loose, a kind of symbolic vengeance that puts things back in order? Signs of problems, passions are also ways of replying: they reflect the questioning of the other, the menace that his or her difference represents, as though exclusive of our own. Why prefer A to not-A if our lot is problematicity, the alternative? If Aristotle advocates the middle course in the passions so that they become virtues, by a kind of *habit,* it is precisely because the middle course preserves the alternatives and all the differences of A or not-A. Do you like money? Very well, if you spend it all, you manifest an incredible lavishness, by the example that you give, and you harm yourself by not having any more left for yourself. You are a tightwad, you keep everything? Not only do you deprive yourself, but you take away from others the resources which could have resulted from your spending. So avarice, like lavishness, harms everyone; both extremes deprive of one and all.

Magnanimity and generosity are the just equilibrium. The desire to possess material goods is legitimate in itself, but becomes a vice the moment it turns into an exclusive obsession, which breaks human contingency by establishing a feigned necessity.

Passions which flow from such excess risk being excessive, even though inevitable, from which comes the role of ethics and, moreover, of politics, which is even more fundamental, since it regulates the ends of the City.

> If so, then we should try to grasp, in outline at least, what that end is and to which of the sciences or faculties it belongs. It would seem to belong to the one which is most authoritative and most architectonic. Now politics appears to be such, for it is this which regulates what sciences are needed in a state and what kinds of sciences should be learned by each [kind of individuals] and to what extent. The most honoured faculties, too, e.g., strategy and economics and rhetoric, are observed to come under this [faculty]. And since this faculty uses the rest of the practical sciences and also legislates what men should do and what they should abstain from doing, its end would include the ends of the other faculties; hence this is the end which would be good for mankind.[15]

This is like saying that passions have a political function by the logic of identity and difference which controls them. An excess in difference, which goes as far as exclusion, leads to disequilibrium, to passionate excess. Disdain, for example, is the expression of a displayed superiority. The reaction could be concern, which causes people to be silenced in the face of the powerful, or—the other case—anger, which is a cry of revolt against injustice. To hurl your anger at those who have disdain for you serves to show that you are not worried about them, that they are not as superior or as powerful as they think they are.

There is therefore a chain reaction in the passionate order, which can go a long way. To live together, as we said, is to negotiate differences with the other in order to arrive at an identity. This is the source of the long list of passions which answer one another, first by being sometimes contrary (contingency obliges, we fall back upon alternative couplings), but as well, and in a less radical sense, by linking together according to diverse modalities. Aristotle gives a list of fourteen passions in *Rhetoric:*

15. Aristotle *Nicomachean Ethics* 1094a25–1098b8.

hatred and *love, fear* and *assurance, calm* and *anger, embarrassment* and *impudence, compassion, emulation, envy, goodness, indignation, scorn.* Passions are interactive in that impudence, for example, which ignores the opinions of others, is a way of reacting to them, in this case by denigration. And we have seen that passions engender the one and the others through complementarity: I love you, you love me; I scorn you, you get angry; you are inferior, but I practice goodness toward you or, on the contrary, I have impudence for you. I am inferior to you, and I'm embarrassed, or I am concerned, and so forth. The logic of difference is necessarily that of equality and inequality, superiority or inferiority.

Despite everything, we feel a strong sense of the arbitrary when faced with this list, especially since the number falls to eleven in the *Nicomachean Ethics* (see 1105b22). Surely nobody would deny that there is a logic of identity and of difference and that this regulates social intersubjectivity. This logic is therefore political. But nevertheless it is not clear why there should be fourteen of them. At the end of the day, there is apathy, restored or original, and Stoicism sings the praises of the calm, wisdom, and consistency of the sage. Everything that carries us, that brings us outside ourselves, makes us angry, is the irascible condition of Plato, the anger. We have the feeling that all passions flow from calm and anger, which are both studied in detail by Seneca, and that beyond that, their combination is forcibly mixed together, and everything meets up. Rage is passion in what it has that is unbridled, if not destructive. This is passion itself: Aristotle employs *thumos* (passion) and *orgè* (anger) as synonyms. There is an anger against myself and against the other which makes up passion, which is to be opposed to temperance, which is indifferent to the exteriority to which I transport myself if I don't control myself. But all of this is already Stoicism, and Aristotle doesn't recognize it. For him, anger is not a part or a function of the soul, as Plato thought. Anger is but one passion among others, and not passion's anti-passion, the guardian. Beside the negative angers, how many positive!

What Are the Ends of Man? Or, the Two Morals of Aristotle

This is, of course, the big question. For Plato, the answer was simple, and it is the one which wins out in History. Even the religions will follow (Plato), and we think here especially of Christianity. Aristotle, through a greater ambivalence in the doctrine, and a greater complexity in the exposition, will remain isolated.

First, Plato. For him, the human being is torn between the external, the world, and the interior which he considers superior. The life of the soul must also liberate us from suffering, from misfortune and temporal decadence. There is a possible hope, at the point where for Aristotle the civil, political society, the one for human beings, carries the weights of human action. Far from being a renunciation of desire, virtue is the framing of it. At least in a certain moral vision, which he will defend, just as he gets closer to Plato in another vision. The soul, even in its purely rational principle, remains interwoven with matter, and this is the condition that gives it form and meaning, at the same time as it is the inescapable law.

For Aristotle, virtue "consists in the verity that corresponds to desire, to correct desire."[16] The ends are given to us through our desires, which present them to us in the imagination as already realized and demand practical reason, by soliciting the means to move from the imaginary to the real. We have therefore the fusion of the sensible and the intelligible of the soul and the body. Harmony of the soul. Unlike Plato, who divided the soul into three more or less autonomous parts, Aristotle sees the soul as divided into two parts, one devoid of *logos,* structured as sensibility, to use modern terminology, and another "endowed with reason."[17] More important, perhaps, is the problem of ends, since human beings immersed in their passions assimilate them to things that are good in themselves: money, power, and honor, or the pleasures of the body. Aristotle doesn't deny the importance of these ends, but he does advocate moderation.

On the other hand, he also thinks that the real ends for human beings should be internal, almost as though they were natural. Only objects of reason have an internal necessity, just as four is necessarily the sum of two plus two. The pure contemplative life would therefore be the absolute Good and no longer an ensemble of passions and desires expressing themselves in moderation, tempered by life in society and by its customs. The sage is master over his thoughts, and this is the sole end that we can possess, master in a natural manner, and therefore give to ourselves. In short, Aristotle challenges himself; human beings live in the *scission* of the means and the ends. The practical syllogism retraces the movement: we move from the ends to the means: I want to heal, *therefore* it is necessary that I take some medication, with the premise which "validates" the practical syllogism, affirming that all medication aims to reestablish health. From here, he says, we don't deliberate *some* ends, but merely *about* them, that is, about the means to realize them through reason. "We deliberate not the ends themselves, but the means to attain

16. Ibid., 1139a30.
17. Other subdivisions in each part are made by Aristotle, but they are not of interest here.

them."[18] Even so, he admits that there is a *discussion* of the ends to be realized, of those which are worthwhile and others, but he speaks as well of what is required for all reasonable people, as though he wished to counter his own relativism, affirming that the ends are *indisputable* (he nevertheless discusses them), beyond *logos,* because they are simply objects of desire.

Torn between relativism and universalism, Aristotle finds himself trapped by the dualism of nature and human nature (the latter being the inverse of the former, despite the word *nature*). "*Everyone* has variable desires," seems to be a formula that destroys the universality of the subject, or, in any case, which empties it of all content. If desires make up the individual and they can differ from one individual to the next, there is no more identity, unless in a statistical form. Let's leave this aside for the moment. What has to be known is that rational thought, in morality, consists of posing absolute ends which are to be pursued, which Aristotle concedes even as he confines them to the caprices of sensible desire for which he is happy to limit the excess by a doctrine of the "middle ground." On the one hand Platonic, on account of its rejection of relativism, Aristotle's translation of diversity, Aristotle's morality, is hybrid, ambivalent, and this is why it has enjoyed a reduced success in the face of the more radical, and more coherent, Platonism.

Further, the idea of the end leads to problems over and above the opposition between relativism and the supposition of objective, universal ends which are natural for human beings. External ends, actions which operate upon means, middle grounds, which regulate practices through social practice, through habit; or else, immanent, necessary ends, which come from *logos* contemplating itself, affirmation of the priority of virtue of intellectuality above all else. We have the feeling that we're dealing with two distinct moralities. But it is difficult to really separate the two sides of this alternative, each of the visions answers back one to the other. To the degree that, in any case, everything that is contingent—like external ends, freely adopted—must reabsorb themselves in the necessity of the immanent end to the act of thinking, we understand that what was disassociated for Aristotle finds itself united, even though this is in reality impossible short of doing violence to the coherence of the respective concepts. As such, Aristotle establishes a distinction between *praxis* and *poiesis:* action and work, if you will. Action is its own end, we did such and such for its own sake; it is not the means aimed at something else; whereas *poiesis* is the inverse, where

18. *Nicomachean Ethics.* [Translation modified to reflect the modifications in Meyer's original. *Trans.*]

we use given means to do something external to the act itself. Lots of ink has flowed from the pens of commentators on the subject of this distinction, ambiguous to say the least, since every action has an end, and even those which are means are pursued as though they were ends, as for example working for a living. In short, the distinction is far from being obvious; it shows, especially in Aristotle, that it is torn between two opposite conceptions of human nature.

The first of these sees humans as social beings, who unlike beings which are simply *natural,* do not have their ends within themselves. They must therefore give themselves ends and find adequate means to attain them. They are multiple, the fruits of their desires, of their passions; morality is therefore a limitation of them. To act is to operate with a view toward something else *(poiesis)*. We don't deliberate ends, says Aristotle, but such a debate is despite everything inevitable, since we have multiple desires. They fall outside *logos,* which explains the fact that Aristotle upholds that we don't debate them, but they are nevertheless clearly the object of ethics. He reproaches certain men for desiring as ends which cannot be such, like businessmen who desire only wealth.

There is as well the other vision of humanity. The end is universal because human beings are gifted with an intellect for which contemplative activity is the natural end. Desires must be subordinated to intellectual necessity. It is the necessity of *logos,* through *praxis,* which is accomplished. The multiplicity of ends find themselves reduced, like the *pathos,* the passions which express them.

Aristotle adds that the unique *Good* doesn't exist, that goodness is made up of many goods. They seem therefore debatable and are obviously not imposed. Goodness is therefore "an activity of virtue"[19] whereby each person exercises his or her own dispositions (= *ethos*), to the *best* of his or her abilities, actualizes his or her desires to obtain a happiness that is rich in elements, and, moreover, in *activities* and in excellence. The diverse passions which push us to want lots of things is in harmony in a general equilibrium, a generalized middle ground. "Let happiness be [defined as] success *[eupraxia]* combined with virtue or as self-sufficiency *[autarkeia]* in life or as the pleasantest life accompanied with security or as abundance of possessions and bodies, with the ability to defend and use these things; or all people agree that happiness is pretty much one or more of these."[20] If Aristotle finds himself torn between two visions, this is because of the propositional obsession, for

19. Ibid., 1098b30.
20. Aristotle *On Rhetoric: A Theory of Civic Discourse* 1360b10, trans. George A. Kennedy (Oxford: Oxford University Press, 1991).

which apodicticity is the law. To admit contingency, *pathos,* therefore passion, is to demean oneself. Passion must be able to be resolved in a universal end which domesticates it, as though the analytical, dialectical order were but a preparation for the accomplishment of the synthesis, which is always apodictic. At the same time, these two orders are distinct, since being is multiple. We fall back here upon impossible dualism, upon which Plato, with his dialectic, had already embarked.

The *pathos* has to be reabsorbed, but it isn't. Passion has to change into reason, and yet it always escapes it. This is the eternal ambiguity, the ambivalence of passion in the history of occidental thought."And the goal is to subordinate the soul to *logos,* to imprint in it a natural necessity, which is that of *logos.* The emotions *[pathé]* are those things through which, by undergoing change, people come to differ in their judgments and which are accompanied by pain and pleasure, for example, anger, pity, fear, and other such things and their opposites."[21] But we have to account for the fact that not everyone desires the same thing, as though we could weaken before the supreme Being, to which we prefer smaller desires. Would Aristotle speak of ignorance, as Plato does, or of weakness of the will? But the Greeks did not know will as a specific faculty:[22] what forces desire can only be reason, while what makes it dominant is passion. Those who are blind to the supreme Good are persons of passion: they refuse to see, and the fact that we explain this refusal by rationalizing it as false knowledge, or passionate illusion which makes for poor judgment or too much desire, and therefore weakly prove that which is just, all of this confirms the baneful character of the passions as such.

The Passions of the Soul

Are passions the fact of the body, which makes them unavoidable, or are they distinct from sensible appetites in order to constitute representations, judgments, which flow from these desires? Is having mastery over passions equivalent to changing an opinion, or to domesticating one's body? Perhaps both? The insoluble problem of interaction between heterogeneous realities surges forth, a problem which we find as such with Descartes, who situates an imaginary gland, the pineal gland, the one which transforms bodily movement into passions of the soul.

21. Ibid., 1378a19.
22. See W. Charlton, *Weakness of the Will: A Philosophical Introduction* (Oxford: Oxford University Press, 1988), and moreover, A. Dihle, *The Theory of the Will in Classical Antiquity* (Berkeley and Los Angeles: University of California Press, 1982), pp. 18ff.

Aristotle takes the word *passion* literally: *passion* is what agents experience, what makes them into patients and dispossesses them of their responsibility. Instead of having its source in human beings, who are therefore no longer *subjects,* action comes from outside to alter, to transform agents we naturally are into purely passive beings. From an ethical point of view, this explains the incapacity of attaining rational ends. We *potentially* know that we must abstain from some action, that we should do another, but we don't know it as an act, effectively, as we would say today. As such, I potentially know that two and two make four, but since I think of other things that interest me more, I don't really think about it. Potential or virtual knowledge is a form of unconsciousness, or of unreflexive consciousness, which can be actualized on demand but which for the time being is not mobilized. I know without knowing, I am in the realm of the un-thinking, which corresponds a passive knowledge.

That will be an image of the passionate domain which will subsist. Passion is born of consciousness which is plunged into the world, turned upon it and away from itself, forgetting or neglecting everything found within itself to give in to externality, and here, Aristotle goes beyond himself in a sense, since there is no longer the issue of choosing between the primacy of a contemplative life and the acceptance of a certain play of passions. Beyond this dilemma, there is quite simply passion as the multifaceted form of our imbrication in the world. But what is required, with Aristotle, is above all a paradox of passions: natural to human beings, they are also necessary in their own way. But they are that which dissolves like a contingent and accidental moment which the generality of being will englobe. Reducible, even as it is indispensable, passion couldn't be really liberated from its conceptual ambiguity except by escaping from ontology, for which passion remains at the end of the day the most vibrant witness of impossibility.

What remains is that passion reinforces in its mark of human nature what makes this nature something paradoxical.

3

From Sickness to Sin

Passion as a Madness of the Soul

During antiquity, and especially after Aristotle, passion resembles in many ways an evocation of madness before the classical age. This must be nuanced, since for Aristotle, passions are not necessarily malevolent. In this sense, his approach was cut off from the rest of occidental thought, which—with Christianity—continued to prefer Plato, who was more clear-cut in his options.

The Greek City is condemned. We feel as though we are no longer the masters of our own destinies; we can only withstand them. To withstand (= passion) returns us to the idea of suffering, as when we suffer from a sickness. We seek the peace and harmony so necessary for ourselves within ourselves. Plato cherished a withdrawal of the soul into itself, but such a renunciation of the political would have been unacceptable to Aristotle, especially since passion leads human beings to disaster. The source of all evil, passion comes to represent more and more an absolute evil. Avoid pain! shouts the Epicurean. From there to the search for plea-sure, which is its contrary, there is but a single step. But the Stoic refuses, since pleasure and pain are still ways of reacting to the external world. Indeed, we must protect ourselves from all dependence upon the exte-rior world, since it is synonymous with sadness and loss. Sooner or later, we must renounce both its good and bad aspects of the tangible, the perceptible *(le sensible)* world.[1] For whom the bell tolls.

Passions have always been the unthinking part of the soul, of the consciousness, the part that seeks its nourishment from the tangible, with the choice of "pleasure or pain" as possible expressions of contact. Madness is basing one's life and one's judgment upon pleasure, in which fickleness and transience oppose themselves to necessity, which is so dear to reason. This is why the word "passion" is so ambiguous: it signifies perception, relationship to the tangible, and desire, which in this domain is always excessive,[2] as though the tangible contains within itself its own dissoluteness when it reflects upon itself. Cicero writes:

> Moreover the emotions of the mind, which harass and embitter the life of the foolish (the Greek term for these is *pathos*, and I might have rendered this literally and styled them "diseases," but the word "disease" would not suit all instances; for example, no one speaks of pity, nor yet anger, as a disease, though the Greeks term these *pathos*. Let us then accept the term "emotion," the very sound of which seems to denote something vicious and these emotions are not excited by any natural influence. The list of the emotions is divided into four classes, with numerous subdivisions, namely *sorrow, fear, lust,* and mental emotion which the Stoics call by a name that also denotes a bodily feeling, *hēdonē,* "pleasure," but which I prefer to style "delight," meaning the sensuous elation of the mind when in a state of exultation), these emotions, I say, are not excited by any influence of nature; they are all of them mere fancies and frivolous opinions. *Therefore the Wise Man will always be free from them.*[3]

Are Passions Natural?

This all depends upon what one means by "nature" and the place that we occupy in it. In contrast to the modern use of the term, nature at that time was not considered the tangible covering of things; but quite the

1. [I'll generally employ "tangible" from here on, but the reader should be aware of the many dimensions of "le sensible," which include sensitivity, tangibility, and perceptibility. *Trans.*]

2. See B. Inwood, *Ethics and Human Action in Early Stoicism* (Oxford: Oxford University Press, 1983), pp. 127ff.

3. Cicero *De Finibus Bonorum et Malorum*, trans. H. Rackham (London: Heinemann, 1931), p. 255.

contrary, it was that which generates the many forms that things assume. The nature of things is their essence, the law of their development, that which assures a certain consistency to the changes that we observe. It is therefore the absolute unity of all things, over and above appearances; nature comes before things and conditions their tangible manifestations no matter how scattered and disconnected they seem. Isn't water liquid, ice, or gas? This is natural, since one understands the principle of all manifestations, which considered by themselves, seem irrational and contradictory. To depart from the tangible in order to render it intelligible consists of yielding to the nature of *these* tangible beings. By the same token the *logos* identifies itself with nature, since it expresses the necessity of that which is. The necessary enunciation of that which is necessary, nature, falls inside itself, a kind of additional obligation where the reflexive statement is conditioned to appear, itself a part of necessity or the providence that it describes. The description of necessity does not come by chance: it is imposed in the evolution of the ways of the world as one moment of this evolution. To believe the contrary would be illusory, an illusion of a liberty and a contingency that creates all passions and which sanctions them as intellectual wanderings, an odyssey of the consciousness and of the *logos,* which therefore understands itself poorly. But if all things emanate from the only necessity, then that which is not itself is not only illusory, but indeed doesn't seem possible. This is absurd, since this generalized *logos* must, in order to exclude the *pathos,* be able to recognize it even if it is like something contingent, born of the illusion people feel a consequence of their being immersed in the tangible. If we wish to explain liberty as the right to error, to illusion, and the passions as that which causes us to neglect the *logos,* haven't we fallen right back to Aristotle, even despite ourselves? So passions are natural because they are, but they are not natural as well, because they are linked to objects which are tangible, and which appear, only to disappear, depending upon the circumstances and upon the individual in question. Be this as it may, passion creates confusion between the tangible and the intelligible, between what is not natural and what is. Passion causes us to mistake one thing for another, it registers the needs of one while at the same time has only the contingencies of the other. This means that passion can be overcome: only good judgment can annul bad judgment. Since nature is the necessity of things in themselves, passions, which change according to the direction of the wind and to those that give themselves over to them, are not natural. As a consequence they can but be the product of the mind, which imagines things as necessary. Far from *being* tangible, appetites are but their reflections in the soul, reflections which are just as contingent as the tangible things they express."Passions in themselves contain nothing natural or necessary, says Cicero."[4]

But the paradox remains: by giving the right to refer to judgments derived from the tangible, passion institutes in its own way the difference between the tangible and the intelligible, but on the other hand it also suppresses this difference, and this is its pernicious side. Since we need to have both its duality and its abolition, it is necessary to have *pathos,* just as it is convenient to condemn it and its falsely natural appearance. Will passion be necessary to human nature, or its denaturation? An inevitable adulteration, or an accidental one? And will this passion absorb itself back into the natural order of things, from which it is but an outgrowth, a mirage which is interposed between ourselves and truth? Or is it the necessary obstacle, peculiar to the human condition, which blocks access to truth and universal justice? In short, Stoicism or Christianity?

Stoicism comes down on the side of necessity, of nature, by expelling passions into the domain of the accidental and the inessential, in short, into the illusory. Where there is passion, there is the Other, with its menacing contingency, its alterity, which people are always looking to conquer once and for all, and which they can but renounce, according to the Stoics. And yet passion finds itself in the will and in the desire, deemed rational, to liberate oneself from all passion. We fall back upon the alternative from which Aristotle, the master of systematic philosophy, could not extricate himself; Aristotle made pathos into the unavoidable contingency of tangible man, a contingency which nonetheless could be solved through the necessity of his substance. By allowing this paradox to exist, by pushing to its limit his concern about allowing concepts from occidental *logos* to survive (which is propositional),[5] Aristotle revealed both its ambiguity and its fragility.

While Stoicism did not succeed in extricating itself from passion, which it reduced to naturalness, from which it made an illusory emergence, Christianity accepted passion as irreducible. Original sin should be without any hope of redemption: it arises from human nature and ascribes specificity to it. But Christianity would not escape entirely from the paradox of passions, since we'd never really know if to discover one's state of sin would permit us to overcome it by faith, which made us aware of sin, or if faith is entirely useless, since consciousness of our state changes nothing about the state itself. We are under the impression that

    4. Cicero *Tusculan Disputations* 4.27, trans. C. D. Yonge (New York: Harper & Brothers, 1894), p. 88.
    5. Ibid., 4.19.43.

Christianity failed in this respect, since on the one hand we have the free will required to save ourselves, while for other Christian writers we are already subjected to preordained destiny because our lives on earth are already condemned by original sin. The passions are in this sense both indomitable and doomed to being overcome by faith, which saves. Here again the contradictory nature of the passions, which we'd thought to have evacuated by settling the original paradox of *pathos* in occidental *logos,* returns.

Passion as an Error of Judgment

It was all well and good that Stoicism has known a number of avatars; from Zeno of Citium to Epictetus and Marcus Aurelius, via Cicero, the main ideas have persisted. And concerning the passions, there is no one more explicit or clear than the good old Roman orator. For him, philosophy was nothing other than a "medicine for the soul"[6] because *logos* must emerge from the ashes of *pathos.* All of the forms that passion takes are "what the Greeks call pathos, and if I could say a sickness, what would be the literal translation, but not respond to our usage. In effect pity, envy, excitement, joy, is a general way in which all the movements of the soul revolt against the reasons the Greeks qualify the sickness. . . . What are you saying? Are you calling attention to the passions, no matter how unstable, of the soul without a doubt?"[7] Reason versus unreason. "When we say of someone that he is no longer the master of self, we mean to say that he is no longer under the control of the spirit to which nature had given sovereignty of the soul as a whole."[8] Physical ailments are felt when the body loses its internal equilibrium, and the same goes for the spirit. Cicero fully recognizes[9] that if a number of passions carry us away, submerge the mind and the ability to focus to the point of chaining us to the world and to its furies, there are simple perceptions, tangible as well, as well as desires, which we would be unable to assimilate to such surplus. There is something excessive in this condemnation of that which is not excessive. But for Stoicism the whole question is to know if such a desire, if it were to be moderated, is natural. The answer is simple; it is negative. By abandoning ourselves to our desires, whatever they may be, we are victims of a judgment which makes them, and their objects, appear indispensable. This is, after all, a simple question of judgment. If

6. Ibid., 3.3.
7. Ibid., 3.4.7.
8. Ibid., 3.5.2.
9. Ibid., 3.10.23.

we were to modify our opinion about what is suitable for us, then we
would no longer have these desires; perhaps others would take their
place or, better still, the desire to no longer have any desire would
emerge. To lose sight of what is necessary, what is natural, results in our
isolation and the loss of our freedom for *logos,* and on this account gives
us over to that which touches the irrational part of our souls.[10] But if
everything is natural, including the denial of this fact, can passion still be
considered "contrary to nature?"[11] We are free to make our own judgments, and if we make an erroneous judgment, by agreeing to something
when we shouldn't have done so, isn't this as natural as the contrary?
We realize that this is the trap, which is in effect natural, of Stoicism.[12]
Evacuate dualism and it comes back with a vengeance, something that
Aristotle himself could have said. From this point on, there is a classifica-
tion in the relations with the exterior world, the tangible, which are just
as much opinions about the world as passions which we endure and
which reflect upon themselves inside of us. This consciousness of the
other in us which is both consciousness, thus reflection, and thoughtlessness as well, since its object is not itself but something outside. This
"contradiction" is passion.

We have four fundamental passions, according to Cicero, whose
source was Zeno. They embrace the fluctuations of exteriority, of which
time inscribes the rhythm of their precariousness in the human soul. Passions are opinions concerning good and evil, and from which we cannot
escape, even if they don't show us what is naturally good or evil on
account of *our purely temporal nature: pleasure* is of concern to the
present, while *desire* (*libido,* for Cicero) is for the future, corresponding
to *pain* and *anxiety.* But we are not dependent upon the outside world
unless we wish to be; and desire, by monopolizing the soul through a
future object, inspires in us the idea that we absolutely require it, thus
rendering us its slave. We can do without anything except the mind, the
logos, which frees us from the exterior world in the sense that it makes
us want only what we can think about, since we are in the end the masters of our own thoughts; everything else can be taken away from us,
or is liable to disappear depending upon the whims of providence. From
the passions flows vice: desires, guilt, destructive opinions, Neronian
pleasures, and so on. A slave to oneself, and therefore potentially a slave

10. Ibid., 4.6.11.
11. Ibid., 4.7.14.
12. "It is natural in effect that everyone searches for what could be good and avoids the contrary, and that is why as soon as an object appears and seems to be good, instinct alone pushes
us to assure us the possession." Ibid., 4.6.12.

to others, subject to their desires, their caprices, their interests and, why not? to madness. To admit one's passions, to neglect the universal, means that in the end we will be destined to perish on their account.

> Such a man takes so exact a survey on all sides of him that he always knows the proper place and spot to live in free from all the troubles and annoyances of life and encounters every accident that fortune can bring upon him with a becoming calmness. Whoever conducts himself in this manner will be free from grief and from every other perturbation; and a mind free from these feelings renders men completely happy; whereas a mind disordered and drawn off from right and unerring reason loses at once, not only its resolutions, but its health.[13]

Do we not see "that all these excesses of sadness and happiness pursue a false idea?"[14] But isn't the struggle for reason itself a passion? "In philosophy itself, the masters would never have realized so much progress in their fields of study, if they weren't consumed by a burning passion."[15] There is a liberty that can be found in us, the liberty to choose to either give in to passion, or to abstain from it. As Aristotle said, passion is always there to support and nourish reason. "For me, all the debates that concern passions, the question, it seems to me, comes back to one single fact that all depends on us, that we contract them deliberately, they are all voluntary."[16] So if everything is imposed by the nature of things, in what sense are we free to resist? Isn't our decision inscribed in the very order that rules over all things?

Passion as Original Sin

Christianity, with the exemplary force of the Passion of Christ, wants to resolve this tension, but in fact it actually represents its logical end. Historically there was in the Roman Empire an increasingly precarious public life, just as there was a precarious private one. It was difficult under these conditions to hope that this world could offer much more; but to therefore detach oneself from it with the intellect, as the Stoics advocated, was not a possibility for everyone in society.

13. Ibid., 6.17.142–43.
14. Ibid., 4.17.41.
15. Ibid., 4.19.44.
16. Ibid., 4.30.65. See 4.35.76.

Passions, which we could negotiate with Aristotle, and treat with Cicero, become under Christianity the sign of radical evil, the embodiment of sin. The idea that the tangible world forms a rational order, for which *logos* rediscovers necessity, providence, and the ultimate design of things, is abandoned. The schism between the tangible and the transcendental is hereby given form. What lies "beyond" is inaccessible to reason. Unfortunately, knowing the difference between good and evil is no longer enough for doing good, for acting upon this knowledge. To even think this is a sign of undue pride; so ignorance as impotence becomes the only established fact. Isn't original sin as much a sin of pride as pretension to knowledge, the fruit of which being the famous apple that Adam and Eve shared? If, as St. Augustine said, the original sin was before all else a sin of pride,[17] this is derived from our illusion that we can know divinity, when in fact the only thing we can really do is love it. Ignorance must know itself. Original sin, by diverting us from a love of God, becomes a sin of the flesh: the only love that those who have turned away from divinity as a means of manifesting their own autonomy is the love that links them to other persons, and this is passion itself. Flesh symbolizes difference, the Other; so passion links us to the Other. Fleshly love is guilty since it brings us to love ourselves (pride) rather than God.

Adam is thus banished from his paradise on earth, for having yielded to his passions. The apple symbolizes the fruit of this garden. For him to have taken it suggests that he considered himself the proprietor, that is, God's equal. This indeed is the sense of *original* sin. Far from being a reflection of a historical evolution, or because things have now changed for the worse, we can no longer hope to negotiate with the other in order to control or divert his violence (we *endure* it), the *original* sin crystallizes the human condition, without appeal. There is no hope of redemption. But doesn't the Passion of Christ present itself as a kind of "amnesty"? But this passion is, without doubt, the witness of the suffering that is linked to sin, that which delivers to innocence us who are in the grip of the passions, which all men feel because they are passionate beings. Isn't Adam, who was expelled from earthly paradise on account of his having abandoned himself to his passions, newly reintegrated into the spirit of God, after the Passion? When all is said and done, isn't Christ an Adam "in reverse"? We *are* sinners, according to our nature; how can we believe in the possibility of escaping our condition by our own acts? The grace that God accords to certain persons is the only

17. Augustine *City of God* 14.12 and 12.6.

thing that can save us, but we cannot know how to attain grace through our acts, by reason of our will, as though substituting our own will for that of God.

The difficulty that arises here is fundamental for Christianity. It relates not only to the meaning that one must accord to the Passion of Christ, but, moreover, to the meaning of the human condition in general. Are we really free or irremediably sinful? To which point can we exercise our own free will; and can we, by the exercise thereof, obtain our salvation?

From Knowledge to Love: The Irreducible Quality of Passion

Something has happened in the troubled times of the history of the world which has shaken thought right down to its very roots: the destruction of the idea, originally Greek, that the *logos* can through its internal resources have access to the apodicticity of the order of things, to their nature, of which we are an integral part and about which we must therefore be able to reflect in order to accede to our true nature. The equivalence between the real and the rational seemed more problematic than ever to people living in this era. Reason withdrew from the world, and the world had thus been delivered to chaos. That which was intelligible remained outside, and the tangible was governed by its own rules, which were nothing other than the rule of unruliness. What was broken was the Aristotelian hope to have a human order which could be absorbed, with its *pathos,* into the universal order. *Pathos* remained free of all shackles, without any possibility of absorption, without the ultimate rationality required to contain and control it. In the face of the ideal of necessity, we were doomed to remain in the wrong, which is nothing other than what the Christians came to refer to as "sin." The rupture with intelligibility, with Reason, with absolute order, made absolute order transcendent. An exterior God, for whom nature no longer permits *comprehension* or intellectual understanding, becomes a God that is inaccessible to reason; and he himself becomes nothing other than will, free will, and sometimes terrible in his wrath. Obedience is the keyword of relations with the divine spirit. There is no longer any question of understanding; from now on, the problem is one of will, since transcendence is outside the rational order of things. Religion, with its postulation of revelation, cannot but take over the place of philosophy in the Greek sense of the term. This makes us think back to Pascal and his rejection of all-powerful reason.

Our will to rediscover the will of God is no longer a question of knowledge but, since passion is omnipresent, one of love. The love of God, the will to bend to his will, to his designs, is the mission, the vocation that humanity must from this point on practice. Greek intellectualism is dead and buried. And yet, this is nothing other than Platonism. We are naturally victims of our passions; translation: we are naturally sinners. We don't know it, we consider ourselves innocent, we must be saved, we don't realize that we are prisoners in the Cave. From now on, the philosopher is to be replaced by the priest.

The Paradox of Fault as a Renewal of the Platonic Paradox of the Passions

According to the Scriptures, we are all guilty as soon as we are born, even if we don't realize it, and even though we couldn't possibly have done anything reprehensible. This is the meaning of original sin, the fruit of the human condition, the inheritance we bear on account of Adam's expulsion from paradise on earth. We see ourselves henceforth as condemned in advance, without hope for redemption, because we are what we are. Whether or not a priest intervenes changes nothing. Only God can save those he chooses, and in whom he invests his good graces. There is no liberty that isn't illusion, no knowledge that isn't pride, as Pascal reminds us in his *Pensées*. We cannot assure our own salvation with our own power, even less so through our actions, even if they are intrinsically good. So what good is faith, or religion in general, if all redemption by persons from original sin is excluded in advance? To know that we are prisoners of our passions delimits the problem that must be resolved, replies the Catholic, whereas the Protestant would no doubt be tempted to affirm that this only makes us aware of the problem which remains, in any event, irresolvable.

The paradox that remains with Christianity is the one already noted with regard to Plato: passion is on the one hand an obstacle to the truth, which causes us to confuse the appearance of things with the things themselves, and that which pushes us to search for the truth, since we only have access to appearances and since the tangible world is nothing other than a trap that we must overcome. Passion is thus the force that blinds and the thing that we know we must overcome, suggesting that we have subtly become aware of our own blindness. But if we are being tricked, we must ignore the fact that we are, without being able to doubt that there exists something to be overcome. We ignore, even as we believe we know, and we don't even look any more; but since passion is also that which we know we should be able to overcome, it pushes us to look for the truth for which it is the obstacle. All of this is of course contradictory, since it is not possible that passion be at once that which pushes us to search for truth and that which impedes our ability to discover it. Either we know that reason is beyond us, or we don't even put into doubt that reason could be other than that which delivers passions. But these two theses are irreconcilable. A passion which drives me to search for what it conceals could never be. In one case I am conscious of the problem that must be resolved as well as the obstacle that has to be overcome; in the other case, I don't even know that there is an obstacle, or that the shadows of the Cave are nothing but shadows.

Things are similar for the case of original sin. If Adam is innocent because he can't tell the difference between good and evil, he couldn't possibly know that he is committing a sin "by biting into an apple." How could we reproach him for anything at all if he wasn't even aware of what guilt was before committing the sin? It is even difficult to understand what it was that drove Adam and Eve out of their paradisiacal serenity in the first place. St. Augustine is well aware of the difficulty when he writes:

> The pair lived in a partnership of unalloyed felicity; their love for god and for each other was undisturbed. This love was the source of immense gladness, since the beloved object was always at hand for their enjoyment. There was a serene avoidance of sin; and as long as this continued, there was no encroachment of any kind of evil, from any quarter, to bring them sadness. Or could it have been that they desired to lay hands on the forbidden tree, so as to eat its fruit, but that they were afraid of dying? In that case both desire and fear was already disturbing them, even in that place. But never let us imagine that this should have happened where there was no sin of any kind. For it must be a sin to desire what the Law of God forbids, and to abstain merely from fear of punishment and not for love of righteousness. Never let us suppose, I repeat, that before all sin there already existed such a sin, the same sin, committed in respect of that tree, which the Lord spoke of in respect of a woman, when he said, "if anyone looks at a woman with the eyes of lust, he has already committed adultery with her in his heart."[18]

Before the original sin, it is clear that Adam should have been exempt from passion, from malignity, and it seems odd that he would suddenly

18. Ibid., 14.10.

abandon himself to it. What is incomprehensible is not simply the discovery by Adam that he is a passionate being, a prisoner of the tangible (Plato) who was unaware of this fact, but that it was this very state that causes the problem. Why passion? There is no other explanation than God's secret design; pride is the sole source of our delusion that we are autonomous in our decisions: "But God, foreknowing all things, could not but know that man would fall. Therefore we must ground our city upon his prescience and ordinance, not upon that which we know not, and God has not revealed."[19]

From there to conclude that "evils are so far under that which is good, that though they be permitted to exist to show what good use God's provident justice can make of them,"[20] there is but one step required to clear the hurdle erected by the need to close the circle of St. Augustine's reasoning.

But the paradox of original sin will eventually spread to the human being in its entirety. We are all guilty, on account of the passions that we are unable to resist, even though we are unaware that abandoning ourselves to these passions is evil, or that these passions are themselves condemnable. As a kind of ontologically irresponsible being, we will be asked to account for our actions. But how could we?

The consequences of the paradox of the passions have marked the history of Christianity and have been at the very root of some of its critical divisions.

Or else, we know that we are stricken by sin, and through this knowledge we are conscious of the problem at hand, which gives rise to two possibilities. Either the fact that we know ourselves to be guilty doesn't change anything, and only God in his "infinite goodness" can save those souls that he will have chosen from eternal damnation; no priest, no action, good or rational, could possibly substitute for divine grace. The priest is useless. What we find here is Jansenism and Calvinism. Or, the fact that we recognize ourselves as prisoners of vile passions gives us the possibility of starting over, by good acts, by confessions of one's sins, at least those that can be pardoned. And here we are in the domain of Catholicism. Or else we simply are not aware that we have been caught in passion's trap. But to assert as much is contradictory because to affirm an ignorance is to situate oneself outside it and to show that it doesn't apply to the very person affirming it. These two either/or situations at least have the merit of illuminating the fact that passion has been

19. Ibid., 14.11.
20. Ibid.

the source of paradox since the dawn of occidental thought, since they reveal each time a point of view outside the realm of passion, which seems to either abolish itself, or declare itself inaccessible. If I know that I have passions which impede my ability to really know, how do I know this? And if I don't know it, how can I even ask a question about overcoming them while at the same time uttering my own ignorance?

The paradox of passion finds itself at the base of great irresolvable oppositions which turn around the confrontation of Protestantism and Catholicism, or that of Jansenism and Cartesian thought. The question that still needs to be posed is to find out how, in all of our innocence, we can be guilty; and if despite everything we could have discovered this, how we could have possibly *acquired* this knowledge. In short, how is this possible for a priest who is himself supposed to be above it all, and to see from there the weakness of humanity? If he is able to do so, he is useless, since the original condition of all humanity cannot be remedied. If he's not, it is impossible for him to fulfill his role because passion would impede his ability to see. How can we affirm and justify the fact that we are guilty on account of our passions given that we are intrinsically unable to discover them? We would have to know in advance that we are sinners in order to realize that our state of sin, as though we could be under the influence of the Holy Spirit, or informed from the revelation-intuition-remembering process described by Plato; but even under these conditions the body would be condemned in advance as a hindrance to this very recollection.

Augustinianism as a Turning Point in the Conception of Humanity

Like the philosopher-king, Christian thinkers consider themselves above the passions they condemn, and able to reveal the passions in the rest of us, who are since our very origins prisoners thereof. Chaste, humble, and poor, they know that they are obligated to struggle against the very essence of passion, as expressed on the basis of the original sin: luxury, vanity, and cupidity. We are not really free, since we are governed, even before birth, by these three elements of the original sin. Can we really liberate ourselves from them, become modest, renounce sensual delights, and live without earthly goods? What is at issue is an asceticism that should be attainable through realization, as though, through it, humanity could regain all of its freedom. But isn't this just a lure?

The Passion of Christ is there to show that the blindness of human beings leads to their suffering. Yet we are within our rights to ask how any man, having been named to the priesthood, was able to place himself above all others, above his own human condition, and then have access to *their* truth which they themselves could not perceive. It is this impossible, superhuman or, better still, inhuman leap that Protestantism exposed in its critique of the Church. But like the Platonic philosopher, the priest who does attain their truth is necessarily relegated to a domain above all others, who remain in total darkness. There are those who receive the revelation, we're not sure how, and those who remain in a state of sin; faith, like philosophy for Plato, is not accessible through rationality but through reminiscence or, in the Christian world, through revelation. There is an inexplicable leap which allows some people to move from blinding passion to sudden lucidity. We can understand that this was only possible thanks to exterior intervention and that reason itself was insufficient, something that Plato, unlike the Christian thinker, never quite understood. If passion blinds me to the real truth, and holds me to the level of appearances, then I can't even have the idea that there could be something beyond appearances, since I can't even know that what I'm experiencing are only appearances. What is needed is a kind of lightning strike, a sudden inspiration so that certain individuals will be able to grasp the passion that is guiding them, and these same persons must then decide to renounce these passions, just as we abandon a practice that we come to realize as malevolent despite its benign appearances.

All of this suggests that revelation presents itself as a blessing accorded to some persons, and refused to most. The task assigned to the chosen few is to convert the others, since naturally, they will be otherwise unable to see the light. And as we know from History, Christian thinkers are no gentler to those they consider infidels than the Platonic philosopher was to the great mass of individuals who were indifferent to philosophy: "Augustine's dark vision of a human nature ravaged by original sin and overrun by lust for power rules out uncritical adulation and qualifies his endorsement of imperial rule. . . . Augustine, on the contrary, having denied that human beings possess any capacity whatever for free will, accepts a definition of liberty far more agreeable to the powerful and influential men with whom he himself wholeheartedly identifies."[21] Therein we find an appeal to constraint as well as the evidence for an Augustinian injunction to physically eliminate opponents like the Donatists. "By insisting that humanity, ravaged by sin, now lies helplessly in need of outside intervention, Augustine's theory could not only validate

21. Elaine Pagels, *Adam, Eve and the Serpent* (New York: Random House, 1988), pp. 118–19.

secular power but justify as well the imposition of church authority—by force, if necessary—as essential for human salvation" (ibid., 125). We notice once again the profoundly *aristocratic* character of this negation of passions. Reason—or, for St. Augustine, faith—are privileges that are rightfully accessible to all, but in fact reserved for an elite group who are able to detach themselves from the tangible world. If passion is an illusion that we can overcome by reason in the Stoic view of things, it is because human nature is not really true to itself until it melts into nature in the broader sense, of which it is but one element. If passion, in Christianity, presents itself as irremediable, it is because human nature detaches itself from the rest of all Creation on account of its failings for which there is no earthly remedy. The paradox reemerges here, since we are by our own nature condemned for our passions, but we can redeem ourselves by effacing our passions through an appeal to Christian faith. What is new in all of this is that we are despite everything beings who are distinct from the cosmos, which makes of the Augustinian viewpoint a truly intellectual revolution in terms of a conception of humanity. Desires for the tangible no longer designate passions in an undifferentiated fashion. They are linked to the original sin and defined by it. Everything flows from vanity, luxury, and cupidity. All other desires are but derivations. Unlike the Stoics, Augustine does not consider that we can or even should live in a state of apathy: this would be to confuse life on earth with life that is reserved for the beatitude that serves to reimburse those souls which have been saved. Could Hell be anything other than "eternal passion"? In short, we cannot avoid our Adamic condition of sinner; and Stoicism, by confusing that which is derived from the City of Man with the City of God offers to us an unattainable hope.

We don't know how to escape from our passions, and this is why to this day, on this earth, it is worth living a Christian life, that is, a life of restraint, in which we consider the hold that the dreaded passions have over us.

> At the same time, we have to admit that the emotions we experience, even when they are right and as God would have them, belong to this life, not to the life we hope for in the future; and often we yield to them even against our will. Thus we sometimes weep, even when we do not want to, though we may be moved not by any blameworthy desire but by praiseworthy charity. That implies that we have these emotions as a result of the weakness of our human condition. . . .

At this point, we may examine that condition which in Greek is called *apatheia,* which might be translated in Latin by *impassibilitas* (impassibility) if such a word existed. Now, bearing in mind that the reference is to a mental, not a physical condition, if we are to understand it as meaning a life without the emotions which occur in defiance of reason and which disturb the thoughts, it is clearly a good and desirable state; but it does not belong to this present life. For it is not the voice of men of any and every sort, but the voice of the most godly, of those advanced in righteousness and holiness, which says, "if we say that there is no sun in us, we are fooling ourselves, and we are remote from the truth." And since this state of *apatheia* will not come until there is no sin in man, it will not come in this present life.

At present, however, we do well if our life is free from external blame. But anyone who thinks his life is without sin does not succeed in avoiding sin, but rather in forfeiting pardon.[22]

This is pride: to ignore that we *are* sinners.

Love as the Original Passion

As Bossuet says, "Take away love, and there are no more passions; put in love, and you give birth to all of them."

Among the three elements that make up sin, sexual appetite is the one most severely condemned by St. Augustine, who makes Adam's actions a carnal sin *above all else;* and this is indeed the image most frequently associated with the episode in the garden. *Love* appears thus, and since the very beginning, as passion *par excellence,* even more than game-playing, avarice, or the lust for power. Terrestrial love is that which turns people away from God, with whom one's relation is no longer intellectual, as we saw, but amorous. The beginning of sin is of course pride, as St. Augustine suggested, but there again it comes in the form of love, the love that we have for ourselves. But the question is to know if condemnation of a theological nature doesn't hide something that is in fact intrinsic to love itself, and which does so by way of passion itself, exemplary and archetypical for all others. Desire, in Latin *libido,* is the mark of passion, but it is sexual desire that fully incarnates it by bringing together all other passions under its guise:

22. Augustine *City of God* 14.9.

Although therefore there be many lusts, yet when we read the word "lust" alone, without mention of the object, we commonly take it for the unclean motion of the generative parts. For this holds sway in the whole body, moving the whole man, without and within, with such a mixture of mental emotion and carnal appetite that hence is the highest bodily pleasure of all produced: so that in the very moment of consummation, it overwhelms almost all the light and power of cogitation.[23]

If the original sin is especially concupiscent,[24] this is derived from the fact that love, more than any other passion, invades soul and body, something which does not occur at the roulette wheel or in the Senate. But through the dependency that love creates for the Other, love renders us not only blind, as the expression goes, but it dominates us to the point at which, and this perhaps more than in other realms, it suppresses and arrests our reason.

Already in the work of Plato, *eros* presented this supra-tangible element of the elevation of desire. Love, which acts to fill in the need, forcibly abolishes the corporal, which is the living expression of this need, which is itself constantly renewed as long as there is life itself. As such, there is a self-abnegation in love-passion, which elevates the soul even as it idealizes the Other. Medieval courtly love, for example, incarnated this idea of nobility of the heart.[25] More to the point, we find in loving passion something which allies itself with the desire to be stronger than desire, and which, according to Rougemont, aims to stir up obstacles in order to exist. Passion shows as well this sense of challenge; the gambler, for instance, repeats his desire as though he were able to force the destiny of the cards or the numbers which, in the end, will commit him to lose. This same loss can be found in love-passion, where we, wholly self-absorbed, end up by giving in to the repetitive obsession which makes us believe that we will eventually arrive at merging with the inaccessible and dissolve into it. Rougemont writes:

Passion means suffering, something endured, preponderance of destiny upon the free and responsible person. To love love more

23. Ibid., 14.16.

24. This is the source of the divine punishment that will be inflicted upon those who are banished from earthly paradise. "It is entirely fitting that this retribution should show itself in that part which effects the procreation of the very nature that was changed for the worse through that first great sin." Augustine *City of God* 14.20.

25. See D. de Rougemont, *L'Amour et l'Occident* (Paris: Plon, 1972), pp. 78ff.

than the object of love, to love passion for itself, for the *amabam amare* of St. Augustine right up to modern romanticism, is to love suffering. Love-passion: the desire of what hurts us and destroys us through its triumph. Why does Occidental man want to endure this passion which hurts him and which all of his reason condemns? Why can't the commotion be just his suicide? It is that he knows himself and tests himself under threat of vital threat, in suffering and at death's door.[26]

We don't experience our liberty except in situations in which we stand to lose it. It is a permanent challenge, in which we gamble our destiny by playing against destiny, against death, just as one will return to the game of roulette in the illusory belief that he can "make it up." This description of us as anti-natural, as anti-destiny, or as liberty, is nothing other than lived passion. We feel, in our irreducible individuality, on the threshold of a challenge thrown out to the universality of death. But there is no victory possible in this case, which renders passion unreasonable: we cannot avoid our own death. The crazy competitor risks death at every moment, just as the forlorn lover or the ruined gambler both finish by hanging themselves. Passion ends badly. In any case, the essence of passion is to bring people to a kind of transcendence which is not necessarily divine, unless this effort is considered as a kind of Augustinian movement, at which point this effort to surpass would become a sin of pride, an insult to the only possible form of transcendence, that of God. But the very meaning of human passion is to throw down the gauntlet to its own condition. Courtly love is a pure and noble love which is gained through combat. Far from being a sin, this type of love ennobles those thereby concerned. We are far from Augustinian morality here, and to its resurgence during the Classical period: "Is it possible that the instinct of man be really become pure, if that he attaches his satisfaction to an ideal object, or that he places his natural warmth in the service of good? The aristocratic virtue can hardly pass up this competition; the Jansenist morality, on the other hand, justifies through the idea of radical corruption of man, his defiance as regards the sublimations of instinct."[27]

The moral code of the hero, wholly aristocratic, is denounced here for the benefit of egalitarianism in corruption, with the well-known critique of self-love as the true motive underlying the most noble of actions.

---

26. Ibid., p. 53.
27. P. Bénichou, *Morales du grand siècle* (Paris: Gallimard, 1949), pp. 115–16.

Jansenism is hereby revealed as a bourgeois expression of human nature, even though it bears the imprint of early theology as a criterion for the definition, if not, paradoxically, for liberation with regard to nobility.

Be this as it may, passion always refers back to a grandeur and an elevation that must be conquered by the stakes which must be overcome or the obstacles which must be conquered. We endeavor to overcome destiny (chance in gambling, conjugal and social mores in matters relating to passionate love) and to affirm our liberty, our virility (from which stems our pride, for which we are reproached) through passion. In this respect passion refers to the problematicity of humanity, to the "necessity" of making up our own minds by resolving problems posed by that which is outside ourselves.

But what St. Augustine's formulation that was cited by Rougemont reveals deserves further attention because therein is revealed a characteristic that is typical of all passion: "Tristan and Iseult don't love each other; they said it and everything confirms it. *What they love, is the fact of loving.* And they act as though they had understood that everything that is opposed to love guarantees, in order to exalt to the infinite in the instant of the absolute obstacle, which is death."[28] Love is the implicit element from one relationship to another which manifests itself in a thousand different ways: by smiles, by gestures and small but tender acts which express love without saying it as such. It is the underlying, immanent idea, the reflexive act which flows from all of this, like an overarching level or an idea which reunites all of the specific acts under a single banner: the Idea of Love. Just as we are able to detect in certain gestures hatred or contempt, anger or compassion, suffering or joy. In every case we are in the presence of an impulse which is itself some passion or another, but which is also the overriding level inside which falls all which characterizes it. Love is tenderness, desire, joy, and so forth, and each of these manifestations is itself this or that particularity: a situated act, like a kiss, a smile, or a gesture. Passion is the higher level within a kind of "hierarchies of types" (Russell) in which the Russian dolls are nothing other than actions which can be piled one inside one another, and at the very end we find the passions which are themselves the meaning of all that came before. They thus extricate themselves, just like reflexes, which bring together a diverse web of actions and subsume them into a single group, which in this case has as overall concept that which could be called, say, love or hatred, fear or anger.

Immanent introspective action is also the reflex we take on from the

28. Rougemont, *L'Amour et l'Occident*, p. 43.

outside, in this case within a single consciousness, which is thereby rendered contemplative by situating itself as an observer of that which overwhelms it. *Pathos* is that which supports movements of the consciousness when it is itself indirectly the object of its concern, having been directly absorbed by a tangible element invading it. Passions constitute those rare moments of fusion between the consciousness of an object and the consciousness of the self, when the self refers back to itself by moods, and is itself immersed in the sensation as though all distance between these two types of perception is suddenly found to be effaced. We here rejoin through the senses of pleasure and displeasure, the aesthetic pleasure which is both contemplated (Kant) and in-thought or spontaneous.

When we suggest, along with St. Augustine for example, that love has no other object than its own effectiveness, that it is in a sense its *real* object, aren't we affirming that the consciousness of an object is always reflexive? In the realm of passion, the consciousness that is turned outward coincides with itself, and in the end that is the end point of passion: to rediscover oneself, to prove oneself, to feel one's existence through sensations that are produced by exterior objects. To arrive at that point, the consciousness creates for itself obstacles that will divert it from the real objective, in order to experience itself alone through these obstacles, which if overcome, would lead to a suppression of passion. Passion is a condition for the impossibility of death in that it perpetuates therein desire in unappeased desire, a perpetually repeated sequence. Passionate desire, being its own object, forces the consciousness to measure everything that irreducibly separates it from the real and from that which it aims to grab hold of through passion, despite the fact that it doesn't have the power to do so. Hence the role of imagination in the state of passion. It has as its mission to resolve a tension which at first glance seems insurmountable. Through it, passion presents itself as a fusion with its object. On the other hand, passion aims to maintain a certain distance, since it amounts to a challenge that is thrown out to the necessities of the real, which cannot assuage us completely without condemning us to die. This is to say that the idea of fusion is imaginary. We idealize the loved one, in much the same way as we partake in gambling more for the play than the actual gain. The imagination allows for a fusion that reality forbids. As we have seen, the tension to which we referred earlier on resolves itself in the realm of the imaginary. The illusory character of passion consists in making us believe that fusion is possible, while passion could never survive unless it renders it impossible. The link to the tangible is thus an illusion, which as a mere imitation of the truth must be rejected as such, as a deception.

If we express ourselves in terms of the consciousness, that is to say in a more modern fashion, we are led to suggest that passion lodges itself into the space that is left open inside the consciousness by the difference between being conscious of an object and being conscious of oneself or, to use the words of the Ancients, between the tangible and the intelligible. These two types of consciousnesses have quite distinct objects, one which applies to that which is external, while the other, the consciousness of the self, has as its object that which occurs within it. Passion is the illusion of the synthesis of these two types into one single consciousness, an illusion that philosophers have spent significant energy in denouncing. Nevertheless, passion fills in the gap in a consciousness which in a narcissistic fashion has no other object than itself. If there is illusion, it is because the consciousness is *not* aware of itself when it is absorbed by a particular object. Take for example a man who is painting a picture; he does not think about the fact that he is painting, which would be tantamount to his undertaking another activity, because thinking about oneself painting and painting are two different activities. He is simply painting, and devoting his undivided attention to *that activity*. In the domain of passion, it is as though these two consciousnesses were but one. It is as though the consciousness of the object, by its nature immersed in itself without having to reflect thereupon, suddenly became conscious of itself, a form of thinking about *itself*. It is nevertheless contradictory that the consciousness be both reflexive and not reflexive: passion is the name of this contradiction or, at very least, this illusion. To introduce the concept of passion is tantamount to abolishing what is nevertheless an insurmountable difference. This clearly indicates the contradiction itself, since all consciousness is necessarily consciousness of self that is condemned to being the unconsciousness, and which the tangible consciousness *is not,* whether we like it or not, a consciousness that is turned toward itself. Consciousness of the tangible is henceforth a consciousness which is unaware of itself as consciousness, as reflexivity, although it remains reflexive because it is consciousness. This is similar to the image of the man immersed in the cavern of his own passions, and who recognizes as much, even as he must remain ignorant because he is the victim thereof; or to the man who is guilty of the original sin even though he had been innocent thereof at birth. We name the problem that must be resolved, and we know that there is a problem even as we remain unaware of it because we are immersed in that which impedes critical thought. This is as though sensible consciousness and consciousness of self as sensible self could be considered something different and, simultaneously, identical.

What one needs to recognize here is that passion is at once the name of the (illusory) distance between the consciousness and the object, and its abolition in the adherence to the self which creates the identification of the consciousness with itself. Passion is an obvious reality, since it insinuates itself into the crux of the consciousness; and it is perfectly illusory, since it is the fabric that the consciousness knits upon the frame of its own reflexivity, as though it could possibly escape from itself and into the object.

The distance is both abolished and maintained in and through passion, and that confirms the paradoxical character of passion within the occidental *logos*. Passion seems to renounce desire through idealizing sublimation even as it identifies with the pleasure of realizing it. Is passion an effusion of joy, is it pleasure, if not the sin, or is it, on the contrary, a sense of resignation and the sufferance that comes from being unable to achieve something? In which case, it is that which signifies the impossibility of doing something; pleasure, perhaps, but only that which emanates from pure reflection, contemplation, a kind of sublime experience, a "thing in itself" that could be found in the domain of action. Or perhaps passion is death, through which we lose ourselves and then meet our end in the sensible world? Or is it life itself, which is the result of the nonfulfillment of desire, always plunged into illusion and working in a phantasmal fashion therein? At the end of the day should we consider that passion opens onto its own annihilation by serving as a foil for divinity in us or, on the contrary, as the most earthly and most primitive form of our true nature? In Augustine's terms, the question is clear: does awareness of the original sin allow us the opportunity to be liberated therefrom through repentance, or does it change nothing in the fact that we are condemned by our very human nature, *a priori* sinfulness? Can our guilty desire transcend itself in the love of God, or is it unavoidable? Both readings are possible, and they have coexisted in Christianity since the very beginning, from the very idea of passion, which is considered to be an obstacle that stands in the way of our ability to overcome passion while acting at the same time as a stimulus for an attempt to overcome it. In terms of consciousness it could be said that unthinking, tangible consciousness is blind to its own nature, and that all consciousness, being consciousness of self, could not blind itself in and by the tangible. We cannot be sinners without knowing that we are, even though we are in all of our innocence, which in itself confirms the sin of pride.

St. Thomas himself attempted to respond to this fundamental contradiction in Christianity, which is fundamental in the doctrine; he did so by reintroducing the old Platonic distinction between concupiscence and the irascible, which conceals the passion that blinds us, including with regard to itself (thoughtless consciousness which is unaware of itself as consciousness), and the passion which distances us from itself, which intellectual reflexivity is by its nature a carrier (consciousness of self). Passion-obstacle, and the distancing of this passion which has become in some ways conscious, passion which the mind can be diverted away from.

The Reasoned Classification of Passions According to St. Thomas

Thomas Aquinas's approach comes in response to a concern about classifying passions in a more systematic fashion than Aristotle, and in a more detailed fashion than St. Augustine, who had rooted his analysis in the single original sin. Thomas, who hereby follows Aristotle, considers that the passions are not in themselves either good or bad, because they represent the modifications that the soul undergoes as a consequence of its being tied to the body. Perhaps in this sense as well, Thomas prefigures the modern era, which will from Machiavelli onward dissociate passions from morality.

This is somewhat surprising, since Thomas came from a tradition which linked passions to issues of good and evil, even if we are frequently under the impression that this is quite simply a way of speaking about that which the soul either desires or rejects.

On the first level, the soul leans naturally toward that which gives it pleasure and away from that which it finds disagreeable, without asking any questions and without going back on its choices. Concupiscence is thoughtless consciousness which allows itself to be absorbed into the pleasure of objects that it lusts after, or that spontaneously pushes aside others. It is at this stage that the passion about which we are not conscious, the passion that we don't even know, is holding us back or tricking us. The soul is in the Cave: it lives passion without reflecting upon it, it has a tendency of taking for good or evil that which appears to it as such.

But there is a second level, where the passion that is rebelling against itself reveals its true nature to the soul: it is an obstacle that must be overcome in order to arrive at reason; in any case, it is so if passion is synonymous with evil. But Thomas considered as well the other possibility that is offered up here, which is that passion allows us access to good; and here of course we think of the love of God. Irascibility is the passion that makes itself known in the obstacle, in the problem that it presents in order to be realized, a good that is difficult to attain, an evil that is difficult to avoid. In short, in the course of this return upon itself that the tangible and emotional consciousness enacts, this consciousness comes to know itself, through difference, through the distance from the very object that absorbed it without its even being aware thereof. Logic of identity and difference, of distance, of the difficulty of enhancing this distance from the bad or diminishing it from the good, the game of passion becomes one between concupiscence and the irascible. The consciousness of the object that knows itself as such measures its identity in the distance that separates it from that which unthinkingly immerses it entirely, in an unthinking fashion.

> *Since passion is a kind of movement,* as Aristotle says, the criteria for contrasting two passions or emotions will be the same as those for contrasting two movements or processes; and these are two-fold. First, two processes are mutually contrary when they stand in opposite relationships to the same term: thus generation—coming into existence—is the contrary of dissolution, going out of existence. Second, two processes may be mutually contrary because they stand in the same relationship to opposite terms: thus bleaching, the process of changing a thing from black to white, is the contrary of blackening, the process of changing a thing from white to black.
>
> Accordingly, there are two possible criteria of contrast between two emotions: one, their having contrary objects, viz. sense-good and sense-evil; the other, their involving a movement towards and a movement away from the same object. Only the first of these can occur among the affective emotions; but among the spirited emotions, both occur.
>
> For as we have seen, the object of the affective orexis is sense-good or sense-evil *sans plus*. Now the good *qua* good can never be the object of an impulse away from itself, but only of one towards itself: nothing shuns the good *qua* good: it is precisely what all things want. Similarly nothing wants an evil *qua* evil: it is precisely what things shun; therefore an evil as such is never the object of an impulse towards itself, but only of one away from itself. Hence each of the affective emotions whose object is a good is a movement towards that good, viz. love, desire and

pleasure; and each of them whose object is an evil is a movement away from it, viz. hatred, aversion or disgust, and sadness.
Two affective emotions are never mutually contrary, therefore,
on the score of their involving movement towards and movement away from the same object.[29]

The passion-obstacle is the irascible. Passion is experienced therein
in its problematic appearance: is it possible to come sufficiently close to
goodness? Is the difficulty that must be overcome insurmountable? Or
can we distance ourselves sufficiently from the evil which draws near?
To ask oneself if obstacles can be overcome comes back to asking ourselves about the possibility of suppressing the interval, that difference
between the tangible consciousness and the intellectual consciousness,
its difference from itself. And being beside oneself is the equivalent of
losing one's temper (irascibility), a bit like leaving oneself.

The passive soul endures a movement which reflects its reaction to
the object, good or evil. In concupiscence, we either have *love* or *hate,*
along with, for the actualization or resolution of the movement of the
soul, *joy* (pleasure) or *sadness,* which completes the *desire* or *aversion*.
Joy, desire, and love have as their object goodness, while hatred, aversion
(*fuga,* flight), and sadness are reactions to what is evil. Some have seen
in these three movements the passage of time:[30] the present (love, hate),
the past (joy, sadness), and the future (desire, avoidance). Others have
seen therein the opposition between the craving movement and its realization, the whole of which comes into opposition with the absence of
movement. That is to say, three passions that have to be split up depending upon the good or the evil. In any case, this is of little significance.
There is in all movement a tendency to orient toward the future:[31] temporality being the leaving from the self *(sortir de soi),* the nonidentity to
the self, which is an integral component of the domain of the passions in
general. The angle of approach could be multiple, something that St.
Thomas admitted (Question 25, article 3).

Concupiscence breaks down into three pairs of passions, while the
irascible remains but five individual passions, which makes a total of
eleven. What are the passions of the irascible? It would suffice to consider once again its nature in order to respond to this question. It is

29. *Summa theologiae* 1a2ae, question 23, art. 2, trans. Eric d'Arcy (London: Blackfriars,
1963), p. 23.

30. E. Gilson, *Saint Thomas moraliste* (Paris: Vrin, 1974), pp. 119–20.

31. J. Rambach, "A propos des passions: ombres et lumières avant Descartes," *Travaux de lin-
guistique et de littérature* 15 (1977): 43–65.

passion that shows itself for what it is: the indication of a problem that must be overcome, the measure of the difficulty in arriving there. From that point on, armed with that reminder, we are in a position to be precise about the contents of the irascible: pure anger, of course, has no contrary, nor any other temporality than the present. It would make no sense to lose one's temper on account of something bad that we don't know anything about, and that is expected to occur in ten years. It would be equally absurd to suddenly get angry about someone, or something, injurious to us ten years ago. Anger, says St. Thomas,[32] henceforth has two objects simultaneously; the correction of evil, which is good, and indignation against this evil. In this sense it is contrary to love, which only pushes us toward a desired good, or hatred, which opposes a good that we flee from. Clearly, there is in the phenomenon of anger a double movement which tears apart the soul or the consciousness, "it carries in itself the contradiction,"[33] and this finally signifies nothing other than the separation of the consciousness from itself in that distance that is formed between the desiring soul and the cognitive one. Through anger, the mind comes to be aware of all that it had not been conscious of previously, and that carried it away. Anger gets carried away as well, but it is aware when it is doing so. Anger is passion that reveals itself to itself as a problem, and it therefore symbolizes a consciousness that exists outside itself; it is torn between two parts, between its reflexivity as regards consciousness and the passionate rage which it wants to domesticate, and which it also perpetuates.

If irascibility presents us with ourselves as being outside ourselves, in divisions and the problematic, it can but return us to the question of its resolution. Is evil difficult to avoid, and good difficult to attain? There are the (inevitable) problems which arise from the recognition of the distance between *myself* and my objects, following the reflexivity that is instituted within the irascible movement. The list of possibilities that arise is as follows: either the difficulty is overcome and the problem resolved; or on the contrary, insurmountable, the problem remains. Since the irascible is the realization afterward of all that separates the two moments of consciousness, like a future possible appropriateness, desirable or dreaded, we have therefore, in correspondence with the future of concupiscence, a sense of desire or aversion, four irascible passions which will be witnesses of this future. As regards desire, we have either hope or despair; for flight (or aversion) we have either courage or fear.

32. *Summa theologiae,* question 46, art. 2.
33. Question 46, art. 1, p. 89.

In fact, hope concerns a difficulty which we deem to be conquerable, and despair reflects an insurmountable problem. Courage reveals a difficulty that can be overcome, while concern is the passion which insinuates itself when we think that there is no hope. St. Thomas opposes hope and despair as contrary recognitions of the distance that needs to be overcome in order to realize one's objectives, like a measure of the distance between desire and the rational possibility of success.

On the other hand, we could consider the *nature* of the difficulty, rather than considering desire or aversion, with its correlative notions of hope/despair or concern/courage. This leaves us with the following:

A difficulty considered surmountable:
Desire→hope
Aversion→courage

A difficulty considered insurmountable:
Desire→hopelessness
Aversion→concern

We could provide more details of this analysis, stipulating that the difference between the unthinking and the thinking consciousness, that is to say A and B respectively, can be measured by the irascible, which is this reflection about a consciousness taken in by the object. The difference AB is thus the expression of a distancing, desired or feared (after having been perceived, which the irascible soul does), which we seek to avoid, or on the contrary, which we demand. Is there, for the consciousness, a possibility of coinciding with itself in spite of, and within, the natural passionate movement?

Through the irascible the soul comes to realize what has happened to itself when it was not aware of itself on account of its having been preoccupied by the evidence of the good that absorbed it, or the evil from which it naturally fled. By reflecting about itself, it reflects about what in itself was unthinking, it *thinks about itself* when it doesn't think, and by doing so pushes itself outside itself to the place where contradiction creates anger. And anger is directed against the self, because one recognizes not having been oneself. Taken in by the tricks that it was trying to avoid, by the contradictions that it wishes to resolve, by its own movement toward resolution that it is trying to achieve, the irascible soul explodes in the face of the obstacles that it discovers, notably against its own passionate immersion which implicated it entirely, even despite itself. This difference that it discovers in itself helps it see that goodness is more or less distant from it, just like the evil, and that it must react, which is the reason for the irascibility. To resolve the problem that is now apparent becomes *its* problem. The soul endeavors, struggles, resigns itself, controls itself, but each time it measures the difference between itself and either good or evil for which it seemed to be naturally well informed without having to think about it in order to achieve it or avoid it. The distance is nothing other than that which opposes a consciousness immersed in the tangible world, with pleasure and pain as norms, to a consciousness which recognizes that it is the prisoner of its own feelings. It rebels against its natural naïveté, to recognize that what it considers natural, is in fact problematic. The problem of good and evil must be considered as distinct from its own consciousness, as is the object from the subject. Would it be desirable, or possible, to get closer to what we consider good, and to avoid what we consider evil?

Once consciousness recognizes that it has been absorbed by its passions, it recognizes everything that distances itself and tears it apart. It is its unity, the fusion that it recovers with itself, that it attempts to achieve by conquering passions, or by consciously accepting what brings it toward goodness.

The coincidence of unthinking and thinking consciousness is the very object of the irascible reaction against natural immersion, and its trappings. If this coincidence is possible, it is a good; in the irascible we therefore have a glimmer of hope if the good is nearby, and of despair if it is still far away, or if it distances itself in order to appear inaccessible. Hope and despair run contrary to each other with regard to this distancing, the distance that separates the desiring soul from its object.

> Now the object of hope, which is an arduous good, is attractive as long as it is considered possible of attainment. It is under this aspect that hope, as implying an approach of some sort, reaches out for it. If the object is considered impossible to obtain, it becomes repulsive because *when men come upon something impossible, they turn away,* according to the Ethics. But this is the reaction of despair, which consists in an act of withdrawal. Hence despair is the contrary of hope as withdrawal is of approach.[34]

And yet, adds St. Thomas, the opposite of hope is not only despair, but also fear, from another standpoint. Hope relates to the good that we

---

34. Question 40, art. 4, p. 13.

consider possible to achieve, whereas fear addresses itself to an evil which is the inverse, and which as a consequence is far away in the future.[35]

We have here two types of vexation, hope/despair which answer to desire, depending upon whether we consider it "realistic" or possible; and then we have hope/concern, which responds to the concupiscence that we reflect upon to evaluate the difficulty in achieving either attraction to the good or avoidance of the evil. Despair corresponds, in a symmetrical fashion, to audacity and courage: if the good is far away in the first case this means that, *a contrario,* the evil that we wish to avoid and which is its inverse, or its mirror opposite, is close at hand.

Flight, or aversion, which represents the movement of backing away from the evil, demands a higher degree of courage if the distance that separates us from it is short; for a greater effort to combat an evil that is nearby.

Concern is more intellectual because the evil is further away and is, therefore, easier to put aside. "Fear shrinks from a future source of harm by which one may be overcome, whereas daring faces up to and seeks to overcome an imminent threat. Therefore it is clearly contrary to fear."[36]

In short, we have hope/despair, according to the type of desire, just as we'd have concern/courage, depending upon the type of aversion; but we'd have hope/concern depending upon the opposition between good and evil, just as we'd have despair and audacity depending upon the axis of good and evil. "In fact we have seen that the contending emotions involve a twofold contrariety. The first is the opposition of agreeable and disagreeable—this is how fear is contrary to hope. The second is the opposition of approach and retreat—this is how daring is contrary to fear and despair to hope."[37]

St. Thomas emphasizes that there are some related implications, since "despair is derived from concern" and "audacity is not a part of hope, but is rather its effect." He explains these relations by saying that concern about an evil that is nearby comes from a good that is far away and that we desperately wish to obtain, just as audacity comes from that which we hope to conquer.

We can therefore set up a table of the four passions of the irascible other than anger:

35. Question 42, art. 2.
36. Question 45, art. 1, p. 73.
37. Ibid., pp. 73–75.

Table 1.

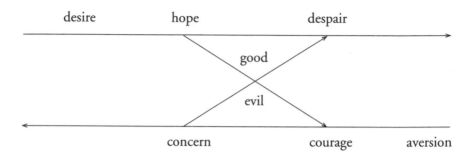

The horizontal arrows correspond to moving closer or further away: as the good moves away along the arrow of desire, the difficulty of achieving the good goal increases, while the evil follows an inverse pathway, which augments the sentiment of aversion or flight. For a nearby evil one needs courage, and if the evil is still far away, only concern that it will approach will increase. The vertical *lines* correspond to the opposites of concupiscence, which express themselves through static oppositions: hope relates to a good that is nearby while evil could, despite everything, appear to be far away, and therefore inspires only concern that it will occur. While the evil that is too close provokes a more violent reaction, in this case courage, we feel a sense of despair as regards its correlative good, which seems beyond reach. The crossed *arrows* represent the dynamics of the passions. In itself, hope is opposed to concern in that hoping for a good is flight from evil, but this process will imply courage if it approaches. By the same token, the concern about an evil that is still far away and that we push away could lead to despair if the desired good doesn't appear. Hope for a good that approaches raises one's courage to flee from all evil which could act as obstacles, just as the concern about an evil that is approaching could make us lose hope of obtaining something which, by the same token, would recede into the horizon.

In conclusion, five passions make up irascibility: anger, which is purely reactive to an evil that is present, or an evil that is absent; and the reflexivity of the passionate movement which follows in the quest for a realization, for a future. Hope and despair correspond to desire and aversion, courage and fear. Concupiscence is like a past stage of the irascible, and cannot see whether it has a future except in the reflection of its "chances for success."

Doesn't the Thomas Aquinas Resolution Put to Rest the Problem of the Passions?

In fact, it simply repeats it, since it is difficult to know how we could reflect upon an obstacle if we aren't already cognizant of its existence.

How is it possible to achieve the irascible when we are immersed in concupiscence and obsessed by natural desires? This is the Menon paradox again, but this time we rediscover it as an impossibility of passing from concupiscence to the irascible or at least to explain how this passage occurs. If concupiscence renders us passionate to the point of being blind, could we prevail over this sentiment with regard to which we lose all ability to be lucid?

The irascible and the concupiscent seem fundamentally different, to the point where they seem devoid of any possible link. And yet we could rightfully object that the search for good, is just as naturally the flight from evil, which makes more than problematic the distinction between concupiscence, which involves an approach, and the irascible, which is the concern about distancing, always *difficult* to solidify with regard to a passion that drowns its victims. Would they be identical, if not redundant, in the sense that going toward a good consists of recognizing the distance from what is evil? Take an example: if I am looking for that which procures *joy* (the passion of concupiscence), isn't it true that I'm going to be concerned about everything that could be considered synonymous with sadness (the passion of irascibility)? Both passions are supposed to grow out of distinct levels of passion, but "all the emotions of the spirited orexis terminate ultimately in those of the affective."[38]

Here, in concupiscence, there is already a reflexive attitude which isolates the consciousness from its object and sets up the distance that must be conquered or reinforced. I know that I am looking in the attitude of irascibility, and since I am not even aware of my own state of passion in concupiscence, by integrating the two of them together, the two that we had previously divided up, we "resolve" everything.

It is true that the criteria of difficulty *(ratio ardui)* remains as a means of differentiating them, but this is subjective. This places St. Thomas in a rather difficult position historically, seen from today in any case, since he comes after a moribund Aristotelian scholasticism and before the advent of modern subjectivity with its concomitant theory of consciousness in which the unlinked dualism, between concupiscence and the irascible are reabsorbed in the unity of consciousness and reason.

38. Question 23, art. 1, p. 21.

4

The Genesis of the Individual and the Eruption of Guilt

Introduction

The Renaissance left its mark on history in the form of a slow dissolution of Augustinianism, which regularly experienced rebirth from its own ashes, as though it were a kind of counterbalance to the letting-go of the passions. One could very well ask what kind of society could possibly survive an enrichment that crushes over a prolonged period of time its weakest members, or which tolerates licentiousness to the point of sadism. What political system could support indefinitely struggles for power and honor in a constant duel of exacerbated vanities? Protestant-ism, like Jansenism later on, subscribed to Augustine's doctrine as a means of convincing the faithful that they must search for salvation instead of vain pleasures in this distraught and condemned world.

All the same, greed, luxury, and vanity take on a different hue, chang-ing if not into positive virtues, at the very least into subjects of study rather than condemnation; that is to say, they became subjects for analy-sis rather than theological judgment. Human beings could seek to under-stand themselves with reference to themselves, rather than through God and his priests. Human reality could reflect upon itself (Descartes) with-out having to make reference to the mythical Fall, the fall which would be like the inverse of the moment before existence, of each existence; the fall which is both the inevitable source of understanding for life on earth and destined to remain inaccessible to reason, just like its Mystery and its Dogma.

In the pursuit of honors and power (Hobbes, Machiavelli) pride incarnates an endless struggle which would have exhausted the participants if they had not agreed to enter into a social contract designed to limit their appetites. They needed to be made aware of this, and of the passions which define or flow from their appetites, in order to permit the establishment of a democratic society. Each one could freely work toward the suffrage of each person, and society would thus pass from absolutism to modern citizenship, and this thanks to the newfound lucidity with regard to real human passions and to the right of all to express them while respecting those of others. To limit passions or to permit them to run freely, that is the political question *par excellence*. How should one choose between Hobbes's absolutism and Rousseau's libertarian will? The basis of this question is nevertheless the same: politics is passion, even when we pretend to reduce passion to silence. To deny political passions by condemning them through theology, for example, leads to indirectly legitimizing their repression, which returns us to a feudal type of power arrangement.

The meaning of greed was also changed. From then on one spoke of economic interests; everyone who endeavored to promote economic interests to his or her own profit would henceforth be assuring, without necessarily being conscious thereof, the interests of the community as a whole (Mandeville, Smith).

Lust became the liberty of the body, the cult of pleasure, which could range from aesthetic tastes to licentiousness. Here again, excesses would find their limits, recalling the opposition between Kant and de Sade, or in the economic domain Marx versus Smith, or in the political domain Montesquieu versus Machiavelli.

The dissolution, if only partial, of Christian asceticism corresponds to the opening up and the enrichment of a world that since the Middle Ages had lived in a state of contradiction. The great majority of people had to concentrate upon their own survival, and the survival of their offspring. The keyword of the era was "renunciation" with a hope, considered quite real, for leniency from beyond. In this sense the Church only justified the obvious for the great majority of people by teaching them to accept the inevitable order of things.

With the Renaissance—and here we're thinking of Italian cities—hope came back down to earth. We aspired to other things, better things, but it was necessary to struggle to obtain and keep them. It became possible to enrich oneself, and the quest for glory and for responsibilities became possible within the order of things. This signified that traditional links were rendered fragile. Some families mounted the social ladder, while others descended it. Wealth and power, like love, so constrained and so codified, raised the stakes, which made them subject to the inexorable swings of Fortune.

Perhaps it is bad to fight against one another for power, just as it is to wish to conserve it at any price or unrelentingly and fiercely attack those who have it; nevertheless, this is the way people act, even when they are acting under the guise of religious virtue. Once we have said that human beings are corrupt and sinful, we've really said nothing; we have simply condemned without comprehending. The expulsion from terrestrial paradise hearkens back a long way, and relates more to myth than to reality. The original sin is undifferentiated in that it affects all people without exception and for all eternity, even though societies themselves change and people are diverse. It would be unreasonable to avert one's gaze in the face of the lust for power, with all of the arrogance and the lucre that comes along in train once one gets it. What a trick for those who don't come to see things clearly! Such blindness would without any doubt satisfy a certain ideal conception of morality, but not of prudence.

In this warning, one recognizes the meaning of Machiavelli's message.

For him, it is useless to neglect the true passions of human beings if we really hope to live among them. The Catholic Church certainly didn't hold itself back from practicing Machiavelli's own ideology. Didn't it manipulate the City States to divide Italy, and by doing so play them against each other for its own benefit? What then is this original sin for the Church, other than a political weapon that allows it to hide its true intentions? Far from a reality based upon observation, the definition of the human being as sinner is shown for what it is: pure ideology.

By denouncing hypocrisy, Machiavelli claims to open the eyes of those who otherwise run the risk of becoming its victims. He was animated by the desire to unmask appearances, so-called virtue, strong sentiments, and generous ideas, and to go beyond the self to where the reality of humanity affirms itself as being singular individuals. Passion is the truth of action, and it must be discussed as a means of resisting blindness. Passion does not trick us, but negating it does.

Pride and Passion: Politics

Everything moves, everything changes, the fortunes of humanity are uncertain and unpredictable. One thinks of King Lear, the very symbol of the certitude of power which supports itself solely upon its own past and, by doing so, blinds itself to its force and its perennial nature because it forgets that we mislead to conquer and that appearances are illusions upon which it is best not to rely. Lear divides his kingdom among his daughters, by asking them if they really love him; but he is quickly caught in his own trap, which turns out to be the answers that they offer up. The beginning of Lear, says Yves Bonnefoy,[1] does not describe something rotten in the kingdom, as was the case for Hamlet, but it is a mysterious evil of the soul, in this case, pride.

Recall the words of Gloucester in Act 1, scene 2: "Love cools, friendship falls off, brothers divide: in cities, mutinies; in countries, discord; in palaces, treason; and the bond cracked between son and father. This villain of mine comes under the prediction; there's son against father; the king falls from bias of nature; there's father against child. We have seen the best of our time: Machinations, hollowness, treachery, and all ruinous disorders, follow us to our graves!" This recalls Hamlet, who is unable to find himself in a world which is turned upside down, in which signposts disappear and appearances stand in for reality. Hamlet, who considers that he is charged with the task of putting things back into their proper place after the death of his father, finds himself confronted with his own weakness. As Yves Bonnefoy says: "Hamlet is profoundly and specifically concerned with the problem of a consciousness that wakens to this condition, previously unknown and unpredictable; of an unstructured world; half, concurrent, and contradictory truths; and ample signification, that occurs rather too quickly, but nothing that resembling a sacredness, or a meaning" (my translation). Thus Hamlet reproaches his mother who married his father's assassin, "to be blind . . . to the point of being unable to distinguish between such dissimilar beings" (Act 3, scene 5). Everything is mixed up in this mixture of similitudes, in which reality changes despite all indications of continuity.

We find this idea in the work of Cervantes, notably when Don Quixote confuses windmills for giants, being unable to distinguish between what he sees and what he believes.

The old order crumbled in Italy long before it did in other nations. Machiavelli sees better than anyone else how passions work for those at the summit of power, where conquests occur, where all things are gained or lost.

But universality is in season: "So leaving aside imaginary things, and referring only to those which truly exist, I say that whenever men are

---

1. Yves Bonnefoy, *Préface à Hamlet et au King Lear* (Paris: Gallimard, Folio, 1978), p. 19.

discussed (and especially princes, who are most exposed to view), they are noted for various qualities which earn them either praise or condemnation."[2]

Each person is master, not of his or her destiny or necessity, but through of his or her own abilities and strengths. Passion is that which expresses our individuality and the maximum amount of liberty accorded by the blows of destiny. Being prudent is appropriate when faced with that which we cannot always control. The game is rhetorical—whence arises the role of blame and forgiveness—in that it obliges us to offer illusions, to turn things around, to show the best face of things, and if we are the Prince, the need is all the more urgent, since we must absolutely command the respect of others. We change directions according to necessity, to go with the flow or to diminish the threat of violence. But the blows of fate—*Fortuna*—are hard to avoid. Social and political mobility doesn't necessarily offer guarantees to the victims of tomorrow, or the heroes of today. As such, *The Prince* is a work that presents a web of advice for survival or, at very least, the rhetorical principles that underwrite prudent action. Therein we find a rerouting of the passions through the passions themselves in the service of "natural" ends: "honors and wealth." There is no constraining logic at work in this *reflection* about passion, but rather a constant evaluation of particular situations, an evaluation that is often assimilated into the realm of opportunism by those who condemn it, especially as regards other persons, as though they could escape its logic.

Be this as it may, to know the necessity of things—*Fortuna*—refers to an ability—a virtue—which allows one to avoid or direct it depending upon the prevailing circumstances.

Machiavelli, or the Rhetoric of Prudence

Ever since Aristotle there has been a clear distinction made between *logic* and *rhetoric*. The former is apodictic; it is a science of certain conclusions because they flow from principles deemed to be absolutely true. The second, far from being a "science of principles," is a theory of consequences. Logicians draw conclusions from axioms stated at the outset, and then follow through with their choices, which are essential on account of the principles that have been adopted; rhetoricians on the other hand are more prudent: if they too reason with premises in order

2. Machiavelli, *The Prince*, XV, trans. George Bull (Harmondsworth, U.K.: Penguin Books, 1980), p. 91.

to arrive at their conclusions, they do so by first examining the effects of these conclusions. They consider their impact before proposing principles. Logic is axiomatic before all else, whereas rhetoric is concerned about ends. Are these particular ends desirable, reasonable, or even just? These types of questions make no sense to a mathematician or a physicist, who deduce theorems one by one, whether one "likes" them or not.

One might well recognize in this distinction the one that Max Weber set up between *the ethics of conviction,* principled and absolute, just like Kant, and the *ethics of responsibility,* so important in the political realm.

Those who speak of an ethics of responsibility speak of a constant dialogue between ends and means. The means are often unacceptable, from which arise the rhetorical ruses that must be set up to justify them. Machiavelli has often been reproached for his defense of the maxim that "the ends justify the means." In fact, this is a form of immorality that is quite peculiar, which exists only if the ends are solely in the service of the individual. For Machiavelli, it is *natural* that we give themselves over to personal objectives, which confers a "Machiavellian" character to the "logic" of prudence, but also confirms its inevitability in the face of human realities.

The "logic of prudence" is, as we said, a rhetoric of passions which defines itself through the rational act of accounting for all consequences, where the issue at hand relates to peoples' decisions and actions. It is opposed to the logic of principles, which refuses to see the implications of actions taken or of beliefs adopted. Brutus assassinates Caesar, but he can be defended for it (or at least we'll adopt that possibility here). Depending upon one's point of view, he liberates the realm by getting rid of a tyrant that menaces it. As Casca says in Shakespeare's *Julius Caesar,* Brutus "sits high, in all the people's hearts: / And that, which would appear offence in us, / His countenance, like richest alchemy, Will change to virtue, and to worthiness" (Act 1, scene 3). There is no doubt that Brutus wouldn't have denied this basic truth according to which "assassins are guilty," but he wouldn't be perceived as a vulgar assassin. The underlying reasoning is obviously *disjunctive:* Brutus doesn't see, cannot see, that a certain general truth applies to him and that his action is nothing other than a particular case. Thanks to this blindness, he is able to hide the consequences of his act, in this case that which would make him like the assassin. He knows that such an act is evil, but since he didn't actually commit that particular act, why should he worry?

Good conscience, rationalization, even ideological closing-down, are all logical practices which relate to "principled thought," the thought we apply to questions that demand that we act in respect of consequences.

The logic of principles ignores prudence: it is *a priori*. Never have those who subscribe to it ever had to ask themselves about the application of its truths. From an ethical point of view, one might call this type of procedure *irresponsible*. One *must* do this or that, one *must* eliminate Caesar, and whatever flows from this action can be ignored, denied, or rendered inessential.

The logic of prudence consists of considering the consequence B before deciding about A, which is the principle. The problem that must be resolved is to obtain B (or to avoid it), while in the logic of principles, we don't seem to be in any way faced with a problem, as though everything were already decided by an immediate or predigested reading. By not having to worry about whether B or not-B will be the consequence of A, one manifests *indifference,* but also a refusal to see the link between A and B. We don't recognize A's relationship with B, or we deny that it has anything to do with A. Brutus could very well have denied that he was a murderer, which would permit him to avoid seeing that A leads to B, that is to say the crime. But he could just as well reject the consequences directly by challenging the AB link, that is, by denying that all intentional homicide justifies capital punishment. The logic of principle is not determined by what follows, as though the progression literally follows from that point, there where the logic of prudence considers derivations, before coming back to the principles which are rational to accept. We would be almost tempted to say that the prudent are the only ones who really reason, while in the two cases we've considered persons of principle save themselves from the need to put forth the AB inference. The question of knowing whether one needs to do A is not even at issue, according to this latter group. A principled and axiomatic logic transforms life into necessity and admits that the course of things is nearly ineluctable, which is inscribed against the elementary rules of prudence and thus politics. One might suggest as well that this logic is tautological, since it condenses one problem, "In light of B should one do A?" into a single identity which consists in identifying A by leaving to the side B, which is nonetheless a part of the action initiated by A. This identity conferred upon A couldn't be anything other than wrong, since it neglects B, which defines A. And the whole procedure is rhetorical, in the bad sense of the term, even fictional, because the discourse that affirms A accords itself an identity *a priori,* without any hope of discussion, and which suits the speaker just fine since he can blind himself through a kind of story which he'll end up telling to himself.

The logic of principle thinks things through step-by-step, without having the end have any retrospective effect upon the beginning, that is, analytically. One does not determine things with regard to consequences, a bit like the man who knows that snakes are poisonous but cannot see that x is a snake, or the man who goes carelessly forward because he denies, *de facto,* that all snakes are poisonous. In this case, imprudence is tantamount to negation. It comes back to denying the consequences of the principle for which prudence demands respect or application, and thus to not establish a link between A and B. One denies that the question A or not-A needs to be asked, so there is no longer anything to resolve because the problem itself has disappeared: A is necessary. In all matters human, however, the course of things is uncertain and problematic: uncertainty of effects must rebound upon the causes by rendering problematic the decisions that must be made. To snap one's fingers at the problematicity of consequences, as though they could be taken for granted, or as though the principles sufficed to guarantee the occurrence, is to deny the very character of history. To set out a problem as though it were already resolved is to enter into a vicious circle. That Brutus denies that he is an assassin without asking himself what he has done to make himself an assassin suggests that he excludes the very question, or that the question finds a resolution in the story that he tells himself to justify the action, which amounts to the same thing. A principled form of thinking shows itself to be as rigid as it is erroneous because it ignores alternatives. It would place those who believed in it at the mercy of the pliability and the ruses of those more wily than themselves. It is nothing other than a form of denial of reality, a negation about the particularity of situations. Experience is neglected because one doesn't perceive it with respect to the general truth that applies to its categorization. The dissociation between a proposal of this nature and the particular case at hand rests upon whatever the subject feels, in short, upon the passions. The passions rend, whereas reason synthesizes. The passions blind us, and it is for this reason alone that they must be condemned. We use them anyway, and exploit them.

The denial of the problematic, through prefabricated or predigested solutions, leads to a misunderstanding of one's own passions. Machiavelli recognizes that princes exploit this situation, but by unveiling it, he offers his readers the possibility of outwitting the ruses, or of using them to their own advantage. Machiavelli opens us up to our own passionate nature, which operates even when we are unaware of it. He does not praise his passion, he notices it. It is more dangerous to deny passions than to follow them, because by doing so at least one is liberated from manipulation by other people. All action is finalized: if A, thus B. To not see this is to act according to a rhetoric of passions which forgets prudence and leads to catastrophe. It is clear that the ends pose the problem of the means, especially of their occultation or their imposition by brutal means, but by being aware of this, one can make informed decisions without hiding from the consequences which inevitably flow from them. For Machiavelli, we must reflect in order to become aware of our passions, and by this act we can liberate ourselves from them, if we decide to do so, or we can abandon ourselves to them, but this time in full cognizance of the cause.

Whatever the case may be, there is no doubt that knowing the rules of the game allows one to play it to one's own advantage. This is indeed the very meaning of the irreducible freedom of the human being. He or she can scoff at means of persuasion once this process has been followed. Ruses and manipulation cannot be eliminated: one could always say to another, "You know I am sincere," and the other can choose to believe or not, just as the one uttering the statement can be sincere or not. To know that we are able to manipulate, and to know how to do so, doesn't impede victims and executioners from finding themselves on the roundabout road of history which repeats itself. This is why human nature, which always thwarts history in order to affirm itself, is nothing other than the return to Machiavellian ideas which we thought we had overcome and unmasked.

The State of Nature, and Human Nature

Machiavelli still represents a decisive rupture for us in thinking about human nature because he undertook his reflections upon a wholly novel basis. For him, we are no longer beings in nature. He sets out a new dualism, that of nature and human nature. He thus creates a gulf between human beings, on the one hand, and nature on the other, which forces occidental thought to consider the relation that exists between them. Descartes does so with reference to humanity, Spinoza with reference to nature, but in each case it is necessary to rediscover the whole and to show that thinking about it is inscribed as a possibility within this very totality. But is it inscribed as destiny, or as a contingency?

What seems increasingly clear in this opposition is the objectification of nature—and not only the new status of humanity—which corresponds to detachment from nature as an integral part of the whole being. It is difficult to determine which of these comes first, however, the objectification of nature or the birth of the individual, of the human being as subjectivity. The dissolution of traditional ontology, which had been Aristotelian and scholastic, probably took it all away. In any case, nature was no longer perceived to be a whole that is woven out of essences which conditions us like it does other beings. To be *affected* by nature becomes a process whereby one is subjected to nature, and no longer one of fulfilling an essence which would be deployed in the order of time and of becoming.

The same goes for being affected by, or having, passion. This becomes the inscription of nature in the human being, in other words, the natural state is being passionate. Reflecting upon ourselves signifies for us the act of seeing ourselves from a distance with respect to nature and its effects; this is equivalent to objectivizing nature and thinking about the state of nature within the self.

Because the whole becomes fractured and does not lay itself open to apprehension through a theory of being, deemed too indistinct and general, a specific conceptualization of nature must appear, and does indeed in the form of the modern physics of Kepler, Copernicus, and Galileo.

What caused problems in the ancient vision was the dualism between the tangible and intelligible. This flower, this tree, this insect, appear to us as natural beings. Nonetheless, nature is above: the nature of the plant is not itself a plant, but what conditions its development, its life as a plant? Is it this becoming which is natural, or is it the object itself? Is nature something tangible or, on the contrary, does it explain the tangible world as a universal, formal and intellectual principle would? Nature comes to coincide with the essence of the thing in question, such as when we speak of the nature of democracy, for example.

This ambivalence about what is natural is one between contingency and necessity. Some authors see the state of nature as a state where everything that happens is contingent upon free choice (Rousseau): others (as we'll see later on) see it as the empire of a more brutal form of necessity (Hobbes). In any case, nature becomes a concept which, by becoming objectified, cannot avoid being seen as a place of contradiction. One way to suppress this contradiction would be to consider that our becoming conscious of the natural world occurs as a consequence of our being part of the tangible: this would be passion. As for the object of this coming to consciousness, this is something purely intelligible, nature in a mathematical sense. Passion is thus nature in the subjective sense of the term, what I experience and what I see, what I feel and what affects me on account of the fact that I am a body among other bodies. We must be wary of passions because they fool us, says Descartes; they lead us to confuse what is objective with what is subjective.

From this standpoint there is more in the idea of the state of nature than a new vision of being or human reality. A mode of thinking which aims to consider humanity in its entirety is hereby being drawn up, because passion is not simply an epistemological obstacle or a foil for theoretical reason: it is also a key concept in political thought. Kant pursued this idea by assimilating the emancipation of the age of Enlightenment to the victory over passion, that is to say nature. The "political minority" is on the level of passion, while the fact of being the majority is a part of the order of reason. Passion signifies passivity, and thus is opposed to liberty:"Laziness and cowardice are the reasons why so great a portion of humanity, after nature has long since discharged them from external direction *(naturaliter maiorennes)*, nevertheless remains under lifelong tutelage, and why it is so easy for others to set themselves up as their guardians. It is so easy not to be of age."[3]

Modern political thinking emerged from a reflection upon the state of nature. We previously noted that to favor a state of nature is an intellectual undertaking that consists of disassociating oneself from such a state, of becoming aware of it, which establishes a distance with nature, but which does so with regard to the person who is doing the theorizing. This is the source of the correlative appearance of subjectivity. This state is interior to and constitutive of the reflection about humanity. Through the state of nature a difference and an identity is established, a transcendence and sense of belonging. We consider ourselves as being determined by such a state, but it is, at most, an origin to which we could want to return, or from which we might wish to be completely separated.

All of the ambiguity emerges from not really knowing whether human nature is above all natural or human, if we should be situated within the general order of nature, or if that which is human should be considered by itself because it is human. Finally, Hobbes isn't any more correct about this than Rousseau is as about Hobbes, because both of their methods of proceeding incarnate two possibilities that are inscribed within the idea of the state of nature. The problem is too clear, and it is unresolvable: if we are nothing but nature, then we are not human; but if we are not part and parcel of nature, then we have none of the qualities of other living beings, and are therefore God himself. If passion is a sin, or if sin is passion, and if being sinful is comparing oneself to God through a sense of arrogant mastery, it is because passion is the point of convergence between nature and human nature, of nature in the human being. Through passion, we lose sight of our specificity as human beings and abandon ourselves to our instincts, as though we were nothing other

3. Kant,"What is Enlightenment?" in *Foundations of the Metaphysics of Morals and What is Enlightenment?* trans. Lewis White Beck (New York: Bobbs-Merrill, 1959), p. 85.

than nature. We forget our humanity, which we naturalize, and turn our desires into derivations of our appetites, rather than detaching ourselves from them. The *human* in human nature is passion, since it is the element that makes us believe that we are above nature, of which we are in fact part, as though we could be on equal footing with God, who also dominates nature. On account of our passion we forget what is natural in us, and what ties us to everything around us. But this is a forgetfulness in which only we can partake, since neither animals nor plants can ignore or even reflect upon their condition. This brings us back to the original sin; passion places us above nature because it prolongs our own sense of it, so it is not pure nature even though at the same time it is.

Passion, whether one likes it or not, is by the same token the *natural* of human nature, that from which it cannot escape because to live is to be compelled to reproduce, protect offspring, and so forth.

With this assimilation of passion to nature in the human being, and to the human in nature, we're no longer sure if passion is corporeal, mental, or both. In any case, its conceptual role is to serve as a ground for human identity, even if passion also expresses a difference. The logic of passion reveals itself as a game in which we are not ourselves except with regard to other things; this, not surprisingly, is the definition of vanity in the work of Thackeray, and conscience for Sartre. The state of nature is therefore this "other" in us, which draws the contours of our identity and reveals, yet again, our alienation.

The result of all of this is that passion is natural and it is not, it is human and it is not. It is the paradoxical concept of coherence which should permit people to be both part of nature and human. This difference is incarnated in passion just as it is turned away by it so that a real identity can emerge.

This leads us to the question of knowing about nature, and about the humanity of humanity. We obviously have the sense that humanism is born from reflections about this question, just as it will die from its noticing the *aporias* that will close off the answer, which is always renewed on account of their contradictions. Doesn't humanism rest upon the evidence of a human nature, evidence that is all the more problematic since these two concepts, human and natural, are involved in incompatible relations?

The Idea of Humanity as a Relationship with the Passions

Very few authors have perceived this relation as essential to the understanding of the idea of humanity and the traditional couplets which have

been passed on to us to assist in our thinking about it: soul/body, des-
tiny/liberty, state of nature / culture or society. In reality, the whole question is known with regard to what human nature should be defined.
According to the proposed answers different couplets emerge, combine,
even link up, and of course, overlap. The dualisms are multiple but they
each reveal an identical structure: human nature is apprehended according to nature and at the same time it differs from it. Nature extends or
is opposed to human nature; whatever the case, it is in each case part of
this duality that contains one natural component and one specific one,
the combination of which creates the very idea of what is called our
humanity. Some authors, and some religions, make this into an outcome,
a center, a kingdom that exists outside the order of living things. Other
philosophies prefer to see in human nature a part of nature in which
laws are identical. Behaviorism, naturalism, empiricism, come down on
the side of the heirs of Kantianism, and work toward a science of humanity: a science of the mind, of liberty, of disciplines deemed irreducible to
other disciplines. These would be the *Geisteswissenschaften*.[4]

The question of whether human nature is more nature than human, or
the inverse, will always be difficult, perhaps even irresolvable, despite
the reinforcement of concepts and the assault of dualisms, which both
unify and separate.

Why this difficulty? We are beings in nature, and we are all the more
so, or else we are something else, because we can reflect upon nature,
something that animals and plants cannot do. This is an old and elementary observation that has brought us, since the dawning of time, to want
to demarcate ourselves from the animal kingdom, of which we are nevertheless a part. We can be naturally ourselves only by being not natural, an
idea that remains paradoxical. Passion *is* the paradox of human nature,
like exteriority that falls inside it, like a foreign body.

But is this a solution? Passion is *a problem* because it casts a spell
which it refuses to break, and it is also a *solution* in that it signifies that
which it should have thought and, by the same token, overcome, in order
to do so. We became aware of passion, and so we are beyond it, we are
liberated. Passion is the problem of human nature just as it is, paradoxically, its solution. Through it, we *look* to tear ourselves out of nature and
affirm as much, but as long as we know it, it is as though we had already
resolved this difficulty. The problem is not recognized as a problem,
and from the moment it is discovered as such, it is as if it had vanished,
because realization presupposes that the veil of blindness has been

4. ["Sciences of the spirit." Trans.]

lifted, and thus we have overcome passion, which naturally impedes this surpassing of the self. The problem arises when we thematize passion, but as soon as we do so, it no longer poses any problem. To resolve the problem of passion, to overcome the dreams that it promises us, implies that we can perceive it; but this is impossible, since passion either chains us down, or else it sends us beyond it to a place where it no longer causes any problems. We cannot hope to overcome our passions or else it is as though they had disappeared, which makes any concern with them useless. Some authors, like St. Augustine, see passion as the insoluble condition of humanity, as that which confronts it and puts it in a situation of contradiction with itself; it is the insoluble problem that we'd be vain to think possible to overcome. Other authors, like Aristotle and Hume, have situated themselves differently with regard to passion, considering it as a space of reflection about the insertion of humanity into nature.

In the meantime, the paradox can only remain, even from this second point of view. This rests upon the idea that passion is both natural and conscious. The difference is reabsorbed into identity, as though human nature were nothing other than natural while at the same time conscious of being, without any sense that this dualism is problematic. In empiricism, it seems that there is nothing more to overcome, and one has difficulty understanding the value of passion, which should be the power to erect a human order in nature (morality) or, at the very least, to have the ability to recognize it. To sum up: when we speak of human nature, either we reduce the difference with regard to other beings of nature by the passion which prolongs it, and we have the passion-identity, which, being human, is just as good as difference. Hence the paradox. Or else we emphasize this difference, and passion serves to express it, also in a fashion deemed natural. Once again the paradox, despite the reversal of point of departure.

When passion is experienced as a problem, we cannot even see how we could perceive it. But when it does not cause any problem (any more), we have difficulty seeing the role that it could have played. Here we think back to Rousseau or Hobbes. For the latter, human beings have passions which, naturally, bring them into opposition with one another. What will bring them to renounce their passion and obey reason? There is a qualitative leap here which remains enigmatic. It suggests that human beings overcome their passions by becoming aware of them, and that they universalize their own position as being that of the other, which is the fear of brutal death. For this reason they must give themselves over to a transcendental power which will assure them peace. But how will they be able to become aware of all this if passion guides them in every case and, in addition, gives them the illusion, that frequently appears, that they will finally prevail because they are stronger than those who will try to outwit them and cheat them? If everyone reasoned like this, if everyone considered themselves to be more cunning than everyone else, then there'd be no chance of leaving the state of nature, which would be made up of vanity and aggression. Notice that a similar problem comes to the fore in the work of Rousseau. There, the state of nature is a state of liberty, where human beings have the right to their own individual passions, which are naturally good. Why would they be led to renounce liberty and bind themselves to a union? Why build a society based on *reason?* It is not that Rousseau doesn't answer this question, but he does so by postulating, as Hobbes did before him, that there is in passion a reaction to itself which diverts it, displaces it, transcends it, making the state of nature into a fiction.

Passion functions by displacing itself and by coming to consciousness; but by the same token, it ceases to be itself, in order to be thought about, if not lost. In order to attain this level of consciousness, it is necessary to be freed from passion. Passion reverses itself but also maintains itself in the objectification that is thereby undertaken because passion is itself the problem (resolved).

The whole question is to know how this leap is produced, or in other words, how we overcome this natural innocence, which, for Rousseau, identifies itself with pure individual liberty without hindrance. If this state of nature is so happy and so unproblematic, why must it perish if not by internal malediction, passion turning upon itself?

This raises the question of passion-identity where the problem is to know how the Ego could discover itself as an example of something simple, passionate, and natural, without the addition of difference?

Passion *is* this difference, just as it is identity. Human nature would be contradictory if passion were not there to condense the paradox of our human and natural conditions. Passion, made up of instincts, of sensations, of desires, is more than all this: it is the feelings and the thoughts that all of these sensations produce that only human beings can maintain, on account of the mysterious effect of these sensations that perhaps cannot be shared by animals or plants. Passion makes us by unmaking us, it links us to nature and our animal nature, which we transcend as it does so because passion is itself a human, and only human, reaction. Nevertheless, passion, being both natural and human, makes of our identity a fruit of passion, as in Hume; it is to forget that we thereby introduce an in-difference between passion, deemed natural, and reason, one of humanity's qualities, which is nothing other than human and which denies the identity of passion and reason.

According to another hypothesis, passion is indeed the difference that we don't want, but which we cannot avoid because it represents identity. Passion comprises us, and by the same token we have rifts, faults, guilt, states that we cannot shake off, despite the fact that by being aware of them, and by speaking of them, a certain kind of liberation comes to pass. But this is a mystery, an impossibility. While in one situation, wherein human nature passively extends the nature that englobes it, the solution is found; we reflect upon our passion and at the same time accept it. But how could we succeed in resolving the problem of passionate blindness, which seems to be a kind of magic? In any event, nature is very generous: the humanity of humanity is reabsorbed even as it affirms itself, and passion forms an identity with difference, and the whole thing abolishes itself in a generalized confusion which we nevertheless deny.

Passion, far from being an obstacle to reason, coincides with it: this is the source of the irrationality that we find in Hume's radical skepticism. Just when passion is recognized as a problem, it disappears. The move from passion to reason, which is deemed impossible by some philosophers, becomes difficult to grasp for others who, when posing the question, abolish the terms of difference.

In terms of resolution, we have the following opposition: I am not aware of what I'm looking for, or there is nothing to look for. Passion is either omnipresent, or else we've overcome it. In the first case, to speak of it is contradictory, and in the second, to speak of it is superfluous. Either we know that there was passion and we couldn't explain this knowledge and the reason why the passion was overcome, or we consider that there was nothing there that needed to be conquered or resolved. Everything followed its natural course, and passion becomes the mystery of the non-mystery. In Hume's empiricism, passion is a kind of purely tangible awareness of self, where the consciousness of this self seems impossible: everything being a matter of nature, the self cannot emerge outside of nature. Passion, which characterizes human nature, ceases to do anything, and thus shows itself to be superfluous.

Human nature contains the problem and the solution in the form of passions. What opposes these two visions is the passage to the solution that is required on account of passion, a passage that is deemed impossible, but is nevertheless the object of affirmation in one of these versions, and a passage that is rendered useless in another, which empties passion of all its problematic and negative content. Nobody is further from St. Augustine than Hume. Yet how could we have been made aware that passion linked us to the tangible by *talking* about it, when in fact it should have emerged from the intelligible, that which empiricism either cannot explain, or simply denies? Empiricism rediscovers the scission that it wanted to avoid and which philosophies of divided human nature constantly repeat.

Depending upon whether passion is seen to be natural or not, given philosophies will perceive human nature as being either a rupture with nature or, on the contrary, as being an extension of nature. This is similar to the whole area of philosophy that associates passions with something unnatural, even as it admits that passion is an integral part of human nature. In this light it concludes that human nature is divided within itself. The passions oppose us to each other, they destroy universality, while they nevertheless remain an important characteristic of each individual. This contradiction, which is that of the passionate falling inside of human nature as its absolute exteriority, should provoke suspicion about the very conception of human nature it implies. After Nietzsche, and thanks to him, we think this way. But we must recognize that this is not the way that earlier philosophers reacted to the contradictory and paradoxical nature of passion. Far from seeing it as an indication of a difficulty that must be taken up, they simply decided to consider this paradoxical quality as itself the nature of human nature. This allows them to simply evacuate the contradiction. Since they cannot resolve this initial paradox, they simply consider it as a composite part of, if not the very foundation, of their vision of humanity. This becomes dialectical, or antithetical. Human nature is conceived as contradictory *on account of* its passions, which are, or are not, natural: this is not on account of our seeing human nature and passions in a certain way, but on the contrary, it is passion itself which arouses the irreparable division of us from ourselves, which ultimately drives us downward. This leads to the idea of sin, for Christianity, of the state of nature, for Hobbes, which is the space of permanent confrontation between human beings, or society for Rousseau, as the inversion of benevolent and natural passions which naturally socialize with each other and, by the same token, degenerate.

Even among those like Aristotle or Hume who consider the passions something natural, and thus conserve for humanity a false unity, human nature remains double-sided. It is natural and human by the passions which one induces over the other, a kind of automatic and unexplained intellectualization of appetites which direct the most socialized types of will and desire, such as the need for justice.

Here as well the dialectic—or moreover, the paradox—is present, since passion is not only tangible appetite, it is the very form that consciousness takes of its relationship to the tangible, thereby overcoming it. Whether we like it or not, human nature remains in contrast to nature because of the types of passion and modes of consciousness that it is expected to translate.

Are Passions More Natural Than Human?

The passions are of course both natural and human, which means that the reality of human nature differs from that of nature or any extension of the natural world. We have been able to point out the two major orientations, one of which urges continuity, the other, opposition. But it is difficult for one to ignore the other, as though human nature must in any event find itself in a state of scission with regard to itself in order to affirm its identity. This situation is the state of passion. This constitutes the humanity of humanity even as it confirms his natural qualities.

We've also seen that some authors are quite willing to make different terms equal. Aristotle, for example, writes: "But the pleasures in activities are more proper to them than the corresponding desires; for the desires are distinct from the activities both in time and in nature, while the proper pleasures are quite close to them and are so indistinguishable from them that men disagree as to whether activities and pleasures are the same or not. Still, pleasure does not seem to be the same as thought or sensation, for this would be strange, but they appear to some to be the same because they are not separated."[5] Despite the confusion caused thereby, one might nevertheless consider that the rupture is an essential component of human nature, causing it to double up, tear away at its very depths, in short, condemning it to the torture of perpetual disharmony. The fall, the sin, the pain, the rupture, the struggle of each against all as universal destiny, which paradoxically gives us over to our negligence toward others and toward universality, are all concepts that have marked the history of human nature as described by St. Augustine, Hobbes, Rousseau, and Plato. Each have proposed dualisms that, like the one between soul and body, verify the scission while imposing an impossible basis for unity.

It would be naïve to affirm this beyond the contradictions that occur. But are we confronted with contradictions in human nature itself, or with contradictions in the concepts that are invoked to describe it? When we are told that passion is both that which irremediably roots us in the tangible world and the awareness of the distance that must be established

---

5. Aristotle *Nicomachean Ethics* 1174a17–20, 1175b33–35.

with it, we aren't saying any more than the following: the rupturing of the natural order of things is inscribed in the very rupture that forbids this rupturing. We have the problem and the solution at the same time, which is to say that we have nothing at all. The situation is irresolvable, except by force. The problem is the solution, there is no problem (or solution); or if you wish, there is a contradiction, and it's natural. We were able to identify these conceptions which situate within human nature the paradox of the passionate, which would be irremediable and avoidable. Faith saves but in the end only God can do the saving. Yet by assimilating passions to that which is specifically human, we have the sense that they can be negotiated, These are judgments, representations, they are in the soul, as Descartes said; and they are no longer just animalistic appetites. The Stoics believed that we could detach ourselves from passion just like we can correct an error; but since tangible nature makes up our condition, it was necessary to suggest, like the Catholics, that evil was inescapable and that human nature is necessarily corrupt. This did not prevent Christianity from imposing spiritual detachment, which it considered impossible to achieve on earth, thereby rendering humanity guilty and punishable. And it has certainly taken it upon itself to punish those it considered unbelievers. Shouldn't we therefore give in to the fact that there is "sin," and admit that we can despite everything live in the world, even in a state of sin? This will be the Protestant doctrine, which is more concerned about the tangible world, but also more ambiguous. We must not forget that in Catholicism we are sometimes able to negotiate sins with the priest, whereas in Protestantism fault cannot be appealed because there is no intermediary to plead for our salvation before God.

What follows from this is the coming to consciousness that the passions, being both natural and human, can certainly be found in a human nature perceived as autonomous from nature, just as they can be found in a human nature that is considered as existing in a symbiotic relationship with nature.

The two tendencies open up, subdivide, according to whether human nature is considered an extension of or something other than nature. It is clear that Aristotle, at least in some texts, tends *rather more* in the direction of continuity, while Kant, on the other end of the spectrum, speaks of a rupture between nature and liberty. Reason is the essence of humanity, and it makes a clean break from what is natural; so even when we study nature, the natural remains inaccessible, the things in themselves, and phenomena.

We must insist here upon the use of the adverb *rather* because the lines of demarcation are far from clear on account of the fact that passion straddles both universes, natural and human. Passion reintroduces what it eliminates, and eliminates what it seems to have accepted; it renders dialectic, turns on itself, and denies itself. The contradiction can appear as a natural dialectic (unless it is specifically human) at the inside of what is systematic. No vision, no conception of human nature can escape being paradoxical, which Christianity understood well—and it is as though each of them had to inevitably find the others, above and beyond superficial differences, at the level of the play of structures that support them. Passion is the key that renders these games intelligible, and it permits us to find unity in diversity.

If nature and human nature can be confounded in order to be differentiated by passion, or are differentiated even as they are prolonged, again by passions, it still remains true that they are doubled up. Passions can be seen as nature, and human nature as either specific or not. We can also conceive of passions as being human, a vision which places us in a situation of identity with nature or, on the contrary, in a situation that rejects this identity.

These considerations are fundamental if we wish to answer the question of whether there exists *a system of passions* in the history of modern thought. It would be a map of possible lines of evolution, a space of divergence between different philosophies, a recognition of the oppositions which could seem arbitrary to the eyes of the profane.

Take an example before coming to the systematization of the passionate: if we situate ourselves in the perspective of a human nature that is out of joint with nature, we have two possible situations that can emerge. Passions are natural, and by the same token, they fall outside human nature, since they are like tangible appetites or animal desires.

The realization of becoming human happens through the domestication of passions. Since it is natural, passion is difficult to control, and impossible to eradicate completely. The struggle against passion permits universality, the essence of human nature is rendered concrete over and above the sense of identity that passions translate. But this is only one possibility, the other being that passions are simply human traits, a contingency, a liberty which, despite being not natural, still affects us; so passion places itself in a situation of power.

By the same token, we can hope to overcome this residue of the animal in the human being, since it is the individual him- or herself who decides to succumb to it, without any determinism. Liberty is verified in its own affirmation, which would be a victory for the need for this liberty against passions, which are in this description only illusions.

The big difference between this possibility and the one that we examined previously relates to the abandonment of a state of (passionate) nature in us; morality becomes disassociated from politics to become conviction and straightforward consciousness. We give morality to ourselves and emancipate ourselves from all that is natural at the point where previously we had to negotiate it. The reader will have recognized both Kant and Hobbes in this description.

In this example we can clearly see a subdivision in the nature/human nature opposition, according to which passion is shown to emerge from an order, such as nature, more so than from the other.

The taxonomy of the passionate thus has four cases which we will now examine in some detail.

Taxonomy of Passions

The principle of the taxonomy is our ambivalence, for we, when thinking about ourselves in nature, become aware of the fact that we are above it because no other being in nature except ourselves is able to do what we can do, notably reflect upon our condition, which suggests that it is *possible* that we could escape it. If the natural is lived on the basis of a predetermined condition, then we, who are able to consider this condition, escape nature, which nonetheless prohibits this type of intellectual detachment. As such, liberty becomes the essence of humanity. But is it natural that we arrive at an ability to think about ourselves in nature, and thus to transcend it? Human nature seems to escape from nature the moment it begins to think about it. Passion is what impedes our ability to escape, while at the same time showing us what this ability to overcome looks like. Passion is natural and nonintellectual, but by presenting itself as such to us, we present ourselves as being beyond passion, which we thereby outflank. There are several parameters, or large questions, that underwrite a taxonomy of passion: a natural trapping, a concept of reason which transcends that which is not reason's own to affirm as such, and human nature, more or less disconnected from nature.

The problem that needs to be resolved for us concerns the realization of our essence, our fulfillment as persons. It is important for us to know who we are, and what we are. Passion is both a help and a hindrance for this project. It is that which renders *useful* the passage from the natural order to the human order, since it is animality, and it too considers itself as the element that renders this transition *possible* because passion is what realization signifies: liberation and opposition, transcendence and humanization. We know what has to be overcome, and we can therefore escape our natural blindness; we also have an obstacle which must be beaten. With passion on our side we have everything we need to define reason, what makes it useful and what makes it possible, on account of the very fact that we know, with passion, the difficulty that has to be resolved. The paradox remains that passion is the invisible veil of nature, that which blocks the passage to reason.

The First Case: Stoicism

We are a part of nature, and in this sense we are perfectly natural. Since everything in us is natural, the fact of saying as much is as well. The truth of humanity consists in finding nature, and living in harmony with it. Nevertheless, we are different from all other beings in nature because we can think in this fashion; we thereby surpass the order of nature, of which we should consider ourselves an integral part. This illusion of reflection is passion, which is what in nature prohibits us from recognizing ourselves as natural. Passion is what is specifically human about human nature; by the same token, it is that which it can control through an opposite form of judgment. The wise person should renounce with the force of judgment all things which link him or her to the tangible. Passion, far from being natural, is the product of the human mind when it forgets *its* nature and *nature*. Passion is a false liberty which we imagine ourselves possessing, a liberty which authorizes us to think that we don't share in the course of things, even though we are in fact unable to escape them. It is necessary to overcome passion because it gives the illusion of liberty, which wouldn't know of what it is made except in terms of its link to universal necessity, to the *cosmos* itself. Our humanity is liked to a passion that is avoidable and condemnable, itself the very expression of an illusory contingency, which suggests that we, through the difference which our reflection and our consciousness constitute, consider ourselves superior, even though in fact we are simply an extension of the natural order of which we are an integral part.

Clearly, this first case illustrates the many paradoxical aspects of passion. Human nature is inscribed in nature by the human appetite for the tangible which nourishes our passions, and which make them into something which is both natural and human. And yet the Stoic considers that passions are above all else human because people reflect about themselves in nature, and passions are impressions concerning natural appetites. This difference which could make him believe that he might be capable of transcending his passions, which he in fact does, is annulled by the eradication of passions which place him above the natural order of things which the passions have themselves described. The problem, which passion represents, is described as though it were already resolved by the Stoic sage, who knows which obstacle he has overcome. The Stoic is in the solution, since the problem has already been unmasked and resolved. Passion is not natural even as it is, and it becomes the false problem *par excellence,* the one that the stoic wise person shouldn't have asked, since he'd already resolved it. Under these conditions, can't the whole world be stoic, since humanity itself is reflected in Stoicism?

Whatever the case may be, passion is the name of the problem that human nature has as such, it is the sign of a difference that must be abolished if we hope to affirm an identity, and by doing this, it reveals that *all* difference is human. Passion prohibits us from being ourselves, and since it is itself a product of *nature,* then keeping it in check is tantamount to affirming one's humanity, because passion is not natural, it is an error of judgment.

Passion is denied, being human, but being natural it is rediscovered by the negation of which it is the object, the very negation that allows us to differentiate ourselves from nature. We do affirm that we are a part of nature, which is akin to re-inscribing passions into the natural order of things, by seeing in it only one modality of natural consciousness. This proves that passion remains perceived as the trace of nature in us, and the interest that we have in putting distance between ourselves and passion presupposes the inhumanity of passion, which, in fact, is located in humanity itself.

Passion, for the Stoic, is thus something of which we are always aware, that we have perceived, and that we can overcome for this very reason. It is the problem of the non-problem, the solution to a problem that no longer exists, but we don't know how it was resolved, or how this is even possible. That which is above passion, which is passion in the first case, comes from a mystery, from a revelation which came to people who were able to go beyond other people.

The Second Case: Hume, Rousseau

Here as well, we see ourselves as being in nature. Human nature is a part of nature, but the passions are no longer human above all else, as in the previous examples. Far from creating a rupture, passions are in this case seen as natural. They prolong nature in human nature, even as they institute a difference which makes up the whole of human nature. Rousseau writes:"Our passions are the principal instruments of our preservation. It is, therefore, an enterprise as vain as it is ridiculous to want to destroy them—it is to control nature,... Our natural passions are very limited. They are the instruments of our freedom; they tend to preserve us."[6]

The Third Case: Hobbes

Human nature is considered in this example in terms of its relationship with nature. There is an implied difference between human nature and nature. This is the source of the apparition of a state of nature that is in nature, and also outside it. Passions are natural, but human nature is difference, and passions are the measure of this difference. The affirmation of a human identity goes through the recognition of the naturalness of passions, just as the case with liberty, with its ability to separate them. Here, we observe that since passions are both natural and necessary, the problem of their resolution seems impossible even as it is resolved by virtue of the fact that we think, then reflect upon our own situations, and cease by the same token to be taken in by them.

The Fourth Case: Kant

By thinking about nature human nature thinks something totally different from that which it thought when it thinks about itself. The rupture between human nature and nature is hereby confirmed. Humanity, which considers itself part of nature, necessarily goes beyond it and affirms a liberty that is irreducible to the natural order of things. It can thus escape to determinism, since it is capable of putting distance between what is natural and what is not and conceptualizing this difference. By thinking about nature, we do something that no other being in nature can do, which is to think about ourselves. This contradiction is resolved by Kant by suggesting that we are at once tangible and intelligible, natural and free. As beings who can think about themselves as different from nature, we display an awareness of freedom as regards natural determination:

> For this reason a rational being must regard himself as intelligent (and not from the side of his lower powers), as belonging to the world of understanding and not to that of the senses. Thus he has two standpoints from which he can consider himself and

6. Jean-Jacques Rousseau, *Emile; or, On Education,* trans. Allan Bloom (New York: Basic Books, 1979), p. 212.

recognize the laws of the employment of his powers and consequently of all his actions: first, as belonging to the world of sense
under laws of nature (heteronomy), and, second, as belonging to
the intelligible world under laws which, independent of nature,
are not empirical but founded only on reason.[7]

The passions, for Kant, emerge out of his reason and are not natural; as
such, people can control them: "[Passion] is always connected with his
reason, and we can no more attribute passion to mere animals than to
pure rational beings."[8] Passion is characteristically human; we can exercise our freedom by refusing to recognize it, or we can free ourselves
from it through rational desire, desire that defines morality.

Recapitulative Table

The road from Stoicism to Kant is marked by a rising gulf between
nature and human nature. For Kant, we can even speak of a rupture
between the two orders which will, as we shall see, pose some irresolvable problems. Passion plays an essential role in each case, especially
when it serves to mark identity when the accent is placed upon difference, and vice versa. A philosophy which aims to underline identity will
consider passion as a difference that is either positive or negative. On the
other hand, a philosophy based upon difference from nature will emphasize the residual identity over passion, either more natural or more
human, more necessary or more contingent, depending upon the case at
hand:

Table 2.

The ambivalence of ⟶ human nature ↓	The passions are natural	The passions are unnatural
Human nature belongs to nature	Rosseau, Hume	Stoicism
Human nature is autonomous from nature	Hobbes	Kant

7. Kant, *Foundations of the Metaphysics of Morals,* p. 71.
8. Kant, *Anthropology,* sec. 80, p. 120.

The Dialectics of the Passions

Since because of the passions human nature is both identical to and different from nature, the passions will concentrate all our contradictions,
for we will have to see ourselves as other than what we are in order to
be who we are. Passion is the problem that refuses all solutions because
it is blind, and it is that about which we become aware as a problem;
this suggests that we thereby cease to be blind, that we are in the domain
of reason, which implies that we can find the solution. In either case the
problem can be thought of as such, either outside the solution that would
abolish it—without it being able to be stated and resolved—or outside
the solution that this problem condemns because it is the problem. The
paradox emerges rather clearly: either the problem is insurmountable,
or we have the solution with the problem: pure insurmountable difference, or else superfluous difference. For Hume, reason emanates from passion, and it is reason's specific difference that becomes unexplainable, as
though it were useless once the passionate game is defined. We can't even
see why reason should exist, since it is as unnecessary as it is problematic. On the other hand, for the Stoic, Christian, or Platonic thinker, passion, or sin, is the determinant of, and inherent to, human nature; and to
even realize this seems impossible, unless through the intervention of revelation's magic wand. Let's not speak of salvation here either, and of the
problem that it represents for us, who being natural sinners, must cease to
be in order to accede to our true nature as creatures of God, which seems
impossible without the divine intervention of God himself (Pascal).

The Antithesis of the First Case

Everything in nature is necessary, so the illusion that passion brings
about is itself ineluctable and natural, even if human. This is clearly contradictory. But how then can passion, which is natural and necessary,
cease to mark humanity? And if this is the case, shouldn't we restore
human beings to the level of other animals and consider them as devoid
of the ability to reflect or to overcome through reason? Passion must be
natural and human, avoidable and unavoidable: and once again we fall
into the inevitable irresolvable paradox of a natural *identity* as *difference*
that is intrinsic to humans. It is necessary that passion be instinct and
judgment if we wish to correct one, even as we admit that it is also the
other. Passion seems like an omnipresent natural element, as the expression of our desires which we can bend and overcome, without in fact
being really able to do this. Christianity, as we know, goes even further

by admitting the naturalness of the sin as that which demarcates human-ity as such (which signifies that passion isn't simply natural), as a conse-quence without any possible salvation, but nevertheless, all is not lost; human beings are what they are but, on the other hand, sin is not natural, though it can be mastered.

The paradox of this first case is that we are human even though we are of nature, whence the difference that is no difference, his passion, which, though natural, is imaginary, an intellectual construction. If passion is the freedom to blind oneself to the true interests of reason and action, how could the possibility of denying that necessity freely appear, when everything comes by necessity? If this necessity is necessarily denied because we are human, and because we therefore have passions, how can we escape the trap that they represent?

The problem here has no solution because we cannot see that there is a problem, or because it is useless to pose the question once it has been perceived.

This unavoidable character of passions-judgments, which the sage per-son thinks he can get rid of, is attested to by Seneca:

> So if one of those who speaks out against philosophy proposed the usual diatribe: "why are your words more courageous than your life? Why do you bow before a superior, do you consider money a necessary instrument, are you troubled when you endure injury, do you cry when you learn about the death of a spouse or a friend, do you admire fame and are you affected by ill-meaning words? From where comes the fact that your grounds in the country are more exploited than is necessary for natural exploitation? That you don't dine in accordance with your principles? Why do you own such an elegant home? Why do we drink wine that's older than you are when at your home? What is the purpose of an aviary? A plantation of trees which only gives shade? Why does your wife wear the revenues of a rich household upon her ears? Why these precious robes upon your children? Why is there an art to setting your table, instead of simply placing them as they come, why is this the object of trained servants? Why do you employ a master of meat-cutting?" You can add as well, if you wish: "Why do you have houses over-seas, and more than you even know of? It's an embarrassment: you are negligent enough to not know the small number of slaves which you possess, or sufficiently fastidious to have too many so that the memory cannot even remember the number of

them!" I would add something to this blame, and would reproach myself more things than you think; but for the moment, this is what I answer: "I am not a veritable sage, and I offer this admission as food for your evil ways, I never will be. Demand of me, therefore, not that I be equal to the best, but that I'm worth more than the worst. It is sufficient that I remove each day some force from my vices and that I chastise my aberrations. I have not come to a recovery, and I never will."[9]

St. Augustine will go even further by establishing an opposition between human passions, which can be modified by the exercise of will, and faith, the spiritual exercise, which by nature make them daughters of God.

The Antithesis of the Second Case

Humanity is seen in a kind of continuity with respect to nature, with respect to the passions, which are considered natural. But to say this is to go further; it is not natural. Passion holds us tightly even as it carries us further, to the place where we become conscious and then free of passions.

For Rousseau, the major problem posed by the passions is that they reduce us to the level of savage animals even as they set us off because we are human. Passion is the expression of a natural liberty from which we cannot see how, or even why, we'd want to emancipate ourselves. And it also begs the question of why pervert this natural liberty, since it was good. From the positive idea of the state of nature will emerge the negative idea of the social realm, which must be renegotiated with a new "social contract." Rousseau admits the difficulty in establishing the demarcation: "For it is no light enterprise to separate that which is original from that which is artificial in man's present nature, and attain a solid knowledge of a state which no longer exists, which perhaps never existed, and which will probably never exist, yet of which it is necessary to have sound ideas if we are to judge our present state satisfactorily."[10]

We are above this state of nature: the diversion of the passions is a *fact,* and as a consequence it was necessary that natural passion socialize. How is it possible that a state of society, whose existence is undeniable, emerged from a state of nature which only knew a kind of happy passionate existence?

9. Lucius Annaeus Seneca, *Works,* trans. R. L'Estrange (London, 1679).
10. Jean-Jacques Rousseau, *A Discourse on Inequality,* trans. Maurice Cranston (Harmondsworth, U.K.: Penguin Books, 1984), p. 68.

Halbwachs, in his nice introduction to *Social Contract*, confirms this difficulty: "It is as Durkheim said, a tour de force from Rousseau that explains how a being so profoundly indifferent to everything that is communal came to found societies. . . . As such, naturally, we leave the state of nature. . . . Society, being outside of nature, is also against nature."[11]

What is clear is that natural passion, when it becomes human, reverses itself, returns on itself, is perverted. It is the affirmation of an ego without compassion, which appropriates and excludes. The struggle of each against the other is the state of society which could be reversed by a fair contract, returning legitimate naturalness to political passions. The state of necessity made them unavoidable, the state of society made of it an insatiable affirmation of each Me. Even if Rousseau made the passage from nature to the social into a contingent phenomenon, like the meeting of two or more liberties can be, nevertheless something will be born from our being aware of passions on account of the other, and it will take the form of vanity and [a concern for] appearances, the fear of appropriation, and so forth.

> The source of our passions, the origin and the principle of all the others, the only one born with man and which never leaves him so long as he lives is self-love—a primitive, innate passion, which is anterior to every other, and of which all others are in a sense only modifications. In this sense, if you wish, all passions are natural. But most of these modifications have alien causes without which they would never have come to pass; and these same modifications, far from being advantageous for us, are harmful. They alter the primary goal and are at odds with their own principle. It is then that man finds himself outside of nature and sets himself in contradiction with himself.[12]

Need and weakness will nourish the social desires, will in fact constitute them. Liberty will change into dependence:

> The point of historical anchorage of human socialization resides in the efficaciousness of need: it brings together men in return for certain circumstances, in return for the favor of chance. Human history asks for nothing else in order to release itself. It would be ill-advised, therefore, to say that man is naturally sociable, since effective socialization depended upon circumstances

11. Jean-Jacques Rousseau, *Discours sur l'origine de l'inégalité* (Paris: GF, 1971), p. 151.
12. Rousseau, *Emile*.

which themselves might not have intervened. And these same circumstances which make us see that human socialization is fortuitous shows us why it is bad, not in itself, but by the fashion according to which it is engaged: need was constrained to play against its nature.[13]

This is the source of the dialectic that we find in this movement.

Passion is only perceived afterward, in the social realms which witness its return and its diversion. Since passions are natural, they recall a kind of lost paradise. Socialization represents the *Event* which can be compared to the expulsion from earthly paradise, as described in the Bible, because in that case as well humanity becomes aware of its passions as of an evil without hope, as an innocence lost forever. With the eruption of the *Event* in the state of nature, Hegel's historical vision points to the horizon. The passions fulfill the humanity of humanity even as they contradict it.

Already in Rousseau we can sense the paradox of passion manifest itself *historically,* even if it turns out to be the fruit of an inexplicable contingence in the course of things. The passions may very well be natural, but to say this, to utter this proposition, presupposes an overview (a "meta-level" in contemporary lingo) which can be defined as being of an order other than that of passion, given that passion itself blinds us, even to its very existence. Thematized passion is a passion that has been twisted, outflanked, objectified, which maintains its identity in the conscious overtaking. This is the source of the paradox of passion-instinct, which is as much a form of consciousness and representation of the natural, and thus what makes passion into something that is above nature.

Rousseau does not escape this paradox any more than all the others, and he places it in the very heart of the development of humanity in its passage from the state of nature to the social realm. Passion is natural and human but, being human, it leads to its own separation in a state of development wherein humanity discovers that the passions are passions, and in so doing also discovers that these passions can play against it in a role that contradicts what they naturally are. We cannot find this neutrality or this lost innocence, since passion is also human and, by the same token, it ceases to be individualized, to become fact for all people. As soon as humanity considers the humanity of passions, the passions cease, according to Rousseau, to be what they are; they *denaturalize,* and their universality becomes synonymous with a proprietor-like affirmation of the

13. P. Manent, *Naissances de la politique moderne* (Paris: Payot, 1977), p. 154.

Me, which is exclusive and agnostic because each individual says "Me." Passion, which is individual, by becoming social and interactive will necessarily have to manifest itself as opposition and vanity. The humanity of passion is nothing other than passion which, to stop being itself, remains nevertheless what it is. Far from seeing in this encounter a contradiction or a paradox that must be resolved, Rousseau, like others before him, saw the process of humanization itself, as though the process realized all the ambiguities of the concept. Rather than liberty, Rousseau spoke of "perfectibility," as though to underline the continuity between nature and human nature. He nevertheless denies this continuity, and passions serve to mark the rupture by their reversal, by their socialization.

The human being who discovers that passion is natural, who finds therein his or her specificity, maintains a paradoxical characteristic which defines the antithesis of passions. These we perceive in order to grasp our humanity, our human nature: they must come out of nature, but they can only be human because they reflect upon the state of nature. How can we even speak about this state, be it as it may, and of the passions, affirmed good by these same passions, without falling into contradictions, without having to describe the very place where we ourselves cease to be, unless we haven't already arrived there?

The Antithesis of the Third Case

In the previous case, it was necessary to suggest that human nature will naturally follow itself, and by doing so accomplish everything through a kind of inversion. Natural passions socialize, and become perverted. How can what is naturally good be a source of division?[14] Moreover, how can we be authorized to say what the passions are, or what natural passions can be, given that the point of view required to say it presupposes the rupture of socialization, which renders the naturalness of the passions just as inaccessible as the lost paradise? If Rousseau didn't hesitate to speak of that which he could not know, since he was irremediably plunged in a state that was posterior to that of nature, then this was possible because he conveyed the ambivalence of passions, deemed at once natural *and* human.

In the third case, the paradox changes somewhat. Even if the passions remain natural, human nature is conceived as breaking with the natural order of things, from which it is both born and cut off at the same

---

14. Jean-Jacques Rousseau, *The Social Contract,* trans. Christopher Betts (Oxford: Oxford University Press, 1994).

time. Passions, natural and necessary just like everything that is natural, couldn't be overcome or beaten without a theoretical blow, which postulates victory simply by suggesting that we are different from all other natural beings because we are able to think as much. This is what drives a philosopher like Hobbes to introduce the blow that must subdue the passions in the very order of their becoming, in their confrontation which is in fact between people who are immersed in nature. The great peacemaker, Leviathan, is reason, which is imposed upon the passions from the outside like a realization of their insolubility. The theoretical blow of a transcendental and exterior reason has become a practical blow which is inscribed in the order of things themselves, an absolute power, which would be equivalent to reason. Reigning absolute, reason will make us conscious of the mortality and the destructive character of the passions.

Even so, passions are natural and we have difficulty seeing how to beat them if they really are. Maybe they are already human, too human, despite the state of nature that defines them. To call the first passion the sentiment of ego, vanity, assurance, the idea of superiority, is to speak of the social and of becoming socialized, even as we pretend that we only have dealings with what is natural. How can a power, even an absolute power, transcend what determines each person through an incontestable need that arises from its being natural? This is the paradox of the *Leviathan*.

On the one hand, reason, which must permit us to overcome passion, seems to grow out of this state of affairs; on the other hand, it seems to be in a situation where it is obliged to act from the outside, as though in a state of rupture from the passions to the point where they become insurmountable and even imperceptible, or to the point where we don't even wish to realize this. On the one hand, the passions lead us to fight wars, to fight to the death, and to also fear this; they as a consequence renounce wanting to assuage the passions which oppose them. On the other hand, nothing impedes us from using trickery with these passions, from manipulating them, in order to convince others of whatever we wish without renouncing our own passions, interests, or appetites. It is necessary, therefore, that a powerful and exterior force come and bring us to think rationally. But here as well the problem remains to know how a passion for reason is born in people, the type of rational thinking that will destroy all those passions which operate contrary to reason. We need to think of a kind of revelation, or the working of a rational and purely passionate reckoning. Here Hobbes becomes the counterpart of Machiavelli, for whom people, by becoming aware of their passions, arrive at a situation whereby they can better mask them and play with them in an endless game where the other, who also is aware of the rules, can participate as well: Hobbes, on the other hand, thinks that it is necessary to conclude that we can get there, that fulfilling one's human nature as a human being implies overcoming natural appetites. But what creates this reckoning which leads to reason if not reason itself? To be clear, it is necessary to know what the passions are in order to know how to combat them: but how can we have this idea if we are tricked by them, to the point of believing that we are stronger than an other who is threatening us with death?

The two basic passions are pride and the fear of death, the consciousness of self and the consciousness of the Other, identity and difference. But how is it possible to effect the synthesis and have the right to affirm that consciousness of our superiority, present in each person, will necessarily allow us to back down on account of our fear of dying? We could never emphasize enough the irresolvable nature of this question, even for the individuals we're discussing here. For Hobbes, people consider themselves superior, but they are afraid of dying: "The antithesis from which Hobbes' political philosophy starts is thus the antithesis between vanity as the root of natural appetite on the one hand, and, on the other, fear of violent death as the passion which brings man to reason."[15]

If they consider themselves stronger than all the others, they will never think that they aren't really, and that they should therefore be concerned about others whom they consider to be superior. Struggle is therefore inevitable, since each person thinks this way, and desires to satisfy whatever craving his or her appetites desire. Fear of dying would seem stronger in this regard, and individuals become aware, through reason, that they cannot hope to defeat it. From this point on, they renounce identity and move in the direction of difference, the Other and the death that he represents.[16] They would stop placing the emphasis upon the ego in order to continue to be, in something, such that the Me would be an affirmation of self and a contempt for others.

This is to say that the sense of vanity and superiority of identity would be erased in the equality of rights for each person, a kind of institutional modesty that is derived from rational peace. Why not? But

15. L. Strauss, *The Political Philosophy of Hobbes* (Chicago: University of Chicago Press, 1984), p. 18.

16. We're not really sure if identity manifests itself in the affirmation of the self, pure and simple, or if one has to conceive of it as an expression of the struggle against the other, of the fear of death that the other implies by his or her very existence. Recall that passions, considered natural for Hobbes, are in fact already socialized.

nothing impedes any ego from concluding that since all the others have renounced the idea of affirming themselves against others, then he in particular finds himself in a stronger position if he decides not to play the game, which would be normal, since he'd be guided by his own vanity. Since this ego could be everyone in society, the war of each person against the other becomes as rational as peace. Since each person can say to himself that the other will want to play against him, it becomes rational for him to play against the Other, and each against the other. Passions alone cannot make reason, peacemaking reason, issue forth. Yet if reason is not born of the passions, it is difficult to imagine from which standpoint it can be imposed: "Although the rationality account of conflict arises naturally from certain portions of the text, it is not the only account of conflict suggested in *Leviathan*. Indeed, one sees many commentaries on Hobbes' work (Strauss and Gauthier) maintaining that human passion, not human rationality, generates warfare in the natural state."[17]

From this standpoint peace seems to be as rational as war; this war is an endless game of passions, a game without hope of victory, without a conclusion that would bring human beings out of their passions, and is thus the very expression of the nature in them and of the necessity that affects them. Passions obey a logic of identity and difference, which manifests itself here in the affirmation of self and the fear of death. To be or not to be: always the great question.

Notice that the state of peaceful society, reason, which guides us to negotiate rather than fight, is unstable, as we saw previously. But this state of society is also irrational without the guarantee from a strong State which would impose peace by its absolute power. Individuals, in order to be themselves, must renounce themselves. They find in the equality of all people in-difference, what impedes them from being themselves and affirming their natural egoism. From this point on, the state of society, without force, becomes a state which denies the ego by abolishing differences: we all want to be ourselves, we inevitably become the same as the other, and want the same thing even as we want to be different (vanity). This is the source of the temptation to wish to impose oneself in the state of society, to affirm a difference, since the other has renounced his or her own force. If each person says this, which eventually implies that vanity is equally distributed in all people, we can but re-descend into war because it turns out to be the only rational solution to natural passions. Rousseau recognized this when he wrote that:

17. J. Hampton, *Hobbes and the Social Contract Tradition* (Cambridge: Cambridge University Press, 1986), p. 63.

It is false to say that, in a condition of independence, reason leads us to contribute to the common good through consideration for our own interests. Private interest and the general welfare, far from being combined, exclude each other in the natural order of things, and social laws are a tie which each man will gladly impose on others, but by which he will not be bound himself. "I realize that I bring fear and anxiety among the human race," says the independent man, whom the wise man throttles; "but it is necessary either for me to be unhappy, or for me to cause unhappiness to others, and none is dearer to me than I am." "It is in vain," he might add, "that I attempt to reconcile my interests with the interests of others; everything you tell me about the benefits of the social law might be true, provided only that, while I observed the law towards others, I could be sure that they would all observe it towards me; but what assurance can you give me? And could I be in a worse situation than to be exposed to all the wrongs that the strong might want to inflict on me, but not to dare to take compensation from the weak? You must either give me a guarantee against any unjust attack on me, or expect me to attack in my turn. It is useless to say that, by renouncing the duties imposed on me by the law of nature, I deprive myself of the rights it gives, or that if I resort to violence, I authorize others to act as violently as they wish towards me. I agree, and the more readily because I am unable to comprehend how, by employing restraint, I could preserve myself from their violence. Furthermore, it will be in my interest to get the strong on my side by giving them a share of the plunder I take from the weak; that will contribute more than justice can to my advantage and my security."[18]

The vision of Hobbes is paradoxical at the very least: everyone wants to consider him- or herself different in order to be him or herself; but to be oneself, it is necessary to affirm a difference that will deny difference when it turns against the individuals. They will not be entirely themselves except when they stop being because the appetite to live will dominate over a consciousness of an exclusive self.

The passions for Hobbes are not only for the most part unnatural, for instance the sense of superiority of each over all others, which is also a

18. Jean-Jacques Rousseau, *Discourse on Political Economy and The Social Contract*, trans. Christopher Betts (Oxford: Oxford University Press, 1994), pp. 284–85.

consciousness of the other in difference, but they are also already integrated in a rational and social fashion:"It may peradventure be thought, there was never such a time, nor conditions of warre as this; and I believe it was never generally so, over all the world; but there are many places, where they live so now."[19]

In fact, the game of passions cannot be decided, and it is for this reason that we need a strong State which will be able to put an end to the Machiavellian ruse of permanent diversion.

Human nature is reason which goes beyond the passions; but since the passions are natural, reason becomes enigmatic because it is impossible as such, unless we imagine it, or reduce it, to the only "inference drawn from passions" (Hobbes). Human nature cannot be itself except with reference to the passions that it pretends to abolish and which always remain an integral part of the whole of human nature.[20] This is to suggest that Hobbes believes in the impossible.

Antithesis to the Fourth Case

Nature and human nature are herein disjointed, just as reason is from the senses. Yet humanity is a part of nature; this is the source of its double nature, to be sensitive, phenomenal, and also to be intelligible, through pure reason or noumenon. Our thinking separates us from nature, irreducibly; and yet we are not separate from nature, and this is the contradiction. Naturally, by our natural constitution, we are brought to think about ourselves, and to see ourselves, as though we were determined by our reason; but by doing so we demonstrate that we are capable of determining ourselves through reason. For Hobbes, the state of nature is already rational, and the reason-game-of-passion made the passions into a space of contradiction and harmony, a necessity that is not one, necessarily.

For Kant, the vision is different but it raises as many questions. We are in nature, and by saying this we reflect as though we were outside it, which is paradoxical. Our passions, though natural, and though an expression and the very mark of nature in us, are not natural, but human. When we think about them, they must reveal themselves to be exclusively human and susceptible to being pushed aside for this very motive. How is it possible to separate oneself from oneself all the while affirming that what is passionate is not the self, even if it is above all possible

19. T. Hobbes, *Leviathan*, ed. C. P. Macpherson (Harmondsworth, U.K.: Penguin Books, 1985), chap. 13, p. 187.
20. "The desires and other passions of man are in themselves not sins." Ibid.

doubt? How can humanity, which is rooted in the tangible world, aspire to the intelligible world if all passageways between them are cut off? How is it possible to achieve this universal nature, to be intelligible, if this universal nature comes from the unknowable, and is found outside the order of things to which humanity is attached? There's no question that there is a freedom to overcome the tangible which cannot be tangible. It can but be freely put into place by its own doing, but since the tangible determines humanity, the project of accessing reason becomes impossible. It is necessary to already be free, and to know that we are able to be free, in order for the idea to exist. The problem is resolved, but we don't know how. In fact, how can we have even had the idea—if not *a priori?* The answer is circular, since it is this very idea for which it is necessary to show that it can be discovered—to overcome the tangible of which it is part, even though nothing tangible encourages humanity to go beyond this? Without doubt, the *fact* of human nature, which is human and therefore different, obliges us to consider ourselves differently from other natural beings. There again, the argument is circular because the hypothesis of a human nature that is radically divided and specific serves as a very basis for Kantian reasoning, more than the conclusion to which we *must* subscribe. Kant postulates a certain image of the self—universal reason or human nature—that we must have, and which will influence our morals. This is the source of the liberty which is a *postulate* of reason. The passion that blinds us, says Kant, is on this very point powerful and haunting:

> For pure practical reasons, the passions are cancerous sores; they are, for the most part, incurable because the patient does not want to be cured and shuns the rule of principles, which is the only thing that could heal him. In prescribing rules for our pursuit of happiness, too, reason goes from the general to the particular according to the principle: not to overshadow all the other inclinations or sweep them into a corner just to please one inclination, but rather to see to it that the inclination in question can co-exist with the totality of all our inclinations.[21]

Whoever said it was a form of slavery? The one who understood where liberty was, but for those who live in passion, this is not slavery, and they certainly see themselves as being free. Wouldn't Kantian liberty seem to such persons to be a supreme constraint, even if the idea to impose it ever dawned on them?

21. Kant, *Anthropology,* sec. 81, p. 120.

In this fourth form of the dialectics of passions, the absence of any theory of the passions, on account of the split between nature and human nature, ineffectively hides its assimilation in a theory of sensibility *(sensibilité)*. The tangible must be overcome, but it cannot be overcome. The passionate incarnates in the sensibility itself and directs the particular interests of individuals. It is like a presence that impedes morality, although it wants to be considered possible *a priori,* solely on account of our consideration of our self, our nature.

We can always issue a decree suggesting that reason is an *a priori,* a faculty or a necessity which must exist or prevail over all other circumstances as though it were an absolute norm. But the passions are there, and with them come diverse tangible interests, like avarice or cupidity, the lust for pleasure, or whatever else. To affirm that reason must prevail over all these things, because it can, is to suggest the very thing that should be dismantled, that is, that we can become aware of the passions and conquer them. This is the question: can we? And once we have become aware that there is a problem, do we have the force to resolve it? Kant already has an answer; he identifies the postulate of a supreme, sovereign reason to his very mode of functioning, which is to act supremely. It is as though the supposition of an exterior reason as solution to the problem of passions and tangible interests were enough to guarantee mastery over them. The *a priori* of reason makes reason into an *a priori* power. In short, we overcome tangible interests and the blindness that accompany them because we must overcome them. Far from proposing a solution, we are thus relying upon an *a priori* belief in a solution, and the fact that it must exist (which would be morality) is no guarantee that it could be, or that it really is, a solution. After all, we find ourselves in the realm of supposition, of the forced resolution, of the postulation of what should be constituted as a model of all duty. When the circular reasoning becomes the need that we must achieve, when it becomes our objective and our norm, and therefore the norm of the Kantian duty itself, then we transform human nature and reflection about it into a natural transcendental element, which it of course is not. The victory over the passions is supposed to be a natural necessity of humanity, who *must wish* to impose it, and the reason that is at work here has ceased to be natural, even as it realizes what is like an essence. What is the source of the universal necessity of reason? The question itself is troublesome, in that human nature no longer has any natural qualities, as though it could no longer be itself by affirming its own identity. The passions are the remainder of a naturalness that reason can overcome by itself, *a priori*. They become useless, they undergo a displacement. All the same, they are at once natural and aberrations of reason, in that we become obsessed with them through irrational desires which prevent us from wanting moral law. This law can always be imposed by the person, which proves that it is close to overcoming these desires. But this affirmation is circular: that reason is able to do this, and not only that it wishes to do so, cannot be put forward except by an *a priori* definition of what one needs to hear through reason, which consists in attributing such a power *a priori* to the mind. Kant's conclusion, that passions are not natural because they are irrational, works out rather well for him because it suggests that we can beat them whenever they render reason blind.

For empiricism, reason is nothing other than the emanation of the tangible. Passion is therefore that which literally makes the difference. It creates the distance and it masks it, and at the same time it makes *useful* a rationality that would otherwise be automatic. Passion is therefore reason that cannot be grasped, the very difference, an unacceptable abstraction for empiricism which nevertheless must be recognized.

For Kant, rationality seems on this occasion to be completely separated off from the tangible. We have passed from an identity, for the empiricists, to a difference that is just as incomprehensible. Reason is an *a priori,* certainly, but for us, who are always plunged into the realm of the senses, this rationality is inaccessible, since it is cut off from the tangible that constitutes our world. This is the case unless we think that passion is the obstacle that must be overcome, the negative strainer that makes us aware of the need for reason, of reason as necessity. On one side identity, on the other difference; in both cases we find a passion to make difference there, identity here, and to abolish that which has been conceded in each case. Empiricism associates reason and sensation, and the difference that needs to be recovered is passion, a form of sensation that is not one. Kantianism turns reason and sensibility into an absolute difference, "transcendental" (inherent to the subject in his relationship with the objective world), but in order to make this passage from one to another possible, one needs a point which would anchor the mind in the tangible, which is passion. Identity must in this scenario be overcome by morality so that reason can recover its rights.

The Kantian recognizes his passions thanks to sane reason. But where does this rational overview come from, the overview that the passions are supposed to prohibit? Reason must be presupposed in order for it to be efficient. Passions are natural but are not seen as such because the Kantian perceives them as passions and could by this ability emancipate him- or herself from them. This is itself proof that they cannot be natural or determining even though they express on occasion an animal desire in each of us because we are human. This *apriorism* of reason overshadows the problem of knowing what led to its foundation: it is necessary to think about it straightaway in an *a priori* fashion, but is this reasonable or realistic? By denying our tangible nature we realize our potential as being intelligible, but we are *just as much* tangible beings. This manifestly opposes that, instead of serving as a strainer for it; unless we accept the idea according to which the sensible is only so for a reason which is made *a priori* different from sensibility, by conceiving of it as peculiar, and by this fact, by knowing the limits of this sensibility, which it recognizes as *a priori*.

In reality, the dual nature of humanity, sensible and intelligible, contains the division of which passion has been the mark ever since the Greeks. With Kant, we have the impression of colliding with the problematics of human nature according to a rupture and of the impossible. To affirm that human nature is intelligible and tangible is equivalent to naming the difficulty rather than resolving it, as though paradoxically nature and humanity must be opposed in order to coexist in the same reality.

An Inquiry into the Wealth of Passions, or How They Became Interests

Ever since the Renaissance, passions have made up an integral part of the observations made about humanity by writers, moralists, and philosophers: "One of the greatest reasons why so few people understand themselves is that most writers are always teaching men what they should be, and hardly ever trouble their heads with telling them what they really are."[22] Their role is to characterize relations among people, for better or for worse. Beginning in eighteenth century passion becomes the sign of individuality, and the nineteenth century goes even further by turning it into the symbol of individuality itself.

The great reversal of Augustinianism, which immersed human beings in guilt, permits the passions to have a place in discourse, which gives them a degree of rationality despite themselves. Here is the paradox of the passions: they express a rationality underneath our own blindness and dissoluteness, they form reason behind the chaos of appearances, and of History itself. The discourse about passions brings reason to bear, it abolishes and preserves them, abolishing them for the observer who leans toward the actors who are tricked by passion. The meaning of history, if there is one, grows out of this passion that is ignored by the

22. Bernard Mandeville, *The Fable of the Bees and Other Writings,* abridged and edited, with an introduction and notes, by E. J. Hundert (Indianapolis: Hackett, 1997), p. 36.

actors who have given themselves over to it. A century earlier, this ignorance was a source of immanent rationality and incarnated itself in the
mechanisms of the market, and one century later in the unconscious:
Hegel finds himself between Adam Smith and Sigmund Freud.

From the time of Machiavelli we have been witness to this confrontation between individuals and vanities. But this doesn't present any rational character beyond the cunning of ends which permit us to promote
them. What is rational is to realize one's virtue, no more. It is only in
English thought, notably with Hobbes and Locke, Mandeville and Smith,
that the idea of an "invisible hand" is born, a hand which will harmonize
private interests within a generalized order that is profitable for one and
all. The market fulfills this very function. From struggle is born harmony
(Hobbes), from competition comes welfare (Smith), from vice comes
virtue (Mandeville):

> Then leave Complaints: Fools only strive
> To make a Great an Honest Hive
> T' enjoy the World's Conveniencies,
> Be fam'd in War, yet live in Ease,
> Without great Vices, is a vain
> *EUTOPIA* seated in the Brain.
> Fraud, Luxury and Pride must live,
> While we the Benefits receive:
> Hunger's a dreadful Plague, no doubt,
> Yet who digests or thrives without?
> Do we not owe the Growth of Wine
> To the dry shabby crooked Vine?
> Which, while its Shoots neglected stood,
> Chok'd other Plants, and ran to Wood;
> But blest us with its noble Fruit,
> As soon as it was ty'd and cut:
> So Vice is beneficial found,
> When it's by Justice lopt and bound;
> Nay, where the People would be great,
> As necessary to the State,
> As Hunger is to make 'em eat.
> Bare Virtue can't make Nations live
> In Splendor; they, that would revive
> A Golden Age, must be as free,
> For Acorns, as for Honesty.[23]

23. Ibid., pp. 34–35.

People enrich themselves by the will to do so, something that had traditionally been condemned: "As for my part, without any compliment to the courteous reader, or myself, I believe man (besides skin, bones, etc. that are obvious to the eye) to be a compound of various passions; that all of them, as they are provoked and come uppermost, govern him by turns, whether he will or no. To show that these qualifications, which we all pretend to be ashamed of, are the great support of a flourishing society has been the subject of the foregoing poem."[24]

The question that arises is to know what could have pushed us to transgress this feeling of guilt, and allowed us to pursue our own selfish interests. The Christian would reply that this flows directly from the corrupt nature of humanity. Since Max Weber, we have a better answer. For him, Protestantism allowed people to invest in the world and to look for benefits. Is it necessary to see in earthly success a sign of divine afterlife? One is allowed to hesitate on this one. In effect, individuals who would consider that their power could substitute for God's free choice would be awfully presumptuous. Pride is the very essence of original sin. It would be to renew it if one were to nourish such a hope. It is important to recognize that individuals cannot buy back this original sin, and that they must expiate it through labor and suffering, that it would be impious for them to pretend to escape it. Only God can recognize his own, but nobody can force his hand.

Human passion is therefore ineluctable, and it would be vain to deny as much. We cannot redeem ourselves by ourselves, and reason consists of admitting it, of accepting this condition and returning to the Grace of God. Work and the benefits it brings are signs of this acceptance and resignation, rather than of election. The moral duty is to carry out one's work because it was after all God who wanted to banish humanity from the earthly paradise of the Garden. Passions are natural, and there is no longer any question of being content with simply condemning them. They will come into opposition with one another in political and economic confrontations. They will limit one another, they must be dissimulated in order to be more successful. They become interests (Hirschman), which suggests that we think about those passions which fit into a specific framework: the calculus of means and ends. Already in the work of Machiavelli we can find that human beings manipulate their passions as they do those of other persons in order to satisfy their objectives, as though it were all a game of chess. Passions that conflict with

24. Ibid., p. 36.

one another and counterbalance each other no longer overflow to the excess that is always feared and rejected. The market or the power game will fulfill the same role as pure moral or religious condemnation of ancient times, and find themselves more efficient in the reciprocal regulation. Interest, says Hirschman,[25] is a passion that becomes rational and which is not pure unruliness as are the more fickle passions. Passion that becomes reason, because it is naturally calculating, is the fact of a human nature that is newly reconceived, and we have studied this genealogy and these structures earlier on.

From Wealth to Luxury

The passion for wealth, like the pursuit of honors, will be made part of new forms taken by occidental society, and they will as a consequence remodel it. The lust for power, like the search for profits, will become secularized and even legitimate little-by-little. Liberty won't stop there. By winning over the body, it will lead to excesses similar to those found in the economy or the management of the City. We think for example of de Sade. But he is only the culmination of this unbridling of sexual relations.

The rehabilitation of affect, the right to express oneself, is organic and corporeal. Through passion we suffer the destiny of the body, of nature, in drives that are sometimes terrifying. Passion is no longer just a political or economic game, it is a game of love, and there as well, the law of passion is that it rids itself of all laws and of all limits: "The *One hundred and five days* proposes to offer an inventory and description of six hundred different passions, one hundred and fifty per month."[26]

There is a combinatorial quality of passions which suggest their acceptance.

If the Sadean operation of passions presupposes their recognition, it continues to shock us, now and forever, not as an example of extreme liberty, but instead as the reflection of a totalitarian exercise of power. Passion is a balance of power, thus *apathy* for him or her who submits. Far from liberating passion, it is the victory of one over another who we then torture because they gave in. Is radical passion violence or universal freedom? The arbitrariness of passion, in passion, is murder. Passion ceases here to be natural. For de Sade, it is passion that considers itself only natural, and who forgets to consider itself as a social and human

25. In A. Hirschman, *Passions et intérêts,* trans. P. Andler (Paris: PUF, 1980), p. 54.
26. M. Hénaff, *Sade: L'invention du corps libertin* (Paris: PUF, 1978), p. 41.

component; passion is the paradox that negates itself in the search for a coherence that is as absolute as it is impossible.

Provisional Conclusion

The closer we come to our own era, the more passion manifests itself as sensation. It is necessary to limit passion, and Kant's critical project attempts to fulfill this ambition through morality. But we can find the same will to regulate passions in economics and in politics. The market, the division of powers (Montesquieu), morality, will all reveal their own limitations in limiting those who wish to increase indefinitely: the quest for wealth, pride, and the will to power. Kant will be but a pause in this evolution.

We must realize one thing: passion is made up of consciousness, and far from being easy to sweep under the carpet with a moral or political stroke, it is here that it flows back in order to better demonstrate its demands.

The whole question now is to find out to what degree passion is a structure of the human mind. To answer this question, it will be necessary to return to the theory of consciousness inaugurated by Descartes, and then follow the thread right up to Kant. Our whole sense of modernity plays itself upon the history of consciousness, right up to when it was overcome by Freud, Nietzsche, and Marx.

5

From the Experience of Passion to the Passion of Experience

Introduction

We last saw St. Thomas when discussing the dualism of the irascible and the concupiscible. The latter expresses the natural desire which passionately directs us toward the sensible objects of which we are in constant need. Consciousness takes the form of unthinking spontaneity, absorption into exteriority. The irascible, on the other hand, constitutes the coming to consciousness, the return to the self. By the same token, the possibility arises of pushing the passions away, winning the day, with the help of anger, which, although reasoned, if not reasonable, is nevertheless anger, and therefore again and always passion.

Such a coming to consciousness is at the very least ambiguous, if not paradoxical. To become aware of passion presupposes that its charm is broken. Since blindness is essential to passion, the distanced and lucid irascible must situate the soul outside the domain of passions. This is obviously not the case, because our becoming aware of our passions is insufficient to break their hold, just as learning about one's illness is not akin to curing it.

If we confront these two theses, they seem contradictory, since on the one hand we overcome passions by thinking about them, while on the other we have not overcome them simply because we have thought about them. By presenting this double constitution the irascible loses all coherence. To present a problem is not to solve it, and yet in this example, to be able to present the problem in the first place required that it be solved beforehand. Recall that it was from this very ambiguity that was born the scission between those who thought that knowing about sin is tantamount to having the means required for absolution, and those who consider that the condition of the sinner is in no way affected by the awareness that we might acquire. If dualism is intrinsic to the Augustinian corpus, it is nevertheless the case that it will offer a true opposition to the doctrine of salvation, the role of faith and the Catholic priest.

Be this as it may, the irascible seems impossible or superfluous. The concupiscible prevents the birth of reason, *a fortiori* its embryo, which is rebellion against passion (irascibility); and if the consciousness that gets angry nevertheless has to be born, it will come too late, because the victory that awareness presupposes to effect over the passions would render useless all struggle. Being conscious of passion, and having passion without consciousness, the irascible is shown to be both too much and not enough. It is too much because everything is contained therein, from consent to rebellion; not enough because we can barely understand how it could operate the passage from one to the other because the first impedes the second by the blindness it incites.

The sensible soul (Kant) excludes the intelligible soul by cutting it off from itself. The mind dissolves into its own impossibility on account of the lack of unity; and it is beyond any doubt that the irascible constitutes an early stage of self-consciousness, just like the concupiscible incarnates consciousness that is directed toward the objects which it seeks (or seeks to avoid).

Descartes is the one who replaces this fractional view with a unitary theory of soul and consciousness, which aims to take into account awareness by the soul itself, through which it becomes mobilized, sometimes despite itself. "For there is only a single soul in us, and this soul has within itself no diversity of parts; the very one that is sensitive is rational, and all its appetites are volitions."[1]

The idea of a consciousness, even when unified by its consciousness of a specific object, which knows itself as such, is nevertheless far from a resolution of all problems. The question that remains is the following: how can a consciousness be directed both toward itself and toward an exterior object even when this object absorbs all of its attention? Don't we forget ourselves among the things in the world because they occupy

---

1. René Descartes, *The Passions of the Soul,* trans. Stephen Voss (Indianapolis: Hackett, 1989), art. 47.

the mind? How is it possible to consider that what is different, and the external consciousness certainly is different from self-consciousness, could make a single entity?

In the evolution from St. Thomas to Descartes, don't we move from one difficulty to another, which consists of abolishing the ascendancy of the passions in the eternal transparency of consciousness to itself?

The Cartesian Dilemma

Cogito, ergo sum. "I think therefore I am." How is it possible to doubt, without thinking, and thus without being something, in this case, something that thinks? This reasoning is well known. What is less well known is what this presupposes and implies.

If I doubt everything, then nothing is certain, even the fact that I am doubting. This affirmation should self-destruct the moment it is proclaimed. Doesn't it too fall into the domain of everything that is doubted? Even so, Descartes claims to deduce this very resolution from radical doubt. In order to do so, he needs to admit that by doubting he affirms something beyond doubt. Rather than the expression of a radical interrogation, isn't doubt nothing other than the following assertion: to doubt is to *say* that I doubt, and saying is a departure from the doubt that is supposedly inevitable. Descartes attempts to ground the possibility of assertion, as well as its criteria; but this is what he presupposes from the start, as though it were a necessity, a necessity based upon itself, but in a circle. If doubting is saying that we doubt, and doubting and asserting are both modalities of thought, then doubting is not just thinking but also knowing and thinking that we think.

By doubting, I think, but by affirming that I think, I still think; in fact, I think that I think, I think of myself as being in the act of thinking, and think of myself, therefore, as a thinking *being*. To doubt is to affirm that we doubt, and to affirm this is beyond any doubt. The Cogito is not only a thought, but also, because of its very nature, a reflection. It is also necessary, apodictic, since to doubt I must think, and from the outset I affirm my consciousness as reflexivity but also as a necessity, the necessity of knowledge, of knowing that we know that we know when we know. To know and to feel the interiority of one's consciousness forms a single and identical reality.

Thought is reflexive, and doubt, being a particular way of thinking, reflects upon itself in the affirmation "I doubt." This signifies that I affirm a necessary thought, and affirm the necessity of thought for itself, a necessity that affirms itself and reflects upon itself in the Cogito. The

Cogito is the first proposition of a chain of reasons, or reason, because it expresses, by its very necessity, the norm of apodicticity which bolsters all rational enterprises. To doubt that one thinks is to think, necessarily: the necessity of Cogito affirms that real thought is necessary, beyond doubt, certain, and apodictic.

Reflexivity, by suggesting the need for reflexivity as being at the base of all possible assertions, makes consciousness into a consciousness of the self, necessary each time.

If all consciousness is necessarily consciousness of the self, it is also a thought that can take on different modalities. Doubt served as a point of departure for Descartes; but he could have said "I experience" or "I want," which are affirmations that reflect upon themselves as such, as though they surpass themselves by affirming that they themselves are thoughts: "Where I have said, this is the mind, the spirit, the intellect, or the reason, I understood by these names not merely faculties, but rather what is endowed with the faculty of thinking; and this sense the two former terms commonly, the latter frequently bear."[2]

In fact, to feel or to think are from the very outset forms of consciousness, and therefore, of reflection. It is possible to be mistaken about *what* we feel if we say "I feel," but we cannot be mistaken if we assert that we doubt; but in both cases, the result is that the proposition "I think" is true: "By the word 'thought,' I understand all those things which occur in us while we are conscious, insofar as the consciousness of them is in us. And so not only understanding, willing, and imagining, but also sensing, are here the same as thinking."[3]

There is therefore an apodictic certainty which is linked to sentiments, identical to a Cogito, because to feel is to know that we feel, even if we are wrong about all the rest.

As we have seen, to know and to feel meet in the consciousness of self; they swallow up the consciousness of the object in reflection and erase the difference between thought and sentiment, and between what is necessary and what is contingent. "I do not see any difficulty in allowing on the one hand that the faculties of imagination and sensation belong to the soul, because they are species of thoughts, and on the other hand that they belong to the soul and only as joined to the body, because they are kinds of thoughts without which one can conceive the soul entirely pure."[4]

2. Descartes, *Third Reply,* in *the Philosophical Works of Descartes,* trans. Elizabeth S. Haldane and G. R. Ross (Cambridge: Cambridge University Press, 1912), vol. 2, p. 62.

3. Descartes, *Principles of Philosophy,* trans. Valentine Rodger Miller and Reese P. Miller (Dordrecht: D. Reidel, 1983), vol. 1, pt. 9, p. 5.

4. Descartes to Gibieuf, 19 January 1642, in *Philosophical Letters,* pp. 125–26.

If there is an idealist enclosure in Cartesianism, it is best expressed here.

Consciousness is consciousness of self right through. Its transparency is so complete that it permeates the child virtually from birth. From the moment the child has a soul, it not only knows that it has one, but it also knows its contents, because for Descartes God made it this way. On the other hand, Descartes suggests that the first ideas that come into one's mind are confused because they are born of the body's imprint.

Nevertheless, we know that we are knowledgeable and by this we know what we know (nativism). There is no more illusion, no more opacity, which we have just admitted as being the zero degree of consciousness:"Wherefore I have no doubt that the mind begins to think at the same time as it is infused into the body of an infant, and is at the same time conscious of its own thought."[5]

This thesis establishes an identity between the consciousness and the consciousness of self. Can one imagine an unconscious consciousness? The consequence of this is radical nativism, which means that the consciousness is filled with ideas that are implanted by God into people at birth because he is God and they are human beings. This is the case for a series of simple ideas, notably that of divine perfection. If we had for a moment to consider the contrary, it would be necessary to admit that "clear and distinct ideas" have their origin not in us, but in the external world. This would be subjected to the various leaps of contingency, while the character of the elementary contents of the consciousness, of the Cogito, is apodicticity. Is any kind of science even possible without it? All mathematics would dissolve if they were deemed dependent upon external sensations for their validity.

We do understand that Descartes wanted to identify consciousness (and what it contains) with a consciousness of self and to suggest that it is impossible to make propositions without the Cogito, which is like its measure and its truth. This is the source of utterances such as "[I can] affirm with certainty that there is nothing in me of which I am not in some way conscious."[6]

Such a viewpoint cannot be upheld. We have difficulty conceiving of a consciousness that is reflexive through and through. We cannot subscribe to an idea according to which the bases of all knowledge is possessed by all from the very outset. And we can imagine even less a consciousness that is omniscient of all its contents since birth, even if this comes with the idea of a unified self. At the beginning of the *Essay*

5. Descartes, *Reply to objections IV,* in *Philosophical Works,* vol. 2, p. 115.
6. Descartes, *Reply to objections I,* in *Philosophical Works,* vol. 2, p. 13.

Concerning Human Understanding, Locke suggests that children are counterexamples who must still acquire reason, and idiots, counter-examples who have lost it. This proves that it is possible, and not that it is innate and immutably so.

It must be possible to learn things we don't know, an idea that radical innatism renders superfluous. It is true that the union of body and soul caused us to forget the clear and distinct ideas that were implanted at birth, and daily actions have led us to be diverted from them. If this is the case, how is it possible to be sure that the soul contains *a priori* the atoms of truth from which science is nourished?

Since we always have, and have always had, bodies, radical innatism cannot be proven because it is based upon a situation that is inaccessible to us, which is to represent what happens in a mind that is isolated from the body. Radical innatism, says Locke, implies an unfounded meta-physics which pretends to know what is in fact unknowable for humans who are composed of flesh and blood.

Descartes is perfectly aware of the difficulties presented by the thesis of maximal innatism. A consciousness which reflects upon itself con-stantly, which has knowledge at every moment of everything that is going on inside it, from the very beginning, is obviously absurd. We learn, therefore we are unaware. We forget, therefore the contents of our con-sciousness get erased, sometimes as fast as they appear. As paradoxical and contradictory as it sounds, consciousness is often unconscious of what happens inside it when it is completely absorbed by an activity or an object. To return to the idea of passion is, therefore, inevitable. Is it possible to give credit to the idea of an unconscious consciousness? Pas-sion comes aptly named.

At the beginning Descartes attenuates his radical innatism in favor of a moderate or minimal innatism: "Finally, when I say that an idea is innate in us [or imprinted in our souls by nature], I don't mean that it is always present to us. That would make no idea innate. I mean merely that we possess the faculty of summoning up this idea."[7]

In other words, we haven't possessed the answer to 986 times 564 since the dawn of time, any more than we have possessed the answers for any other questions since the dawn of time. We only have an innate ability to produce answers. These are innate faculties, not the contents of our consciousness. If the Cogito is the first of all answers, it is not because it has all others in an immediate and *a priori* fashion, but rather that it is the first in the order of answering which it constitutes in the

---

7. *Objection III with replies*, in *Philosophical Works*, vol. 2, p. 73.

forms, which is the necessity. The form of answering is thus given by the Cogito, but the matter comes from elsewhere. If we look closely, this is the very position that is assumed later on by the English empiricists. Empiricism is the logical consequence of Cartesian thinking, the very price of its credibility and coherence. The tongs that hold Descartes are clearly recognizable: either we have radical innatism, which preserves, through divine necessity, its mark upon us—the Cogito—the apodicticity of knowledge, of mathematics; or else we have the acceptance of a consciousness that is nothing other than the form of knowledge which accumulates, little by little, through material contact with the external world. Contingency and fluidity mark the contents of consciousness, and as a result, we will have lost the apodicticity that is indispensable to the foundation of science, just as it is to the method for acquiring it.[8]

How is it possible to maintain the apodicticity of science while avoiding the unacceptable consequences of radical innatism? But how is it possible to soften this innatism without sacrificing the necessity of scientific propositions to empiricism, which is only aware of contingence and probability?

By defending both a strong and a weak innatism, Descartes hoped to escape from the consequences of both; unfortunately, they are as inevitable as they are incompatible. The theory of passions is the way around the contradiction that threatens him. *Passion will be the maximum amount of empiricism that he will admit in order to avoid having to become an empiricist;* he uses his passion by instituting a degree of un-reflexivity into the mind, which will allow for a degree of contingency despite everything. Passion becomes in this instance the consciousness nourished by the sensations of the body, a kind of external consciousness that forgets itself to the point of considering itself to be the truth, but which knows as well what it contains, and thus reintroduces reflexivity to the point where it no longer has a place. Since a consciousness is always a consciousness of self, it is normal that reflexivity be continuously present; but how is it therefore possible to differentiate a consciousness from the necessity of a sensible consciousness if both are required to really think about what is happening inside? The illusion of passion is situated in this permanent reflexivity—which should dissolve all possible confusion—which gives the impression that ideas that come from the external world have their origin in the soul. The reflexivity that is unique to consciousness is the one which renders the passions as certain and true as mathematical propositions and other innate ideas;

8. On these points, see Meyer, *Science et métaphysique chez Kant,* pp. 72–73.

this is, of course, absurd: "Thus, because we do not conceive the body to think in any way, we do right to believe that every kind of thought within us belongs to the soul."[9] The problem of their difference always bubbles up to the top because the illusion is natural, just like the passions, and to conquer them is just as difficult as to eliminate the illusion: "Then I also take into consideration that we notice no subject that acts more immediately upon our soul than the body it is joined to, and that consequently we ought to think that what is a Passion in the former is commonly an Action in the latter. So there is no better path for arriving at an understanding of our Passions than to examine the difference between the soul and the body, in order to understand to which of the two each of the functions within us should be attributed."[10]

The confusion will cease, even if we don't succeed in liberating ourselves from the hold of the passions, even though they are natural: "For experience shows that those who are most agitated by their passions are not those who know them best, and that the passions are numbered among the perceptions which the close bond between the soul and the body renders confused and obscure."[11]

The idea of following the analytical order in the examination of passions, whereby the most simple elements will be revealed in order to deduce the most complex ones, as Descartes did in his metaphysics, permits us to recover a certain degree of mastery over thinking about thoughts that come from elsewhere.

If passions are natural, then the will to overcome them is illusory. If they are only judgments, then analyzing them should resolve them; but Descartes himself recognizes that this is not so easy on account of the fact that they originate in the body and in "the movement of the minds." It is as if to say that these are no longer just judgments. Here we fall back upon a dualistic model: natural passions and human passions, a two-sided board upon which our ancestors play on both sides simultaneously, and hence in a contradictory fashion. The unity of the human being as the union of two autonomous substances, soul and body, reveals all of its problematicity in that we don't really know if the relationship between them is corporal (caused by the action of the pineal gland) or if it obeys the intellectual rules of the will which domesticates through reason everything that happens in the composite that is the human being. Sometimes we describe passivity as being that which constrains us and makes us weak (or even sinful) by nature, sometimes we recognize the

9. Descartes, *Passions of the Soul*, art. 4.
10. Ibid., art. 2.
11. Ibid., art. 28.

power to advance victoriously upon our passions, as though they were nothing other than the products of the soul. Descartes doesn't escape from the ambivalence of passion.

Is There a Cogito of Passion?

Descartes's problem is obvious: either he admits that there is a form of consciousness that is nourished from the external world and that the Cogito, which affirms the immanence of consciousness for itself, is therefore in great danger; or else he rejects this form of consciousness and falls into a radical—and incoherent—innatism. Descartes is, therefore, forced to admit that there are perceptions which come from outside and which are mediated by the body. The problem is to figure out what status to ascribe to them.

The soul that must put up with the body cannot have anything other than involuntary representations, which are unrelated to knowledge. Knowledge is voluntary and freely produced by the mind on the basis of its own innate contents. The illusion of the passions, the one that philosophers have tried to overcome ever since the very dawn of philosophy, is a sham, because nothing resembles a thought as much as another thought even if one is the real truth, and its imitator nothing more than an appearance. This is true because of the contingency and the fluctuating nature of everything corporal and empirical. A passion is useful to help us avoid displeasure or find pleasure, but in no way can it be assimilated to knowledge.

For Descartes, passion is the "body in the soul"; it is not a sensible impression that is experienced in the body, but rather the effect of this sensation in the actual consciousness. Passions are "the perceptions that are referred to the soul alone ... whose effects are felt as in the soul itself, and of which no proximate cause to which they may be referred is commonly known."[12] This is the source of the illusion which consists in our believing that they have their place there.

Passion is thus what will be later be called external consciousness, sensible consciousness, or for convenience, *sensibility:* "Now even though all our perceptions—those which are referred to objects outside us no less than those which are referred to various affections of our body—are truly passions with respect to our soul when this word is taken in its most general sense, nevertheless it is usually restricted to mean only those which have reference to the soul itself."[13]

12. Ibid., art. 25.
13. Ibid.

In a state of passion the soul has to deal only with itself. It represents a sentiment to itself, it thinks, and it knows that it thinks. Hunger, thirst, hatred, love, and whatever else are known as such by whoever experiences them. This is where the necessity of a consciousness of self comes into play, just like in science, and which leads to the fact that a man who thinks that he is in love or that he is hungry cannot be wrong about the fact that he is thinking, or about *what* he is thinking, whether that be about knowing that he is in love or that he wants something to eat. The Cogito rediscovers its rights in passion. The consciousness, even the sensible consciousness, necessarily knows that it is sensible.

This "affective Cogito," to use Jean-Luc Marion's term, is confirmed by Descartes variously in the *Treatise*. Even if passion is leading me on, yet I think, necessarily: "Now as to what concerns ideas, if we consider them only in themselves and do not relate them to anything else beyond themselves, they cannot properly speaking be false, for whether I imagine a goat or a chimera, it is not less true that I imagine the one than the other."[14]

In short, passions "are so close and internal to our soul that it is impossible it should feel them without their truly being such as it feels them."[15]

Thanks to the recognition of the Cogito effect in passions, Descartes manages to save the Cogito as the truth of consciousness, which is to be ever conscious of the self even in the case where the consciousness is manifestly turned toward something other than itself. In fact, the concept of "another thing" is a concept that delineates origin, but which does not effect the nature of the representation, which as a content of consciousness, lives in itself in the same fashion, whatever the origin.

By putting forth such a thesis, Descartes assures himself of an analytical mastery over the order of the passions, and all the more so since he then goes on to enumerate them from the most simple to the most complex.

Unfortunately, some of the consequences of this approach are unacceptable. All Cogito expresses a necessary proposition, and even affirms the necessity of the thought that is in the consciousness. But this is not true except in science, or in mathematics; it is not true of sensible truths, like the passions. Passion is precisely this moment of consciousness which is unthinking, spontaneous, and where things aren't voluntary or constrained by the soul. In fact, if we consider that passion is a form of Cogito, then the risk that one takes is to witness the abolition of the

14. Descartes, *Meditation III*, in *Philosophical Works*, vol. 2, p. 159.
15. Descartes, *Passions of the Soul*, art. 26.

difference between truth and appearance, interiority and exteriority, knowledge and experience. How would it then be possible to even talk about passion—or action—if everything is nothing other than representation and immediate thinking about this representation? Descartes himself evokes this very confusion, this amalgam: "And though with respect to our soul it is an action to will something, it can be said that it is also a passion to perceive that it wills. Nevertheless, because this perception and this volition are really only a single thing, the denomination is always made by the loftier one, and so it is not usually named a passion, but an action only."[16]

The distinction between actions and passions seems to be purely verbal as regards the consciousness which experiences, feels, and thinks. "Thus, even though the agent and the patient are often quite different, the Action and the Passion are always a single thing, which has these two names in accordance with the two different subjects it may be referred to."[17] This is true unless of course the origin is scrutinized; but this is beyond the consciousness, which reflects when it is conscious of something, since this involves searching for the *reasons* for having what it has inside, and not simply enduring it.

This immediate Cogito, which has no distance from the self, and which is present in scientific knowledge just as it is in passionate spontaneity, is incapable of distinguishing between them, and offers no grounds for recognizing them as such. To speak of illusion suggests a state of super-, supra-, or meta-consciousness, which would permit us to analyze consciousness, which was the very meaning of the Cogito: to be able to differentiate between the contingent and the apodictic, the corporal and the empirical.

By wishing to save the Cogito as the constitutive text of all possible consciousnesses, Descartes must place it in the empirical consciousness, which thus becomes apodictic without becoming knowledgeable, to the point where his passions-contents "can sometimes be caused by the actions of the soul, which determine how to conceive of some action or another."[18] It is as though this time the consciousness produces its own passionate qualities by itself. The Cogito was beyond perfect: here it is extending to the passions even though it cannot even distinguish them from pure truths unless it is able to leave the realm of the consciousness, which was supposed to be its foundation.

16. Ibid., art. 19.
17. Ibid., art. 1.
18. Ibid., art. 51.

Descartes could not follow such an idea to its logical conclusion. To admit that there is an empirical consciousness is one thing, to align it with or reduce it to the Cogito is quite another. Further, if consciousness is entirely determined by the Cogito, why wouldn't passion be felt and thought like all other thoughts are, passionate or otherwise? The question is to know how to proceed despite the difference between the *I think* and the *I feel*, between an apodictic consciousness and a sensible phenomenon, which one must worry about in order to avoid being trapped by the representational contents that it conveys. Do we have to renounce passion as a distinct form of consciousness? A passion is not the same as an opinion, and to consider it such would in fact be absurd. So does one have to dissociate passion from the Cogito and turn passion into a simple unthinking sentiment or state, not thought out as such, which obsesses the consciousness precisely because it doesn't retract back into itself when passion comes and impairs it? This would of course preserve the Cogito's primordial function, which is to assure through its apodicticity the necessity of the propositional norm as science. But by instituting such a difference passion ceases to be a consciousness, a reflexivity that necessarily knows itself as such; it becomes a mood which is devoid of consciousness. This is what Descartes must challenge, because if it were so then the status of passion would become completely problematic as regards the nature of consciousness: "The subjective character of passion is such that, although we can be wrong about its cause, we can't be wrong about its existence. The evidence of passion participates, in this sense, with that of the Cogito. If I feel sad, my sadness can rest upon false reason, and I can be ignorant of its corporal causes, but it remains in any case certain that I am sad."[19]

I know that I am sad, I couldn't be otherwise, and I could even be wrong about what I feel, though not about what I *believe* I am experiencing, unless what is being suggested is that I experience what I think that I experience, which is that the sentiment is the thought about sentiment, which would make this sentiment into something as true as a mathematical truth. Descartes cannot subscribe to this idea: "Just as in thirst the sensation of the dryness of the throat is a confused thought which disposes to the desire for drink, but is not identical with that desire."[20]

If passion recognizes itself to be passion, such a necessary knowledge cannot be confused with its object, and the Cogito is saved, as is passion, which could neither take advantage of, nor sweep away, the soul. When I

19. F. Alquié, *Commentaire aux passions de l'âme*, in *Oeuvres de Descartes*, vol. 3 (Paris: Garnier, 1963), p. 973.

20. Descartes to Chanut, 1 February 1647, in *Philosophical Letters*, p. 209.

feel, I know that I feel, and these are two different things, two different levels of consciousness, that of reflection, and that of the absorption in the sensible world. There is no unknown passion as such, but instead it is always taken into account in a reflexive fashion, without any possible confusion, as though the soul were always conscious of the tiniest movements.

Passion is both lived without being thought—which it cannot be, since it is situated in the soul—and thought without being lived, since it is always thought. By combining these two theses, Descartes is able to turn passion into something that is thought about and conscious, even as he insists upon its unthinking and involuntary character, that is, even as he unmasks passion for what it really is.

From the Cogito, which instills a sense of transparency, we have moved to the Cogito as the immediate adherence to the self, which means that we've confounded passion and reason, and we've made a therapy of desire necessary, which no Cogito could ever establish. Could the Cogito be the criteria for apodicticity, or is it a possible combination of apodicticity and contingency, knowledge and sensitivity?

From Which Standpoint Does Descartes Speak?

If passion is the result of the union between soul and body, and if Cogito is a property of the soul in that it plunges into itself, then to speak of the Cogito, to carry this out, seems nearly impossible, since this presupposes our ability to ignore our own bodies. In fact, if there is passion, how could there be reason which goes beyond it and negotiates it, unless one postulates the possibility of an overview which is *a priori* inaccessible?

If all passion is derived from reflexivity, and therefore placed under the aegis of a Cogito, then it could not be mystifying. In terms of an innate approach, the idea that passions have a hold upon us is impossible because we always know that we feel, and what we feel, over and above any other doubt or hesitation. When I'm thirsty or I'm upset, I know it, and I know that I know that these are passions and not representations that the soul draws forth from its inner self in an innate fashion through pure reflection. If consciousness is this Cogito, like the one we find from the very beginning of the *Metaphysical Meditations,* then passion could never act upon us at our own insistence. We are innately, and from the very outset, able to distinguish what emerges from the soul from what comes from the body, and we can get around the obstacles to the union of the two as though they never even occurred. And yet we are human, and the union is real. *From which standpoint* does Descartes speak, therefore, in order to assume an exterior viewpoint, that of pure mind? According to the *Meditations,* the question that arises is that which concerns the possibility that we must doubt, and rejects in a radical fashion sensible illusions in us. These are either operations which arise without our even realizing that we must doubt them, or else they are always already overcome by the consciousness, which renders superfluous the need to pass through radical doubt. To doubt is to know that we doubt; it is thus no longer an act of doubting, but rather an affirmation of something that is without doubt.

In order to bring to our consciousness the idea of things in doubt, of the deceitful sensible world, it is necessary to provide for oneself an idea of truth, something that Wittgenstein confirms later on in his *Of Certainty.* This overview presupposes an affirmed liberation—we don't know how—from the yoke of passions, from the influence of the body and the sensations which it brings to the soul, a knowledge of the passions and of the confusion that they induce. The affirmation of doubt and the possibility to express this same doubt comes from a lucidity of an overview, of a detachment which through nature passion impedes because it is not easy to forget one's body as much as rational will might require. To know that we must doubt is already to know that we think and that we are made up of a thinking matter because doubt doesn't become conscious unless we are already over it, unless we've already overcome the obstacles that face us. The Cartesian resolution recalls the Thomist irascibility, a coming to consciousness of that against which we must struggle.

The impression that remains after a careful reading of Descartes is that we are constantly dealing with the idea of innate reflexivity, which is on the one hand upheld, and the other refuted. This will remain a problem as long as the presence of the body is unavoidable, even despite the supposed autonomy of the thinking matter vis-à-vis the body. In an order of reasons which follows its own necessity, the child must know everything and the adult must learn nothing; but to think this is to forget the confusion of sentiments which trouble this pure reflection, and which is denied the moment it is proclaimed, and this on account of the unrealistic nature of the initial thesis.[21] Passion is thereby creating doubt, but also impeding us from becoming conscious in the way that would be required.

The *Meditations* begin forcefully with the consciousness of this fact, which is as much as saying that this fact is at the basis of the postulation,

---

21. Descartes to Chanut, August 1641, in *Philosophical Letters,* p. 203.

similar to the way that radical innatism and total transparency are. The problem is to arrive at this "beginning"; this is the mystery of Cartesian thinking that is taken up according to the "ordering of reason," even though it reveals itself when we envision it according to the ordering of the passions.

We see at this point a consciousness which surprises itself, and which reflects upon its own surprise, in the emergence of the new empirical fact, the contingency of the world. It examines itself and finds admiration in this doubling effect. Under the influence of this sentiment of admiration, consciousness absorbs itself and, in a contradictory move, finds itself lost in the object as though in an illusion, which a methodological pathway of reason would have eventually unmasked: "When the first encounter of some object surprises us, and we judge it to be new, or different from what we knew before or what we suppose that it should be, this makes us admire it, and we are surprised."[22]

In other words, the commerce with the world becomes passion when consciousness is invaded by surprise about what is contingent: a non-empirical definition of empirical consciousness which permits Descartes to avoid empiricism. If consciousness submits itself to the sensible, it does not reflect. And if it reflects, does it still submit itself to the sensible?

Does the Cogito, which affirms itself in the consciousness of self that is the product of sensations, distinguish real knowledge from sensations, or does it confuse the two because it originates in the senses? And if there is no Cogito but instead nothing other than a simple emotion that is experienced by the soul, then the Cogito is saved as a vessel for knowledge and necessity, but emotion becomes by the same token a domain without consciousness. Suppose that there is a Cogito in passion: if the consciousness is aware that there is passion, then passion is abolished, unmasked; and if it is unaware of this, then truth and illusion become merged and the Cogito is transformed into a space of uncertainty. So from total transparency, we move into opacity.

The Cogito's function is supposed to be to enlighten us, to offer us methodological guidance; but all of this seems rather difficult if it offers verification of itself in an indiscriminate fashion in either the consciousness of doubt or of sentiments, or in the illusions in which it plunges us. And yet the Cogito does differentiate between the two sorts of consciousness, since consciousness of doubt is no more dubious than consciousness of sentiment. I know that I feel when I feel, and I don't imagine myself simply feeling. Feeling is thinking and not thinking. The difference

22. Descartes, *Passions of the Soul,* art. 53.

is only verbal, assumed. We can have doubts about what we feel, but not about whether we are feeling. The Cogito renders contents indistinct as a means of affirming only itself, but we can consider it as implying other things as well.

In short, if I necessarily know that I know when I think, I can be in possession of the truth or not. Because of the passions, my certitude is identical in both cases, but who would miss the gulf that separates certainty from illusion? This undecideability will lead Kant to opt for a double consciousness later on, sensible and intellectual, in order to allow him the possibility of saying that the consciousness knows itself knowing other things. But from the Cogito we move to the transcendental analysis, which is characterized by the examination of faculties and the relationship between them. "Passions are perceptions that the soul brings back to itself. There is in fact the psychological characteristic of affective facts. Descartes doesn't perhaps fully explain this character with as much tidiness as might be desirable."[23]

So isn't the truth just another form of affection of the soul, and the affection, a form of truth? "But if I deduce this from [the action of my mind, or] the very sensation or consciousness of seeing or of walking; the conclusion is completely certain, for it [the premise] then refers to the mind which alone perceives or thinks that it is seeing or walking."[24]

To summarize, the Cogito seems to impede passion-induced illusions by unmasking them, even as it remains present in this illusion just as it does in any other fact of consciousness. If this is true, then the consciousness is reflected in every intellectual act it undertakes, which undermines the Cogito's underlying force as regards reason and its necessity. Descartes plays on both fields in order to preserve the Cogito, and thus in order to distinguish reason from passion, even as he considers it as a fact of always reflexive consciousness. The Cogito, the consciousness, is *that which makes* the trap of passion by mixing it with reason and creating confusion. The Cogito also demarcates it, which disallows all confusion.

Nature and Liberty

According to Descartes, the passions are natural to the human being, just as the unified body is natural to the soul. To believe that one has shed one's passions is as illusory as it is useless. "For we see that they are all in

23. O. Hamelon, *Le Système de Descartes* (Paris: Garnier, 1911), p. 361.
24. Descartes, *Principles of Philosophy,* vol. 1, pt. 9, p. 6.

their nature good."[25] Further, "they dispose the soul to will the things nature tells us are useful."[26]

Such a conception is difficult to reconcile with the one that is traditionally associated with Cartesian thinking, which attributes an autonomy to the thinking substance on which all clear and distinct thinking rests.[27] But passions are not perceived as such. They are related only to the soul, as though they originated there; this is the source of their ability to fool us. Here we'll change languages: the order of reason asserts its authority over the order of utility. Passions cease thereby to be valued because they are the source of the unhinging of judgment. To realize this requires an act of liberty, a coming to consciousness, of which the source can be nowhere other than in an act of will as regards truth, which brings ideas back to their original source; but what is the proper origin of the will?

To aspire to truth, one must begin by assuming that we don't have it; but the essence of passion is that it gives the impression that we already possess it. How could we even imagine that it is necessary to exercise our liberty when we don't even imagine that we are enslaved? The question of knowing whether understanding precedes will, or if the two coincide is, unfortunately, impossible to resolve: they must be distinct even though they cannot be. I must want to know in order to be successful in the quest for knowledge, but I cannot want something without knowing that I want it, and what it is that I want. It is as much to say that the will to set out the reality of the thinking substance and the supremacy thereof are already based upon this idea. The Cogito has no other origin than the will to establish it, which coincides with its very installation. And the problem in wanting to cast away bodily influences, which is natural, remains intact in its very possibility. Reason must be postulated in order to be, which makes its very foundation mysterious, if not entirely outside all reason. Isn't Nietzsche already inscribed within Descartes in the form of his realization of ultimate hopelessness? A certain conception of reason, which we have called propositionalism,[28] is hereby put to rest, but not rationality itself, which can't be reduced to this self-proclamation of analytical reason, which ignores what is in fact an obstacle to its very possibility.

Following Descartes, we are of the opinion that passions can and must be overcome so that the reflexivity of thought can be exercised. The

25. Descartes, *Passions of the Soul,* arts. 211 and 52.
26. Ibid., art. 51.
27. See J. M. Monnoyer, *Traité* (Paris: Gallimard, 1988), p. 47.
28. See Meyer, *Of Problematology.*

human order melts into the order that has been established by God, and this thanks to the Cogito, which rediscovers God's order in us. This is when we should forget ourselves and repress our passions, on account of this very procedure. But can we, given that we are human beings, and not God? We must abolish passion, but this is impossible, since by doing so we would thus cease to be human. If the order of reasons for Descartes differs from the order of things as they've been created by God, it is because of our humanity, our absolute freedom. But what are we suggesting here? That the passions, which are the effect of the body upon the soul, which would otherwise be the reflection of the divine intellect, are absent from this order of truth? By eradicating the passionate, an act that is ontologically impossible, we could bring together analysis (human) with synthesis (divine). But aren't the *Meditations* proof that the Cogito opens up a space of truth outside all passionality, which is *a priori* overcome? Reason's objective, which is apparently realized, is to extricate itself from this passionality, which prevents it from being deified. Doesn't the Cogito contain the idea of God? And yet the human must remain human, just as divinity must remain divine. This is what differentiates Pascal from Descartes. For the former, we are naturally sinners, and since we cannot be God, passion affects us, whether or not we realize it. For the latter, realization liberates, at least in principle: our pride would be reason, its optimism; Descartes would call it our generosity.

Passions, once perceived as such, fall outside the domain of our search for truth. In fact, they've never really been a part of it, since the Cogito can affirm itself straight away, in a doubt that cannot be posited except beyond itself, in the assertion that creates no doubt whatsoever, and which no longer brings us to that passion associated with unfounded beliefs.

Passions impede our ability to conform to the natural order of things, and yet they themselves are of that order. They are an indication of a difference which differentiates us from the natural ordering of things even as they inscribe us within it. On the one hand, we by the pride of our reason, hope to coincide with the work of God, and this identification begins with the purging of the passionate from the sensible in the soul. On the other hand, the analytical order which reflects the pathway of human reasoning remains distinct from synthesis, which is founded on God, instead of being like analysis which ends up with God. Passion is absent from analysis unless it manifests itself from the very start in the beliefs that arise from the sensible world, those very beliefs which are attacked by doubt. Passions are there like beliefs to be questioned, and they express what is human. Freedom consists of admitting the states of passion, and adhering to the ordering which is made such that we are susceptible to passions,[29] rather than suppressing them, which is generally futile. Descartes adds that "even those who have the weakest souls could acquire a quite absolute dominion over all the passions if one employed enough skill in training and guiding them."[30] To free men from their passions to bring them to reason, the Cogito, which leads to God, is both necessary and impossible, a fact that revives the paradox of passion. We recognize passion once we have become able to defend ourselves from it, but since it blocks access to our coming to consciousness which weighs upon the difference between passion and action, this difference becomes inaccessible. In his "Treatise on the Passions" Descartes plays upon this very ambiguity. Passion, which obsesses our mind, which confuses it with all other forms of representation because the person doesn't have the faculty of reason necessary to grasp its corporal and exterior origin, coexists with passion which is known as such, within a consciousness that is upheld by the Cogito, and which makes up the difference. This difference allows for liberty and intellectualism, as well as the more or less partial domination of passions as false judgments which are brought back to the Cogito, where the difference is always made. The Cogito can establish the dissociation between passion and that which comes from the soul itself; but doesn't passion prevent the Cogito? Cogito can only be a postulation, since it is necessary to want to doubt, and to surpass doubt, in order to be successful. But why would someone want to doubt unless he already knew that he needed to doubt? Doesn't passion reveal itself on the basis of the Cogito, which distinguishes the necessary from what is simply contingent?

Through liberty I can nevertheless dominate the desires which are within my own power, and resign myself to all others, without unleashing passions that are as negative as they are useless.[31] Only desire what is within your power, and try to give up on the rest, advises Descartes.

On the other hand, the identification of will with understanding, which are considered distinct, emerges from the same paradox as the one that affects passionality in occidental thought. Through the dissociation of will and understanding, we understand that access to the Cogito is useful, if not necessary, since we must first desire the truth before we can see any reason to seek it. But to know about what we are searching for, it is necessary that will be understanding, which renders the search

29. Descartes, *Passions of the Soul,* arts. 41 and 45.
30. Ibid., art. 50.
31. Ibid., art. 146.

useless. In the first case, since will is distinguished from real knowledge, I can't even know what I want, and in the second case, I know too well. I know and I don't know; this is the paradox. Understanding itself wants itself in its own establishing, or else the mind is blind. This is the problem concerning the foundation of reason; founded by reason itself, the process is circular; founded by something else, it is irrational or blind.

Is liberty an integral part of the ordering of things to the point where it denies its very existence, thus reinforcing the mystery of its specificity? Or is it a severing force and thus one that stumbles blindly upon the ordering of things from which it escapes, and which it could not redis-cover except by miracle? In terms of passions, the dilemma is as follows: if humanity is free in its will to transcend its passions, then the passions are not natural; and if it is not, how is it possible to speak of them, since they make us blind? Liberty in this sense seems either impossible or superfluous. It expresses the unexplained of the nature of humanity, the Kantian "thing in itself." Liberty is impossible on account of the irre-sistible and blinding force of passion. And it will be superfluous if we can become aware of the passions and thus overcome them. Passion could obviously be this weakness of the will of which we are free to become conscious or, on the contrary, which we can follow without asking too many questions. We know, and we don't know, we know and we don't want to know, we deny the passions in order to be able to give way to them and, by doing so, we confess as much as if we had expressed them.

This solution has the advantage of presenting the two alternatives: consciousness and unconsciousness, both subordinated to the weakness of the will by which we wish to ignore the nefarious consequences, even as we know that they are their real nature. Passion is known as such, and it remains a blinding force, which is paradoxical. The weakness of the will explains the unconsciousness and the inconsequence, the blindness.

By the weakness of the will we are aware of the passion that inhabits us, the passion that we cannot overcome. It blinds without blinding, since we know it without being able to overcome it. Later, Sartre will refer to this as "bad faith." By our liberty, we can abandon ourselves to our passion, or else we can struggle against it.

In reality, the idea of the weakness of the will, which seems to offer an explanation for the insoluble, in fact does nothing other than name the problem. We know about passion and we give into it on account of our weakness. And since we are able to exercise an effort of our will, liberty becomes the bedrock for the doublings of the consciousness.

The question that remains is to know how we can be unaware of a passion even as we know of its existence. If I am not aware that I am a prisoner of a passion that must be overcome, how can I say as much? And, if I know it, then the evil is unmasked, and I am unaware of nothing. The intermediary state, where I can be ensnared, blinded, even as I know about what's going on, could very well be called the weakness of the will. This warrants further explanation, one which doesn't recover both terms of the alternative and as a consequence renders them incompatible and co-present at the same time. Why am I "weak," why am I "strong"? Isn't there a passionate negation, a nefarious characteristic, which leads me to continue drinking or smoking even though I know that both are bad for me (just as gambling or making love can be bad for me), even though I don't feel concerned by the *delirium tremens* or by cancer? In the rationalization of my habits there is a stronger passion which haunts me, which eclipses all others, one of which I am in a way conscious but nevertheless unable to combat.

Descartes's Genealogy of Passions

By virtue of what we've just said about the passions in the Cartesian system, it is possible to unveil a general principle to classify them, at least as far as the primitive passions are concerned. As for the others, they flow from the composition of elementary passions, which are *admiration, joy* and *sadness, love* and *hate,* and finally, *desire*.

At the base of all passion we find a consciousness that is turned toward the outside, which draws thoughts from sensible impulses from the outside world. In short, perceptions. Is this consciousness, which is turned away from itself, still consciousness even though it does not define itself through reflection from its inner source, from innate ideas? In order to avoid this question, Descartes speaks of the passion of the soul (and not of the consciousness) even as he confronts the problem by placing a Cogito into passion and thus abolishing the distinction between consciousness of self and consciousness of the sensible or else, reinstating this difference, between action and passion, while all the while affirming that the passionate consciousness is unaware. The Cogito would unfold, and once again we would have a kind of consciousness that would not know that it was not ensnared, even as it knows as much (because of Cogito and that the Cogito respects the difference). Passion thus becomes impossible even as it has been rendered possible.

It remains the case that passion is a consciousness that is surprised by the external world, which it must discover and also confront. We are not surprised to learn that two plus two is four; it cannot be otherwise, and this truth, at its basis innate, would only be considered surprising to

someone who is crazy, someone who denies what is obvious. But that it
is warm outside, or cold, or that I am meeting John and not Paul, and so
forth, this is necessarily surprising, because it doesn't *have to be,* it could
only happen on account of pure contingency.

External consciousness (passion) reflects the contingency of things,
the sensible, the corporal, of the external world. Passion is linked to surprise, just as the truth that comes from the soul is linked to the necessary
unfolding of an order of reasons.

But there's more: in surprise, the soul surprises itself because it is not
determined by reflexive necessity. It thinks about itself as invaded, passive, in a state of rupture with regard to *a priori* evidence. Admiration,
like spectacle, is the consciousness that catches a glimpse of itself and
finally finds itself surprised by its nature, and by what can occur in itself
without it wanting this to happen:"And since this can happen before we
know in the least whether this object is suitable to us or not, it seems to
me that Wonder [admiration] is the first of all the passions. It has no
opposite, because if the object presented has nothing in it that surprises
us, we are not in the least moved by it and regard it without passion."[32]

Passionality is henceforth the doubling-up of consciousness, which
reflects upon itself but this time in order to become conscious of its own
duality. The world is passion from the moment it strikes my senses, my
body, in order to awaken ideas. From that point on we understand that
admiration, as surprise, is at the origin of all possible passion. We would
say today that passion is the symptom of the problematic: an object or
unexpected event raises a question, and this question awakens in us a
range of responses.

Consciousness that surprises itself and examines itself at an interval
from itself can only be marked by time. The time of the world, some
would say. We observe that a consciousness, from the moment that it is
absorbed by an external object, is unaware of itself, and when the subject
reflects upon what it is doing, or had been doing only a moment earlier,
a certain time lapse had occurred. Reflection comes after the fact. It's
the same consciousness that knows what is inside itself and which is
unaware, but this is not contradictory, since this knowledge and this
ignorance don't occur at the same moment. Scrooge, while in the act of
counting his money, doesn't say what he's doing because by doing so
he'd stop doing what he's doing, that is, he would be engaged with
describing what he's doing rather than actually doing it. But he is not
unconscious, since he could answer if someone asked him what he is

32. Ibid., art. 53.

doing. Passion, which in this example is the seduction of money, doesn't become consciousness of passion except when the object that is at the basis of this passion is rendered distant. Descartes recovers the unity of consciousness, which passion puts into question, through the temporization of the field of passions, of the soul joined with the body. Consciousness does not remain identical to itself except with regard to time. It is the same consciousness that busies itself with counting money and which can afterwards affirm what it had been doing. An immediate intuition of the self would be an instantaneous consciousness of the self, or else a consciousness of the object and a consciousness of the self fused simultaneously, outside time, in the same and identical instant. The Cogito exemplifies this time of psychic reality, and if we direct our attention to the arguments that affirm its presence in the passions, then we could speak of an "affective Cogito" and of a reflection by the self on itself that is immediate and that has no distance from consciousness.[33]

All the same, the truth of passionate consciousness is elsewhere. This consciousness is held inside the object, and it is only afterward that it becomes the consciousness of self. It is memory. By this, the consciousness recognizes itself, and this at the very moment when nothing else could certify this, which is the source of uncertainty as regards external information. "And it can be said in particular of wonder that it is useful in making us learn and retain in our memory things we have previously been ignorant of. For we wonder only at what appears rare and extraordinary to us."[34]

Wonder is the grasping of what is novel, and not simply of what was unexpected. Consciousness turns back upon itself and deploys a movement of reflection which plays its part. It realizes that an object has appeared and has captured its attention, it concentrates its attention upon this attention, it reflects the novelty that has arisen in itself, and it does so after the event has already passed. The object has been imprinted in a forceful fashion within the soul, and the soul cannot avoid thinking about this movement, which in itself is a new movement of the soul, a prolongation of the initial impression which creates a continuity within the consciousness. Reflection for the consciousness consists of becoming aware of what it has just experienced, and the passions cannot miss this but rise up in all their specificity. We are a long way from a Cogito that mixes together passion and action in the same representation, thereby misleading the consciousness about what has come from

---

33. J. L. Marion, "Générosité et phénoménologie," in *Etudes philosophiques,* 1988.
34. Descartes, *Passions of the Soul,* art. 75.

itself, and what is nothing other than some kind of fluctuating "knowledge." When consciousness reflects upon itself passionately, time has
passed, and this temporal difference permits us to realize that there was
a sudden appearance that came from outside. But in this case can we still
say that there is a place for a passion which unconsciously invades the
spirit and could mislead it? Does it still make sense to speak of passion if
not mechanically or physiologically? Shouldn't we discredit all information that comes in from the outside because it is necessarily misleading,
even if useful, or even necessary to our need for knowledge, but without
ever being able to identify itself with this need?

Passion must be a consciousness, a kind of Cogito, a form of reflection, and also a confusion of the soul, which passes off contingent information as apodictic knowledge. We are not beyond the dilemma even
if the limpid style of Descartes's writing sometimes makes us lose sight
of it.

Consciousness that is surprised by itself reproduces temporarily the
appearance of things in their own emergence, which is itself temporal.
This is the source of our sense of the appropriateness of the consciousness that finds itself "subjected to," and the object which has entered into
the mind. Isn't there despite everything an impression that the distance
between self and self, and self and object, has been effaced, which creates at the same time an amalgam between passion and knowledge
(which comes from a voluntary and innate action of the soul)?

Whatever the answer to this question, which is insoluble inside the
Cartesian framework, what is important here is to understand that consciousness is reflexive in time and time structures consciousness in
passion.

The real problem of this consciousness that is touched by passion is
to rediscover the identity with itself: this is *its desire,* subjective perseverance, the concern with sticking to the self for as long a time as the
passage of time will permit, moment by moment. The sense of *joy* will
be the result of this fusion with the object, herein the consciousness
itself, but this could relate to any other object (and would lead to *love*).
Sadness, on the other hand, would be marked by a failure of symbiosis.
Joy and sadness, as coinciding with the self, plunge us into a domain outside time by the very fact that they situate the soul at the end of the
process. We can feel pleasure, or feel sadness, with regard to a thing that
has occurred in the past or in the present, just as we imagine the success
or failure in the future (hope or despair). In this sense, joy and sadness
consecrate a relationship between consciousness and itself, a Cogito that
experiences joy, where the soul experiences itself. But is it possible if the

interval between passion and reflection remains insurmountable, and must even remain so, so that the Cogito won't destroy itself by losing the very apodicticity that defines it? It is necessary to preserve this reflexive aspect and this passionate immanence: love and hatred will fulfill this role because the soul considers a good thing that it would like to get close to, or an evil that it rejects, and thereby puts the passionate logic to work at either identifying or differentiating. Love is fusion, conjunction, whereas hatred is disjunction. Desire is a force of avoidance of evil in the search for the good, but love, like hatred, requires the usage of the will, which plays on consensus and judgment. "Now all the preceding passions may be excited in us without our perceiving in any way whether the object causing them is good or bad. But when a thing is represented to us as good from our point of view, that is, as being suitable to us, this makes us have Love for it, and when it is represented to us as bad or harmful, this excites us to Hatred."[35]

Desire seems blind and thoughtless, even if the distinction doesn't seem so clear. Desire could be a love or a hatred that is made temporal by the future, but it constitutes a primitive passion: it is not able to proceed from the combination of other passions, such as love and hatred.

Of Generosity

Passion arose as a consequence of action upon the body by the soul, a mechanical action that was analyzed by Descartes with reference to a physiological model. According to this model there is a mysterious gland that transforms the sensible into mental representation. In the course of the *Treatise* he changes his approach somewhat, as though passion for him only belonged to the domain of the soul, of judgment and, at the very end, it fell into the moral domain. "But because these passions can incline us to any action only through the mediation of the Desire they excite, it is that Desire in particular which we should be concerned to regulate; and the principal unity of Moral Philosophy consists in this."[36]

As a result: "As for things which in no way depend on us, no matter how good they may be, one should never desire them with Passion—not only because they may fail to come about and thereby afflict us all the more, the more we have wished for them, but mainly because, in occupying our thought, they divert us from casting our affection upon other

35. Ibid., art. 56.
36. Ibid., art. 144.

things whose acquisition does depend on us."[37] The passionate man knows that only that which is in his power merits being sought: "And there are two general remedies for these vain Desires. The first is Generosity, which I shall speak about later. The second is that we should often reflect upon divine Providence, and represent to ourselves that it is impossible that anything should happen otherwise than has been determined by this Providence from all eternity."[38]

We are aware of our free will, of our power, through generosity; but we are also made to be aware of the consequences of actions upon beings for which generosity-passion applies. A universality is thus established which is not that of scientific *cogitationes* but which is linked to it. Generosity allows us freedom from the opinions, reproaches, and envy of others by giving us confidence in ourselves when we take care of others. Generosity shelters us from excessive or nefarious passions and guides us toward a greater sense of self, or at least as much as passion will permit. It signals what is in our power even as it delineates barriers. This passion-virtue reinforces the taste for liberty and is the contrary of pride, which resides in a false image of the self and which is often negative with respect to the other. Pride is arrogance; generosity is acceptance. Generosity is the love for others, while pride is the love for the self, something represented by superiority and exclusivity.

Passion as the Difference Between Human Beings and God (Spinoza)

The Cartesian viewpoint suffers from a profound ambivalence. Human beings had to rediscover the divine order through a consciousness of self that is devoid of all passion (the one we find in the necessity of the Cogito); such a liberation was found to be impossible, or illusory, because we are what we are, we have bodies and souls that are influenced by the sensible. We are natural beings, and everything inside us is natural; therefore, it is vain for us to wish to eradicate our passions: "Hence it follows that man is always necessarily liable to passions, that he follows the common order of nature and obeys it, and that he accommodates himself to it as much as the nature of things demands."[39] Spinoza's approach is rooted in this idea, which aims to question the Cartesian point of departure, from which we must be able to free ourselves of everything that

37. Ibid., art. 145.
38. Ibid.
39. Benedictus de Spinoza, *Ethics,* trans. Andrew Boyle (London: J. M. Dents & Sons, 1989), IV, prop. IV.

creates doubts (beliefs that come from passions) without our knowing how we could come to doubt the sensible things that necessarily affect us. The Cogito seems to float in the air, as though under the effect of an unfounded approach because it wishes to be spontaneous. The Cogito is between the passions and God, as though we could abolish the passions and melt into the Other:

> I know that the most illustrious Descartes, although he also believed that the human mind had absolute power over its actions, endeavored to explain the human emotions through their first causes, and to show at the same time the way in which the mind could have complete control over the emotions: but, in my opinion, he showed nothing but the greatness and ingenuity of his intellect, as I shall show in its proper place. For I wish to revert to those who prefer to abuse and ridicule the emotions and actions of men than to understand them. It will doubtless seem most strange to these that I should attempt to treat on the vices and failings of men in a geometrical manner, and should wish to demonstrate with sure reasoning those things which they cry out against as opposed to reason, as vain, absurd, and disgusting. My argument, however, is this. Nothing happens in nature which can be attributed to a defect of it: for nature is the same, that is, the laws and rules of nature according to which all things are made and changed from one into another, are everywhere and always the same, and therefore there must be one and the same way of understanding the nature of all things, that is, by means of universal laws and rules of nature. Therefore such emotions as hate, anger, envy, etc., considered in themselves, follow from the same necessity and virtue of nature as other particular things.[40]

For Spinoza there is a more serious difficulty: the Cartesian circle taints the choice of Cogito from the very beginning. What is the nature of this circle? Despite the fact that this subject is reasonably well known, it's worth mentioning again briefly.

The certitude and verity of my ideas can only come from God, he who renders possible their appropriateness to the order of things which he has created. On the other hand, in order to prove that God fulfills this function, and he is himself everything that has been said about him, it

---

40. Ibid., III, preamble.

is essential that we be sure about our ideas about God. In short, God himself guarantees the ideas that come from the Cogito—which has the necessity and the truth of these same ideas, but God himself is an idea of this sort. To be sure that God is, we have to be sure about the veracity of our clear and distinct ideas, but since God is the one who establishes the objective values of these ideas, we can no longer be sure about anything. To dissociate the two orders of truths, one issuing from God, the other from humans, analysis and synthesis (Descartes), the order of reasons and the order of things, resolves nothing, since one must emanate from the other, and must adhere to it and reflect it. So how is it possible to think that we could view them autonomously?

Spinoza rejects this circle from the very outset by making as his point of departure that which imposes all necessity, and which conditions all possible necessity that flows from it: God, or Totality. We can thus affirm that God contains thought of the self, analysis, the thinking which forms itself about God, without having this conclusion flow from any kind of Cogito. The point of departure has changed: it is no longer a question of thinking about passion as a weakness of the Cogito, as previously described, but to use God as point of departure, which allows us to perceive human beings as a less-than-God, and passion is thus revealed in terms of this inferiority, in terms of *desire*.

God is thus the source of the thoughts that we think about him, that is, our own understanding. Everything is necessary, including the illusion of believing the contrary: there is a certain degree of liberty which is identified with ignorance, and it is this liberty which confronts humanity with opposites, to irritations, and leads it to lose sight of the necessity of things, which is of course the divine order. It is in the essence of this order to consider oneself born of this essence, and doomed to represent it by representing the self: "The order and connection of ideas is the same as the order and connection of things."[41]

This is a fundamental proposition which illustrates the need for thought about necessity as thought about God.

The passions, for Spinoza, are the result of an inadequacy, of an inevitable or amendable lag between humanity and nature, the Whole, or God, a kind of forgetting of principle which leads us to react through ignorance with "inadequate ideas," which our relation with God is supposed to abolish. But can human beings, by bringing everything to the All, to God, suppress everything that makes them human beings rather than God? "We therefore see that passive states are related to the mind only in so far as the mind has something involving negation: that is, in

41. Ibid., II, prop. VII.

so far as the mind is considered as part of Nature, which cannot be clearly and distinctly perceived through itself independently of other parts."[42]

We consider things in isolation as though they were their own source of support, as though they were substances, instead of seeing the necessity of the course of things, which implies that we bring things back to the chain of causes that issue from God. There is in passion an incomprehension of causality, or a bad attribution of causes. If for example we find ourselves victims of a car accident, then we will take it out on the alcoholic who in his drunkenness made the error that led to the mishap. Is this appropriate? It is in fact sterile in the sense that it changes nothing in the order of things that provoked the accident. It is normal that the two cars meet in the instant of the collision because that event was preceded by a chain of causality that led one party to the accident to drink and drive, and the other to take the same route as the drunk driver. Everything has its cause, everything can be explained, and to be angry with the order of things makes no sense, and can but injure and distress without any result. Whether it be God or nature, one must if not celebrate this chain of events, at least accept it as inevitable.

So, is conquering passions nevertheless possible? To think this is to forget that there is a range of passions which emerge from affections of the body, with which we all must live. Everything that relates to the effort required to continue living, the "life for life sake," everything that overcomes the principle of inertia and determines vital movement, is passion or, more precisely, desire. The sentiments that we experience are those which affect our ability to act, those which we consider without being completely aware of them; we experience the corporal world without necessarily being able to relate it to God.

In contrast with Descartes, who placed the source of passions at a reflexive distance from consciousness, in a weakness which plunges the soul into a state of admiration for the exterior world that submerges it, Spinoza prefers another point of departure: God. We are such that we lack reflexive immanence, total transparency, the immediate perception of the Totality, because we are not God; we have bodies and we must perpetually fill in this original lack in order to continue being what we are. This is a task that God avoids by reason of his perfection. Desire, and not admiration, is the original passion according to this synthetic ordering whereby God is, and must be, the necessary measure for all things. Passion is the rupture in the mind which makes us forget, neglect, or

42. René Descartes, *The Ethics*, III, prop. 3, scholium, in Descartes, *The Ethics and Selected Letters,* trans. Samuel Shirley, ed. Seymour Feldman (Indianapolis: Hackett, 1982).

ignore God, as well as the whole chain of causality which unites all events. To singularize, to isolate, to cut out reality, is a passionate action that responds to a corporeal, human need. Can we overcome it? This is the eternal paradox of the passions, which give the illusion of a victory that is possible by a knowledge of the higher kind, as though one could become God and thereby cease to be human. If passions are natural, then it is useless to struggle; but if the source of our passions is defective reasoning, then coinciding our spirit with God's should offer up a solution. Here we return to the Cartesian dilemma about the passions, which are deemed both necessary and possible to domesticate. But the two theses cannot be reconciled: Spinoza does not count admiration among the emotions, saying that "I recognize, therefore, only three primitive or primary emotions, namely pleasure, pain and desire."[43] Love and hatred, so difficult to conceive as primitive in the work of Descartes, are defined by Spinoza in terms of joy and sadness, since they emerge "from the idea of exterior causes."[44]

Desire is truly fundamental because it is the very effort that we manifest in order to be and to remain what we are.[45] Desire is the essence of our passions; when fulfilled, they procure joy, and when unfulfilled, they lead to sadness: "Desire, says Spinoza, is the appetite accompanied by the consciousness of itself."[46]

This means that the body, by being what it is, engenders the *idea* of what it is, which makes up a part of its determination to act, and which provokes an awareness of the power of action, which is a source of sadness (if it is weak or if it diminishes) or of joy (if strong or growing). Passions aren't necessarily the act of desiring as the fact of enjoying for *oneself* some object or another. This passivity, this dependence, nourishes the imagination and not our reason. Reason gives back to the mind a burst of activity and of mastery, not as regards exterior things, but as regards the self, because it leads to an understanding of what happens. But: "From this it is clear that we are in many respects at the mercy of external causes and are tossed about like the waves of the sea when driven by contrary winds, unsure of the outcome and of our fate."[47]

A sense of satisfaction can only procure the joy of pursuing the quest that procures it. A passionate acceleration affects desire, which becomes its own object, a kind of pre-Nietzschean will to power.

43. Ibid., III, def. IV.
44. Ibid., def. V.
45. Ibid., III, prop. LVII, demonstration.
46. Ibid., prop. IV, scholium.
47. Ibid., prop. LIX, scholium, p. 140.

Passion and Servitude

It is well known that passions enslave. We are caught up in the whirl-pool of things that affect us, and that give us the impression of pleasure. In fact, autonomy is fallacious and dependency is real: true liberty is a conquest that consists of knowing our place in the nature of things. But are we really less affected by this if we have such knowledge? Is it possible to overcome servitude, even when decoded, or does this knowledge change nothing? Aren't we simply aware of natural necessity, from which we cannot escape? Does knowledge of our enslavement constitute our overcoming thereof? It's sure that knowledge makes us less its victim: we've already seen the hope of belief, or belief in reason, in the course of this study.

On the one hand, we live in accordance with nature through our passions, and we universally seek what best accords with our nature as human beings. On the other hand, the fact of wanting something can only deprive the other from having it, which destroys the natural harmony just now proclaimed. Passions push us to combat one another, and then push them to reunite. Isn't this contradictory? To call one of these actions Reason and the other Passion doesn't make this process any less enigmatic. The problem seems to be resolved, but it is resolved only verbally. The decree does not explain how reason overcomes passion, by overcoming or by constraining it. In short, it is not enough to juxtapose reason and passion to show how one can be overcome by the other. Can passion be overcome by reason? This is the eternal question, which is found along the whole line of reasoning of occidental thought. Here again the simple fact of recognizing passion as such signifies that the traps had been avoided, and that passion had been abolished in the name of reason: "A passive emotion ceases to be a passive emotion as soon as we form a clear and distinct idea of it."[48] As a result:

> Since there exists nothing from which some effect does not follow (Prop. 36, I), and all that follows from an idea that is adequate in us is understood by us clearly and distinctly (Prop. 40, II), it therefore follows that everyone has the power of clearly and distinctly understanding himself and his emotions, if not absolutely, at least in part, and consequently of bringing about that he should be less passive in respect of them. So we should pay particular attention to getting to know each emotion, as far

48. Ibid., V, prop. III, p. 206.

as possible, clearly and distinctly, so that the mind may thus be determined from the emotion to think those things that it clearly and distinctly perceives, and in which it finds full contentment. Thus the emotion may be detached from the thought of an external cause and joined to true thoughts. The result will be that not only are love, hatred etc. destroyed (Prop. 2, V) but also that the appetites or desires that are wont to arise from such an emotion cannot be excessive (Prop. 61, IV). For it is very important to note that it is one and the same appetite through which a man is said both to be active and to be passive. For example, we have shown that human nature is so constituted that everyone wants others to live according to his way of thinking (Cor. Prop. 31, III). Now this appetite in a man who is not guided by reason is a passive emotion which is called ambition, and differs to no great extent from pride. But in a man who lives according to the dictates of reason it is an active emotion, of virtue, which is called piety (Scholium 1, Prop. 37, IV, and second proof of that same proposition).[49]

Perhaps reason has the power to unmask passion, which is a tautological statement, since passion is a concept of reason, but Spinoza forgets here that passion has the power to impede reason. It proceeds as though the power of unmasking it could be identified with the one aimed at annihilating it even though passion is in the final analysis natural. Isn't this the same illusion that he criticized in the work of Descartes? The postulate remains the same: passion only works when masked; as soon as it is recognized as such, it is no longer present, it is known for what it is, and the mind finds itself either beyond or outside its power. But isn't saying this a way of attributing to knowledge, to truth, a force that it unfortunately seldom has? We recognize here the repetition of the model from two standpoints. The model is discredited when we accept that passions are natural, something which makes them intellectually as well as physically unavoidable; and this is the model from three standpoints whereby we know what must be overcome, and not that we have overcome because we know.

One question remains: that is, what could ground Spinoza when he says that, despite everything, reason can emerge from passion, and against it. Everything is necessary, even the illusion which denies it.

49. Ibid., prop. IV, scholium, pp. 206–7.

Spinoza's response is not any clearer: if thinking about being is inscribed in the very order of being, if thinking about being is the being of thinking, there is, nevertheless, a difference between thought and being, a difference which consists in the fact that thought can come from being, because being, which obeys the laws of necessity, is not thought and mind. The comparison shows that this is not a form of identity, which would abolish the very terms which must join together and fuse. To consider the natural order of things may be seen as being natural, but this is not any less a reality that is specific as regards the whole of things, and which would permit us to oversee it with the mind, to understand what is wrong by thinking about it. It is true that the ideal is to exercise this liberty by thinking about its necessity in the order of all things, to consider its relationship to this order, and to destroy all obstacles which come between us and our wholeness, which happen to be the passions. The freedom to abide by God is complete, which nevertheless raises the question of knowing what renders possible such a liberty as regards this divine Almighty, necessary by and in nature.

If we examine it carefully, liberty and necessity are opposite sides of the same coin. If I say to myself that I am free to smoke, or to abstain, this statement is not any truer than the one that affirms that I am determined to smoke because of some factor or another that leads me to do so, even when I think of myself as being free to continue (or to quit), and this judgment is the result of factors which result in my believing something, and saying as much. By the same token, if I stop smoking, I could believe that I'm engaging in an act of liberty while in fact several different things condition my decision, and condition me to believe the contrary, which makes me say and think that I am free. The freedom to quit smoking becomes an illusion which consists in my considering spontaneous that which is in fact nothing other than the result of a group of factors in a long chain of causality. To believe that I am free, and to affirm as much, as action that is in accord with my will, is caused by events of which I may not be conscious, even though they are quite real. Such persons, who are willful and determined, will affirm themselves as free in their choices, but where does this willfulness and determination come from, if not an education and a character which predetermined their qualities, and which make them affirm and exercise the weight of these determinations?

To be sure, we could just as much support liberty as universal necessity, the former a part of the latter as the opposite side of the same coin.

Reason, for Spinoza, consists in becoming aware of this equivalence; reason is the fruit of passion, just as liberty is the fruit of necessity, but from another standpoint! Passion governs us blindly, but the very fact of being able to see it, in order to move forward (= *conatus,* perseverance at being and the reflection upon this effort), is inscribed in the order of passion, which becomes the order of reason, which is a reflection upon passion. So commences the liberty of seeing necessity in this liberty, and with this vision the power of determining the self through reason like a determination which becomes autonomous even as it attaches itself to the Whole of things.

It is clear that this solution is not ideal because a necessity which gets translated into liberty and a liberty which is but an illusion as regards the profound necessity which affects us continuously do not help us see more clearly because this would suggest that passion and reason could only be differentiated in the paradox which links them together.

Passion is an opinion, and in this sense it emerges from an inferior kind of knowledge, which sane reasoning permits us to correct. Passion is an illusion of liberty, which is only ignorance of causes and the necessity which regulates them. In this sense, Spinoza is situated within the domain of Stoicism. From another standpoint, Spinoza makes passions into natural forces which envelop the movement of the body. We find here the ambivalence of the passions: since they are natural, they are unavoidable; since they are human, they emerge from our essence, from thought and from judgment, which goes beyond them. By making an equivalence between liberty to modify one's judgment and the necessity of having passions, we convert the enslavement by passions into liberty through reason, and we maintain our passionate nature as a fact of human nature. But we obscure the distinction between passion which tricks us and reason which saves us. It is necessary to maintain this difference, and Spinoza does this effectively; but it is also necessary to abolish this difference, and there again we have the sense that reflexive passion coincides with the establishment of sovereign reason.

Passion is a necessity, and Spinoza reproached Descartes for pretending to be able to transcend this necessity; but like Descartes, Spinoza follows the same pathway by showing that reason is finally inscribed within passion, as a phenomenon of consciousness. From this point, passion is free like reason, and it is necessary, as is everything else. Passion contains its own capacity for overcoming itself, but this ability to freely overcome itself is illusory in that we necessarily go beyond passions which have liberty only in the illusion caused by ignorance. True liberty is that which allows us to find our own reflexivity, our independence, thanks to the universal love of God. Passion is thus reason seen from the perspective of autonomy, an autonomy which leads us to neglect the

universal, upon which we must adjust ourselves, rather than limiting ourselves to considering particular things and forgetting to see the great
causal chain, knowledge, God. On the other hand, reason is passion envi-
sioned according to this same universality, according to the order of
nature, which creates accord and sublimates different beings by rendering them independent of this or that in order to better relate them to
God. In short, rational desire:

Again, it is to be noted that these unhealthy states of mind and mis-
fortunes owe their origin for the most part to excessive love for a thing
that is liable to many variations, and of which we can never seize the
mastery. For no one is anxious or cares about anything that he or she
does not love, nor do injuries, suspicions, enmities, etc. arise from anything else than love toward a thing of which no one can truly be a master. From this we can easily conceive what a clear and distinct knowledge, and principally that third kind of knowledge whose basis is the
knowledge of God, can do with the emotions, namely, that if it does not
remove them entirely in so far as they are passions, at least it brings it
about that they constitute the smallest part of the mind. Moreover, it
gives rise to a love toward a thing immutable and eternal and of which
we are in truth masters and which cannot be polluted by any vices which
exist in ordinary love, but which can become ever greater and greater
and occupy the greatest part of the mind and affect it extensively.[50]

Reason and passion are like liberty and necessity: they are another
way of seeing nature, which is always unique. True liberty is such that it
sends us back to reason, which confronts us with equivalence, equivalence which makes us take for liberty what is nothing other than a
mask, and which makes us take as necessary what is nothing other than
contingent.

At the end of the day reason is free to determine mind and action
because it doesn't recognize any necessity other than that of the nature
that made it possible. Human beings who are won over by the spirit of
liberty are liberated; they will free themselves from one object or
another that affects them at some moment or another, in order to find
themselves; but by doing this, they perceive their own nature, therefore
God and nature, and they adhere to the necessary order of things.

Passion is contingent and can be thought about, abolished, without
really being abolished. It is not by a *postulant*, once again, that reason
can overcome passion and that we can consider ourselves as victors,
something which is in fact denied the moment it is proclaimed, because

50. Ibid., prop. XX.

passions, even when thought about, are much more powerful than errors in judgment.

Passions as Experiences of the Consciousness

One property of rationalism is that it cannot rid itself of the relationship it has with the body, any more than it can explain it. A consciousness that is closed up within itself, turned upon itself, and which misses nothing, is not at all compatible with this form of the soul which pushes us toward the material world because it lives within it. How is it possible to assimilate this consciousness with the other, which was described as being the whole of the consciousness? Passions enter the game to explain the inexplicable. Without them, rationalist systems don't hold water even if, on account of passions and with passions, it is necessary to quit them.

What rationalist systems have in common, despite the great diversity of viewpoints,[51] is that passion is an external and non-reflexive consciousness of which the consciousness is aware. In passion I know that I know other things than myself, I know myself as not being a being of pure knowledge.

For certain thinkers, like Pascal, this is what indicates our natural weakness. There is as well the pride in wanting to seal off this breach of passions, and to believe that we can overcome with reason what escapes us by nature. Passion as an object of knowledge would then fall into the domain of a reason that affirms its all-powerful nature as regards this original fault, from which God does not allow us any escape.

We find here again the irreducible dilemma of the theory of passions. To discover them is but to assure that they are indeed there, that they are necessary. Faith, hope, or even reason changes nothing of this. The certified report of the accident doesn't override the existence of the accident that was observed.

But we find as well thinkers for whom becoming aware of passions nourishes the optimism of reason: since passion entraps the mind as to its very existence, to discover passion is to denounce the trick and, by the same token, to liberate oneself from it. By knowing our sins we can save ourselves. We know that the problem is to explain how we come to this lucidity, to this "state of reason" without ever postulating it. This is the source of the idea of turning passion into an illusion, an irresistible

---

51. See A. Levi, *French Moralists: The Theory of the Passions 1585-1649* (Oxford: Oxford University Press, 1964).

force, and turning the idea of this force into the awareness of its presence. Then reason has a chance to be able to struggle through will and rigorous morality against the abuses of passion. But whatever the force of the will, or the belief that saves, we still believe that passion is both unaware and fully aware, that it is natural and that it is but a product of judgment that can be corrected through this same judgment. It is this very ambivalence, if not this ambiguity, that poses the real problem. A number of authors, like Descartes, cultivate both theories at the same time: passion blinds me, therefore I am in possible error, and I know this, thus I am over and above passion because I am knowledgeable of its true nature.

The opposition remains: is knowing that a problem exists the same as having erased it through the solution that this knowledge expresses? or is it in fact to have simply reproduced it in another form? To know that we are sick and of what disease we are suffering does not mean that we are cured, unless we believe that this sickness was the fact of ignoring the sickness. This explains how we were able to go from resignation to struggle, from joyful resignation to religious hope, in matters relating to the passions.

In short, we could have spoken more about Sénault's *De l'usage des passions* (1675), or of Malebranche, or Coëffeteau, or Cureau de la Chambre, but we would not have added anything to our discussion except a few minor details that emanate from the small original points that each one of them make. We couldn't have added to the reading of this text by adding a thousand and one different genealogies of particular passions and specific details of the type we find already in the works of Descartes and Spinoza.

Our interest is elsewhere. It is important to explain how the consciousness operates in a type of thinking that uses it for support, and to see what is missing and why. What is outside is not the consciousness, since we are obliged to maintain coherence, but rather passion, something that is easy to depreciate.

Even Spinoza's work, which turns desire into the primary passion, unlike Descartes who began with admiration, there is this idea of thought which knows that it is something other than pure thought and pure intellect because it has for its object extension and the affections of the body which change into the passions *of the soul*. That this comes from our absence from God in terms of desire (Spinoza), or the presence of ideas other than those which are deemed innate (Descartes), our rationalist authors share the same defiance as regards the singular contributions that come from outside, and upon which consciousness tries to reassert its mastery. Passion is this natural place wherein the empirical forces the doors open illegally. Moreover, it is necessary that the law regain its rights. It is clear that the consciousness of the world, experience, would insinuate itself into this form of consciousness, without God and without innate ideas, which would slowly invade all consciousness, to the point where it would become identified with the whole of the passions for them?

The Ego becomes passion itself, in that it is dominated and flushed with experience. And from experience of the passions we will have moved to the passion of experience. Kant, by going beyond the first, passes up the second.

The Uncertain Consciousness and Its Reunion with Itself

Whether we are willing to admit it or not, rationalism leads to the insecurity of consciousness. Passion is this consciousness which gets lost in the object and introduces exteriority in what is supposed to be nourished from itself. Passion obeys the demands of identity and difference because it is aware of a difference within itself. Contempt and veneration, love of self and hatred of the other, all name as many relative positions which mark these identities and differences which can never really wipe each other out, or be filled in.

If passion has to be invoked to explain external consciousness, it is because this rationalism defended the idea of a total transparency of the self, which is deemed reflexive and nourished with or by God. Since we can't know everything at once, the thesis itself has to be amended; we have forgotten the ideas that were implanted within us originally, and which are innate. But how can we be so sure that the ideas of which we are not conscious are nevertheless in the mind, and that they are not purely and simply *absent?* How is it possible to prove that we don't know what we should know, precisely on account of the transparency of the consciousness as regards itself? Reflexivity makes known all of the contents of the consciousness because consciousness = consciousness of self; and what does rationalism suggest if not that there are ideas which are innate but not conscious, that is, forgotten? Isn't this to overcome this total reflexivity and make another hypothesis which nothing, except specious metaphysics, can justify?

Total reflexivity and nativism are opposed to each other. If we have to renounce one of these options, it has to be the second, since it cannot be proven. On the other hand, that consciousness is consciousness of self, and not unconscious, is a thesis that is difficult to contest. Nativism doesn't hold up. If we don't know everything at a given moment, rather than saying that we are ignorant, we should suggest alongside of the rationalists that we forgot it from the moment when God placed it into our minds. But this position is not verifiable and should be sacrificed long before the preceding one, as Locke suggests: "It seeming to me near a contradiction to day, that there are truths imprinted on the soul which it perceives or understands not; imprinting, if it signify anything, being nothing else but the making certain truths to be perceived. No proposition can be said to be in the mind which it never yet knew, which it was never yet conscious of."[52]

Reflexivity of the consciousness which makes of all consciousness a consciousness of the self forbids the opacity that comes along with innate ideas. Coherence demands that when we know something, we know that we know it, and since we cannot know everything at once, we must conclude that the consciousness is empty of what it doesn't know at a given moment, t. It is nourished from the outside world, little by little, through experience.

Thus is born empiricism, of the contradictions and also the coherence of Cartesian rationalism. The Cogito is the first answer to all possible questions, the point of departure of reason, not because it contains all within it (nativism), but because it reflects and establishes the form that all other responses must take which must themselves come from elsewhere. That knowledge accompanies consciousness, no empiricist would deny; but that consciousness already possesses the chain of reason that it institutes represents an untenable thesis. Since it doesn't itself contain successive replies, consciousness can but borrow from the exterior world.

The real problem of empiricism resides in that which it defends: experience. As Kant says later on, to found the cognitive role of experience with reference to itself doesn't get us very far; at best, it's a vicious circle. From Locke's work forward the problem is posed.

We are under the impression that consciousness has a direct understanding of the object through the sensations that it communicates. The sensible qualities are thus transformed into ideas, and from the physical realm we pass into the mental one. It is clear that not all qualities have the virtue of being objective in themselves. A number of them do nothing other than translate the subjective effect of things in us. Heat, for example, is a relative notion which is not to be found in the object, but

---

52. John Locke, *An Essay Concerning Human Understanding* (Oxford: Clarendon Press, 1924), p. 18.

which our relation expresses to it. Or dimension: this man seems small from far away, but when he's close he is twenty centimeters taller than we are and seems immense. Does this mean that being large or small are intrinsic qualities? No, and they are not in *us* either; they are subjective, relational qualities, measured as regards themselves.

On the one hand, we get perceptions or direct ideas from objects; on the other, the effects of these ideas on us, which are other ideas. Locke calls the latter group qualities, secondary qualities, which describe the qualities of objects themselves, the primary qualities; these are like the essences and the accidents as regards the objects themselves. The solidity, extension, movement and rest, number and form, are all intrinsic qualities of the matter, while coloration, heat, and size are all variable qualities which depend upon the first ones, but are different from them on account of their permanence. Locke thinks that he can thus explain how the components, the atoms of the matter, with their inherent qualities, affect us in terms of various sensations of taste, smell, heat, sound, and so forth.

At first sight the distinction between the primary and the secondary qualities does not seem to cause any problems; the ideas which emerge from it are thus objective, scientific, in that they represent the matter itself.

And yet, it is this distinction which constitutes the burden of the newly minted empiricism. In fact, if all consciousness is consciousness of self, the only real object that can be born in the mind is an idea. To postulate, like Locke, that ideas may be related to qualities of the things themselves is without any basis. The equation of idea = sensation is dubious, which is a problem, since all empiricism rides upon it.

Berkeley goes to the very end of this equation even as he preserves the basic idea of a consciousness identified with a consciousness of self. Finally, he says, we are certain only about our ideas, and nothing, if not God, could assure us that they have objective value. As soon as we feel a sensation, we should try and discover whether this is a primary or secondary quality without falling into the *petitio principii*. To suggest that solidity is objective and that heat is not is risky business, according to Berkeley. Solidity works for me, diminishes for a stronger person, and diminishes to the point of making no sense whatsoever for a hypersophisticated machine. On the other hand, when it's 100 degrees in the shade, just try to convince me that this is but a sensation, and that the exterior world is not in fact hot.

Berkeley makes Locke's position radical by searching out coherence, and he concludes that consciousness, which is transparent to itself, only knows itself through sensations, and that therefore nothing permits him to affirm that they have a substratum which supports them.

Skepticism was not far away: if we do away with God, we leave Berkeley and arrive back at Hume.

One might reasonably ask what relationship exists between this and the theory of passions. At first glance, nothing. In fact, what has to be explained here is the relative absence of the passions in empiricism, right up to Hume, who relies heavily upon it when he introduces the Ego and the human person into his system. The response to this apparent enigma is simple: from the moment when the philosopher closes consciousness upon itself and no longer conceives of it except in terms of lucid adherence to the self, there is no place for the passions. Locke speaks of uneasiness to signify a hiatus which divides the consciousness, but the role that he accords it is of little importance, for it is true that reflexive transparency is as unfounded as thoughtlessness. We don't evacuate passionality, even when its explicative function is weak.

It is finally with Hume that the passions surge back with force.[53] For Hume, consciousness doubles up by sensible impressions and relations that reflect them. From there emerge abstraction, concepts, and ideas. The external consciousness and the consciousness of self must be distinguished here. For rationalism, passionality is the sensible rupture; for empiricism, passion could only be the consciousness of self, a tiny island in a sensible sea. In any event, it is the Other *par excellence,* and is that which seems to escape the general premises. Passion is empirical, and is a way of transforming into the sensible that which manifestly refuses to be reduced (reflection).

Although Locke distinguishes between sensation and reflection, he nevertheless brings them back to the ideas that the mind forms by observing its own contents, a conclusion that Hume did not consider empiricist.

For him, ideas are derived from impressions. They double the impressions, rather than becoming substitutes for them. The consciousness is first and foremost sensible, and therefore thoughtless. While Locke brings together the operations and the contents of consciousness into ideas, Hume reserves this term in order to designate the contents that are peculiar to a reflexive consciousness.

Since the consciousness of self becomes autonomous as a non-sensible support for sensible impressions, it is necessary to reduce this secondary

53. I have dealt with this at length in the introduction and commentary to David Hume's *Réflexions sur les passions* (Paris: Le Livre de Poche, Classiques de la Philosophie, 1990).

consciousness to the primary one without annulling the differences that exist between them. This is the squaring of the circle, the nth example of the paradox of the passions. Passions create the difference that is not supposed to exist, and which occurs in a single and undivided consciousness that is turned toward both the external world and itself.

For Hume, passions explain humanity, morality, society, and justice as well as egoism. As many notions as there are passions, says he. Passions arise out of the sensible, and they are sensible without being.

Reason is itself the fruit of passion, like a non-sensible reaction to what is sensible. It serves passion, extends it, and is its very instrument: "What we commonly understand by *passion* is a violent and sensible emotion of mind, when any good or evil is presented, or any object, which, by the original formation of our faculties, is fitted to excite an appetite. By *reason* we mean affections of the very same kind with the former; but such as operate more calmly, and cause no disorder in the temper."[54]

Passion permits us to give a certain consistency to a personal Ego, which empiricism condemns to an uncertain status. If everything is but a sensation in the soul, then is the soul itself just another sensation, or is it something beyond us, necessarily incomprehensible to an empiricism which by its very nature knows nothing that exists beyond us? Consciousness of self is both natural and empirical, without being either, because it is *not* the sensible consciousness. A sensible reflexivity always remains a contradiction in terms, something that Hume himself admits: "But upon a more strict review of the section concerning *personal identity*, I find myself involv'd in such a labyrinth, that, I must confess, I neither know how to correct my former opinions, nor how to render them consistent.... For my part, I must plead the privilege of a sceptic, and confess, that this difficulty is too hard for my understanding."[55]

The Ego that brings together perceptions without being one itself forever causes insoluble problems for empiricism. Passion aims to resolve it in terms of *I feel*, and this by a range of methods as diverse as there are objects that affect us. I am not interested in objects in the external world except as regards the effect they have upon me, in terms of what I'm looking for and what for me is useful. Reason in this sense is the daughter of passion, and my Ego is always the indirect object: this either flatters me or it doesn't, pleases me or it doesn't, honors me or it doesn't, enriches me or it doesn't, and so forth.

---

54. David Hume, *A Treatise of Human Nature* (Oxford: Clarendon Press, 1896), p. 437.
55. Ibid., pp. 633 and 636.

In short, passion solidifies the contradiction of a non-sensible entity in a doctrine which contains only sensible things. It evacuates contradictions and incompatible couplings, like the empirical Ego, the consciousness of the sensible self, the reflection as sensation, which are hereby gathered up into one unique notion, passion, which is destined to create coherence where it is difficult to find.

In rationalism I wasn't aware of what I was looking for because passion acted as a screen, to the point of making us forget even its presence. This is the source of the thesis of a passion which must reflect upon itself and, by doing so, points out that it is itself an obstacle that must be overcome; as such it renders reason both useful and possible because through it reason knows what it has to overcome. This is to forget, however, that everything is a given, even victory. Is it useful to once again demystify passion if it is already so on account of the postulate of reason which was able to establish itself on its own, as though by miracle, and thereby propel itself *beyond* passion that forbids it and *in* passion that makes it conscious? We began with the impossibility of reason and we are now into its uselessness, because illusion has been unveiled as such, suppressing by the same token the obstacle that was the source of blindness. Here passion must be both ignored and understood, or by the combination of two contradictory positions, it must be known but without letting knowledge of it change anything, on account of the weakness of the will. Morality compensates for reason, which is powerless. But isn't morality rational? How is it possible to convince someone to stop drinking when he is too weak to stop, even though he is aware of his lethal passion?

Beside this we have the thesis of the empiricists, for whom from the sensible stage I already know everything I can and must know. There it is useless to reason; hence the role that passions play. They make reason useful because they make it distinct from sensibility.

These are debatable solutions, because the passions concluded by rendering reason impossible, because they lead us to blindness. And in empiricism, even though reason emerges from passion, it is so difficult to distinguish them that we have the impression that reason is thereby abolished. Hume's skepticism becomes at that point inevitable.

If we look closely, we'll find that passion serves to reverse the tendency in rationalism as it does in empiricism; it is necessary to render possible the impossible, render useful what is useless. Passion was useful for rationalism because it became that which had to be countered; for empiricism passion is necessary because reason would otherwise be rendered useless, incomprehensible in fact, with regard to sensible impressions. Passion is, and makes, difference. There is no longer any question of denigrating it, and Hume is consistent in this regard.

Passion is supposed to resolve the paradox of Menon, but in fact it simply reaffirms the paradoxes it tried to eliminate. Through passion I cannot but ignore what I seek, but if I know it to the point of unmasking it, I no longer need to search for truth, which has been found. The problem of Menon remains intact.

Passion is the difference, the problem that (propositional) reason itself creates in order to render itself useful and possible: it is ignored and known at the same time, ignored in order to be operational, known in order to be surpassed. But isn't this a bit much?

Be this what it may, passion for Hume aims to account for a consciousness of self that is aligned with the sensible consciousness, which leads to and blocks fusion. It orients us toward the other-than-self even as it makes us feel the self, a self that remains inaccessible despite everything. The problem, even though the inverse of the one we found in rationalism, resurfaces: it could but demand that both of these basic tendencies be overcome.

6

The Mirrors of the Sensible

Morals, Aesthetics, and History

Beyond Rationalism and Empiricism

Rationalism placed all of its emphasis upon the consciousness of the self, which is exteriorized by passion. Since this passion represents a form of consciousness without being conscious, but consciousness all the same, passion is deemed to be a fusion of illusion and a kind of alienation. Passion is therefore an impossible synthesis of two different levels of consciousness; it maintains the identity of consciousness through a kind of necessity, a destiny that is destined to fail.

Similarly, empiricism, which is based upon the sensible consciousness, turned the consciousness of self into the locus of passion *par excellence*. The era of the sentiment was thus brought into existence, with the point of origin being sensibility.

Passion becomes the difference that creates the *Ego* in the tissue of sensations, of which it is part, without the power. The enigma of the Ego,[1] for Hume, is the enigma of passion, which makes of reflection a kind of sensibility. Reflection is as necessary to empiricism as it is impossible.

For Kant, consciousness is not more sensible than intellectual; it is both. But the problem remains of how to articulate them. Understanding and sensibility, if you will. The unity of the subject demands this, but

---

1. [I'm using "Ego" to correspond to the author's *Moi* throughout. *Trans.*]

whether it be reason or imagination that incorporates sensibility and understanding, the passions are integrated in a pure subjectivity which dominates everything.

Kantianism expresses the universalization of this subjectivity, a subjectivity that empiricism scatters into discrete units, each deemed "passionate." There is no more subject in all of these "subjects," and each one is now devoid of links to the others, with the exception of this absence of community. Morality, like science, finds itself under attack on this account. With Kant humanity is above nature, but it nevertheless remains a part thereof. By thinking about it, human beings show themselves to be the ones who can consider it from the outside, from the exterior, if only on account of the concepts of the imagination. This is the source of the metaphysical character of the human condition. All the antinomies of reason, which lead it into contradiction with itself if it's not careful, flow from this double inscription: human beings are in nature as natural living beings, but outside nature on account of their thinking because there is nothing natural about saying that one is natural. In this sense, reason affirms their liberty and gives them a proper determination with regard to the determination which rules over the natural order of things (determinism). A double reality is implied here for humanity: as natural beings, they are limited by the sensible, which affects and determines them; but as intelligible beings, they think about the fact that they think about nature, which situates them outside these very determinisms: Kant's view, expressed in *The Metaphysics of Morals*, is that the concept of an intelligible world is nothing more than a *point of view*, which reason is obliged to adopt outside phenomena *as a means of conceiving of itself as practice*, which would not be possible if the influences of the sensible were determinant for human beings.[2]

This liberty, which human beings express by thinking about themselves, is the result of the fact that they are alone in nature as being able to reflect, and this is not in itself a natural fact, a determination that is inherent to physical or chemical laws. Against Spinoza, Kant affirms a real liberty as being beyond nature. Nevertheless, human beings are double in the sense that they are determined and free to determine themselves, so the question remains to know how beings that are guided by their affects and by their passions, their desires and their interests, could be bought to renounce them (affects, passions) in the name of moral reasons, of self-determination. It is clear that the autonomy of the

2. Kant, *The Metaphysics of Morals*, IV, trans. Mary Gregor (New York: Cambridge University Press, 1991).

will expresses the (metaphysical) *possibility* of putting moral duty to work, but this autonomy is quite hypothetical. If morality is possible as an application of norms that issue from the intellectual or intelligible part of the human reality, which escapes from determinism and which could impose its own laws of how to act, it is nevertheless the case that human beings have a sensible part that is the source of multiple pleasures and personal interests, which they are unwilling to let go of easily. So when they demonstrate this reluctance, are they not acting in accord with their nature? This would have to be the case unless we imagine that it is in our nature not to have a specific nature, which is paradoxical, just as the transformation of will into moral will. Morality is a pure metaphysical given.

Kant delimits three spheres of human reality that emerge as a consequence of this transcendence.

First, there is the one that thinks about human beings thinking in nature. This reflects the fact that human thinking as such situates human beings outside nature, as intelligible beings. This is like saying that human beings transcend nature and by doing so nature remains inaccessible to them. The only things they can grasp, from their external point of view, are things as they appear to them. The phenomena and the noumena, the knowable and the unknowable, the appearance and its ultimate substratum, remain inaccessible to humanity. Consciousness, which comes along with all possible knowledge that humanity could have about the world, can but return them to this transcendence as regards nature. It projects categories that are un-natural, human, which consecrates the dividing line between nature in itself, which remains a mystery, and what humanity can actually perceive in nature. Since they are a part of nature, their thoughts about nature must correspond to what nature is, according to the constraints of sensibility, which imprints the limits of the possible separation between pure and limitless projection and the mechanical reflection that is conditioned by the object. The *Critique of Pure Reason* is the study of this knowledge of nature and of its limits for humankind.

By the same token this is revealed to human beings themselves as beings in nature. This is in a certain sense equivalent to affirming a liberty toward natural determinism, awareness which is the fruit of distance, all intellectual, indeed, and expressing the objectification of which human beings are capable *a priori*. In reality this transcendence reflects the moral fact, auto-determination, auto-affection, which pushes human beings to transcend sensible conditions. But human beings are free to be not free, as they are free to be free. And the use of liberty extends to not exercising it, paradoxically. *The Study of Practical Reason* is the study of this possibility for auto-determination of the will.

By discovering that they are free, above the grasp of nature, human beings reveal their natural belonging, if only to orient themselves. They show themselves that they have desires, ends, in the fashion of every-thing that exists in nature, but their objectification permits them to perceive themselves as naturally desiring beings, even if the desires themselves are not natural, and are not naturally determined. Desire is perceived as such by human beings, which is not the case for a plant, and by the same token the ends are exterior to their desires, which leads to the fact that desire imposes itself *as* desire. An immanent end would have abolished desire as such, desire which is defined only as a lack, a distance of which the end, which comes from the outside, is the sign. Desire is a tension that difference with its end maintains as such to the mind. Desire which surprises human beings who contemplate their own natural exigencies puts them into the presence of what they will call "human nature," which constitutes this desire as the expression of what is natural *and* transcendent.

There is in the faculty of desire (Kant) that which reflects upon itself an awareness of liberty as regards external ends, but there is as well the possible universality of desire. This is the meaning of the Kantian imper-ative in morals; to make it such that a particular will be universalizable. Human nature only becomes human if this occurs, and it tears itself away from the natural world in order to effect this movement. Humanity is nature that is no longer natural. In this sense, we can speak of humanity as an unstable concept. Desire that we bring to consciousness is a notion that situates us in nature, and also liberates us from it because we reflect upon this desire as such, with its immanent non-realization and the satis-factions obtained on account of the end which falls beyond our reach. Desire is therefore universal because it reflects us as free with respect to the sensible and particular world. Particular desire appears as a contradic-tion in terms, a conceptual error, which pushes us to act inappropriately on account of a lack of metaphysics and of adequate reflection.

For Kant, we are situated between nature and history, in a problematic field of rational desire as foundation of action. To think about nature, and therefore desire, is to situate oneself beyond nature by universalizing desire as practical reason that is common to all humanity.

But a third dimension emerges from the simple reflection of human-ity concerning its nature.

We contemplate our nature in its pure transcendence, freely and with-out taking into account our knowledge of nature or our possible action upon nature; in short, we contemplate nature for our own pleasure. The pleasure of reflecting upon our "nature," that is, of our humanity, is the object of Kant's third *Critique*, devoted to the faculty of judgment. The mind contemplates its own reflexivity for its own sake, and it discovers the play of its faculties; it gazes at itself, but this is not a Cartesian admiration, because this contemplation is passionless. By examining ourselves, we observe what is universal and project this universality upon specific things that we find "to our taste." The aesthetic judgment is born of this reflection; it operates in the faculty of judgment when the subject takes itself for a pure object not for self-knowledge, but as free subjectivity which discovers what it can do as such. The word "object" is perhaps not well chosen, if we wish to speak of this unknowable (only knowledge has an object) which is the subject for itself.

Three *Critiques*, three faculties, that of knowing, that of desiring, and that of judging with regard to the sense of pleasure and displeasure. Notice that the passions should appear in the domain of sensibility on three levels: that of knowledge, that of interests, and that of pleasure. Yet each time sensibility, even though it was exalted, has been brought to heel. Divided among these three functions, it nevertheless belongs to the general unity of the subject and, as such, expresses it. Nevertheless, the Ego integrates sensibility, and since it was the locus of the passions, the Ego becomes in its very activity a passionate being. Romanticism points toward the horizon. To have a passion is no longer to just manifest a passivity, but hereafter it is a part of the very activity of the self, of its nature and its character.

Kant is the source of this reversal, at least for the domain of philosophy. Yet the least we can say is that he is no friend of the passions. He doesn't have to use them as part of his system, since the external consciousness and the reflexive consciousness, transformed into faculties of the mind, integrate into the unity and the identity of the pure subject.

Reason Above All Passion

With Kant we speak only of sensibility. It is now an *integrated sensibility*, which signifies that it is now subsumed to reason, and thus to universality (the rule of morals). We are outside passions, since we think about ourselves *outside nature* when thinking about nature. The problem of the passions is evacuated and with it goes the problem of access to morals, to the universal, and the renunciation of sensible passions. But what makes us wish to effect this renunciation if not the moral law itself? How could this emerge if not from the renunciation of all passions that it requires? The circle is complete: reason imposes itself. Kant will make of this liberty a kind of incomprehensible mystery.

Let's go back to the theoretical issues raised in the *Critique of Pure Reason*. Kant's work articulates the relation to consciousness in a new way. The consciousness of the self and the consciousness of the object are both different and identical, since they form the consciousness; this is the eternal problem. What is new here is the way that he takes it up. It is necessary that the object be already given so that knowledge can take possession of it—and know that this is even possible—but it is also necessary that this object be unknown from the start, so that this very process be rendered useful. These two theses combine to form a paradox, the paradox of the object, a singular and double object.

Kant is obliged to say that it is the same object that is given to the sensible consciousness and to understanding, *and* he has to further contend that this is not the same object, which means that this intellectual, reflexive, and abstract consciousness is useful. Two objects which make one, this is the phenomenon and the noumenon, the thing as it appears and the thing in itself. Two consciousnesses which make but one, that which manifests itself in the sensible world and that which unifies by, or through, understanding. The global unity of this subjectivity is unknowable, since it is itself a nonphenomenal entity, pure reflexivity at work, if you wish. The unity of consciousness, like that of the object, is very enigmatic. It can't be the object of knowledge. The consciousness is at once conscious of itself and of other things. To make an amalgam of them would be to fall into a *paralogism;* but what else is there to do? By admitting identity and difference, Kant doesn't have to appeal to any theory of passions in order to restore coherence, because he thinks he can establish it by evacuating in the supra-sensible whatever is contradictory and paradoxical.

If passion seems useless in the framework of Kantian thought, it is because the human mind is always beyond what passion is supposed to impede—reason. The difference between reason and passion is incarnated in the scission between understanding and sensibility. The noumenal identity of the intelligible consciousness, as consciousness of itself, guarantees *a priori* the overcoming of this difference.

It is true that what is left is the whole practical domain. There, clearly, the passions guide and mobilize those of us who don't give up our confrontations with one another. Sensibility delineates itself through strong inclinations and interests, sources of pleasure that are always desired. By thinking about nature, we show ourselves to be beyond it, but only on account of our reason, because our sensibility roots us in a nature that can but affect our very *humanity*.

Emancipated human beings are those who can liberate themselves from passion's grip, as opposed to the political minority of humanity which remain its slave.

History hereby explains the accession of the reign of reason, that is, the overcoming of the natural in human beings. But how is it possible to take into account the possibility in us of going beyond what is natural in us? For Kant, how to explain this is precisely the problem that we cannot resolve.

In order to motivate transcendence as regards the sensible, for Kant, it is necessary to have an interest and a pleasure that is related to the accomplishment of moral duty, but it is impossible to understand, that is, to explain *a priori* how a simple idea, which contains in itself nothing sensible, produces a sentiment of pleasure or pain.

Kant doesn't explain how one goes beyond the sensible to take possession of moral law: it is necessary to want to be moral in order for moral law to occur, but this very will could not rest upon moral law alone, which makes it good. Even if this critique of Kantian morality is well known among specialists, it is not any less important here because it illustrates the consequences of the *a priori* evacuation of the passions, which are there but ignored, in a conception which situates itself in the mysterious domain of the intelligible, rational, and abstract.

What remains is the metaphysical or historicist hypotheses, which consist of noting that we situate ourselves through our nature, through our reason, above all that is natural, and that this moment of coming to consciousness happens on account of emancipation, to the political majority of human beings: the *Aufklärung*. How is it possible to prove that we are the beings in nature who are not natural, *in our very essence?* Kant himself admits that this is inexplicable. All the more so since this represents a paradoxical formulation, just like its inverse, which would affirm that it is in nature of human beings to be only natural, which assigns them to a lost paradise, and an identity that they must rediscover.

If it is in the nature of humans to transcend nature, then it is a universal function, which turns moral imperative into an ahistorical universality. Nevertheless, Kant attributes the ability to overcome passion to the politico-historical emancipation of humanity. Through atemporal ethical formalism, he seems to take back from history that which he'd already credited to it, something that Hegel would later see in his suggestion that passion be considered the present of a History that has been assimilated to reason, which thus overcomes passion through the force of time.

Deprived of any content, taken from History or from sensible matter, the categorical imperative is necessarily purely formal on account of its formal content; the form of moral law is necessity (apodicticity), which applies to everyone (universality), but unless it is a goal in itself, as Kant suggests, it takes but the empty form of norms which escape it. In this sense, Kant doesn't defend any particular morality, he establishes the conditions of all possible morals. But as soon as he makes universal imperative into a goal, that is, the content of the morality, he begs the question, the petition of the principle, then he defends *a priori* a certain morality of the universal in the name of reason, which expresses the human in human nature:

> Don't we have a problem here? How can Kant reconcile this new principle (that the will cannot be determined without a concept of ends) with the more fundamental ethical principle of knowing that a will which is determined by an end is "het-eronomous"? . . . The problem of the translation from formal law to the final concept of sovereign good emerges from a specific difficulty. Kant insists upon fact that the moral law itself establishes the final goal and that it does so *a priori*. Yet it is clear that the idea of a sovereign good isn't derived from the concept of pure will as such. It comes from a philosophical reconsideration of diverse empirical factors such as man's natural aspirations toward happiness; or the natural interest that he has in the result of his actions and, more generally, the empirical conditions of the world in which will must act.[3]

In this Kant puts aside the sensible and the particular. Prior to emancipation through reason, wisdom must go through the rejection of the passions. With emancipation it is necessarily beyond the self; it can ignore them, since it is beyond the self *in principle* (naturally?).

> The principle of apathy—namely, that the sage must never be in a state of emotional agitation, not even in that of sympathetic sorrow over his best friend's misfortune—is quite a correct and sublime moral principle of the Stoic school; for an affect makes

---

3. Y. Yovel, *Kant et la philosophie de l'Histoire* (Paris: Méridiens-Klincksieck, 1989), pp. 41–42.

us (more or less) blind. But it was still wisdom on nature's part
to implant in us the predisposition to sympathy, so that it could
handle the reins provisionally, until reason has achieved the necessary strength; that is to say, it was wise of nature to add to our
moral incentives to the good the incentive of pathological (sen-
suous) impulse, to serve as a temporary substitute for reason.[4]

If emotions present some positive virtues, for example, when reason
guides enthusiasm and imposes its mark upon moral sensibility, they
bring with them the formation of negative passions. They are in fact per-
versions of reason, in that they are the product of reflection, which reinforces *natural* emotion, by transforming emotion into pure judgment.
From there, "*Affections* and *passions* are essentially distinct; the first
comes from *sentiment* in the sense that it, preceding reflection, makes it
impossible, or more difficult."[5]

Since passion is constituted through reflection subjugated to the sensible, "it is always connected with reason."[6] In conclusion: "It is easy to
see that passions do the greatest damage to freedom, because they are
consistent with the calmest reflection, so that they need not be thoughtless, like affects, and consequently stormy and transitory, but tend to get
themselves rooted and can co-exist even with subtle reasoning."[7]

The Ambivalence of Kantianism:
From Integrated Sensibility to Romantic Sensibility

In Kantianism, the restriction of sensibility is clear. It was necessary to
save reason from various efforts to erode it, from empiricists to skep-
tics. The era in question here is not one that rejected passions, either
in practice or in theory. "Nothing great happens without passions," says
Helvetius, a formula taken up by Kant, to contest him, and Hegel, to support him. Diderot writes:

> People are forever declaiming against the passions; they attribute
> to them all the pains that man endures, and forget that they are
> also the source of all his pleasures. It is an ingredient in man's
> constitution which cannot sufficiently be blessed and banned. It
> is considered as an affront to reason if one ventures to say a

4. Kant. *Anthropology*, sec. 75, p. 121.
5. Kant, *The Metaphysics of Morals*, VI, p. 408.
6. Kant, *Anthropology,* sec. 75, p. 133.
7. Ibid.

word in favour of its rivals; yet it is passions alone, and strong passions, that can elevate the soul to great things. Without them, there is no sublime, either in morality or in achievement; the fine arts return to puerility, and virtue becomes a pettifogging thing.[8]

For Kant, on the other hand, even aesthetic judgments reinforce the universal. The subjectivity that is at work is the one that we all have or, if you wish, the one that we all have in common, in communication, the one that we have with all others.

But on this side, we cannot but feel a profound ambivalence, which consists, on the one hand, of a search for the universal, which determines the sensible or which reflects (this is the difference between knowledge and aesthetics), and on the other hand, of a transformation of the sensible into a key element of subjectivity. The most particular sensible passion becomes an integral part of Ego. Romanticism is born of this identity of the subject and its sensibility, creating an intellectual symbiosis with what can never be intellectual. Even restricted, sensibility becomes a critical part in the redefinition of the human being, making of the passionate Ego an active Ego, which abandons itself deliberately to what pushes it to the depth of itself. We realize our passions, just like we search for something, in a movement of agitation, excitation, which mobilizes all existence at one moment or another.

We understand from that point onward the tension that runs through Kantianism. On the one side, the universal is dominant; on the other, sensibility is an integrated sensibility which affects the Ego. It even limits it, at least in the theoretical domain. It's sure that Kant postulates a human reality that is outside nature, which situates people outside themselves, in the abstract universal, without passion; but it cannot deny the sensible and particular nature of the human that it characterizes so well. This empty humanity, all metaphysics, which acts as the base of action and which nourishes reflection to the point of nourishing aesthetic pleasure, has difficulty resisting this question of its own reality, if not of its establishment in a manner that is neither ideal or formal.

History and Aesthetics; or, the Explosion of the Universal

All objective perspective upon nature situates us outside nature, in a transcendence which, although unknowable, is nevertheless thinkable.

---

8. Diderot, *Philosophic Thoughts* 1, in Diderot's *Early Philosophical Works,* trans. and ed. Margaret Jourdain (New York: Burt Franklin, 1972), p. 27.

Is the kingdom of the intelligible, of the supra-sensible, where we are all equals, accessible here?

The whole question is there: what is the status of the surpassing that is reduced to the Idea? If we hold to Kant's ideas, then we must distinguish ourselves from that natural world for the benefit of the universal, of the human, and we mustn't lose sight of the fact that the natural world is there, and that this world affects us. To square off "human, typically human" against "human, too human" is a difficult game to play; but Kant decrees that it is possible *a priori,* necessary in fact, but this is but a decree, of reason for reason's sake.

Transcendence in human beings is both postulated and denied, divided between two worlds, the sensible world of nature and the world of ideas, which is the reign of the most abstract universality. Since our nature draws us in a gravitational fashion toward the sensible, which is undeniable, then the empty universality which dogs Kantian thought cannot survive the critical question of its own foundation. This transcendence leading to aesthetics is a fiction unless we can make this into a historical emancipation characteristic of the Enlightenment. History or aesthetics? Kant brings everything down to the level of the abstract universality of the moral idea; so he establishes himself within a rationality that is rendered empty, without natural content, which is always a product of the world and contingent necessities of the real world. The romantic return to natural sensibility becomes inevitable in these conditions.

In fact, two visions emerge and redouble upon themselves in response to this unreferential transcendence that is found in Kant's work. As we said, the *first* postulates what exists beyond nature as historical fact, as becoming; the *second* postulates that it is an aesthetic overcoming, because it restores the rights of sensibility, a sensibility that has become fully aware to the mind, with passions that absorb it or are absorbed into it. Historical universality and aesthetic universality find their respective counterparts in historicism and romanticism, where the individual becomes the norm and the measure. In morality Kantianism is hereby opposed to Nietzscheanism, and the historical universality of Hegel has as its antithesis a certain romanticism, deemed historicist or naturalist, but which privileges the particularity in each case. The aesthetic particularizes, just as ethics and history do.

If what is *natural* is perceived as being before the *universal* being, then the overcoming[9] will be singularized, and if it is historical, then we

---

9. Kant postulates this overcoming in his result without absorbing the question of the movement which drives it. For him, this is a mystery, like metaphysical liberty.

will have historicism, and if it is aesthetic, we will have romanticism. At the end of the day, the two will mix together.

On the other hand, if what is perceived as *natural* manifests itself in us in a *particularized* fashion, then the overcoming thereof which is always historical (but never historicist) becomes the seat of a renewed rationality, necessarily universal, as in the work of Hegel or Marx. Notice that this overcoming, as dialectic, spills over the relation with nature; it involves in a more general sense of a link with everything that is individualized in us.

Finally, if this overcoming of nature is natural, then it becomes a fiction, because this overcoming is an extension, just like morals and savage nature are in the work of Nietzsche.

We who overcome nature, who overcome All, exist in a space where there is nothing other than metaphysical fictions, appearances, and fables. Individuality is now nothing more than instinct and the will to affirm, if nature is *particularity* and it is furthered in us as individuality. It is natural to overcome nature and, in so doing, to repeat it in an "eternal return of the same."

On the other hand, if we keep the *universality* of nature, as though to say "what is natural for all people," "what everyone should need and should conform to," then what is beyond nature, which is the domain of the human, becomes the singular affirmation of this natural state (as though it represented what is beyond itself). In the first case, we have the ideas of Nietzsche; in the second, romanticism.

We must consider that even if we make the natural into something universal, we necessarily fall upon the particular because nature is both one and the other. Each one, being singular, is finally like all others, and all others, since they are affected by sensibility, reveal themselves as being different one from the other. *Nature,* as nature, shows itself to be Nature itself, and the particular becomes the prerogative of all things. Romanticism and historicism end up joining together.

Kantianism

The starting point of this denaturalization is Kant, who sees human beings as affirming themselves as such, even if historicity and aestheticization are contained in them, and lead them to abandon this universality as a means of realizing it. We are liberty and desire, but also contemplation of ourselves in that we are not necessarily outside nature. Thinking thinks about itself, as a *faculty of judgment* or as pure and disinterested reflection. Humanity is its own end in that the mind derives pleasure

from this spirituality, without any practical will or adjacent interests.[10]
Nature is most certainly universal because it is determined by laws; but
the fact of thinking about them and of reflecting upon us thinking about
them implies for Kant a free universality made up of the relation to
understanding which mires sensibility, and mires itself, while doing it
under the aegis of an all-encompassing faculty of imagination. The universal reappears in this reflection that we address to our own subjectivity as human beings: "Now this merely subjective (aesthetic) judging of
the object, or of the presentation by which it is given, precedes the pleasure in the object and is the basis of this pleasure, a pleasure in the harmony of the cognitive powers. But the universal subjective validity of
this liking, the liking we connect with the presentation of the object we
call beautiful, is based solely on the mentioned universality of the subjective conditions for judging objects."[11]

The radical break of reason with the sensible coincides with the eradication of passions, but the unavoidable character of the sensible ends
with the rendering of passions into aesthetic entities. Universality swallows everything, including natural differences. It is no longer necessary
to struggle against that which we can *a priori* avoid, both theoretical
and practical. This is true in morality, in science, but also in aesthetics:
"A pure judgment of taste is one that is not influenced by charm or emotion and whose determining basis is therefore merely the purposiveness
of the form."[12]

But we cannot eliminate the passionate without seeing it surge up
elsewhere, in the unavoidable breaks of consciousness and reflection.

This displacement is particularly visible in certain key ideas of Kantian
aesthetics. Consciousness that feels surprised by the *sublime* majesty of
nature necessitates a doubling of this same terrorized consciousness.

The distance between sensible consciousness and intellectual consciousness gives birth to this sentiment of the sublime:

> For what is sublime, in the proper meaning of the term, cannot
> be contained in any sensible form but concerns only ideas of
> reason, which, though they cannot be exhibited adequately, are
> aroused and called to mind by this very inadequacy, which can
> be exhibited in sensibility. Thus the vast ocean heaved up by
> storms cannot be called sublime. The sight of it is horrible; and

10. Kant, *Critique of Judgment*, I, sec. 6, trans. Werner S. Phular (Indianapolis: Hackett, 1987),
p. 139.
11. Ibid., sec. 9.
12. Kant, *Critique of Judgment*, I, sec. 13.

one must already have filled one's mind with all sorts of ideas if such an intuition is to attune it to a feeling that is itself sublime, inasmuch as the mind is induced to abandon sensibility and occupy itself with ideas containing a higher purposiveness.[13]

Naturally, the sublime rattles and destabilizes the consciousness by making it aware of its own shaky character:

> In presenting the sublime in nature the mind feels agitated, while in an aesthetic judgment about the beautiful in nature it is in rest-ful contemplation. This agitation can be compared with a vibra-tion, with a rapid alteration of repulsion from, and attraction to, one and the same object. If a thing is excessive for the imagina-tion (and the imagination is driven to such [excess] as it appre-hends [the thing] in intuition), then the thing is, as it were, an abyss in which the imagination is afraid to lose itself. Yet, at the same time, for reason's idea of the supersensible is not excessive but conforms to reason's law to give rise to such striving by the imagination. Hence the thing is now attractive to the same degree to which formerly it was repulsive to mere sensibility.[14]

The passions follow suit: "For when we judge something aesthetically without a concept, the only way we can judge a superiority over obstacles is by the magnitude of the resistance. But whatever we strive to resist is an evil, and it is an object of fear if we find that our ability to resist it is no match for it. . . . Hence nature can count as a might, and so as dynam-ically sublime, for aesthetic judgment only insofar as we consider it as an object of fear."[15]

The mind experiences its limits, outside nature, as mind or, rather, as a faculty of reasoning that is capable of looking upon infinity:

> And since in contrast to this standard everything in nature is small, we found in our mind a superiority over nature itself in its immensity. In the same way, though the irresistibility of nature's might makes us, considered as natural beings, recognize our phys-ical impotence, it reveals in us at the same time an ability to judge ourselves independent of nature, and reveals in us a superiority

13. Ibid., I, sec. 23.
14. Ibid., sec. 27.
15. Ibid., sec. 28.

over nature that is the basis of a self-preservation quite different in kind from the one that can be assailed from attacks by nature outside us. This keeps the humanity in our person from being degraded, even though a human being would have to succumb to that dominance of nature. Hence if in judging nature aesthetically we call it sublime, we do so not because nature arouses fear, but because it calls forth our strength within us, to regard as small the objects of our natural concerns: property, health, and life, and because of this we regard nature's might to which we are indeed subjected in these natural concerns as yet not having such dominance over us, as persons, that we should not have to bow to it if our highest principles were at stake and we had to choose between upholding or abandoning them. Hence nature is here called sublime merely because it elevates our imagination, making it exhibit those cases where the mind can come to feel its own sublimity, which lies in its vocation and elevates it even above nature.[16]

The Cartesian admiration led to an awareness of the limits of consciousness.

The question which must be asked, and which should lead us to the third figure, Nietzsche, is to find out why transcendence when considered as regards nature must belong to the field of the aesthetic. Until now we have assumed, following Kant, that this was obvious. We have a (natural?) tendency to reflect upon ourselves in our own subjectivity, which tears us away from nature, even if it means terrifying us into about what such a "forgetfulness" might lead to. Nature, in its majesty and its constraints, won't disappear for very long.

The response to the question asked is short. The exterior position that we take in our contemplation of nature means that through this contemplation we escape the Wholeness of things of which we are naturally a part.

This overview, as an unnatural surpassing of the natural, as a working out of the Idea, beyond the impassable sensible world, cannot be anything more than a fiction for each of us, who in fact live in the sensible world. To reflect upon it as such is *imaginary*. The aesthetic founds itself in this fiction and in this imaginary. To describe the sensible from this point of view is not a question of truth, because this is illusory because the mind is above it. To think about the sensible as such is not a matter

16. Ibid.

for science, but for aesthetics. Is asserting truth the indication of the greatest error?

The human condition is tragic: to think about nature in which we evolve, we necessarily leave this same nature. By thinking, we survey the Whole of which we are part. But this is not possible, since outside the Whole, there is nothing, which is proof that this is a fiction or that, since we thought that it was possible, that it is metaphysics. Is there another world that is above our own, and which would allow us to perceive the limits of our world? This is nothing other than a story, an illusion, and even the priest's withdrawal is situated inside nature as a mode to dominate nature and other persons. Everything is natural, including the fiction of believing and making others believe the contrary.

This explains the fascination that Nietzsche had for the sciences. But he also defends the opposite thesis. The truth implies that we describe nature and the Whole from the inside, a proposition which autodestructs as soon as it is uttered because, to utter it, we must make nature into an objective Whole, and situate ourselves outside nature in order to accomplish it. What was analytical, partial, and immanent truth emerges from a point of view which is nothing other than appearance. There are two alternatives, either truth remains defined in the most classical manner imaginable, and it rests upon a fiction or it is fiction, and art in general, which becomes the most authentic truth. Immanent truth is now nothing more than a tricky illusion, which postulates a world (Nietzsche) which doesn't exist in order to make its point valid. Absolute immanence requires a transcendence in order to speak out; fiction from the outside, is in fact a reality from the inside, which is not recognized. Absolute transcendence, which is illusory and which sends us back to immanence, sends us into a kind of endless ping-pong game between truth and appearance, illusion and knowledge, art and reality.

The passions are natural for Nietzsche, and they are also the concept of an illusion, of a condemnation; in short, they are part of a rationality and a morality which occults the passionate, which they express as the will to power.

The paradox remains; passion is natural and it is a construct, for which demystification should signify suppression. But if the passions are the very nature at work, are they still the construction of a sick and powerless reason?

As for morality, it finds itself in the emptiness of natural overcoming which disorients us, deprived of our traditional reference points. The hero, the creator, and not the imitator become for Nietzsche the symbols for the reversal of values or, if you will, for the creation of other values.

History, or How the Real Becomes Rational (or Vice Versa)

We reveal ourselves as above nature because we are, from a historical standpoint.[17] This natural state is singular; it is both present and individual at the same time.

The distance imposes itself here as a fact of History, the veritable and concrete space of reality and human actuality; this History is the living incarnation of this transcendence, while passion divides, individuates, and by so doing marks present time. Reason, on the other hand, reconciles by overcoming the natural contradictions of humanity: "Passion is first of all the subjective side, being the formal side, of energy, of will, and of activity, the content or the goal being still undetermined. It comes as well from personal conviction, personal thinking, and personal consciousness. . . . I would say, therefore, passion, understanding from this the particular determination of character in terms of these determinations of will, doesn't have a uniquely private content, but constitutes the driving and energetic element of general actions."[18]

As for the goal, the materiality of passion, it manifests itself as existence which incarnates and realizes particularity: "Calling interest a passion, as the whole individuality, by placing all other interests and ends that we have or could have into the background, projects itself into an object with all the interior fibers of its will, concentrates in this end all of its needs and all of its forces, we should say in a general fashion that *nothing great is accomplished in this world without passion*. As such, two elements intervene in our subject: one is the idea, the other, the human passions."[19]

History transcends the shock of passions, and makes them equal in a rationality that comes *after the fact*, and which gives them meaning; this is a well-known thesis in Hegel's work. What is worth underlining here is the universal aspect of this historicity, a universality that is concentrated in the State, which brings together and coordinates individual wills. Nature, and therefore passion, finds itself surpassed in History, which permits us to render nature objective from a point of view that for it is exterior.

---

17. It is the case for Hegel that nature is not reduced either to a particularity or to a universal, even if the natural is linked in humanity to a biological and individual existence. The passage to the universal is hereby conceived of historically, rather than *a priori*, as was the case in Kant. The result is universal, and that is what counts here.

18. Hegel, *Hegel's Lectures on the History of Philosophy,* trans. E. S. Haldane, 3 vols. (London: Routledge & Kegan Paul, 1955), p. 31.

19. Ibid.

A New Vision of the Natural, or the Return of Instincts

The natural is seen as particular, as being constantly differentiated. Individuals are naturally above nature even as they are inside it, since, according to Nietzsche, it is in their savage nature that they best reestablish their perversity, that is, their spirituality.[20] We don't return to nature, as Rousseau suggested; we are naturally moral because we are simply natural![21] Individuality is in all of us, which renders the process universal and which seems to denaturalize it at the same time. This is the origin of Nietzsche's "moral naturalism," which consists of "translating moral values that are apparently emancipated and denatured, according to their "nature," that is, their "natural immortality."[22]

There is no longer any nature, only individuality which affirms itself: dissociation no longer has currency; nature is "indifferent" and dumb.[23] Life is this individual struggle that has no model.

For Nietzsche, everything is natural, including the rejection of the natural, that which the priest practices or extols through his ideal of ascetic renunciation. "Consciousness," that is in this case morality, is therefore a deception, but also an illusion. Sublimation through consciousness remains, and can but remain, as a form of the *will to power*. Sublimated consciousness is ignorant of its own origin, an occultation which makes of consciousness an unconsciousness, a difference through which it is constructed so that it can institute its own identity. In fact, moral asceticism is a mark of superiority and individuation in a nature that undifferentiates beings, and pushes them to selection, to differentiation.

Don't criticize passions, they incarnate the truth of humanity; or attack them, because they are issued from reason in order to sublimate passion by rationalizing the renunciation. There is in passion the trace of condemnation and morals, of decorum which is nothing but vulgar taste. Consciousness is, therefore, the false rupture between nature and its human extension:

> Assuming that nothing real is "given" to us apart from our world of desires and passions, assuming that we cannot ascend or

20. See Friedrich Nietzsche, *Twilight of the Idols,* trans. Duncan Large (Oxford: Oxford University Press, 1998).

21. See Nietzsche, *The Will to Power,* sec. 124, trans. Walter Kaufmann and R. J. Hollingdale, ed. Walter Kaufmann (New York: Vintage, 1967).

22. Ibid., sec. 99.

23. See Terry Eagleton, *The Ideology of the Aesthetic* (Oxford: Oxford University Press, 1990), pp. 249–50.

descend to any "reality" other than the reality of our instincts (for thinking is merely an interrelation of these instincts, one to the other), may we not be allowed to perform an experiment and ask whether this "given" also provides a *sufficient* explanation for the so-called mechanistic (or "material") world? I do not mean the material world as a delusion, as "appearance" or "representation"..., but rather as a world with the same level of reality that our emotion has.[24]

As for the consciousness, it loses sight of its own point of view ("from where it speaks") by communicating what it has to say; it puts itself in the position of judge and master, a humble master in that it is content with reflecting the real, from which it emerges and which it thinks to be able to arrive at overcoming. This unconsciousness of its origin, of its "genealogy," is the essence of this consciousness which is made from an identity with itself through the distanciation of one's own point of view. The eye does not see itself seeing:

> The problem of consciousness (more precisely, of becoming conscious of something) confronts us only when we begin to comprehend how we could dispense with it.... For we could think, feel, will, and remember, and we could also "act" in every sense of that word, and yet none of all this would have to "enter our consciousness" (as one says metaphorically). The whole of life would be possible without, as it were, seeing itself in a mirror. Even now, for that matter, by far the greatest portion of our life actually takes place without this mirror effect; and this is true even of our thinking, feeling, and willing life, however offensive this may sound to older philosophers. *For what purpose,* then, any consciousness at all when it is in the main *superfluous?*[25]

Passion becomes what is natural in consciousness, instead of being a sign of its fissure, if not its foil. But it disappears as fast as it surfaces, in its own negativity, since it was there only to establish pure reason or, moreover, purified reason. Isn't the superman the person who is above reason and passion? Passion is perhaps the superior form of reason, and both passion and reason mutually abolish each other as difference:

24. Nietzsche, *Beyond Good and Evil,* trans. Marion Faber (New York: Oxford University Press, 1998), p. 35.

25. Nietzsche, *The Gay Science, with a prelude in rhymes and an appendix of songs,* 354, trans. Walter Kaufmann (New York: Random House, 1974), p. 297.

"The unreason or counterreason of passion is what the common type despises in the noble."[26]

Morality is the unconsciousness of consciousness, the value that supports it. With the will to power that reproduces it, by affirming itself in an eternal return, the true identity of the self, which is completely natural this time, could be exhibited. Passion is no longer inscribed in the depth of identity, henceforth recognized as undiscoverable by the consciousness.

The natural occultation of what seems to escape nature—moral conscience, asceticism, which pretends to be superior—inverts nature, muddles up the genealogy, and makes passion appear as what it is not: a product of reason, as the Devil is for God. We see in this inversion of nature as morality, the opposition between action and contemplation: "Understanding kills action, for in order to act we require the veil of illusion."[27]

By considering that one is above the world, we are still in the world, and on account of this departure, we refuse to act in it. But this is in fact a part of the world, a tragic and "Dionysian" part, as Nietzsche puts it, since the *hubris* of transcendence is heroic.

Romanticism

A nature that is conceived of as universal cannot be surpassed except through particularity. The individual is the truth of life; the biological, the vital instinct and sensibility, find themselves in the affirmation of the Ego, an Ego that is thus rendered universal.

Transcendence coincides with the isolated Ego. Particularity, if not eccentricity, is hereby considered exalted. Nature prolongs and modifies itself because it is our nature to consider ourselves outside universal nature, legitimizing the most diverse particularities: the group, the nation, the past, or more precisely, *our* past.

Since each person is in the same situation, romanticism becomes a kind of universalization of sentiment *but,* as well, the universalization of the self; this leads some to think that Nietzsche emerges directly out of romantic thought.[28]

In any event, romantic exaltation appears to be the expression of the

26. Ibid., 3, p. 78.
27. Nietzsche, *The Birth of Tragedy,* trans. Francis Golffing (New York: Doubleday, 1956), p. 51.
28. See H. G. Schenk, *The Mind of the European Romantics* (Oxford: Oxford University Press, 1966), p. 282.

difference between persons, that which "is not done," precisely because it is part of all persons; this creates frustration, despair, and struggle. Nostalgia takes possession of souls.

But romanticism eventually dissolves into historicism on account of its rejection of the universal. The relative, the singular, the values, all occupy the forefront of the theory scene. Individualism, being the fact of all persons, becomes once again natural.

The overcoming of Kantian thought, which is by its postulates inherently unstable, leads from Hegelianism to historicism and to romanticism, which came to dominate in the nineteenth century.

To overcome nature naturally could not but deliver humanity to a romantic and passionate singularity, to moral or aesthetic universality, to historical overcoming. The reflection of universal reason as being beyond all things natural in us leads us to reassert the value of sensibility, of singularity, even of irrationality. Passion is the locus of identity with nature, which has the effect of making what is natural unnatural, and by the same token consecrating a human, concrete, and very real transcendence of our nature in nature.

But for history to become passionate, or that "pathos" find its rightful place as the free expression of the singular individual in his or her sensible nature, there has to be some movement in the way that nature is regarded. This movement impedes the inscription of transcendence as simple dogmatic postulation, on account of a kind of rupture that is decreed but never explained. To think about nature is to situate oneself outside it, in History, and the access that humanity has to History is more or less natural, that is, it is made through passion or else it is progressive and civilized (politicized). There again passion affirms itself as the filter between the human being and nature; it maintains contact with nature, reflects it, and also humanizes it. *Pathos,* the sensible, is for the historian the mark of the "new" human being. It is the expression of our unchangeable relationship with nature from which we detach ourselves; by doing so, we are no longer only individuals. Passion is therefore the singularity of each person, but being in each person, and therefore in everyone, it is rendered dialectic and it becomes a characteristic of humanity in general, like the universal form of what renders the individual singular (Hegel). It is the place where anti-universalistic romanticism, which cultivates a strong taste for nature which it does not wish to discard, meets universal history, which sees in nature the seat of individual passions. Between naturally overcoming nature, which it always expresses, and the historicizing of the individual, there is a gap which hereby disappears. In its wake, history is transformed into the natural inscription of human nature and the free affirmation of sensibility is transformed into a historical phenomenon that has no other rationality than its own affirmation (Nietzsche).

Narrated Passions

Ever since Aristotle and Longinus, the author of the first treatises on the sublime, passions have been recognized as part of aesthetics. The contemplation of humanity by humanity, the spectacle that we put on for ourselves, is as passionate as it is impassioned. We *endure* our history by narrating it. The action is played out by the passions, which bewitch and obsess us, to the point where we are made to forget the story as story. And we know very well that it's all a "beautiful fable" anyway. It's a bit like children who scare themselves by horrible and blood-curdling stories that they in fact don't really believe in. Passion is precisely that which captivates the spectator even as it makes him or her aware that it isn't real. Passion that is unaware of itself and passions that are aware of themselves as passions meet in fictional action.

The spectator is passion that turns back upon itself. Ignorance, sometimes tragic, that affects the hero doubles as a consciousness that is very real for one who, from the outside, sees this passion put itself into place and become unhinged. A partial identification is born of this acting out of passions, but as well a sense of distance and difference. From there, said Aristotle, pity and concern are combined in the tragic domain, just as laughter erupts when the relationship between spectators and heroes is such that what was superior and tragic becomes inferior and the comic. If spectators fear that they are being talked about, and in observing the play have pity for the hero, they derive aesthetic pleasure from the contemplation of their own passions, over and above actions which are now considered nothing other than play. We make believe to be afraid, like we make believe in order to laugh. The identity of Ego is in this equilibrium between the inferior and the superior, between the comic and the tragic, between the ridiculous and destiny. The game of passions is reassuring because it distances the aesthete from the action which brings him down and from that which elevates him too high and leads him to his downfall.

Aesthetics is the privileged domain of passions, since the consciousness is given space to see itself therein, when it incarnates itself in the other, but since it is only a fiction, the whole thing remains a game that we believe in without really believing in it, that is, the "willing suspension of disbelief."

The representation of passions has a pedagogical role, what is usually called the "moral of the story," which is derived from this aesthetic point of view because it allows us to become aware of that which is unconsciously explained by the subject.

If there were a simple identity in us, there would be neither fiction nor aesthetics. A consciousness that is perfectly aware of itself, in perfect accord with itself, leaves no place for passions that would obscure its actions. This is the result of a difference and a gap wherein subjects experience themselves as out of touch with themselves and invaded by a universe transformed into destiny and necessity, which they must endure. This difference is linked to inequality, tragic or comic, heroic or burlesque, which elevates us in the spectacle of ourselves, or diverts us from a model deemed ridiculous. The sublime corresponds to this elevation; it amplifies the sentiment that we have of ourselves. This occurs within the spectacle of nature because it engenders terror without pity, unlike the tragic fate of ancient heroes.

The rhetoric of the passions coincides therefore with poetics. Passion itself is avoided on account of this process of aestheticization which is no longer received and which, nevertheless, procures sensations which arise through rhetorical form. This form consists of ordering figures which amplify or shorten the action of the individual. The figurative involves the one which is the object, either directly or indirectly. Projection disappears in the literal discourse, the one of common sense, of science, that banishes the subject from history by using mathematical symbols, demonstrations, and models. Metaphors bring the reader closer (to the action), or moves them further from it, creating a connivance of the enunciator and what is uttered in the enunciation, revealing the enunciator where, it would seem, there is nothing but discourse.

The sublime and the beautiful, the supra-sensible and the sensible, the metaphysical and the physical, the pure subject and the empirical subject, are all distinctions that are held dear by Kant.

But as early as Burke the beautiful and the sublime are opposed to each other.[29]

As for Hume, the sensations of pleasure and pain are associated via reflexive impressions or passions, which establish through a kind of passionate logic a form of sympathy between persons, the precursor of Kant's *common sense,* which is a source of universality in difference. This is because the passion we feel originates in a difference which

---

29. E. Burke, *A Philosophical Inquiry into the Origin of Our Ideas of the Sublime and Beautiful,* 1757 (Notre Dame: University of Notre Dame Press, 1968).

strikes the senses. And even the reaction of in-difference is a passionate one because it occurs through being stubborn, or on account of prejudices, ignorance, or a lack of concentration.[30] The biggest difference, the one that threatens the very identity of the one who experiences it, is terror. The sublime creates this threat, something that the beautiful doesn't do.

There is a representation of passions, which is a manner of living without them without having to do so, which "touches" and concerns individuals. Being-in-nature could be assimilated to the Beautiful, and transcendence, which comprehends it, could be identified with the sublime. Isn't it terrifying, and therefore sublime, to have to think about one's supra-sensible nature? Or, if you wish, to have to think about everything that is beyond the self, and which escapes imitation?

The aestheticization of the passions makes passions quiet or mute. Reflexive judgment is hereby at its highest level of *pathos*. The aesthetic is a vaccination against passions, which are hereby rendered contemplative and reveal the universality of human nature. In this there is a perfection of the approach originally set forth by Descartes.

Passion is this sensible consciousness which is not consciousness even as it is, which creates fusion and which immediately casts doubt thereupon by showing it to be an illusion, a dream. It is a kind of condition of impossibility (Kant) of consciousness, but it also assures this unity, as in empiricism where it assures an intellectual function in a universe of consciousness that is solely sensible. Passion is therefore sensible here (for intellectualism), and there (for empiricism); it represents a fissure of consciousness, of the universal and of the particular, of nature and of human nature. Passion is necessary and superfluous in the sense that it *must* account for that which undermines personal identity and at the same time erase itself, disappear before this identity, because nothing can *a priori* question such an identity, which expresses the very nature of the consciousness of self.

Finally, Kant's pure consciousness is nothing other than a fiction, an internal rupture, an admirable and terrifying fragmentation which questions the consciousness of each and every person. The dialectic between the one and the many resurfaces: human nature is only individual, but it is *the* human nature, which is contradictory to the idea of individuality. Conversely, if each person is an individual, then everyone is, and we fall once again into the mysteries of the universal. The dialectic doesn't

30. Ibid., p. 24.

solve the problem: the pure subject can explode, as it does with Marx, Nietzsche, and Freud, which opens the pathway to the metaphysical or ethical despair of the contemporary world.

The Death of the Subject

Kant displaced passions into the aesthetic, the supreme form of reflection, where consciousness doubles back upon itself and projects itself. Particularity and the sensible are thus framed by the universal, but they had to come back *for themselves,* despite their express thematization in Kant's work or, perhaps, on account of it, because in his system they are focused upon a realm. The sensible can but keep its rights because nothing motivates the renunciation of passions except for the postulation of human universality, which is both transcendent and present in all of us. Moral law has no other motivation than itself, since it is the end in itself, the ultimate end (Kant). The pure subject, upon which it rests, is an Idea of Kant to which particular people have no access as such in their undeniably sensible lives (finitude).

Unless, of course, we transform universal reason into immanent reality. In this sense we think of the well-known passage at the end of the *Critique of Pure Reason:* "What pure reason judges *assertorically* must (like everything that reason knows) be necessary; otherwise, nothing at all is asserted. Accordingly, pure reason does not, in point of fact, contain any opinions whatsoever."[31]

Passions are what constitutes the difference between the philosopher and the layman, as we said at the beginning of this work; if we deny this difference, then we also deny the importance of passions as, for example, in conflicts with reason.

Subjectivity is empirical on account of its immanence. This is a paradoxical assertion because to speak of *the* subjectivity is to postulate a universal unity at the very moment when one denies it.

This contradiction will be quickly identified to this newly formed subjectivity: the will to power, in Nietzsche's writings, with its battles between the strong and the weak, its "morality of slaves" which tempers the effects, and with its universality as ideological umbrella, a universality that Marx denounced as fictive.

Marx, Nietzsche, and Freud are the three names that come to mind

31. Kant, *Critique of Pure Reason,* trans. Norman Kemp Smith (London: Macmillan, 1961), p. 335.

when we think of the de-fundamentalization of Cartesian consciousness; they are names associated with a foundational crisis that is discussed at length in *Of Problematology.*

The reflexivity of consciousness is theorized as being partial, if not illusory, for all three thinkers. Freud maintains that consciousness has a reflexive function and an immanence, which maintains the coherence of the idea of consciousness even as he identifies it as inappropriate as a regulator for his old empire. To explain what is missing from this reflexive and conscious lucidity Freud proceeds by recalling the idea of the unconscious, rather than introducing the concept of passion, as was the case in Descartes's work. "The *Ego* represents what may be called reason and common sense; in contrast, the *Id* contains passions."[32]

Are the passions all unconscious and repressed?

Since passions are the concept of the Other of consciousness in the consciousness, they should have disappeared with the primacy of consciousness. This does indeed happen, in part: passions appear as a secondary notion.

Yet with the erasing of pure subjectivity (and not only of consciousness) and the assimilation of the subjectivity to the individual, passions couldn't but reappear as expressions of individual differences. If universality still existed in Marx or Freud, or even Nietzsche, then the questioning of all anthropological reality other than the one associated with the individual, and the meltdown of ideologies, would nevertheless have undermined the universality that was the rampart for passions. The tolerance of the Other, which we sometimes call "human rights," eventually admits the passions, at least at some theoretical level. But to what point, in law, as in fact?

Today, the question of passions is crucial to contemporary reflection, in its ethical and political aspects; but also when there is the problem of redefining rationality and the role of the consciousness which it implies.

---

32. Sigmund Freud, *The Ego and the Id*, trans. Joan Riviere, ed. James Strachey (New York: Norton, 1962), p. 15.

7

Toward a Critique of Pure Passion

A Conclusion in the Guise of an Introduction

Throughout the previous chapters we have studied the history of philosophy in order to help us with the subject of passion. Some people might ask, Why bother examining the past for a study of passion?

History is in reality a heritage: we couldn't accept it except from the perspective of an inventory, because it determines us without our being aware of it by making us see things in a given way; so it is good to reflect upon it from a critical standpoint.

That is the way we have proceeded. It was out of the question either to give ourselves over to a glorification of particular authors, or to examine in a tedious fashion one author in particular, which could lead to what I, following Nietzsche, might call the "philological mind/split" (cf. Nietzsche). This approach would have *reduced* the problem of passion to respectful commentary on what some thinker or another had said in some earlier moment in time.

In fact, the examination of the past is more a continuation of the problems at hand, which are linked according to a particular logic, than a catalog of solutions for which we offer a eulogy.

Where does a question come from, and how is it articulated? What are the arguments that constitute the backdrop, the arguments that are often unavoidable? This is the style of interrogation that best suits the method we have followed thus far. And what have we discovered? That the opposition of passion and reason is something so obvious that few would contest it from the very moment that they proclaim, rightly, that we need to live with passion, if not from our passions. Where does this apparently obvious fact come from, which is so enmeshed in contradictions? The past, whether we like it or not, is in the present, as other intuitions that we have about passion show us. Everyone can feel that this is the place where humanity meets its animal nature, where individuals, with their desires and instincts, meet society, without anyone really perceiving the link with the ethical or political questions, or solutions, which flow from it. Here again, the history of philosophy cast light upon these links, as it does upon the diverse replies which may be conceived, and from which we have not yet extricated ourselves.

At the end of the day, the real question that emerges after this analysis is: what is humanity? Its violence, cruelty, impulses, judgment, even its rights, individuality and altruism melt into the theme of passions as a river flows into a sea.

One thing should spring to mind: a certain conception of reason is hereby rendered null and void, the vision which has exhausted its own possibilities and for which passion is the product and the inverse, a paradoxical product. What is this rationality of which we are the inheritors, and which so many among us have trouble casting off despite the many insurmountable difficulties that it poses?

We are referring here to propositional reason.

Propositionalism replies to the most fundamental question that exists: what is an answer? This demand supersedes and models all others, for the solution that is brought to bear applies to all other possible solutions, since what is at issue here is to determine the nature of a solution in the general sense. Since questioning opens up a number of possibilities, the reply, being one possible option, evacuates by the same token *all* possible alternatives, and therefore *all* possible problems.

It is in this little word "all" that the paradoxical nature of propositionalism is affirmed. It establishes as a general *answer* the very *abolition of answering*. The eradication of the interrogative becomes the very foundation of *the* rationality, and makes its "answers" into simple propositions. It is an answer to a problematic that comes by the evacuation of *the entire* problematic, as though propositionalism existed by its own accord. This explains why the deduction that oversees the propositions, and the intuition which engenders the first of them, find themselves as the guarantors of the propositional autonomy; and in the process, induction ends up addressing itself to experience.

There is in propositionalism a denigration of its very foundation: a question that it evacuates, which is its real but hidden foundation, and to which it replies by doing so, thereby instituting this suppression of the problematic as the criteria for rational discourse, for *logos,* for reason. This reason will make the exclusion of alternatives into its ultimate truth, without even worrying about establishing this requirement, finding out where it comes from, and why we *necessarily* need such a necessity. The necessity is nevertheless the master word of this *logos:* what excludes the alternative (the problematic) is necessary. The guarantee of this necessity is codified by a certain interpretation of the principle of contradiction: "A *or* not-A," which is to be understood as saying "there is no alternative but a single proposition," and so the circle is closed. To counter the sophists who practice the game of alternatives by defending contrary positions, Plato proposes the Idea of the Good, a foundation that is necessary to necessity, just as later God will be, or the subject that affirms itself, or Being which cannot not be ... Being.

One could object that we must respect the principle of noncontradiction, that propositional deduction passed the required tests, notably in the realm of science, and that there is no reason to reject the norm of resolution which consists of leaving to the side all questions that have been resolved, because they were resolved. It's clear that there is the foundational problem here, but isn't this a minor criticism in the face of the possibilities and the efficaciousness of this rationality?

No one could deny that the resolution of a question *could* come through its elimination; what needs to be asked here is whether this should apply to *all* answers. The necessity which excludes the alternative couldn't constitute the model of the response, as though all other forms of answering should either be in complete accord or disappear. In short, who would reject noncontradiction? It is only its interpretation as propositional structure that is at issue here, not to mention its foundation. Must we read noncontradiction as the simple eradication of the alternative, or should we instead interpret it as follows: "Every alternative (= every question) A/not-A, has a solution which precludes any possibility of the alternative," and the suppression of the question is but one way of answering among many, in any case never the only one? As such, to reply could consist, for example, of producing an answer for which the opposite is not excluded, and which lends itself to debate; this is a manner of saying that the answer doesn't eliminate the problem, but puts it on the same footing. The elimination of the problematic is not the panacea, and even less so the one and only possible resolution.

By the same token, what can be deduced, rather than being exclusively the discourse of "necessity," frequently takes over from, and is explained by, related questions which intervene in the course of the progression of answers provided. This does not form an homogenous and self-sufficient tissue, as is the case in mathematics, which has for a long time been considered the model for rationality. Today, few people would support such a thesis. It is rare to be able to fix from the very outset a solution that is preestablished through itself (where would it come from if not afterwards?), and to be able to treat it as though the issue were a question, and to deploy the solution, which is, moreover, the demonstration. The reality of our reasoning shows that questions emerge in the course of the questioning, and that the answers that emerge have no demonstrative qualities, but are answers nevertheless. Do we have to prefer their rearrangement *a posteriori,* with an autonomous propositional texture that is closed down upon itself? Isn't it finally artificial in many cases, even if it is discursivity that is privileged by certain sciences as a means of exposing its results?

Propositionalism suffers only from its absolute qualities. Demonstrativity and necessity are both excellent forms of discourse, but they couldn't be the only ones unless we reject all others in the gloom of the irrational. And there, propositionalism destroys itself, since it doesn't consider itself except upon the exclusive nature of its exclusions. The reason for this is simple: to accept plurality in the reply is the same as admitting that the problematic and the multiple can be inscribed in it, and resurface in the form of questions in the answers themselves. Propositionalism emanates from the necessity of *affirming* the necessity, which *affirms itself* in a circular fashion as regards itself, but also excludes all that is not apodictic. The foundation of propositionalism couldn't be found in the questioning that it presupposes, even by denying its existence, since it is instituted in the will to deny it. This is paradoxical, since it consists in taking as point of departure what we cannot accept as such, and to therefore reply even though there is no space for replying, which is a manner of considering the proposition with regard to the questions posed. Propositionalism only knows one entity, the proposition, or the judgment, which is a way of replying as well. Propositionalism refuses to think about the proposition, refuses to think about itself, since it needs to be modified to its very root, *in its very foundation*. Since it can but support itself, it needs to institute a guarantee of its own autonomy, a role that is played by God himself. He needs to be the *causa sui*: he causes himself to be because he is the cause of everything, which is what Nietzsche denounced as a contradictory utilization of the concept of cause, that which cannot be applied to itself without self-destructing. The *affirmation* of God can only rest upon a first intuition (or revelation), for it cannot rely upon something more rational to found rationality.

Whatever the angle of approach we adopt, propositional reason, even though it endured beyond the Greek era, still finds itself in a tight spot. By providing an answer to a problem that it denies exists as a means of offering a resolution, it ends up destroying itself. It is the answer that it cannot be, the answer to the question of questioning that it negates by even taking it on. It has as an authentic point of departure a problem, but it invents yet another one in order to allow it to deal with the first. As an answer that suppresses the problem as such, it is a living paradox: in the will to assimilate reason to apodictic discourse, occidental rationality right up to Husserl expresses a will that must be situated in an anterior position as regards the apodicticity that it wishes to effect, and by doing so places itself on this side of itself in order to become itself. It is this fact of being on this side, this non-apodicticity that presides at the apodictic foundation, that has to be explained by rationality. This is why discourse about passion and the discourse of passion are on this side of reason, inside of reason, and destined to account for what precedes it, and falls outside it.

Since this rationality is and remains paradoxical, passion is also the space where the paradox of propositionalism, as well as its foundation, is crystallized. This paradox is better known as the paradox of Menon: I need to know what I'm looking for in order to find it, and I don't know about it so that it will be useful. In fact, we know that this doesn't pose any difficulty: we find what we are looking for. The paradox refers to the reflection, the "glance," that I find in the conditions of this successful quest, and I explain them. It is at this level, where the issue of the understanding of the phenomenon of knowledge itself, of rationality, that the paradox strikes reason most adroitly. How could I both not know and know something, in this case, the very object of my quest? It is imperative that I not know what I'm looking for, but that I also know what I'm looking for: this must be the same thing, and must also be two different things, since otherwise I would know everything as soon as I begin the quest, which would render the whole research endeavor rather useless. A difference must coexist with identity. Propositional reason will therefore create its own difference: passion.

On account of passion I don't know what I'm looking for, in fact I don't know to the point of being ignorant of not knowing, which I don't even suspect. This is too much: it is thus necessary to nuance this and suggest that passion is known by those who are its victims. The innocent are thus rendered guilty. By the same token, we know that we must search. This is where the trap and the illusion are located! Passion is ignorance and the knowledge of ignorance, the desire and the consciousness of desire (Spinoza): through it, I am not aware of what I'm looking for, but I know what I want. Passion becomes the very *object* of my quest, the name of the problem that has to be resolved, to be overcome and which is already overcome. If passion blinds me and renders its own annihilation useful, it is also what I know that I must overcome. As such, reason is anti-passion *par excellence*. The condemnation of passion is inscribed in the propositionalism as a condition for its institution. And the paradox of this institution comes along in train, since the "solution" proposed through passion is not a solution, especially in the terms proposed. It is sure that what I know and what I don't know must be paired up, hence the duality of passion, the lieu of ignorance, and reason, the place of knowledge. But when I *look for* something, I know and I don't know at the same time: I know that I am looking for something even though I necessarily don't know what I'm looking for. In these conditions passion is reason without being, or reason contains passion as its (motivating) principle. The whole problem is this: passion is ignorance, it submerges me and it blinds me, so I cannot even know that I must look for something; so I'm like the prisoners of the Plato's Cave who already believe that they know everything even though in fact they are living an illusion.

Furthermore, passion doesn't blind me, since I have already recognized its characteristics in the course of my struggles to engage it: I had to leave the Cave for this reason, so that I would *know* that the reality lies elsewhere. In short, in passion I ignore what I must look for and I don't ignore it: I know what I am looking for, but to have found it in the overcoming of passionate ignorance, it was necessary that it stop operating on me. There is too much in passion: ignorance and recognition, the blinders and the truth that tears them away. How can I be abused by passion when I have unmasked it, and how can it be unmasked when it functions to impede all lucidity? It is necessary to recognize from the outset what I am ignorant about, so that passion can play its double role, which hereby recalls the paradox of Menon. Passion presupposes the reason that it must incite me to acquire, even as it is precisely that which generally holds me back from doing so.

Reason, once again, had to be initiated by its own initiative, we don't know how, in order to overcome the passion that made it useful and necessary in the first place, which is paradoxical. Kant adopts the only possible "solution" when he affirms, as a necessary evidence that reason is *a priori,* that it is there by itself, with its own necessity, that it is its own end, and that it is a break with regard to that which is not itself, because it originates in and by itself.

One needs to recognize that such a break makes the idea of the inaugural moment of reason into a pure postulation, and if we recognize the role of passion, it in fact becomes an impossibility. Kant doesn't care about that, and he is, unlike his predecessors, perfectly coherent about this issue. Reason thus becomes a mysterious object through the rejection of the *question* concerning this inaugural moment, because the question is *quid facti* or factual, empty of any interest for a philosophy that wishes before all else to justify, rather than to go back to original sources of things. But despite everything, passion is there, implicitly, even for a faculty of reason that can create or found itself. It is the *useless opposition,* the scarecrow that can be set up to create a good attitude, if not a good content. It is what I know I must combat, even though the very knowledge that I must do so suggests that I've already been victorious in the fight. This is another way of saying that nothing remains other than really wanting it, without weakness: reason becomes passion once again, since it is akin to strong feelings or rational will. The weak individual is the one who has other reasons than reason, another motivating force than *the* rational force which makes him weak-willed *(akrasia)*. What remains is the passionate, considered as the discrepancies inherent in a consciousness that is both reflexive and un-thinking, a discrepancy that, by going against the unity of the consciousness is fictive or, moreover, aesthetic. A displacement or derivation of the passionate, the logic of the difference at the interior of the identity of the consciousness is inscribed as the sense of the sublime. The mind contemplates itself and is surprised that it is able to do so, and thus finds itself overwhelmed; what overwhelms it brings it to consider that which is unreflexive, to think of it as such, as though it were a coincidence. Aesthetic reflection defines itself as being the domain of "as if" (Vaihinger) of this appropriateness of the self, the space of contemplation, without passion but not without pleasure.

If we follow Plato and others, passion is the Others' reason, a reason that unlike our own, doesn't lead us to our reasons, and thus to *the* reason. Rhetoric could perhaps convince them, if we refer to Aristotle, but it is more likely that they will be resistant to reason because they are politically and socially beneath it, and this because they work and make their minds work by obeying partial and precise imperatives (Plato). Passion is the blindness of those who are affixed to their social position, and are left out by those privileged few who have access to innate reason.

There is a social confrontation played out in the process of rejecting passion which manifests itself as a kind of intolerance to the Other's point of view, as we see in, for example, religious wars; but there is as well the thesis according to which social differences are simply insurmountable. Passion creates an impassable blindness in those it affects, as "others" can see, be they who they may, who are by their very nature or essence above the rest. Passion thereby becomes the keyword for the impossibility of leaving one's condition to become elevated, just as it reveals the point of view of the lucid exteriority.

Christianity is more universalist than Plato, and makes this impossibility into a condition that is inherent in the *humanity* of human beings. A Platonic human being would have had passion that could be overcome if such a person, who would be both universal and abstract, existed, because there are beings which can perceive it in others, and thus become liberated: evil is involuntary for the passionate person, but this evil is not evil, it is lack of knowledge. For the Christian, passion is a fact of life, it is universal, equal in each person, it is sin itself, and the evil is in this (false) natural innocence which cannot be cured, either by social or political means. Evil is no longer linked to ignorance. But there again the paradox rebounds. I am guilty at my very origin, therefore I am innocent, since I am ignorant at birth, but I should know this as well, since I am a human being, and I know that I live as a fallen individual; I can save myself by overcoming my sins by the fair exercise of faith, and I cannot save myself because whatever I do won't change my original sin.

From this flows an unavoidable alternative: either people ignore the evil that affects them in an original sense, they are innocent, and in the worst case scenario, they are irresponsible; or they know what evil (and good) are, so they can differentiate, and the faults of passion do not blind them because they've already gone beyond it. If they know what evil is, contrary to their nature, why do they commit it? And they are ignorant of, innocent of, in what sense there is evil and, moreover, how to go beyond it, because they simply have no idea of what the problem is in the first place. Unrecognized evil is ignorance, and evil that is known as such has been overcome. Evil comes from ignorance; it is accomplished without our being aware of it; but is something that we don't recognize as evil still evil? We must admit that evil is in humanity and that human beings are ignorant of it, and that only something from the outside can bring light upon it, or constrain it to do good in the case of when one refuses to see it. From passion we move to coercion, in a short step: the one that involves our recognizing blindness in the Other.

The problem returns and is reversed, and projection reveals it for what it is. Isn't passion in the eye of the one who condemns it in others? It is the fruit of a false universal in which the other refuses to participate, intentionally. Passion represents itself as the projection of an idea for which the proclaimed necessity would be far from effective. It would be like the negation of our own historical anchorage, either social or cultural, a way of denouncing that of the other, upon which we project our particularity which is denied, since it is imposed upon the other. We are never sufficiently sure about a point of view until we affirm it as being something other than a simple point of view, and until we attribute to the other the particularity of the affirmations for which he or she is the author, which makes them passionate because reason excludes all particularity on account of its will to universality.

Passion is a concept of projection and, as a consequence, a rhetorical concept that permits us to precisely classify the propositions of others as "pure rhetoric." It is the notion of rhetoric that allows us to pass one's own rhetoric and denounce that of the other; this is the source of the polemical and argumentative polemic of the passionate domain, already mentioned by Aristotle.

Passion therefore links with rhetorization the questions which consciousness must confront, that is, with what allows for their annulment as new problems in previous replies. This principle of reduction or analogy of the new and the old shows that passion is the instrument of suppression of all problematics, which it renders purely formal. From that point, we must conclude that passion is the concept, if not the process, which maintains the continuity of consciousness in the face of the shocks of reality: a universality which consists in integrating messages that come from the outside, interpreting them in a preestablished, or even closed fashion. Passion is the closing of the consciousness to that which puts it into question in its very openness: it is the level of integration that is required to treat what refuses to be integrated. Paradox? There is no question about it, if we take literally the phrase "integration of the un-integratable," but here we must hear the statement just as we hear that "it is sad to be happy," or, "He criticizes France, like a typical Frenchman," or "He says that he has nothing to say," and other such affirmations which are paradoxical only on strictly literal grounds. Passion manifests itself from that point on in a figured or figurative sense, since we cannot take literally what is apparently contradictory. By going beyond the literal, we explore a higher level, where reason recovers its rights, by realizing the apparent contradiction by demonstrating that it is an admissible co-presence. These are the mechanisms of the rendering rhetorical, of the hierarchization and the re-literalization upon which we must now concentrate, since they constitute passion as we now understand the term today. It is the figural of the literal, the meta-level of the zero point.

We have surveyed the diverse aspects of passion that now must be taken up anew: the theory of consciousness, the ethico-political aspects, and the rhetorical/argumentative dimensions, which are all linked.

Consciousness and consciousness of self form a single unitary consciousness, even as they remain distinct. Passion is the locus of this difference, but in this regard it is also the name of a problem rather than a solution.

If we had to be systematic about what follows, I'd have to suggest a tripartite model that emerges from what we have just said: there is a domain of individual consciousness (or the Self) which has a specific passionate quality; the relationship with the other, who also happens to be imbued with passions (conflicts, or else *compassion*); and finally, the relationship with objects, which is also riddled with passions. All of these passionate regimes will interact, and passions will change as a consequence. To take but one example: love comes to be known as sexual desire, or will to enter into a symbiotic relationship when it links two beings, and it will be called greed when it relates to a thing, like money.

But let us turn now to the theory of consciousness.

The Passionate Coherence of Consciousness

The paradox of Menon is the result of denial, and therefore of the displacement of questioning as such through propositions where it can be found, even though it is not really there. To resolve this paradox, it is necessary to take it up from the idea of interrogation. By asking a question, by accepting the question from the very beginning, I know what I'm looking for, because I know the problem I have to resolve, and I am ignorant of what I must find, since the question is the expression of an ignorance and an unknown. From that point forth, the difference between the question and the answer imposes itself as the solution to the paradox of Menon, and it will be incumbent upon us to apprehend, on the basis of this difference, rationality and its inscription within passion.

This applies as well to the theory of consciousness. We have seen the difficulties that this theory has encountered when it attempts to define the unity of consciousness, and to make reflection coexist (without contradiction) with unreflexive consciousness, which seems to escape its own nature (which is to be reflexive).

In the phenomenon of the consciousness, there is always the faculty for replying that is at work, even in reflection, which is in fact a reply to the response to a certain question. Let's take an example: the grocer who tabulates his take at the end of the day is absorbed in his accounting and is conscious of what he is doing, not because he says to himself in a reflexive fashion "I see myself counting"—since by doing so he would stop counting, but because if we asked him what he was doing, he would say without any hesitation, "I'm doing my cash." He wouldn't have given any attention to the matter of what he was doing, nor would he realize this, which suggests that there is a difference between these two activities.

There is, nevertheless, a certain equivalence to be made between these two levels: one is a direct experience, which links us to objects, things, or beings, and the other, which is a reflection after the experience is already accomplished, which is destined to notice it. These are the two distinct levels which form a single unit, which is assured by the difference between the question and the answer (the *problematological difference*). In fact, by responding to the answer, we express it as such, that is, with regard to a question that is also a distinct entity. In the example just cited, the grocer replies to the solution which he brings to his accounting problem by responding in a literal fashion to the question posed—by his wife, perhaps?—who asks him what he is doing.

It is interesting to note that, even if not all the answers have a conscious origin, they nevertheless end up being treated as though they did on account of the fact that the subject answers a question that is posed, and could respond to what had been answered. There is no other origin of the unconscious effect which produces certain representations than this terminal phase of answering, whereby the subject knows *that* he answers, and *what* he answers, through a second level of discourse that always remains possible. Often, there is the ideology or the unconscious working behind the answer; the question of how it works must also be posed. The explanation of why there is this illusion that consciousness is transparent relates to this final stage, where this answer is considered by the individual who thinks he mastered it because he replied to a question and created an acceptable relation by doing so, one which is often influenced by the exterior, despite the real adequacy of the answer. But isn't there work upon the question, as there is upon the answer, from the very moment when the question is formulated?

The Ego maintains a relationship to reality, which has its own obligations, its specific problematic: the continuity of the real is maintained by perception, but also by reflection, which interprets what happens as being stable. This is the source of the idea of substance, which haunted the philosophers and thinkers of earlier days. What needs to be explained is that behind and despite the multiple changes that we have observed in reality, there is something stable that remains in all possible modifications. If contemporary science renounces the idea of a substratum, the idea of common sense still functions on the basis of a theory that there exists an identity between things and reality that it has to deal with, and this for excellent reasons.

A continuity of the real is beyond discussion, even if everything is moving at a faster and faster rate, and if points of reference have a tendency of being erased in the process. How is it possible to assure this continuity? Every new problem is viewed on the basis of questions that have already been resolved, and apprehended as a function of answers that were brought to bear upon them in previous times. The new questions become rhetorical questions, in the sense that they are presented as interrogative forms of truths previously accepted. Nothing could put them into question, since they serve to resolve all possible questions. Through these questions the "answers" are re-confirmed. Prejudices have no origin other than this mechanism whereby questions are made rhetorical, which abolishes the real problems posed thereby. If questioning could be suppressed as such ever since the dawn of occidental reason, it is because of this problematic that human beings have, which is to wish to live in a feeling of assurance and security. This problematic nourishes a sense of "being right" which is relentlessly reconfirmed, and upon which all ideologies and unconscious constructions are pinned. The paradox has it that there is a certain rejection of the real when we attempt to take charge of the real, simply to allow us to live within it. But reality is a function, not a content. This will be modified by force the day that answers which are served up are put into question; and this putting into question itself must be questioned, in order to permit us to elaborate other answers. There is no precise level in the putting into question to which we can fix the abandonment of existing solutions. This is the source of the debate and the arguments between people, but it is also the source of violence in history, which obligates us, which pushes away that which resists this process of putting things into question. Passion is essential to this rhetorical process, which permits the real to maintain its stability despite diverse changes in how it is considered. It is the *price* that is paid by the consciousness to gain a foothold over reality without getting lost therein. Passion is thus what allows us to exist, a kind of reaction to time, which is destined to annihilate it with the passage of time, like so many shocks that eventually have to be cushioned.

The symbolic of passion is the subjective version of the process of rendering rhetorical, which is "logical" because it is made up of reasoning and rationalization.

The passionate is reactive, it is the safety valve, the way out, of necessity, for which reason we often equate it with liberty. But passion is also, if not mostly, a manner of assuming time which separates moments of consciousness, consciousness of self which returns upon itself. Recall the ambivalent process of the passionate: it is a reaction to necessity and a struggle against it, the first presupposing what the second rejects.

Passion will be deployed, moreover, in the rhetorical reaction: a man *perceives* a snake in the desert (fear), *sees* an automobile which goes the wrong way up a one-way street (surprise; if we have to admit surprise as a passion), *observes* one's best friend's wife in the arms of another (anger), is *stopped* by a policeman who beats him into admitting who knows what (pain), and so forth. Behind these observations, perceptions, events, there is a manner by which things are taken in charge, which is the role of passion. We should have taken more edifying examples, perhaps; the policeman who drags you from your wrecked car before it explodes, the glass of water in the desert, the voluptuous woman who approaches and makes eyes at you, and so forth.

Let's take this a bit further: in order to function in reality, and to continue to experience it as such, we must react with passion, passion which disassociates the subjective from the objective, and permits it to impose itself upon the mind without any confusion. Passion, in a sense, diverts the subject from itself, but by doing so, it can also make it blind to what is but a particular point of view, making the subject take for objective what is subjective, because it could not consider passion *as such*. That passion can blind us is clear; that it orients us in the *objective* world is also clear; and indeed these two ideas are linked.

In the rendering rhetorical of questions about the real, we don't consider them rhetorical even though we make these questions rhetorical: this is a question of efficacy, since we have to act as though the rhetorical question were in fact not one, as though it were really resolved. The question shouldn't seem rhetorical because in this case the solution could only be dubious because it simply repeats the question that it is supposed to resolve. The unconscious is the rendering rhetorical of the process of making rhetorical, which annuls the problem at hand, for which the objective is to know how the new question that had appeared rhetorically was taken up, and resolved. The consequence of this rendering rhetorical is that the subject lives under the impression of an immediate and real, if not automatic, resolution, which thus expels passion into a realm that the consciousness, which seeks resolution, wishes to avoid.

Passion is here unconscious, in the sense that we are ignorant of the standpoint "from which we speak" when we speak; we are blind to our own point of view, which is, therefore, but *one* point of view. The problematic of its resolution doesn't appear to us, and by the same token, neither does the solution, *at least as such, that is, with reference to this problematicity.*

This subtle dialectic of repression permits us to assume history by denying its existence, integrating what is new as though it were the simple repetition of what has occurred in the past.

Rhetorization on the basis of which the Ego gives itself to itself, without saying as much, there is of course a construction of the self which is engendered and elaborated. As rhetorical, this elaboration is a history that individuals produce about themselves. As long as we haven't understood that the Ego is history, we won't resolve the major problems concerning subjectivity that have been posed ever since Descartes and Kant. On the one hand singular, on account of this history it recounts, the Ego is in a state of forced intersubjectivity because the text is destined for the Other, and therefore to each person or, if you wish, to everyone. This is the image that we present of ourselves, where what we are is mixed up with what we want to be, where the false joins the true in variable proportions that can be explained in each case. Does it still make sense to want to be "authentic" or "true to oneself"? Does it still have content, other than the empty form of universality? How can one be purely oneself when doing so always consists in telling a story that one constructs as one goes along, a story that is composed of elements of the ideal and the real? How is it possible to purify the story that we are, what we are beyond all history? Can there be a self that is beyond the text, the partition that *makes it up?*

Again, is it possible to have a pure or transcendent subject that stands behind, or inside, each empirical subject? There again, the answer flows from what was just said: as history, the Ego couldn't be strictly empirical, but what history tells us certainly is, since what is at issue is a particular individual who puts forth his or her own singularity.

Rhetorization is in the end the coherence that a subject gives to itself, and this rationalization of the problems banishes the problematicity from the consciousness which sees only the solution and the resolution. By passion, we make ourselves right, and justify our very justifications. Only *failure,* and not *truth,* is the measure of history, even if the likelihood of something is already related to the success in achieving it.

A weird self-image will likely lead to failure, someone who lives out of synch with the demands of realism. The idealist is, therefore, the person who has the courage of his or her own morals, the morals of his or her own story. But woe to those who tell too many stories to themselves and neglects their own, as was the case for poor Oedipus.

Passion assures the coherence of reason, and permits it to establish itself by repressing passion through difference. We think here of the person who gets angry because he is humiliated, which is a way of assuming the un-assumable, to "deal with it."

Passion is the reaction of reason to what it is not, to the irrational, but the term here is relative. Passion is indirectly present in reason, as is its opposite, which assures its closure and its coherence, the survey that explains it, the inside and the outside. But without the return of the self, passion doesn't appear as such to the one who lives it, and it thus becomes entwined with reason.

Passion and reason are only differentiated when there is reflection. They disintegrate as a couple when they show what the couple is. Otherwise, one is in the other, which leads us to take reason for passion. This is where the illusion begins, and ends. Reason is rendered autonomous and disassociates itself in reflection, where the rhetorical becomes conscious, and with it, so too does the point of view, unilateral, if not biased, from which the individual speaks. The problematic emerges as such, and so does the debate. The difference is explained in the return to the self. Otherwise, we continue to consider two completely different phenomena as though they existed on the same plane.

Passionate coherence coincides with rationalization. To be angry, for example, signifies that we are responding to another or to some fact, and to "deal with it," we react, we reflect upon what we should have experienced, we take our distances, since here passion is conscious. Anger is that which allows us to deal with a given reality. We could also attack someone in order not to have to deal with ourselves in a situation wherein we would be dramatically put into question. Passion is an escape valve, which reestablishes an equilibrium where there is none in order to avoid further difficulties later on down the line. Passion reestablishes equilibrium in the psyche, it regulates the relationship with reality by integrating it.

By anger and disdain, or by love and joy, we take some comfort—or provide comfort for ourselves—in our judgments, we reconfirm and verify ourselves. If we are made to reflect upon what we endure, then we take a survey of the situation around us, which in fact suggests another way of defining it, modeling it, or simply living it. The solution to a problem passes through the process of rearranging the problem, to the point where rejecting the solution is still a way to answer it. Passion is this answer, an answer imposed *upon* what is problematic, that either explains it or responds to it: through evasion, flight, survey, passion can situate the person in question outside, and by doing so, it offers up a kind of liberty in the form of illusion. But passion is reality as well, for we experience it, even if the answer that it provides to a problem doesn't in fact resolve it. Consciousness can therefore continue to function thanks to passion, even if this signifies for it a work to be done on the problematic of the real that it makes rhetorical through its passionate solution.

Coherence of consciousness, which permits us to assume reality as it unfolds, as though it remained consistent, is a passionate mechanism of permanently restoring equilibrium, of "homeostasis" as we say today. Passion is a kind of reaction to a situation because it propels us outside where we are through the intellect, since passion annuls changes even as it betrays them through the intermediary of "opinions and beliefs" that it articulates.

We go from *emotion,* which situates people in duration, to *passion,* when the subject can no longer assume the situation and the problems raised thereby without having to reflect expressly upon those problems. These problems may well have their origin in the original situation, but they nevertheless establish a certain transcendence on account of the solutions that cannot be rendered rhetorical, that they demand in the face of the situation in question. The reaction modifies the context, alters it, without which passion would have as its effect the rejection of that which in this context conditions the impossibility of resolution. Let's not forget that to respond to a problem by affirming that it is unresolvable is still a manner of resolving and dealing with it. Nothing stops us from "putting it into question," literally this time, by another question which expresses it more adequately. Passion reflects this continuity in the response by assuring that the question is rendered rhetorical as "preliminary answer" which stabilizes the real through the continuous projection of an unthinking point of view, the projection of which has a price, which is the passionate reaction. *Emotion* links together passion of diverse fluctuations and contradictions such that the solution becomes a concentration of these *emotions* which themselves originate in sensations, thus the natural of the senses. From *sensation* to *passion* there is a movement of acceleration which takes possession of the mind and mobilizes it.

In order to reduce the problems that are asked of the consciousness, there needs to be a process of rhetorical possession, and reasoning which rationalizes what must be confronted translates passion that is at work in this rationalization. It is the subjective condition, partially conscious or not. The permanence of a point of view, of a perspective, and the transcendence of the Ego, can be illusory, but so is passion. It is useful, it permits us to live, and nobody is exempt from it. It makes exterior the interiority of human beings, and their immanence to an anterior context. But passion runs the risk of being more explicit, even more violent, when subjectivity attempts to delineate itself from the situation that entraps it.

The paradox that remains is that passion undertakes the taking hold of the real as such by a sort of illusion projected upon it. But doesn't this annul the reality of the real and make of it but an *a priori* emanation or, in other words, what everyone would like to see rather than what is really there?

Passion and the Real

On the one hand, passion is consciousness which affirms itself in the objective relation it has to the real world, the source of objectivization and literalness, which differentiates the subjective from reality itself. Passion is the difference between the reading and the reader, and it serves to decode the real for what it is by putting it outside itself, like the moment of consciousness when it no longer deals directly with itself; it is the indirect object of its own discourse, but it is nevertheless distinct. Passion is that which allows us to "take in" reality, to accept it as such, to accommodate ourselves to it, if not to entirely adapt to it.

On the other hand, passion is also a glance upon the real which annuls all problematic, placing us in the domain of pre-constructed answers, making us perceive reality as a function of the *a priori* that denatures it on account of the partial and biased viewpoint it provides, a viewpoint that accentuates some aspects while downplaying others, rejecting consequences, becoming blind to the self, to others, and to the world. From passion as a condition of reason we come to the level of passion which makes passion pass for reason, along with its train of rationalizations and justifications.

To explain this brutal reversal in the function of the domain of passions, it is worth returning to the notion of problematicity and the problematological difference, which serves to demarcate the problematological from what it is not. The negation of the problematological difference leads to the establishment of the duality of passion and reason, the passion being under the orders of the denied problematic either as an *answer* that is presupposed, which exists because the problem is denied *a priori,* or by underlining what creates *problems* for people via a solution that has been imposed, and to which they must respond.

The problem that is posed here is to know if passion is ignorant of itself but nevertheless determines itself, or if it is known as such. In this case, we fall back upon a model in two or three steps: the knowledge of passion presupposes the reason that it unmasked and therefore overcame; or else, we contest that such a coming to consciousness leads necessarily to any victory whatsoever. Knowledge of passion as such is not sufficient for overcoming it, just as knowing what disease we have is not the same thing as curing it. We still need the force of will, an act of liberty. Aristotle, for example, oscillated between the two conceptions, while Christianity endured them as a basic schism.

Is passion therefore the name of a problem that is unaware of itself, or of a solution whose goal is to ignore the problem? Is it the solution or should it lead us to it? Is it ignored, or known?

Questions are paradoxes and circles for propositionalism.

Passion is a way of responding to certain problems by denying them, and by denying oneself. But the question-answer or problem-solution differences are present in the mechanism of the passions, which goes from stimulus to corporal response, right up to intellectual and affective response that passions engender at the end of the process. These passions operate according to the order of the answer, which can go from the repression of the question that is to be resolved (and thus of itself as answer) to its thematization in the most passionate interrogations about the self that humanity can encounter, at certain crucial moments of its existence. What propositionalism calls passion, in the paradoxical alternative which opposes passion that we are unaware of to passion that is known, under the grip of a mechanism which is mysterious because it is impossible—rationality or, moreover, faith—doesn't exist in the framework of interrogative thinking. Passion about which we are unaware is still an answer to problems, a mode of implicit resolution, which we wish to ignore for reasons of comfort, if not conformity. We take as reason that which passion dictates to us, a passion which is sometimes reaction, of anger or enthusiasm, of disdain or sympathy, so that we won't have to put into question, and put *ourselves* into question. Little rational passions punctuate this wise reading of reality. Everything can continue in its proper order.

Passion is no less existent in this hypothesis as an answer to a problem, even if we shouldn't reflect too much upon one in order to not have to ask about the other. Ignorance, which is almost calculated, can destroy if it doesn't work. We've said it before: the criterion of passion is failure and success, not truth, which is reserved for reason. If we need to talk in terms of knowledge, we would say that in passion I know and I don't know, but not on the same level, otherwise we'd fall back into the domain of the paradoxical. I know what I'm looking for, I know my problem, but I know as well that it is a problem: I love a woman passionately, for instance, I *want* to be with her, I *ask* myself how I'm going to go about it, I *search* in order to find myself on the same road as her, or even to occupy her existence and respond to her own interrogations to make myself needed by her, and so on, and I know that this is a problem. My passion reveals my obstacles to me and makes the process leading up to the resolution of this problem into a useful exercise.

Failures, difficulties, changes which affect people, will all react and affect our otherwise tranquil passionate characters. This is what will upset the problematological difference and reveal it to their actors. They will discover that they didn't really know what they thought they knew, and that they make their problems rhetorical even as they abandon themselves to "small explosions" in order to be successful. This is not sufficient, and passion, which serves this purpose, is going to detonate it all, not by a long-term resolution but by a problematic for which it will be the object.

In the end, passion which keeps the subject out of the question because *indirectly* in question will present itself *as passion*. Reason must be elsewhere than in the rationalization and in histories uttered in and through passion. Ignorance, which is very useful, can become problematic and conscious of being so. It emerges as a problem at the scene of an answer which urges us toward a questioning and a series of new solutions. People always presuppose answers to a range of questions that they don't like having posed: *where, when, how,* and especially, *who,* questions which affect them because they situate them, or make them aware of situations that are not necessarily all that pleasant. Passion permits us to assure continuance, but it can also lead to a break therein, before flowing into a new sealing-off of existence upon itself.

What a problematological analysis aims to show is the mechanism's variations. This ends up by ceasing to oppose "Reason" as a singular and indivisible ideal to a paradoxical passion, paradoxical because passion presents itself as a residue, as a projection of reason, a reason that ceases to exist in order to exist.

Passion is both known and ignored, because it is the knowledge of our ignorance, which can be erased to allow for pure knowledge, or be denatured to allow for pure ignorance. It is neither the solution without a problem, nor the problem without a solution, it is the response to a problem which could go as far as its own annihilation, simulated or sought, right up to its express theme.

What we call blinding passion is this state where no differentiation is made between passion and reason, which is in fact a way of dealing with their difference, the way that expressly *aims* to avoid dealing with this difference.

The problematological analysis attempts to show that we prefer to not have to ask too many questions, something that the ancients were quite aware of, even if they found this rather rational, because passion is always wrong in being the "wrong solution" to the question that must eradicate all questions. Only necessity does the job, not passionate contingency.

It is worth noting that the passion that gives us some sense of comfort, in inarticulate and happy contentment, is not seen as a kind of dogmatism over which reason should triumph, but rather as a simple response. Common sense is defined by this very ahistorical attitude, which annihilates the future in the present by prolongation and repetition. What propositionalism called the blindness of passion is what we are calling the comfort of reasons, those which we give ourselves when we don't care to look, or when we're looking for some ready-made solution. It is in the concern for repressing the history of each moment of History that we recall human nature (a kind of reply, if not a form of survival) which helps us forget, as Nietzsche suggested. But there is in this human nature which responds to history in order to support it a kind of illusion that it is a necessity, and this leads us to the worst form of blindness, the worst kinds of compromises. History comes back to haunt those who ignore or bury it.

Passion is always realistic, it is a kind of constraint that we reject, as though we were free as regards reality and transform it by ideals or even by action. There is a *reason* in the taking of a position that is purely passionate, which makes us see the real in a certain manner in order to assume it. In this sense, passion is and always will be realistic, even if reality, whatever it is, is something other.

Passion which is reason is never really reason on account of difference. It is the sign of a partial reading which never says so, but which, by manifesting itself, integrates what it denies, thereby going against the insensible and external character of rationalized reality.

Passion, as that which represses the problematological difference by taking it over in the guise of displacing it, plays a role which is ambivalent and historically variable.

In a conception of reason which denies questioning, and which falls into the paradox of Menon, passion is the inverse of reason, since it is that which impedes reason and makes it necessary, that is, it is that which makes reason both impossible and useful. From the point when we overcome such a conception of things by explicitly integrating the problematic as being objective and recognized as such, passion loses its meaning as a concept of opposition and reference as regards the reason that founds itself. This is why we don't have to oppose passion and reason as though they were enemies. So under these conditions, does the idea of passion still make sense? The question is pertinent and unavoidable. Passion is, and remains, that which deals with the problematic as though it were resolved. The problematological difference is present but denied in the construction of a reality deemed continuous. The problematological difference could of course be made explicit: we think here of the scientists who ask questions of reality, who only see the real through the questions that they pose and the resolutions that they bring to them. There are no passions in those answers even if for them, the answers were made with passion, like passion that is inserted into the act itself over and above its ordinary content. The difference between reason and passion is clear, and since the problematological difference is constantly present in the mind of a scientist, the articulation of the problems and their solutions is undertaken in a rational fashion.

It is not necessarily like this for all of us. We cannot, nor do we wish to, verify everything; neither can we constantly put everything into question at every moment, if only for pragmatic reasons. The utility, efficiency, and speed of action rests upon accepted ideas, inherited from education and the ambient milieu. In the end, the argument of authority is still the most widespread rhetorical structure. We have faith before doubting.

In other words, we act in this sense with passion because we apply a preliminary and unquestioned solution to any new question, a point of view, a perspective, that allows us to see, but not to see ourselves. In this sense, the negation of questioning has its roots in anthropology and in human action at large: History which evolves cannot but make us aware of the phenomenon, but not abolish it, at least not at all possible levels. Passion, which is the process of rhetoricizing these problems, is unavoidable, whether or not we thematize the problematological difference. What this implies is not without consequence: passion is no longer seen as an illusion or an obstacle, but as the very difference of reason, a reason wherein we question and reply, and where we reflect in secondary responses upon the questions and answers of the first round. Passion is at once a manner of responding to problems and of thinking about them, answering them, and taking a distance from them. Passion is inscribed in the framework of the problematological differentiation, and not against it. It is the form that this difference takes for people. Even when someone denies passion, he puts it to work, just like the passionate person who ignores his point of view even as he expresses something as obvious *about* the world, if not *from* the world. What reflection about questioning shows is just that: the assurance of an individual's rhetoric is nothing more than the expression of his or her problematic, a reply which could be known and modified but which, if ignored, blinds those who abandon themselves to it. Passion is the reaction that people have to the problematological difference: they assume it by denying it, hence the postulation, which is a form of reason which refuses to admit that it is, but which purges itself of the assertion it has justified by justifying the assertion. Passion is the explanation of difference by the secondary reflection which it brings to the occultation which we experience each day. It is an immanent and unthinking rationality which makes us reply without questioning by transforming the process of questioning into that of responding.

Passion is therefore the answer to this concern about not answering, which is of course to answer. Knowledge gives to passion a reality that is complementary to that of reason: reason is blind when it is inhabited by propositionalism, which makes it suppress all problems, and also lucid as regards this blindness, a lucidity which permits reason to prevail by integrating the passionate as the unavoidable character of all points of view, whether stated or not. Passion is, finally, the necessity of consciousness, which answers without asking itself about this answer, that is, it is reason which offers no further reason for answering as it does, if only in "justifying" itself *de facto* through the factual nature of its perspective, a perspective which it cannot explain or justify.

The passion-answer *to* a problem, which it redirects into presupposition, or *about* a problem, which it expresses and amplifies, recalls the old opposition of passion which is unaware (and makes unaware) and passion which imposes itself as the awareness of an obstacle. These are the ongoing variations which result from the problematological difference as it can either manifest itself under the shock of reality and, finally, History itself or, on the contrary, hide itself in the stability of the real thanks to the act of converting experience into rhetoric.

Passion is the continuation of reason through other means, and it can also be what is furthest away from it, even though this is not the impression that subjects themselves have.

The Rhetoric of the Passions

How does rhetoricization happen? Consider a few examples:

1. A man is on trial before a war crimes tribunal for actions he does not deny having committed, but which he refuses to consider criminal. He insists that he was simply doing his duty by serving his country. He acted, therefore, [in his opinion] in a moral fashion.
2. Another man knows that snakes are poisonous, but he goes out into the desert anyway. He refuses to see this object, which is approaching, as a snake, or he simply refuses to accept that this snake is dangerous. It's a bit like a child who knows that too much chocolate isn't good for one's health, and yet continues to eat it, and by doing so denies that the general truth about too much chocolate could possible apply to him, that is, refusing the consequences of a truth that he'd otherwise admit.
3. Think then of the university professor whose scientific credentials are dubious, but who is nevertheless co-opted by his colleagues on account of arguments made concerning his value. His youth is used as a reason for the errors in his work, just as these same errors would be used against him if the colleagues thought it best to be rid of him. Behind the defense of this colleague is passion: the fear of quality, the concern about comparisons, the worry about one's own scientific (in)activity and the dangers posed by the hiring of someone who may be significantly better than the lot of them.
4. The next example comes from Shakespeare, in *Othello* III, iii, 345: "He that is robbed, not wanting what is stolen. Let him not knoweth, and he is not robbed at all."

How could someone who has been robbed not have been robbed?

Answer: because passion is the de-literalization of language, where the figure is the only recourse to contradiction, to paradox, giving meaning to the literal by creating a "manner of speaking," which means something other than what the person has in fact said.

The syllogism of passion manifests itself in all of these examples, wherein we see what is called the transformation into rhetoric, what I've been calling the *rhetoricization,* or, if you wish, the passionate inference. Rationalization, like ideology, abounds in similar inferences.

The first step relates to the language order, something we'll return to. For the moment, it suffices to see that the qualification of acts and things is important: the choice of one term, the rejection of another, as we saw in the examples above, is important because the very naming of things has implications. To call an action a crime necessarily has the connotation of something that is not a *duty*. From that point on, to know how to catalog things, acts, persons, events, and actions can no longer be seen as purely neutral. It means taking a stand about certain questions that are related to their resolution because the solution to the questions posed follows other decisions, rational or not. We can arrange internal questions, or their answers, in the domain of the implicit, which are projected upon the situation, and which give a kind of coherence to the entirety of experience. We could speak of the logic of "by the way": a crime is, *by the way*, this or that, and in the situation described in number 1, this "by the way" plays very strongly to qualify and motivate the condemnation of the accused in question. The circularity here functions in that the denomination *anticipates* the implications that must follow, those which were known *by the way*. Passion plays itself out fully in the reasons that are offered up, since these reasons are admitted from the outset, for external and anterior reasons which are never mentioned. Formalism is, therefore, very important, as any jurist knows very well.

Criminals justify their actions by making them fall into the rubric that renders them innocent; accusers, on the other hand, suggest the very opposite. What is interesting in the first case as in the other examples is the logic of the justification, which comes from the capacity to resolve all problems automatically, which proves that the answer is known even before the question is asked, which has the effect of nullifying it as a question. As such, the university professor who is up for a job is either too young, or not young enough, depending upon whether the committee wants to hire her. They cannot say, for example, that "I fear this woman because she is better known than I," or "I envy her," or "I am looking for prestige and the comparison with others will weaken my own position." We simply say that we cannot support her candidacy, despite the arguments offered. Is she too young? This shows that she hasn't proven herself. Is she too old? This proves that she's no longer capable. And so on. According to the thesis put forward, which is passionate, all questions become rhetorical according to the thesis, and all of them confirm it. Further, the very same argument, "she is too young," could as well go in the direction of "she is a good candidate," the very opposite, which shows the degree to which the statement proves nothing, it is a kind of common statement which could be put to the use of contradictory desires. "Passion doesn't look for itself, but proves itself through reasoning. From an intellectual point of view, it is reason that is warned, so sure of its principles that it doesn't cast doubt about their verity, that it cannot admit that no experience, no reasoning, can prevail over them."[1] Passion is given by the problem in the name of which all other problems are rendered rhetorical. It cannot be uttered, but it is the real reason behind all reasons, which are nothing other than rationalization, the resolution that is postulated for a problem which excuses the subject and which it does not want to, or is not able to, offer up as such. The argument of youth is ideological (we say that the question is closed) in that it can be used to justify either the hiring, or not, of that same candidate. It cannot decide because it serves both sides at the same time. It resolves all questions from the outset, rendering such questions illusory, since it serves as a pretext for pre-ordained ideas which are themselves *out of the question*.

In this process of *ideologization,* all questions are found to be resolved *a priori* by a process of naming that is pasted upon the phenomenon in question on account of the taking of sides, where we can see passion at work. And the debate as well, since the whole thing is to know whether or not a crime was committed. The "by the way" is crucial in the resolution of this question. War criminals act out of cruelty, but habitually they refuse to admit this passion, but instead invoke other reasons to define the acts they committed. And yet cruelty is defined by the exterior signs of the act in question, signs which permit us to recognize it as such.

In the case of Othello, jealousy makes him see what is not there, and makes him believe what he has not witnessed. Passion, once again, leads to a rather strange form of logic: all of Othello's reasoning consists in picking up on certain characteristics and considering them as proofs. Literalness is deceiving—and all of Shakespeare is wrapped up in the confusion of appearances which blind people and lead them into disaster, and the figurative is the key to all realist readings. But uncertainty remains, since inference is only probable. It is passion which renders inference unproblematic. Othello wants to confirm that Desdemona is guilty, and at any cost. The problem is therefore already resolved; all that follows is beyond the answer. Othello rationalizes his passion in his reasons, and makes no difference between them, and thereby indicates that he has no idea of the problematicity of what he sees, thinks, and feels. What is pleasure is pain, reality is but an appearance, and at the end of the day, the contrary of the truth becomes "the" truth. The rhetoric of the passions proceeds along the line of this inversion

1. L. Dugas, *La logique des sentiments,* in *Nouveau traité de psychologie,* ed. G. Dumas (Paris: Alcan, 1938), pp. 9–10.

whereby the problematic destroys itself in order to transform itself into unshakable certitude, as though by the touch of a magic wand.

The qualification is already marked by passion: Desdemona's mouth is hot from kisses of betrayal. This affectionate look is not for Othello, love is not love, it is lasciviousness. Everything means something other than what it really is, and Othello attributes to this figurative sense the reality that he denies to the literal. He has a sense of reality that is purely constructed and at work in passion, whence comes his idea that Desdemona is unfaithful, but which rests upon his refusal to see the indications around him as questions.

According to Othello, he is less passionate than Desdemona: he doesn't see his own passion, but instead projects upon the other the lack of confidence that is in fact his own insecurity: his insecurity, the color of his skin, which makes him an outsider despite his military conquests, are as much the problems that Othello evacuates by forcing upon the other the interrogation and the doubt that he himself suffers. Problematicity of existence is for him unbearable, and it cannot be escaped: Desdemona *could,* indeed, be unfaithful to him. He prefers certitude, even in error, as regards a question, which is the certitude that he is for himself, which he wants to reaffirm about the other, who is much weaker than he is. Desdemona's apparent passion allows him to ignore his own passion, making her own the cause of what he is suffering: "All passion has, just as love does, a blinder over its eyes: this blinder hides what it doesn't want to see, but allows it to see even more clearly what it does want to see, that is, what it imagines. Passion is therefore both unreasonable and logical, and more unreasonable than it is logical."[2] The syllogism of passion resurfaces in the second example, wherein the individual refuses to see the consequences of what he seems to implicitly follow.

If in the case of Othello there is nothing which is not interpreted as infidelity, in the example of the snakes, the problem is the exact opposite: nothing confirms the initial proposition, and the passion-driven idea about the snake impedes the person's ability to foresee consequences. This "will to not know" manifests itself in many regrettable, if not dramatic, examples. History would not repeat itself if people were a bit more lucid, or if they had the courage to see things to their ends. We've often heard that the Germans were ignorant of what Hitler was doing. In the strict sense of the word "knowledge," this is true, but once linked to the cult of war the hatred of Jews could not have led anywhere else. To have failed to figure this out is more than just ignorance.

2. Ibid., p. 11.

From consensus to consent, what we see without seeing, because these are only the consequences, which are a step away from the actual action. In the example of the child and the chocolate we find the same kind of "ignorance." Weakness of will? It is more a question of effect-passion, which is another type of reason to act or not to act despite "reason."

To pose the problem in a given way is equivalent to already taking an option on the explanation that we attribute to it. To speak of x as a crime, or as one's duty, is not the same thing, and yet it is the same x in both cases. The implications are different depending upon the category of the person, in this case the criminal. To say that "this is a crime" is to say that "this is punishable," or a hundred other things. By the same token, to say that "this is a snake" is to say that "this is dangerous," but also "this is long and slimy," which could refer to other objects than the snake, which is the source of the implicit refutation of a person who admits that the serpents are poisonous and then classes them with other animals which aren't. In the determination of the observed fact, passion is already present, that is, the idea that guides the qualification of the fact that is *in question*. The will to punish is in the accusation of crime (vengeance, resentment, punishing), just as fear is in the identification of the long slimy creature as a poisonous snake. We suppress all debate with this identification, unless we let it return at some later point.

Passion, in all of these examples, reveals itself in the rational closure, in the lie that one tells to oneself and to others.[3]

The mechanism of inference is always the same. It consists of concentrating on an aspect which can make a passion into an obsession that constantly reconfirms one's point of view, and which projects it upon all other problems. It does so to the point of denying the rest, *a fortiori*, everything which could question the point of view, the solution, or the passion, which anchors this solution over and above all others; it is a form of reason which doesn't admit that it is. "This is where reason enters passion, and we can speak about a logic of sentiments. This sentiment is not born until it calls reasoning to assist, to apply to it: it covers an abstract form, it becomes an idea; it establishes itself in principle, it sets itself up as an end."[4]

This is the source of this circular process, whereby conclusions are hidden behind the principles that contain them. The question is resolved in advance, such that there is no question except a rhetorical one. The

---

3. Cf. J.-F. Kahn, *Esquisse d'une philosophie du mensonge* (Paris: Flammarion, 1989).
4. Dugas, *La logique des sentiments*, p. 6.

discourse of passion, like its reasoning, is rhetoric. There is a specific quality of objects and facts which is privileged, or patched over, and this privileging or patching over creates the templates to be used for reading the situation, for it is inscribed within a network of implicit ideas which validate the interpretation, especially since they offer themselves up as the verification of the Idea proposed *a priori*. What makes these passionate inferences plausible is that they are chosen among the qualities of x which relate to, or evoke, the preexisting passion. The part stands in for the whole: this woman arouses a form of love through her smile which recalls the love of one's own mother, so all of the other properties of her face remain unseen, or simply don't count. This man displeases us on account of a word that recalls to us everything that we are not, or that we would like to be. So what we are left with is envy, malice, or even hatred toward him. Among all the attributes a, b, c, d, of x, only one is used to identify x.

X is a, but could be a, b, c, d, or something else, and if the selection is made by passion, it is based on what x really is. The same process is at work in the example of the snakes and the chocolate, wherein we ignore what doesn't please us, interest us, or accord with the subject that is for us of interest: x is long and slimy, and could just as well have been a y or a z, if no other property of it is examined. The snake, for instance, may very well be a long, wet, rope.

Passion acts by helping us deny the consequences that we are trying to draw, the ones that we refuse to admit because they contradict the idea we had from the outset. "The mind is stubborn, closed to all objections, or if it sees them, it is closed to admitting them, to give itself over to them, or to take them into account."[5]

The logic of passion is a logic that is an amalgamation of properties and the subjects of properties, a logic of contagion and contiguity: x is A, but "to be A" also applies to y, which is B, thus eventually z as well, and so on. By distinguishing the subject from the predicate, x from A, we assure a kind of univocality, an answer which doesn't plunge us into an endless list of possible answers. But all individuals are at once what they are (hence their attributes) and beyond these determinations, things in themselves which are unknowable for this very reason. The paradox of propositionalism resides in this identity which conceals an insurmountable difference, consecrating the proposition as an entity which articulates the impossible coupling, at least when the point is to reflect it in a coherent fashion.

5. Ibid., p. 62.

The rhetoric of passion is therefore a logic of substitution: jealousy can become hatred, disgust, envy, pain, and so forth. In any case, it consists of taking for cash what should in fact be considered in a problematological fashion, that is, as expressing a problem rather than a single solution. Projection becomes certitude and truth.

As for the formalization of this process of substitution, we can in fact show it with the aid of a diagram (Diagram 1): x is A, just as A applies to y; then x is y, on account of A, but since the y is also a B, then A is B; but since B is also z, which has other properties, like B, then we can link the x, the y, and the z. Or to put it another way, the A, B, and C can be linked by snapping our fingers at everything that separates them. If we aren't worried about dividing up the properties of their subjects, then Diagram 2 follows.

All rhetorical figures work this way: "Richard is a lion," the classic example of the metaphor, which signifies that Richard is courageous, because he, x, like y (the lions), is courageous (A); we suppress the properties that differentiates him from lions, like B, C, and D, and maintain this one property, A, and thus make an equivalence between y and A. This means that we annul the subject-predicate distinction: "to be y," or "to be a y" is the same thing, even if we know that the lion reflects courage, one of its principle attributes.

The reader could suggest that this is rather far from a discussion about passions. In fact, this is not the case. A man falls in love with a woman who has some appealing characteristic, worries about a young person who looks dangerous, and gets angry at an attitude that he finds vexing. In each case, the individual in question is loved, hated, or rejected

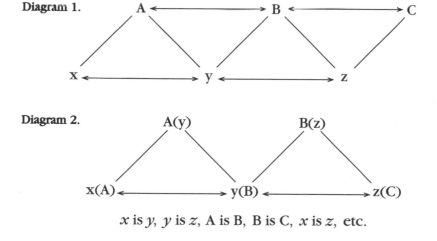

Diagram 1.

Diagram 2.

x is y, y is z, A is B, B is C, x is z, etc.

because of specific character traits which are part of a much larger system of characteristics, which encompass violence and love, for example. The idea and the passion come together. *Do we feel more a sense of being put into question than one of being confirmed by one's responses, if not by one's answers?* This is the principal question which underwrites all other passionate reactions, which demand closure and the exclusion of the other, or the reverse. The man who falls in love with a woman because she has green eyes, which he associates with Femininity (his mother or his first love), characteristic of love: x is A, y is B, and since B is also A, x is y: this woman has green eyes, his mother has green eyes, and she represents love, so this woman with green eyes also represents love for this man. This syllogism of passion reveals traits of rhetoric. It shows that other characteristics of an object are lost from view in light of certain significant ones, but that different people would be looking at different traits. This leads to a deformation of reality, because it is given a facade of passion. Lucretius writes:

> Their mistress is Black, she's a dazzling dark woman; dirty and disgusting, she loathes finery; shifty, she's Pallas's rival; thin and mangy, she's the darling of Menal; she's too small, she's one of the Graces; she's too tall, she's majestic; she stutters, she's amiably shy; she is taciturn, it's the reserve of modesty; she's carried, away, jealous, prattling, she's a wandering flame; dried-out on account of her thinness, she's of a delicate temperament; she's exhausted from constant coughing, she's a languishing beauty.[6]

The logic of this substitution, which makes specific properties undifferentiable from the subjects which have them, and then redistributes them as propositions later on, either inferred or not, operates on the idea of resemblance and partial identity, often subconsciously: "A Frenchman smitten through naïveté falls in love with an Englishwoman because she stammers in French; he associates childish ideas and candor and, having as he does an infantile soul, he loves a woman who speaks like a child. It's the same as a young girl, who passionately loves her father, is taken by a man much older than she because he knew and loved her father. She associates, or even confounds, filial love with romantic love, and one leads to the other."[7]

6. Taken from J. Rony, *Les Passions* (Paris: PUF, 1961), p. 69.
7. Dugas, *La logique des sentiments*, p. 14.

In fact, what happens is less of an association of the mind than an identification where a property which serves as the Idea which, once evoked, functions as the crystallizing principle that underwrites passionate reasoning. The candor of our Englishwoman includes his way of speaking and being, inside the idea of love, to which the candor is identified, or of the age in the second example. All differences are blurred before the idea that is awoken by the real, which finds a coherence that inference will put into form: "The artificial and childish link that exists here between the ideas doesn't have any logical character either. Surely we can always lend reasoning to passion and make it speak the language of Aristotle: there is nothing easier than clearing away and strengthening the syllogism according to which the link supposedly begins, or according to which it develops."[8]

Passion is an idea that comes from the crystallization before being shored up by circular reasoning that confirms it *a priori*, without any possible contradiction. The very obstacles that passion invents are there to comfort it, to root it in the passionate which presents all of the characteristics of absolute necessity (apodicticity). Passion, which constitutes itself in reason outside everything by dissolving into it, loses the excessive character which it has, irreducibly. Passion is what is beneath *logos*. Logos can capture passion only by respecting the problematological difference which gives all meaning to the process of taking charge of the problem that we are for ourselves, and which passion expresses in a range of irreducible ways.

The same type of argument which confirms the subject in its passionate beliefs, sometimes its obsessions, finds itself in all *concentrated* forms of representation. Symbolism affects the subject by one single ordinance, reducing the plurality inherent in multi-sided interpretations that are rooted in the "truth," whether figured or figurative, but always plural. Crystallization, according to Stendhal, consists in finding in things and in beings the signs of pre-formed answers and, when this fails, of creating obstacles to these answers, which are destined to be overcome so that the Idea-passion of the outset can be confirmed.[9] The deliriousness of persecution, jealousy, apology, or rationalization follows the same construction. Affective reasoning is metaphorical in all of these cases, even if, formally, it may look like scientific reasoning. Someone could say without any doubt that by unmasking the origins of this reasoning,

8. Ibid.
9. Which proves the problematical character, herein repressed, of passion.

which is affect or Idea, we demystify passion in reason. In fact, we must look for the problem that is at work in reasoning, since if this problem, which is at work in reasoning, is abolished as such without any possibility of being reconsidered as a question, because of the solutions which suppress it *a priori,* reasoning finds itself closed off, in contradiction to science. Passion obeys a logic which, to be explained, requires a problematological analysis. Since the experience is always interpreted, it is not enough to "make the difference." The passionate absolute is the result of this concentration that we spoke of earlier, and which comes out of a problematic that is followed in the fashion of a permanent resolution, outside time, and thus outside the future, leading it to secure a kind of eternity that Alqiué considered essential for passion, even if this reaction to time is but a derivation.[10] What is at stake here is more of a compulsion to repeat, which is destined to transform an existence which is hardly central to others, to History, or to the *cosmos* (since our deaths, like our lives, change very little in the overall order of things) into something essential, something eternal. In short, passionality is inscribed as the challenge issued to time, to laws, and to social conventions. Human passion is a struggle against death, a will to surpass itself and to achieve the impossible: it is the affirmation of this identity as outside time. This is the essence of all challenge which defies us to *be* more, to push us to will for the sake of willing, as Nietzsche said.

Passion, by suppressing the problematological distance, is the answer that forbids us from seeing the interval of reality, which is the very opposite of the scientist who is constrained to re-problematize his or her answers. The passionate reality sometimes allies itself with magic: we think for example of the greedy, who see each object in terms of value, price, exchange potential; for them, the world is but one giant marketplace. Is this reality? Or isn't it simply one more way of apprehending without distance, in complete immersion? Who hasn't understood that objectivity implies the demarcation of what is subjective, and that science is not identifiable except through problematization, which permits us to distinguish the different methods of taking on what is problematic, with its real solutions and with the others, which simply annul the questions without even thinking about them? Passion is at work in all problematization, from the very outset, from the very moment that we *formulate* the question. Science recasts the problem without perpetuating the solution *a priori,* where the act of rendering ideological, or the rationalization, pushes apriorism to its very limit, by neglecting one side,

10. Cf. F. Alquié, *Le Désir d'éternité* (Paris: PUF, 1943).

wanting to see only the other side, which is a state of constant interpretation without any appeal.

The woman we love is beautiful, intelligent, and charming; everything is there to confirm the love that these qualities are supposed to incite in us. But we don't love people for their qualities, because we know that these same attributes, though present in others, don't have the same effect as our loved ones. We are often incapable of explaining why we hate one person and love another. Intelligence when present in our child is a positive attribute, whereas if it is found in a rival it is unbearable, and for the very same "reason." Doesn't passion preexist reason? No, in this example it *is* the reason for what is happening. The circularity here is complete, but real.

Notice that in the examples cited at the beginning of this section we find the passionate logic that has been of concern to us all along.

The war criminal reasons as follows: "I am obeying orders when I kill people; to obey orders is to fulfill my duty; therefore, I am serving the collectivity by murdering people on demand." This reasoning leads us back to a particular manner of considering murder and sadism: but the fundamental principles which are violated here are completely ignored. We ask whether Brutus, who killed Caesar, was an assassin, which would mean that he should be punished, or whether he acted in the public interest by eliminating a tyrant, which would mean that he deserves to be honored and exalted. The answer can vary, and so too can Brutus's fate: acclaimed as a liberator, or punished as a murderer, it all depends upon how we consider the death of Caesar. The naming of the act *in question* involves a reason, and it is in this sense that passion, in the very act of judging, is also reason. The motivations of the act that Brutus committed change, as does the explanation for it, if not the very perception we have of the act he committed.

To return to our war criminal: his act x could be understood as an A or a C, and the As contain y, which means that through identification, x is y: x is the dutiful act, this particular x is a murder, thus this murder is the fruit of a moral obligation. It is not, therefore, an assassination. The accusation doesn't proceed any differently: x is C, and the Cs are zs, thus x is z: it is a murderous act; and murderers are guilty so this makes the person who committed the act, guilty. To choose to qualify x by A rather than C is obviously problematic, but the only way to decide remains this "by the way": the external criteria must allow for the testing of stories that are told, and the answers that are put forth. We'll know whether or not Brutus wanted to liberate Rome, even if things are always more complex than they seem. We could evaluate how irresponsible the assassins were, like those who permitted the assassination to go forward, even if the boundaries are still a bit fuzzy. What, indeed, does "permit" mean?

By the same token, the snake that is not a snake, the scientist who is not a scientist, or is too much of one, give rise to passionate inferences, all calculated on the model of a rhetoric which passes from individuals to properties, or from properties to individuals, on the basis of one trait or another which relate different individuals, and at the expense of differences which are rendered unessential or invisible, which allows substitution to occur. Is this x, which is in that particular form, a snake? Is this x, which is indeed chocolate, bad for one's health? Was this x, which is the death of a man, a crime, a legitimate defensive gesture, a medical experiment, or euthanasia? Is this professor a scientist or an impostor? As many questions as qualifications: we can not avoid one without passing to the others; where passion, which is inevitable, becomes guilty as if, by the absence of questioning, in light of the apriorism of "solutions," interpretations are taken as truth.

This literalness, rather than the figural, opposes a passion that passes for reason to a reason which completes the passion. This leads us to the question of the language of passion, or, how we find figures in language.

Language and Passion

Passion is also an effect of language, if not a language game. The consciousness of the subject is always indirectly present in all transitive relations with reality. By transitivity I mean the consciousness which is itself when considering things other than itself. We are indirectly in question through this relation, we are like subjects who say something without saying it to *themselves*. Passion is the subject of the enunciation of utterances.

The density of the language originates in the fact of consciousness. This consciousness is what it is when directed to other things: symbolically, it is a by being other than itself, say, b. It represents the world by coming out of it, and by the same token, the formula of consciousness leaps out: "a is b." Consciousness thinks about itself thinking about other things: the table, the neighbor, the enemy, the lover, all leap to mind and are there, in all their presence, which is finally just intellectual. We only have consciousness of them when we forget that it is only a question of consciousness: they seem to be so close that we forget that it is not the actual objects that are in our mind. My consciousness, a, is not itself, except when it is b, that is, the consciousness of an object which loses itself from sight in order to lose itself in the object. This passion of the real is the judgment "*a* is *b*": isn't this the very structure of the proposition? If the unconscious is language, what can we say about consciousness?

Passion is what wants to be uttered in and through speech acts: the meaning of the utterance found in the enunciation. It is the *manner* in which the subject of the enunciation gets involved that is the passion. There are lots of passions: they are dispositions to diverse emotions, to corporal compensation, with pleasure or pain as the key ones. Few affirmations come without passion in some form; it is generally a sentiment that is trying to become asserted through the affirmation itself. This idea is not a new one. Hobbes writes: "And first, generally all Passions may be expressed Indicatively; as I love, I feare, I joy, I deliberate, I will, I command; but some of them have particular expressions by themselves, which neverthelesse are not affirmations (unlesse it be when they serve to make other inferences, besides that of the Passion they proceed from)."[11]

The subjunctive refers back to deliberation, the imperative mode to hope and aversion, with a whole gamut of passionate modalities. Obviously, nothing assures us that the subject who manifests these passions really feels them through language. We can fake passion, just as we can manipulate it in the other, with the help of rhetoric.

When we find ourselves in the face of such banal statements as "Jacques has a pretty wife" or "he's a real bull on the field," the presence of passion hardly seems evident. It is clear that there was someone there making these judgments, who is not without his or her passions, but the one who inhabits that body doesn't give the impression of *appearing*, in the large sense of the word.

Yet when we look more closely, this is indeed what is happening. Passion is in the enunciation of each statement as the imprint of the subject. It is a problematic imprint as regards this utterance, but if we make the effort to problematize it, to not limit it to its literalness, which would be its end point, then passions leap to view.

Let's return to our examples. To say to someone that he has a lovely wife, or to say it to someone else if we hadn't asked him, is to respond to some other question.[12] The question that must be asked concerns the problem of the speaker, and for this reason we would qualify the answer as *problematological*: it is of this type of answer that the discourse of passion is composed.

11. Hobbes, *Leviathan*, pt. 1, sec. 6, p. 128.
12. We have described our theory of language in various texts, English and French, including the edited volume, *Questions and Questioning* (The Hague: Walter De Gruyter, 1988).

We could also imagine that the suggestion concerning Jack's wife obeys certain passionate imperatives (jealousy or need) to raise a question the interlocutor, who, let's say, is married to an unattractive woman, would rather not have evoked, and so on. Here, a plural reading is required, which sends us back to a range of the subject's characteristics, not only in terms of personal disposition, but also as reactions to the situation at hand, which they transform by the suggestion of what is possible. Passion is defined by a set of possibilities, and when we say "there is a bull in the field," we could just as well be raising a question as giving a warning. Each time we find ourselves confronted with a disposition of the subject, with a problem for which the solutions are multiple and which the subject must deal with simply because he succumbs to a situation *which captures him,* and thus puts him into question. Passion is a way of replying, a kind of symptom and sign that there is a problem. Fear, jealousy, threats, or whatever else, have to be resolved unless they are resolved by virtue of their having been expressed.

If the discourse of passion is the indirect language of the statement which captures the enunciation, then passion which speaks for itself permits the person to regain a correspondence with him or herself which the gap between the literal and the utterance creates. Recall St. Augustine's "To love is to love loving," a statement that applies beyond love to many passionate states; who doesn't suffer from suffering, who doesn't have an aversion to aversion, who doesn't enjoy enjoying"? It is as though in each case we return to the literalness of the fact that to love, for example, is loving to love, reflecting in a passionate manner the fact of passion, rendering it completely adequate to itself? Reflexivity, which passion contradicts, would reappear, in the way language expresses passion.

Didn't Descartes suggest that if we doubt our own doubt when we doubt, then we still doubt?

We can nevertheless express a certain reservation about the generality of the fact that we have just mentioned. After all, we can derive a certain pleasure from our pain, in order to feel even guiltier about certain sentiments. But pain makes us suffer, and we experience the suffering of this suffering, even when it is mixed together with other sentiments. The pleasure of pain, for example, is not any less a pleasure from which we derive pleasure. The pleasure in pain thus becomes one state of consciousness which contains another, and this state has two distinct levels which makes them compatible and, paradoxically, in some ways relatively bearable. People who like to complain seem to enjoy the terrible things that happen to them, as though to feel themselves existing in the vicissitudes of life which they unmask, and from which they wish themselves lucidly distanced. The pleasure of this pain stops being contradictory even if, in a sense, it remains unbearable, especially for others. In the reflexive transparency of passion, which provides comfort for *itself* at the same time, subjects find themselves, and know *what* they know or don't know, endure or don't experience, and create their own negations at a level of affirmation which expresses them, and where they don't really play themselves out. In short, they create in themselves a fault line which, rather than breaking them in two, allows their dualities to live consistent with themselves. At the same time, they affirm themselves in pleasure as though having pleasure for pleasure's sake, as in the earlier example, and by doing so, they find themselves at a level of expression of the self, where they live, and thus reflect upon themselves thanks to passion, which permit them to do so.

Let us now confront the language of passion with the language which is lacking therein. A sentence like "It's nice outside" seems to be devoid of passion. We say it to express content; the Ego affirms what it says and signifies nothing else. The conclusion is clear: the reflection adds nothing, since the *reason* for saying what we say is in the saying itself, without any possible role for the afterthought. The passion of truth affirms itself in this adequacy.

It's easy to realize that this is but a possibility. We can easily conceive the inadequacy of the Ego and of what is said, the enunciation and the utterance. Passion reveals itself as irreducible to the figure of the Ego because discourse is no longer literal but figural (or figured, or figurative). We could wish to say that Napoleon lost the battle of Waterloo when we say that he lost Waterloo. But we could be signifying that dictators all lose eventually. There we find an excess of signification as regards the literalness which offers explanations through a collection of ideas or images associated with Napoleon or with the battle of Waterloo, which plays on the fact that the question that is asked isn't "Who lost Waterloo?" or "Who is Napoleon?" (i.e., "the one who lost Waterloo"), but another question, for which the literal response would be "Dictators end up being toppled, sooner or later," which is what the speaker really wants to say. The discourse here is a figuration of this truth, unless it is this truth which is found in the figure of the battle of Waterloo. Passion is this will to say—anger, indignation, love, joy, fear, etc.—which underwrites what is said, a kind of answer to the problem that the answer resolves, and which animates the speaker. This answer could go from the duplication of this answer as such ("You said *x* ..." or "*what you said is* ...") right up to the providing of evidence, through him, of the problem, to the one who did the speaking. This return to the self, wherein we separate ourselves from what we say, to point only to the problematicity, illuminates the game of passions.

A simple example will allow us to illustrate the phenomenon of the passionate lag. Anne sees Sandra with a new jewel and says:

1. "Sandra is wearing a Cartier."

In itself, this utterance has nothing passionate about it. And yet we can find in this utterance a range of passions at work, like figured or figurative readings: envy, for example, or admiration; the joy of friendship or hatred; aesthetic pleasure; or other indirect messages.

The test which reveals the presence of passions is quite simple. It is sufficient to confront a passionate reading of the first case to that same utterance. For example:

2. Anne is jealous of Sandra.

Compare this with another utterance, which apparently contains no passion:

3. It is one o'clock,

which means that "it is one o'clock" because the question that was posed was to find out what time it is. On the other hand, in the second case the question wasn't, "What did Sandra just purchase?" but rather "What does Anne feel when she says what she says?"

By comparing 1 and 2, we could observe that 2 is not the content of the utterance of 1, but is but one derivation, among others, of it. This is the source of the plurality of possible interpretations of subjective readings, which delimit what we want to say, and want to think.

The difference between 2 and 3 is identity: "It is one o'clock," which signifies that it is one o'clock. By contrast, what is signified by the utterance "Anne is wearing a Cartier" is not *that* Anne is wearing a Cartier, but something else. If there is identity, it is situated at another level, the one that speaks situates herself at a second level as regards the first. To say 1 is to say 2, just as to say 3 is only to say 3. This saying creates an identity, but a purely metaphorical one, since it seems improper to assimilate envy to 1, except in a purely figured fashion. To *say* 1 is to say 2, but 1 does not in itself say 2.

Passion reflects this gap between the metaphorical and the literal. We are not tricked by passion unless we create confusion, assimilating reason that is offered in and through what is said, with the true reason. The figurative unmasks passion by imposing a difference, even if there is, despite everything, an identity that gets perpetuated, one that would consist in identifying the envy that Anne feels for Sandra to the remark that describes 1. There is an identity which we couldn't consider literally; it reflects subjectivity as such. With the passions that inhabit it, in its lack of correspondence with what is said, there is an independence from passion. The identity of passion and reason is nothing more than a manner of speaking, an identity which is realized figuratively, and which aims to make passion into reason outside "the" reason, the reason of reason. Passion assures reason the literalness that it needs, permitting the subjective motivation to pass by in the background, by imposing itself as such in its specific identity. The consciousness keeps its coherence and its structure.

What is striking here is the role that the figural plays as the inscription of the passionate difference. It is profound reason, and the real of what is said, which is problematic when passion is at work. This requires an appeal to another answer, which makes the first one nonliteral. We assist here in a multiplication of possible answers, which are as many figured answers to the problem at hand, and which cannot be reduced by a simple literal and referential substitution. In terms of consciousness and consciousness of the self, we can see very well that there is, in the language of passion, a form of nonidentity of the discourse to itself, wherein plays subjectivity. Passionality, particularly aesthetic passionality (which is but one possible form of it), is the measure of the individuality and of the subject. Passion is reason which doubles back in reason which is lost from view in order to better affirm itself. Is its innocence guilty? Without doubt, since subjectivity is occulted in a reason that is not one, and which must be taken by default if we wish to eventually find the real truth. Passion says the same thing as reason in a difference that impedes all definitive conclusions: Anne envies Sandra, or perhaps admires her, or perhaps both, and this is the reason why she noticed her jewels (or, say, her award for scientific achievement). But on the other hand, we see very well that we couldn't be mistaken about the *problem* which animates Anne *in* her answer even if, explicitly, there is no question of one passion or another. Passion rediscovers its traditional meaning, subjective unthinking consciousness, carried out by or toward an object. The ascendancy of a spontaneous sentiment manifests itself in the judgment made about this object. Passion is this dynamic of consciousness, whereby it absorbs itself in the Other by a motivation which makes of it the indirect subject of its own activity. The speech act that would emerge therefrom, if it explicitly manifested itself, would be the carrier of difference, of the non-correspondence of self and consciousness, making of passion the hybrid tissue of our mind, both conscious and unconscious at the same time, self and other, judgment and emotion.

Passion is the consequence of a problematization: the answer that is differentiated from it, or upon it, witnesses a difference that language consecrates. Notice that the realization of the problematic leads to an answer to the problematic which, and there the problematological difference demands it, posits as distinct what is in question in what is said, be it through its form. And the problematic, despite everything, remains, in that we can never be assured of the real passion which makes reason out of the utterance. We imagine it, we infer it, but it remains in principle plural, as in the second example above. Passion makes the saying appear as an answer. The discovery comes in the recognition of the adjacent problem.

In the selection of facts to which the utterance refers, there is therefore a passion which is the reason for saying what we say, and choosing to say what we say and in the fashion we choose to say it, privileging some things and ignoring others. What is forgotten and what is played up are the fruits of passion, which make the fact objective *in fact*. Passion is constitutive of factuality, and when passion reveals itself as such, subjectivity shows itself in its very specificity.

What passion brings in its train is this confusion of levels, where objects are one of their properties, integrating others into a grouping that abolishes all differences. The woman will be beauty for one, tenderness for another; the man will be strength for one, generosity for the other, or intelligence, or wealth. There are as many Ideas that are consecrated to passion as to love, and which manifest themselves in the language games of passion. The concentration of emotions generates passion, as it does here for love. But the combination of properties which are rendered pertinent and subjects which are, from the beginning, but supports for these properties ("the lion" = "being a lion," thus $b, c, d, \ldots$) are not sufficient in order to make passion operate despite ourselves if consciousness didn't proceed on the basis of the same confusion between the reflexive and the unreflexive, between the consciousness of the self and the consciousness of the object, between the metalevel and the external level of its own working. This signifies a consciousness which takes itself as objective even though it's not. The logic of the propositional amalgam is ignorant of itself as such in the absence of distinct reflection: passion is repressed in its own effect: "The passionate dialectic is subjective, but it doesn't appear to itself as such."[13]

---

13. Dugas, *La logique des sentiments,* p. 13.

The Two Forms of Consciousness,
or the Role of Time as a Unifying Factor

We have covered two images of consciousness, which combat each other and must nevertheless be able to coexist. The first is the consciousness-reflection, wherein we represent (to ourselves) objects. The direct and transitive consciousness is directed to these and at the same time, reflects upon itself as consciousness, in a perfect identity with itself, a kind of immediate intuition of ourselves contained in all reflection we make about external objects. This conception, which dates back to Descartes and Locke, is well known, and we have already discussed it at length.

From this perspective, it is as though the consciousness of the self adds nothing to the consciousness itself, since it *is* the consciousness, which always reflects back upon itself. This is the source of the idea of representation, but also the paradox of passion which consecrates the difference, rejected, of the consciousness and the consciousness of self. Passion is the interval of consciousness which expresses the nonidentity to the self, the unthinking absorption, or the consciousness of this un-reflection. Passion is the expression of a telescoping between these two levels of consciousness, which creates the confusion between the part and the whole. Passion becomes the literal version of reason, which no longer sees itself seeing, and which projects upon things without any distance, which would give it a kind of figurativity; and it is as much the consciousness of this figurativity and of this difference, in the consciousness's return to itself.

In fact, the consciousness of something is not the consciousness of itself directed toward something, since it is toward itself that it turns: to amalgamate the two is to take both sides, to mix together the metalevel of the consciousness which applies to itself with the direct level, the one that makes thematic the external object. This mixture suppresses the asymmetrical "*a* is *b*" by creating a kind of identity which is only recognized later on as being figurative. The un-differentiation of consciousness, which is both objective and reflexive, creates the impression that the subjective expression of reflection corresponds to the objective validity of the glance that is directed toward the outside. Passion, to be perceived, must be comprised between this mixture of consciousness of self and unreflexive consciousness. It must be re-differentiated so that passion can find its positive side. Passion which errs brings the un-differentiation of levels of consciousness *and* the inability to know this un-differentiation, or else, the impossibility of escaping, on account of paradoxes that have been studied by the Palo Alto School![14] When we say that "it is true that this statement is false," we are in the presence of a paradox which places the saying and the said on the same level, thereby rendering linear what really should be hierarchical. The statement that applies to itself, even as it says the opposite, evokes consciousness which reflects its own unreflexive self, by thinking of it as nothing, or impossible. Passion is the name of this impossibility, just as it is the space wherein this contradiction is reabsorbed. When we suggest that "to say nothing is still to say something," passion consists of not seeing the differences of the levels involved, as though becoming aware of our passions leads us to the realization that even if we say nothing at all in total silence, we still signify something. We hereby express what we feel, and deal with a question from which we cannot escape, but for which we don't utter the reply as such.

Coherence demands that we abandon the classical theory of consciousness in favor of one that admits to the difference between unreflexive absorption and the moment that consciousness returns to itself. Passion becomes the truth of consciousness, it accepts, or not, what it "experiences," and enjoys or suffers it, depending upon the circumstances. If consciousness remains identical to itself, when it reflects upon itself after having been submerged, then this is the result of the passage of time. In fact, temporality assures through memory a continuity which makes it such that the mind knows what it thought before we asked it. Recall in this regard the grocer counting his money at the end of the day.

Temporal difference is the identity of consciousness. The un-reflexive consciousness is distinct from the consciousness of self even as it is the same, and is therefore consciousness, because it does not occur at the same moment as the return to the self and the forgetting of the self. Passion insinuates itself into this gap, thereby admitting the time of consciousness. To live one's passion is to live one's temporality. There is no conscious living being which does not bear the imprint of the passionate. To overcome passion therefore becomes the objective of the person who wishes to dominate time, and the passion of eternity, or pure immediate presence, is inscribed into the flesh like the illusion that passion can be destroyed and abolished. A whole vision of passion emerges, as we have seen previously. The reaction (which is itself passionate) to passion is a trap; it passes itself off as rational, forgetting all that reason owes to passion. From this perspective, what assures identity to consciousness

14. Cf. P. Watzlawick, J. Beavin, and D. Jackson's work on the logic of communication.

is the victory over the passions, its difference from itself. This suggests that the consciousness of self and the external consciousness could coincide, and that the time of their lag is abolished. The passionate must be expelled from conscious life, which it nevertheless characterizes. The unity of reason thus confers to us a timeless presence, as though we could extirpate ourselves from time. This is only possible under the condition that the shock of History be sufficiently feeble to be erased. Passion represents the illusion of adequacy rather than its condition of impossibility: passion procures the sense of immersion in the world and the forgetting of the self by a strong sense of existing in an immediate and unreflexive fashion. By passion more than by reason, the part invades the whole (as passionate logic demonstrates), it submerges and invades, monopolizes and mobilizes.

The paradox has it that passion is as much the veil of difference as the real fusion. For Descartes, passion is an obstacle to reason and to intuition. In the romantic period, we saw the reverse: it was passion which made the Ego, creating the identity that reason impedes.

For passion to assume this double role it must be intrinsically ambivalent in propositionalism. What we are seeing here is the reversal that marks the difference between Descartes's day and our own, a reversal in which romanticism plays the critical role.

Everything comes from temporality. Descartes thought that he'd be able to annul it, and with it, to reject outside consciousness passionality assimilated to time and to its returns. These become unavoidable with the acceleration of history, lived in revolutions, through thousands of deaths, in wars, or in the simple speed of careers, which accelerates in all societies wherein people are more mobile. So it's the identity of consciousness which causes problems, not the difference. Un-thinking wins the right to be named, and at the end of the day the unconscious, which constitutes the most radical form of this difference, this time without the identity which recuperates it as consciousness. Passionality is the measure of the difference made by translating consciousness that is not consciousness of self, which integrates passion to consciousness. The taking-over of history and time is marked by the life of passion. But the paradox bounces back, since time is also what makes it so that I, who had been unthinking previously, become conscious today of my consciousness of yesterday, which assures a global identity of the subject. Passion gives me the *sentiment* of this identity in time, a kind of permanent presence, a presence of self outside time. Haven't we once again annulled it by our assuming the inevitable?

Time has thus been lived differently from the classical age to today,

where *lived* signifies *passionate*. This lived life is more or less stabilized
by passion, which renders the shock of time and denies it by the identity
that it establishes against time (passionate moments where nothing
exists outside passion).

For a long time it was held that time was something that could be
isolated, a kind of in-itself which existed outside consciousness, or that it
was a kind of pure form, a homogeneous grandeur, or not. We are "in"
time and we speak *of* time, as though it existed wholly outside. Some
thinkers even oppose "objective" and "subjective" time. In short, we have
had the sense of being plunged into a time which preexisted us, and
which continues afterward, a sentiment which offers some solace for the
conception that we make of our consciousness and its identity as either
logical or transcendental (Kant). The exterior and the positive elements
of time rest on the impression that all of us have, which is that whether
or not we exist won't change anything in terms of the evolution of the
world: personal identity goes along with the sense of being inessential.
Passion in these conditions represents the exteriority of consciousness
for itself, what cannot be it, which leaves us with a sense of futility. Passion is all the more powerful because we perceive time as an acceleration. We have to struggle against ourselves to be ourselves. The challenge
against ourselves as well as against others (sports, games) follows along
in train. Passion is pursued actively and assures the identity with a consciousness which seeks itself through history, through its own history.
To live passionately is to invest the time in challenging the time, to build
ourselves outside the time, through the concern about a present which
we constantly repeat, like a game where we constantly put up all our
winnings after each hand.

Passion assures the identity of the Ego, as romanticism pointed out,
because it confirms that the consciousness is single and indivisible in
time and through it, by creating over and above temporality this subjective identity. This presupposes a bearable historicization, that is, one
that can be annulled: the Ego is established *a priori* in an affirmation of
itself which excludes the passionate. This at least applies initially, since
in our time History is moving so fast that passion can no longer be
annulled, and indeed it is passion that incites the Ego to think about overcoming temporality, even if such a goal is illusory and based upon false
hopes. But does the passionate man really fool himself? In any case, the
passionate reversal aims to give the Ego an identity that History increasingly takes away. Passion thus is part of consciousness itself, and it is
the identity of the Ego outside time that causes all the problems. Memory
has become passion, the master of time is no longer the remembrance
(Proust), but the permanent denial that occurs through incessant activity.

When the Ego discovers passion as the truth of its inscription in time, it leads to a passionate reversal whereby passion can no longer be denied. It reflects the phenomena of consciousness, where we grasp afterward what was experienced but not understood earlier on. Passion is this temporality, which confers to consciousness an identity through time, even though we have the feeling that we have a constant identity *a priori*. But now we know all that, and it is no longer possible to consider this equivalence to ourselves in any other fashion than as a consciousness of passion, an identity which is not one, if only through memory. Passion appears like the moment when the difference of self from self is abolished; and the consciousness of this passion appears as the realization that what was at issue was in fact a difference. Pleasure and pain function here as regulators of the system: pleasure (and therefore success) reinforces history, which we forge and create as we go along; on the other hand, pain operates as a difference which threatens the equilibrium of these orientations, put them into question and brings on instability. The more we enjoy pleasure, the more we look for it through the means that brought it in the past, which is a sign that the repetition of the present, however fleeting, is nevertheless possible. As for displeasure, it breaks continuity to render History (from which all questioning was erased) fictional, passionate, in a word, illusory. It is always our own story that we recount, or that we search for, through the spectacle of the Other, of difference, of suffering.

In short, it is no longer possible to extract oneself from passion, it is unavoidable in order to allow one's self to live up to its potential as Self. As a necessity of existence, passion creates the necessity of the self which no Cogito could possibly render. At the end of the day, identity is nothing more than a fiction, and passion is the only reality, the reality of our evanescence, made up of moments that we consider eternal, even though they are incarnated in smaller ends (Kierkegaard).

Passion, therefore, is the quest of existence: it is the question of what I am for myself, what implicates me directly, or indirectly, in all that is: the world, beings, things or events. (Good) conscience is situated behind the literalness of perceptions.

Passion as a Reply to History: From History to History, or the Individual as Reflexive Presence (to Him or Herself)

The whole question is to find out how the theory of consciousness was modified between the classical age and today. Isn't there any possible unity which could account for and integrate opposite conceptions of consciousness?

On the one hand, the consciousness of self and the consciousness of the object, although distinct, are coherent, can be compared: this is because of reason for Descartes, passion for the romantics, but consciousness for both. At the moment when consciousness reflects upon what happens in it, time passes, and it considers itself as having thought about something. Time renders coherent realization, and assures it the duration necessary for its identity. This identity is not immediate, as it used to be thought. But nothing proves that the fact that we become conscious of what we had been conscious of before doesn't alter consciousness itself, because at the moment when we return to what we thought, we are thinking something else and nothing is like it was previously. Isn't irreversibility the very mark of consciousness, as it is for physicochemical systems? Or, is it possible to go backward as if nothing had really changed in the interim? This possibility that consciousness would have to return to the truths of yesteryear and find them still intact, in their purity, if not in their completeness, was one characteristic of the previous era, but flies in the face of contemporary thinking. When I become aware of what I was conscious of yesterday, certain things have already changed and my consciousness has even been modified, so there is no question of returning to the original state of things. What I have therefore is a consciousness of myself having a *quest,* which is to recall what I had been, what I had thought, and what I had lived previously. If time passes slowly, there is some hope of finding an adequate representation of what was previously thought, or at least to believe this to be possible. Cartesian thinking represents this moment of relatively weak historicity. On the other hand, we can recall that to become aware of things which, during the process, are not any more modified than my own awareness, leads to a (relative) impression that the world around us is stable.

On the other hand, romanticism teaches us that there is always a gap, even if consciousness wants us to overcome it. Today, we would be more nuanced about this idea, since the relative speed of events, of life, and of what is outside us, counterbalances this hope, and sometimes either concretizes it or renders it illusory. Our perception of time has changed: it is relative; we evolve at the very moment when we perceive the outside world as being inside ourselves. Consciousness, far from being apprehended as a substance, for which passions would be affections (attributes), must be understood as a quest, an interrogativity, which articulates itself in terms of problems. They express the quest and are already answers, in the form of passions. An unalterable and objective consciousness *(res cogitans)* which detaches itself from the world of which it is part in order to position itself in the face of the object, as an un-namable entity, or as an in-itself (Kant), something different, are characteristics to reject. The Copernican revolution changed the fixed point, whereas the Einsteinian revolution demands that three is more: if the earth orbits the sun, it nevertheless orbits itself as well; just like we humans who evolve even as everything around us changes at a speed that is more or less different from our own. This gap makes us realize the existence of time, which desubstantiates things and people and confronts us with the very passions which a rationalist or propositional conception had pushed away or devalorized. Passion is what permits us to lose sight of our own history, which leads us to constitute one, to imagine personal perspective as personal, and to consider ourselves as emerging from a transhistorical community defined by co-presence. This fixed nature assures people from a particular era a *common sense*, if not a communal sense, of morality, which is possible, since we are unaware of the fact that the point of view from which we speak is nothing but *one* point of view. Passion is action in that the fact of thinking about something, without thereby modifying it, is nevertheless another fact which is different in that it is not perceived in the act of perceiving the real inside of which it is inscribed. Identity is maintained in the difference between the two facts, since identity is *in fact (de facto)*. In this sense, passion is a difference which establishes the identity of the real *for us*.

What is important here is that over and above the oppositions that direct History from Descartes to postromantic modernity is rationality, which supports this movement and which gives it a certain coherence for us. The result of this is a way of living and reflecting upon temporality. The logic of identity and of difference penetrates consciousness and its reflexive nature to become materialized in diverse passions, the passion *for* passion, or *of* passion, which becomes a way of thinking about time which passes, and to make it objective as a means of trying to better control it. To live time, to think time, to find one's identity in the difference that time creates within us, between us and others, is the effect of passion which, since it cannot be denied, must be recognized and imposed upon the human mind confronted with History. Time appears as something exterior, like passion; it was lived successively as regards a fixed point in time for a subject whose identity seemed similar to the identity of mathematics entities. Perception of endless succession doesn't bring us back to an endless succession of perceptions, because the subject operates an immediate and reflexive synthesis of its own character as an object. The hypothesis here is that the subject *reflects* objects, facts, and events as they occur and in the manner in which they occur. Or this, at least, is what we come to believe.

If a gap is created, which the mind cannot bridge by bringing the new back to the old, then we suffer a lost of simultaneity and stability, and this puts into question the possibility of rendering it rhetorical. Rationalization and ideology will be reflected as they are (Marx), and passion will be assimilated, either to the continuation of the occultation of the new by the old by subjects who are oblivious, because they cannot, or would rather not, see that the old has lost all meaning, or, to the passionate disassociation that results from this new temporality which cannot be assimilated, which shows the gap in its own irreducible nature; passion becomes the subjective *par excellence*. The past, as the norm for rhetoricization, becomes unacceptable. Passion is conscious of itself: it is the form that talks to the consciousness of the self in this reaction that aims toward autonomy.

Simultaneity and stability are relative evolutions which are produced at the same rhythm, leading up to the idea of a subject and object which are separated, one sending back (and annihilating or exteriorizing) the temporality of the other at the very scene of its own temporalization. The consciousness of succession coincides more or less with the succession of consciousness, creating, with the inevitable lag between them, the sentiment of the past, the present, and the future, which permits us to annihilate History, to submit without knowing that we are doing so.

The idea according to which consciousness reflects, literally, in its returns upon itself, the ruptures and evolutions of events around us confirms an exteriority and an inessential quality of our existence as compared to the world. We are passive spectators, not influential actors.

We must distinguish this approach from the one which consists of seeing passion as the reactive constant, *the* answer to what changes. Cartesianism seems to us a particular case. And when passion is reflected by consciousness, this phenomenon plays itself out, since what is at stake here is our awareness of the problematic when everything, or almost everything, is put into question, without any hope of bringing the future to a present which is simply prolonged. We could give ourselves over at this point to a "relativistic" interpretation of passion, or even a "quantum" one, just as there was a Cartesian one. The first would consist of integrating the passionate point of view of the subject as having a perspective that hovers over history and surveys it, as though the subject could really become detached, whereas the second would simply deny historicity. Even the facts of saying what the subject says, thinking what he thinks, acting as he acts, are already the fruit of a historical point of view which escapes him, perhaps, but which, seen from the outside, allows itself to be deciphered. Passion which is reflected sees but one point of view, without this implying any renouncing thereof, since this reflexivity makes up a part thereof, so that the relativity doesn't impede objectivity.

One step remains: when passion modifies the point of view that it expresses as it reflects upon itself. It integrates itself into History by thinking about this point of view. It offers itself the freedom to modify its own point of view as it reflects. The reality that it makes rhetorical acts upon the rhetoricization process itself and poses the *question* of knowing whether we pursue this rhetoricization or whether we abandon it. It is in this sense that passion acts upon the world, and that it is not only the fact of dealing with it. The observer works upon the observation itself by realizing what it observes, and this affects him or her in return. This surely changes the idea of believing that the observer has a point of view which intersects with reality. Passion, perceived of as a mechanism of rhetoricization, as true reason that stands as the figural behind the literal, puts the literal into question as soon as the role of passion becomes conscious. From that point we are *free* to change our perspective, or to consider it as truth itself. The subject in a passionate state becomes aware of this, which leads to a new state of consciousness, if not a new passion—unless it prolongs the old one. This makes the relationship to change dynamic and passionate, and counters this relationship with a coherent history-rationalization, whatever the events. Passion must become its own object so that the common sense, and the community as a whole, can keep their identity. Passion is the buffer which absorbs the shocks by sending them back, transforming them, and generally transforming the difference into an identity in difference: anger as regards the world and the beings within it, scorn, rejection, or else love and joy, are all answers which transform problems which we encountered into *individual* challenges which don't endanger the ordering of reality, an ordering which lived History nevertheless destabilizes. We let loose through anger, just as we idealize through love; we ignore what is displeasing, just as we accept what survives in joy. In short, we put individual dispositions to work, and the body becomes subordinated to it all through numerous sensations. These dispositions translate the identity of each person, *his or her* way of reacting to the differences that time imposes, and his or her way of maintaining this identity against time and new problems that it carries along with it. But since these reactions are numerous or intense when we become reflexive about them, then they lead to a modification of the individual. "Who am I to put up with such hatred?" "Who am I to have become so bitter with the passage of time?" or "What have I done with my life, and what can I still accomplish?" All of these questions answer the passions which, when manifested at particular occasions, surface as passions. Passion is like rage, which leads us into History, events, other people, and even fashions; passion imposes itself as the answer that must be imposed upon the problems from which the passions emerge, so that they don't show, even though they'll continue to produce them. Passion represses the historical for the benefit of individual reactions and seems to be nothing more than an answer unaware of itself, to a problem which in fact doesn't exist, but reality catches up to those who live in it and plunge them back into it. It does so by making them aware that the disorganized movements of this very consciousness had their own problematic, outside it, which made individuals believe that they were determined by a kind of chaos and irrationality. Conscious passion is this return to the self which modifies the self. The world in which we live finds itself changed by this very action, if only on account of the manner of perceiving and apprehending it. We call this imagination. The relationship to others, to values, to ends, evolves even if the material world isn't thereby modified. To see the clouds from a poetical perspective and not on account of the effect they have upon precipitation doesn't change the clouds themselves, but what we say about them, the sensations that emerge from this new perspective, the implications of this new way of seeing, are all the product of this passion which transforms into another passion.

For some people, the consciousness that people have of themselves obliges them to reject passion as being suffering and boredom, as though consciousness were pushing them to reject passion, understood here as action for its own sake, as an overflowing that aims to give the illusion that the struggle against the vanity of existence is workable. Death from this standpoint exists to back nihilism. Passion through which we attempt to leave a trace upon society, family, or history is nothing more than vanity.

We have recognized that consciousness-reflection leads to nihilism because it reflects without adding anything. Its temporality remains external to it, since it cannot perceive itself as lagging behind itself. In reality, and romanticism shows this, time is negotiated less and less through the affirmation *a priori* of this identity of self in and through consciousness.

In fact, consciousness is never an adequate reflection of itself, and when it returns upon itself, and when it turns back upon itself, it is no longer what it was previously. Passion doesn't send us back to the subject, it modifies it, inasmuch as a subject can exist outside what affects and recreates it, each time differently. Such is personal identity. An identity which is never given, but always in quest for itself. Identity therefore is the quest itself, nourished by the alternatives which follow along in train.

What is remarkable is that passion solidifies identity and difference. So that the contradiction not appear, it is necessary for history, which marks us with difference, to be lived in the identity of the self and the world, repressed all the more powerfully, since it is itself imposing change. This is common sense. Passion is History within us; we endure it, feel it, and nevertheless attempt to remain who we are, as though nothing had happened, with the maximum of in-difference, as the victims will point out, justifiably.

Passion is the reply to history which permits us to evacuate the problem. We are in History, conditioned by it, and the very fact of thinking this is itself a fact of History, what we wish to ignore in the empty affirmation of our supposedly free subjectivity. Passion incites us to see ourselves as isolated from history, as though our subjectivity constituted an autonomous totality that is folded back upon itself with all the others around it. We live history by ignoring it as much as possible: this is the sense of the present that is lived as continuous within ourselves.

But we must understand that passion is the answer to History which makes of this answer a problem, a "problematological answer," the realization of an alternative at a meta-level of thought, which permits us to forget that History exists, in favor of our own history, the one we tell ourselves and others. Passion transforms History into history or narration, where a relationship reflects upon itself which establishes an origin, which defines the problems that must be resolved later on. Individuality is the result of this answer, and passions are the dispositions. We need to know it in order to act, to better nourish ourselves with History and demystify our liberty, which is often purely theoretical.

Individualism reinforces itself all the more as History accelerates, and so it becomes an existential (if not ideological) way out, that which alters the content of subjective identity to the point of rendering it problematic in its very possibility.

Each person responds to History by repressing it: we each live in what we might call "our own time." Such a repression implies the constitution of universality as value and, at the same time the answer remains individual because each person is at issue historically. We each want to be ourselves, but since the whole world wants this, each one is Other by wanting to simply be him- or herself. The answer to History situates us in it, but this answer is the very negation of the problem that it poses. Shouldn't we thus be speaking of passion here? Passion reveals itself according to an inevitable ambivalence: on the one hand, it wants to be

considered as being the mark of our irreducible individuality, our subjectivity, and our desire to reinforce it (or simply desire); on the other hand,
it translates the universal fact that *each person* proceeds in the same
fashion, abolishing the irreducible singularity of the individual quest. If
everyone want to be themselves, and to be oneself is to be different from
the Other, then each one would be identical even as they refuse to be so.

The Social Logic of the Passions:
Identity and Difference in Practice

The problem of passion is the problem of the Other: the Other in us, the
Other that we are to ourselves, and the Other that we are for others. Our
identity is at risk in this game, like a broken mirror, the pieces of which
we hope will be gathered up by the Other before we then smash them
over his or her head because the Other did it for us, that is, because the
Other answered the question of who *we* are for ourselves.

Passion is often the anathema that we throw in the face of our neigh-
bors to signify their unconsciousness and their blindness. Their motives
make them act outside all reason, from the moment that they are regulated by the empire of passions. This prohibits all reason, which we alone
would have possessed, and which permits us to understand and give
the true reason for the actions of the Other. Passion becomes unreason
in the Other, just as our reason is passion for him or her. Passion is the
instrument of difference and opposition between people, it is the rhetorical argument that acts out their difference by being the common place,
the *topos,* which rationalizes the superiority that each person claims to
have over the Other.

From such a standpoint, or such a practice, there is no such thing as
communal reason. The argument of passion is made in the service of a
reason that I would possess, and that the Other would be deprived of.
But what is reason if it is nothing other than passion that blinds me to
the eyes of the Other? We find ourselves in a reason from which others
are excluded, or which no one possesses, since everyone lives outside
it, because of passion. In such a scheme, either reason is impossible, since
it is nothing other than disguised passion, or there is no value in establishing it, since it emerges from a kind of miracle.

We think back here to Hobbes's problem: people who face each other
in an endless game of passion cannot find peace without the intervention
of an all-powerful Leviathan, who comes from who-knows-where, and
who establishes reason, that is, peace to people who would otherwise
continue their reciprocal ruses and endless struggles. We think as well of

Rousseau, who, *a contrario,* saw in the natural game of passions immanent and universal rationality of the heart, which abolishes all differences
between reason and passion. Reason was impossible (without forcible
intervention from outside) for Hobbes; it becomes useless for Rousseau.
Will reason be installed on the basis of its own impossibility, or through
its express lack of utility? This would be completely paradoxical, and the
paradox would threaten a moral reflection in its very foundation. If there
is no more reason because everything is passion, reason is what places
us beyond the overflow of others, as though by personal revelation, then
no rational ethics could ever possibly emerge in the world. Passion considered as reason that we have but that others don't have is indeed the
theoretical source of evil. It is what nourishes criticism, and condemnation, and we, who are conscious of the weaknesses of others, draw as a
consequence the conclusion that we are their natural superiors. This
sentiment is, for the Other, the proof of *our* blindness, and therefore our
own passions; each person feels superior to the other, more lucid and
without passion, and we therefore are stuck in a kind of ping-pong game
without hope for a Leviathan, or a hypothesis of a preestablished harmony that is natural, or finalized by God or History.

To establish moral reason is the real problem, which is formulated as
such: if we are all ourselves by not being the Other, we are what we are
not, since we are each the Other by only being ourselves. Passion is this
desire to be different, and this inability to put up with differences. Identity defined as such recalls the Other into which we melt, even though
we were hoping to differentiate ourselves from him. Passion is reason in
the service of the negation of the Other, the affirmation of the self as
superior: it is a mysterious or impossible reason, undifferentiated from
passion to which it is opposed, a propositional reasoning because it
simply erases the problem for which it is the solution, which is to justify
its point of departure by an auto-foundational intuition that comes out of
an *a priori.* We postulate that there exists a universal without being able
to demonstrate it except by a bid for power, or a vicious circle which
sets forth the universal as norm, and the nature of the relationship that
individuals have with each other.

In reality, we realize that if we all want to be ourselves by differentiating ourselves from others, which brings us back to acting like them,
then violence is inevitable, and no State could possibly be constituted
unless it existed previously somewhere else (Hobbes). No society could
be born, be it by a "social contract" (Rousseau), without an accident of
History which would lead to voluntary cooperation of individuals who
are determined, concrete, and yet blind to what they are (Rawls).

So that compassion can come about, it is necessary for each of us to be able to be ourselves, and that others be able to be themselves, paradoxically; for if to be oneself means being different, then the Other is *a priori* the enemy of the Other because s/he wishes to delineate himself from the Other; this is impossible because by doing so everyone becomes identical. To be the Other is indifferently the answer to the problem of each one, and the problem itself. In this problematological indifference, all reason is impossible, including in the domain of ethics.

The question of the Other must be posed as such, without any prejudice, that is, without any *envy*. Envy is put into question by the Other, but this Other is no longer really Other, he or she cannot answer, being condemned, as it were, by envy. This Other is put into question with the impossibility of answering. I am the Other, this is neither possible nor bearable. Envy, in the conditions we have just described, is the original passion, original because individual and distinct from others, and identical to them because individual. When desire is the desire of the Other, passions which are born of this desire are but the modalities of envy. This is the inverse of reason, and passion forms with reason therefore a *Janus bifrons:* my passion, according to the Other, is for me reason, and vice versa. The passion-reason difference is individual and relative, and if we add together the various points of view, they fuse and end up in confusion. Reason corresponds to the passivity in action: to want to be what the Other is, to want to be the Other, and, as a consequence, to have what the Other has, to prevent the Other from rendering him- or herself different, since we experience such an action as a questioning of our own being.

Why speak of envy? It is a modern form of self-love and was obviously present in all human societies, although never as strongly as in our own. This suggestion deserves some elaboration. Envy is the natural sentiment of the *petite bourgeoisie,* just as honor was for the aristocracy. In both cases, self-esteem has its specific historical form. This sense of Ego, of authority *(auctoritas)* hereby takes different forms at different eras and in different places. "Upon close inspection it will be seen that there is in every age some peculiar and preponderant fact with which all others are connected; this fact almost always gives birth to some pregnant idea or some ruling passion, which attracts to itself and bears away in its course all the feelings and opinions of the time; it is like a great stream toward which each of the neighboring rivulets seem to flow."[15]

15. Alexis de Tocqueville, *Democracy in America, The Henry Reeve Text*, corrected, and edited, and with introduction, notes, and bibliographies by Phillips Bradley (New York: Alfred A. Knopf, 1987), bk. 2, p. 95.

The petit bourgeois has invaded the mentality of the contemporary world: it is incarnated in accounting-style reasoning. No more credit than debit: everything has to balance. No excess or unbalance, being proper in everything, this is what regulates the regard of the other who establishes the average of things. What creates value, originality, creativity, and invention raises suspicion and jealousy. Competence is defined by a bureaucratic definition, rather than a sense of personal excellence: at issue, therefore, is the "competence" of a dean, a minister, or a postal worker.

So that envy can be made bearable, given how generalized it is, it is necessary that everyone recognize that we all "have rights": the petite bourgeoisie likes to listen to itself speak in its commissions, meetings where everything is decided in advance, but where we are made to believe that at least we exist in the eyes of the other, who have the same problem. Being collegial reassures and provides comfort for the bureaucratic status. It canalizes envy and makes it collective; or when the means are sufficient, it allows for a distribution to everyone "so that we don't distinguish."

The violence of this egalitarianism hits those who think they can escape from it. The mechanisms of exclusion for those who are different are multiple, but History is there to show that the petite bourgeoisie doesn't hesitate when things aren't going very well to resort to systematic massacres. The difference is for them, not for the others.

There is in this an extreme solution which shouldn't hide the many forms that the hatred of difference takes in groups of a given identity. Here, we return to the pacific and daily domain: the fear of the Other makes us cultivate conformity, hollow ideas, the "look" that fits the situation and the members of the group to which we hope to belong, or that we want to meet. And at the same time, the more we go toward identification, the less we feel ourselves, and the less we are at ease in this permanent representation made of trademarks, fashionable places, and ideas which are à la mode. Everyone wants to differentiate themselves from the others they imitate, and with respect to whom they try to act superior; but in the logic of all this, victory herein is impossible. "To envy beings that we disdain; there is in this embarrassing passions that which is required to poison a whole life."[16]

It is necessary that all the fashions change quickly so that we'll have the sense, fleeting though it may be, of having the chance to be different from others. The rules of the market and the money that circulates therein allows us to establish differences, often insurmountable, between

---

16. F. Mauriac, *Le Noeud de vipères* (Paris: Livre de poche, 1971), p. 32.

individuals. The consumer society becomes a regulator for a situation that otherwise could give rise to violence: if we slow down growth, attack the bureaucratic and social status of individuals, then the violence which springs from envy will incarnate a providential man changed by establishing order, that is, literally and paradoxically, by reestablishing difference for *everyone*. This applies to those who are excluded and can no longer bring themselves up to the status of those who have surpassed them, which is itself unjust, given that we're supposed to be equal; it also applies to those who approach those they had previously detested on account of their inferior social status. Examples abound in, for example, the scorn of the bourgeois as regards the worker, the hatred against the Jew because he has been successful, the scorn felt by the worker for immigrants, and so forth.

To wish to be oneself, being within the reach of everyone, makes for a situation whereby a society becomes impossible if envy rules. Envy is but one way, which is benign at its first stage, to negotiate the identity and the difference between individuals. Aspirations take other forms, and so that we can be ourselves and affirm difference, without it being annihilated in the more generalized social struggle, we need to have both the dissociation of identity *and* a sense of difference. To be a oneself in independence from all others or to be what we want to be without having to go through the look of the Other, or upon the Other. Equality has it such that everyone has such a possibility, and liberty, such that everyone *can* succeed by simply obeying their passions. To liberate our social passions of all envy, to purify morality of all resentment, to differentiate between what we are and the aspirations of others, and to not model our own aspirations upon those of others, all become the new order of the day. Choose our own ends. All of this suggests that we dare to be ourselves without looking behind us to see if what we've done has been approved: these are passions which are difficult to assume, but they are the only ones that allow passions to be dealt with rationally, with reason, deemed different and necessary.

In short the question of what we are and what we want should be authentic, and it should not already have an answer that emanates from other persons.

Many will consider it to be a wish: a group is constituted through identity, and personal identity passes through difference, which is reabsorbed when it is affirmed by each person. This is true: no society can escape from the perils of its own dissolution.

There is no less of a solution to what would be no other than the paradox of the origin of the social. This solution is the Law. The capital

"L" in this case suggests that at issue here is not solely positive laws, which regulate some aspect of social life, such as the highway code or the tax law. The Law is the universal structure which establishes a relation between the identity (of each) and the differences (with others). Envy crushes identity through differences, just as pure ambition does the inverse. Equality encompasses a vision of liberty, albeit to deny it, and liberty is as well a way of apprehending inter-subjective relations. The law that we want is that which allows each person to do what his passions dictate without having to worry about those of others, be they what they may. Univocal, the Law must be incarnated in positive and social laws.

The Law is the universal of humanity, and if it swallows up difference, it necessarily becomes a space of envy and desire, and a place where differences are equaled out, or the place where one tries to model oneself upon the other. A *contrario*, the Law can be liberating, if it allows each person to follow his or her own questioning, and makes of this liberty a reality for all persons. In short, everything is in the interpretation of universality. What we have to see is that the Law does not come out of a contract, nor of a despotism from a Leviathan. It is the very structure of human consciousness: Law is what it is when it is based upon something other than itself; "*a is b*"; asymmetry, difference, are therefore integral parts of the consciousness. To be aware of something is to know the difference between oneself (thus the consciousness) and this other thing; it is to know that one's consciousness is subordinated to difference so that its own identity can be deployed. The concept of this difference, which constitutes identity, is the Law, which imposes alterity upon the mind. Each person, in wanting to be him- or herself vis-à-vis the other, entertains an idea about the law, and therefore about justice, which could lead right to the elimination of Law—*for the Other*. Such persons would often consider themselves justified even if others condemn them. As long as the Law, which is the Other in us, the symbol of socialization, as long as it assures my own identity independent of that of all others, then universality can constitute the group and regulate it. Passion which generates antagonisms, the passion of the *Other*, which *I* locate using *my* reason, is a degeneration of the Law, a universalizing and logical rationalization of my inability to be Ego without being Him or Her.

What is important here is the question of historical conditions, since it relates to the Law's ability to incarnate the equilibrium of identity and difference. It is not an *a priori* given because it rests upon the questioning of individual problematics, which act upon conflictual or disjunctive passions, rather than harmonious or conjunctive passions.

Historical conditions of free social mobility should allow individuals to express themselves in society. This wouldn't be the case if the access to given posts were to remain limited or frozen, based upon pre-constituted groups who use them to advance their own interests: this type of organization exists in birthright or partisan groups. Even if morality or justice cannot be reduced to such questions, they remain nevertheless crucial.

Who speaks the Law? It is in each of us, since we are each members of a given group. The Law is the form that the social takes in the individual; it rests upon conjunction and disjunction. Absolute conjunction undifferentiates and thus leads to conflict, while disjunction dislocates the group. The Name of the Father, or the *no* of the Father, inscribes the difference that it represents just as the ideal of the Ego incarnates the structure of identity.

Those who speak on behalf of the law speaks of the identity of those to whom they speak, but in that respect they are different from them because they situate themselves above them. René Girard, in *Violence and the Sacred,* suggests that by violating the law of the group for which one speaks, the speaker places him- or herself outside the law, and will be sacrificed for this very reason. Speakers of the Law act more subtly: they don't speak the Law as though outside it, but rather speak a universal law that is supposed to include them as well. If the speakers are priests, then they know the word of God, and know how to interpret it better than others, but this word still applies to them. If they interpret History, this time we're dealing with members of the Party, then what they say applies to them as well. In short, universality is tough on those to whom it applies, but it protects the legislator from the violence of others because it applies to everyone. So some form of control is necessary.

In democratic societies, the separation of powers is supposed to verify whether or not the Law applies to those who utter it, and that the legislators don't attempt to place themselves above it. Is this peculiar to democratic regimes? We mustn't forget that in the ancien régime the king was only given divine right because the intellectuals had accorded it to him. In exchange, these same intellectuals received significant recompense. One group speaks on behalf of the legitimacy of others, who in return, favor them, so that no one seems to stand outside the Law, even though it seems arbitrary. The "division of labor" between power and the intellectuals is in fact a division of this power, such that those who legitimate must seem themselves legitimate without giving the impression that they can escape from what they say, or say something of which they are the only source of legitimacy. So one group utters the legitimacy from which they don't directly benefit, the others benefit without being able to utter it. If this division of labor disappeared, or could not work in the opinion of the group, then the legitimator, by becoming illegitimate, but nevertheless the source of the law, would run the risk of death, rebellion, or sacrifice.

Universality can thus be in the service of liberty as it can be its negation: in itself, it could not sum up moral requirements. Universality, when invoked by those who wish to mount the social ladder, is the means of affirming absolute equality, and rejecting the differences which create envy. This universality can serve to justify the use of some form of protection against those who wish to cause problems in the name of resentment.

The affirmation of particularities, of individuality, of its difference, opens us up to the same contradictions. The non-respect for the universal, in the name of individual rights, give rise to passions as violent as those that come from a leveling universality.

Universality can justify those who rise up to demand the rights that they assimilate with privilege, or it can be invoked to protect us from those who wish to deprive us of our rights on account of their belief that they have a more legitimate claim to benefit from them.

Without a theory of justice, universality remains an empty ideal, since it is a concept to which those who are looking for protection against envy can have recourse, just as it is a recourse for those who struggle to attain the posts that their envy demands they have. Universality is both the cement of society and the weapon that permits us to eliminate differences and singularities. All rhetoric is from this standpoint universalist, one way or the other. So is it the universalist-as-demagogue or the universalist-as-guarantor? The moral is decided elsewhere, in the possibility of affirming the self in society, and of climbing the social ladder thanks to free access to positions, accorded to the most competent, in respect of the equality we all have to acquire them. Liberty, or liberties, like the meaning of the Law and the universal that it presupposes, returns us to the complex link between liberty and equality, particularity and universality.

Equality is equal access, the freedom to aspire to social positions, and not the right to occupy them. The more we move in the direction of the contrary, the more interchangeable individuals become with a form of interior norm, more the idea of competence would be a bureaucratic one, and the more envy would nourish envy, frustration, frustration. Envy is oriented upon the answers of others, and so must make place for problematics which can be nourished from within.

What counts is to see that we can give ourselves over to a quest for selfhood conditioned by others, with the passive passion known as

Philosophy and the Passions

resentment, or that we can give ourselves over to a search for selfhood which establishes its own objectives in respect for other goals, but also for our own interests. Passion that we credit to others in order to show our own superiority, even as it is rejected by the others, comes from a projection, a kind of community in rivalry, which goes from scorn to jealousy; in this scenario, scorn reflects the fact that the grapes are too green, envy because they are too ripe. Universality gives over to this same reciprocal blindness: reciprocity of difference which must be affirmed to save an identity which holds up solely on account of this difference.

The Law is a factor that brings resolution: it permits us to be ourselves for ourselves, and for others. This is the answer which authorizes the fact of answering, but it is not the content, as Kant thought. In this sense, the Law is an answer outside the moral question, but it is not the whole answer. As an absolute difference which posits identity, the Law is the formal condition of social mobility which must allow each person to express his or her free vanity and his or her Ego, protected from the effects of envy. Moral reason that acts has as guiding principle the freedom to be; in a society characterized by equality, it is rendered social thanks to free access to the positions that society needs to have filled, and this on the basis of real ability rather than privilege or relations.

Can we stop people from considering that social destitution is unjust, and from being affected by passions of envy, and the will to constantly make comparisons with others, which empties them of their own substance and of their quest for true individuality? Will we ever eliminate envy and rationalization through reproaches that are masked by grand principles?

Nothing is less certain. We have to accept that envy will always be more or less present, like weakness, since we have to accept the need to engage ourselves and struggle against ourselves, in order to exist without making our passions into the echoes of passions of others. After all, we can always invoke injustice and inequality which prevail in the most just society in order to reduce the guilt that we feel on account of our being someone other than the person we had hoped to be.

The infernal quest for honor and success is simply more destructive in a universe where each person has access to given posts without necessarily having the necessary abilities simply because they have the right family, friends, or birthrights. So a terrible question emerges: "Why not me?" Egalitarianism, which aims for more justice, is transformed into an argument where everybody has equal value, and when abilities are similar, it becomes possible to substitute *a priori*. Each person is the Other, and what we are will always be as unjust as what the other is, because we are not ourselves.

We'll never stop people from having ambitions, self-esteem, a desire to succeed and to be enriched, but we could hope that envy will not eat away at us to the point where it destroys the whole society and restricts all progress on account of a collective or even collegial cult of self-assured mediocrity. Envy is not an ingredient that is intrinsic to the Ego, a fatality, but it can become so and thereby contaminate a whole way of thinking if we are not careful. And the more that envy is generalized, the more that those who have benefited from social circulation will feel threatened, and this spiral can become an infernal one. The bridge between those who wish to climb, and those who have already arrived, has to lead to violence if the economic means are insufficient to satisfying all persons, or if these means are absorbed at a speed that is greater than the social movement itself.

Such a situation, paradoxically, engenders in many persons a sense of cowardice, which is the very incarnation of negative passions, since they endure the envious look of others even as they feel reinforced thereby. These individuals look to counter this envy by flattery, by aiming at being pleasant to others, at not upsetting other people's plans, or by looking for approbation of others because what they are depends on others. The violence of those who don't fit into this game has as much chance of succeeding in its goals if other players are affected by weakness, leading to implicit consent, and to cowardice, pure and simple.

Is There an Aesthetic of Passions?

Passion converts facts and events into history, into relations which make what we have endured in terms of shocks and changes into something bearable. This is a way of always being right or, at least, of living with destiny. Passion involves a point of view which does not account for its own relativism, which it rationalizes through projection. This is a way of denying History through stories, our own, which situate us in the present and the contemporary, among others, as though this History and these events that mark us should no longer give rise to subjective responses, to other persons or to ourselves.

The Greeks, and in particular Aristotle, were not ignorant of this "unconscious" of point of view and of the action it involves. The role of theater or fiction consisted of confronting spectators with points of view which were ignored by those who were determined by the points of view. The spectacle of passion is supposed to edify and warn the spectator with the assumption that they'll be more lucid about what's going on when what is at issue is the passions of others. Oedipus is the victim of his own destiny, he fulfills the prophecy that his flight was supposed to avoid; he kills his father, and then marries his mother. The abolition of differences in a damned identity which is put to work through the most unbearable difference imaginable, killing one's own father, defines this passion that is pushed to its very limit. The *catharsis* of Aristotle corresponds to a psychoanalytic effect, whereby what is repressed is brought up to the level of consciousness. Pity and fear, for tragedy, and laughter, for comedy, confront us with ourselves.

Passions which are in question over and above the literal, and which give meaning to it, are incarnated in the stories which we tell, as much to ourselves as to other persons. Thanks to this, we put a point of view to work which is rendered legitimate, out of the question because set forth as an answer. The discourse of our passions ally with repression; what we don't see, or what we don't want to see, is found in this discourse indirectly, just like *what is in question* in the very fact of saying what we say. As for the moral of History, to recall a term from the domain of fables, it lodges within this rationalization, and it orients toward an *a priori* and adjacent meaning, one which can nevertheless be discerned by those who wish to really listen.

This is where the idea of value enters the discussion. Whoever mentions value refers to a way of measuring, a structure of proportion that exists between different elements, like the exchange value (price) that can find a relation between people and pears, lemons and wine. The value is that which confers unity on possible variations, and establishes relations between them, and evaluates and structures differences with respect to each other, establishing each in terms of some consistent principle. These are figures: a figure of a Same which moves, which is buried within a story, and which articulates it profoundly. This figuration makes History into a form, and, more precisely, a metaphor of the value or the values which are hereby expressed. Metaphoricity expresses passions, which are like a code for reading. There is approbation, or disapprobation which is not strictly rhetorical, but also moral.

The aesthetic character of passion is an intrinsic component of it. Passion is the spectacle of itself. It allows one to see, by being seen. It is the rupture of consciousness with itself, the questioning which is often displeasing and therefore which we prefer to endure for others rather than for ourselves. But it is also the tissue of our own story, the one that we tell ourselves and which we refuse to consider as being but a story, as though it were truth itself. The passionate is focalized as an implicit problematic, which becomes destiny if witnessed from the outside.

Values create this focalization and reduce variations to modifications of initial and structuring values.

All this explains why we believe in stories even though we know that they're just stories. They reveal ourselves to ourselves, without confronting us directly with a sense of who we really are; we believe them without believing them, we are captivated by the "story," in this case the construction and the unraveling of the problematic in successive resolutions.

The Great Passionate Articulations

Propositional rationality corresponds to a reason which we either have or we don't, but what's not clear here is how to obtain it if we don't. Recall one of the first questions of this book: how does one become a philosopher? This question was posed concerning Plato. Passion forbids the arrival of reason, but only those who have reason already can possibly make such a claim. Passion ties people to their condition, and just above them, we find the philosopher, the exceptional individual, in some sense. Rationality conceived as such denies any chance for interrogation: there is no question of putting things into question; the theory of Ideas must be substituted for Socrates' practice. Is this the truth of all, *in* all persons? We could believe this, but if we do then passion is not an obstacle to reason and everyone is potentially a philosopher. Rationality, far from providing the questions which help people progress, must be seen as that which suppresses alternatives and problematical affirmations for which the Sophists are the bards. Passion is interrogative: rather than being based upon knowledge, it translates ignorance, and therefore blindness.

Interrogative rationality is opposed to propositional rationality. One is constructed on the problem that aims to suppress the problematic, and it is paradoxically made up thereof; the other accepts problematicity as a point of departure. But these are more than theoretical conceptions regarding the nature of reason: they are ways of living. Propositionalism consecrates a kind of immobility: there are those who are, and those who are not; we don't become rational as though by magic. Reason is extended through faith. This is the way to react to common sense, with its pre-formed ideas, its taste for what is useful and agreeable, its rejection of all difficulty. Reason is there, and it doesn't really matter where it comes from. The paradox is such that this reason be outside common sense, since it represents itself as though it were above it, if not opposite to it. Plato is not gentle for those who flirt with the tangible, and indeed he wasn't the only philosopher like this; and when they were, they lost the rationality in the name of which they made their judgments (Hume).

Propositional rationality makes philosophy superfluous, it is immanent, and when we make it explicit, we're just illuminating useless concepts. From Kant to Wittgenstein, we have often seen philosophers speak of their activity as though it were therapeutic, as though they should deal not with common sense, but with other philosophers, who refuse it a place in their work. Propositional rationality is the common sense which reflects upon itself even as it shows no real need for this reflection. Since it is different from, and cut off from, the daily life that it analyzes, reason overcomes it, which is paradoxical. In reality, reason is split off from the passion that falls into it, which is the source of the split of philosophical reasoning and the society that it describes; for this reason, it transcends and annuls the mirroring that it hoped to accomplish. This is why reason is opposed to passion, which it explains and which it surpasses, through recourse to a kind of transcendence that is inaccessible to passionate people. A similar paradoxical split can be found with the theory of consciousness, where reflection is applied to the unthinking consciousness *that it is not,* and for which it will be the truth. Rational consciousness prolongs passionate consciousness, even as it opposes it.

Plato is not blind to this paradox. Reason is useful because it unmasks passion, but passion is reason for those who are practicing it. Reason, for Plato, is inaccessible to the passionate despite the fact that they are its very object. This is the crux of the paradox: reason for Plato is reason for everyone, but the sensible person *cannot* recognize it without ceasing to be who he or she is. Nonphilosophers are the universal men and women, cut off from their own rationality, and living in the tangible world; they are in need of the philosopher to guide them. Since they can't understand him, though, or aspire to be him, they can but obey.

Propositional reason is the common sense that we reflect upon as that which never reflects *on account of its very nature,* on account of a fundamental impossibility. It is therefore me and not me; and it is probably as such that we reason most of the time, even if we are not otherwise Platonists.

Propositionalism immobilizes, it consecrates answers without asking questions, and it passively accepts whatever comes in train. Its subjects are bored even when they aren't (Pascal), and they are living in the hope of showing off all the envy that they feel on account of their being less than others even as their Ego, the supreme answer, has them believe in their own natural superiority. Passion, according to propositional reason, is the appearance of reason manifested in the other, and therefore it is the very place of opposition to them, since we are made to feel superior, and so they are.

Propositionalism is the conception of this manner of living and thinking and, as such, contests it by being more than that because it reflects, it goes beyond absorbed and absorbing passionality. This is why propositionalism breaks with itself; its truth is its error. What it describes is just, but since it describes it, it ceases to be so.

True rationality questions and interrogates about itself: to appoint itself is not to abolish itself, or to render itself impossible. Passion is the name of a problem, and not the code that makes it impossible to resolve it. All our existence is made up of problems which the passions express partially and resolve for one part, which is more or less substantial depending upon the individual and the era, under one form or another for one person or another. Passion *is,* because *we* are, and *should* be. There is a passion of reason in the reflection of interrogation, which transforms *both* reason, which reflects and reflects upon itself, *and* passion, which changes its very face.

If we are all immersed in common sense, we nevertheless perceive that there is a manner of responding, even if this consists of losing our own point of view, willingly or not, and the problems that the common sense hope to offer a solution. Generalization forces us to see in it a way of addressing problems, and therefore to consider interrogative rationality as anterior and fundamental, since we once again ask when we ask how to suppress problems.

The passionate is not opposed to rationality except in propositionalism. This rationality carries with it, however, a certain vision of passion and a certain sense of how it is lived.

The logic of passions governs three domains: the relationship with the self, with the other, and with things (or with the world, in more generic terms). Propositionalism makes this logic into an anti-problematological relationship: there is no questioning in the putting into question of the three domains. This has consequences (see Diagram 3).

Diagram 3.

	Self	Other	Things in the world
Passion according to Propositionalism	passivity *guilt*	weakness envy	certitude possessiveness
Passion according to interrogative thinking	resolution affirmation of liberty	courage love	*responsibility* putting into question

Rationality as manifested in propositionalism must be considered as a particular case of the other, as a particular way of interrogating the self, which is centered exclusively upon the answering. Passionate poles which are typical to the interrogative proceedings find themselves propositionalized, and they manifest themselves as affirmations or solutions which are unaware. As a consequence, passionate poles of the second line can shift to the first and line themselves up under the passionate poles thereby emphasized.

Further, we must realize that the great propositional matrices are ways of affirming ourselves, of returning to the self through the other; they are in the end equivalent, since passions are the figures of the subject, figurativity in action. Putting things into question requires courage, and this produces a certain lucidity about the self.

What the diagram shows is not that there are fundamental passions from which all other passions flow, but that there are matrices of passion. Passivity characterizes a kind of people, but it refers as well to attitudes expressed in replies, which the most resolute people know very well. At the same time, to read only the first line of the diagram shows that it is necessary to conceive of reason against passions, but we must also realize that being passionate, which this propositional reason decries, justifies this rationality and falls, therefore, into it.

In passivity we find an attitude of submission, weakness, which can lead to the worst kinds of compromises even if they are unjust. The goal is to preserve our certitudes, our image of ourselves and of the world where there is self. How many people would rather conform to the ambient norms in order not to have to feel guilty when they refuse consensus-based truths? A questioning is an act of rupture which is unbearable and cannot be assumed. The Philosopher-King or the priest are there to give direction to the passive individual who is thereby led along and guided. Passivity is to be rejected if it makes us neglect what can give us consistency. And the denunciation of passion is the strongest criticism, as though propositional reasoning becomes, when it reflects upon itself, an interrogative rationality, which will nevertheless not be aware of being so.

By becoming activated passion makes a conscious rupture with consciousness at the inside of consciousness. This questioning recalls the irascibility of the ancient Greeks, the only difference being that the context is that of the question, and not that of evil or goodness (St. Thomas). If envy is a form of cowardice, of mediocrity which hides in order to avoid showing itself, then love, on the contrary, accepts the Other in his or her difference, and accepts the community that the loving self shares with the Other. Love allies itself with generosity, just as revolution does with enthusiasm.

From the basis of the matrix previously discussed, we can see how hatred, despair, joy, scorn, or embarrassment can be apprehended. These are ways of dealing with what is at issue with subjectivity: embarrassment is a questioning of the self, while joy or pleasure annul interrogativity even though there may be joy in affirming this but it is still a way of responding. The passions can be mobilized in order to question the world, or to solidify answers and confirm our own thoughts through them. This is proof that the question-response relationship is the key for understanding passions, right to the passion of denying it, and which we for a long time called *reason*. There is, therefore, a real joy in love, wherein we recognize the other as a problem, just as there can be joy in denying the other. Love puts the impersonal role that we're used to playing into question, and envy rejects the difference that love consecrates.

Ruptures of the consciousness (desire) create a difference which separates the problem from its resolution, and sends the mind to the range of possible alternatives: hope, fear, and so forth. Despair is the answer which poses the problem as though without any answer, and hope, of course, is the opposite of this. Desire imagines the solution to the problem, but in itself it poses the problem in its pure form, exempt from hope.

There is a double sense of passions: they respond to a problem, and they can answer *to* a problem by translating and expressing it. We answer through hope, but hope can also consist of our taking a position on a problem that we wish to resolve. By thinking that the problem will be resolved, hope situates itself in the order of the solution, and more precisely, of the one who postulates that the problem has disappeared. On the other hand, hope can also line up on the side of problematization, to which it consecrates a certain openness. Hope therefore expresses interrogation, if not the very interrogativity of existence in action, and it answers this interrogativity with uncertainty of consciousness as regards the solution. In any case, hope makes statements about the problematological difference, about the difference between the question and the answer; it translates, it expresses this difference and it renders it exterior through its identity with an answer.

We could proceed using the same reasoning for a discussion of concern, which relates to a problem and its resolution, a process which would put us into question, at the same time as this same concern responds to a problem that a situation creates for us. In this sense, concern is both unthinking consciousness, which expresses our absorption in a situation, and reflexive consciousness, wherein to judge a situation constitutes a problem that must be resolved, the concern, therefore, being the judgment that is brought to bear upon the solution-problem that was at issue. For this reason, we understand that there was a fusion between these two types of consciousness, as well as a difference. But the fact of speaking of them in terms other than unthinking-consciousness-which-thinks-without-the-ability-but-doing-it-nevertheless, avoids the implicit paradox.

Passion is problematicity at work in existence, and it is thus through the problematological difference that we take it on; this difference expressed in an identity of an answer preserves this identity, and affirms, or reveals, a psychic if not existential unity. As such, if I am concerned about something or someone, I am concerned that a specific question be posed, and that a solution be imposed upon me which I consider nefarious. I am also concerned about my own concern in that the fact of feeling the concern is unpleasant in itself. The idea of pleasure or suffering, "loving or not loving," which should reduce all of the passion to this bipolarization (Hume) expresses only the fact that in all passion there is a Self who is implicated, and who finds itself put into question indirectly, *even as it denies or refuses all questioning, all questions, all problems,* precisely to avoid the displeasure of the effort, the difficulty, the struggle, the possibility of failing and seeing oneself contested. Pleasure and pain are ways of feeling the "I love" and the "I don't love," the *yes* or the *no.* If propositional reasoning is the one that most people use in most circumstances, this is because it brings to the concept our need for facility and agreement, comfort and conformism, answers which are beyond question, which passions disrupt, unless they are their extension and confirmation, the lid over the problem, in short. It's a strange answer, and a strange reason, which must contradict itself in order to conform to its own goal. People thus avoid having to place themselves into question, or re-think their reasons, and therefore inquire about their own reason.

Passion is *one* answer (identity) to a question and its answer, even as it answers without considering this relationship. There's no more paradox here: the difference is admitted and is even recognized as constitutive. And the dual sense of pleasure and displeasure (which are so important to empiricism) is considered as a corporal or noncorporal reaction to problems (a kind of response to the stimuli), and as a judgment, an answer to this very answer.

Propositionalism presents itself as an existential *demand* for certitude; it is an aspect of the answer which still presupposes questioning, if only for its eradication, an eradication upon which propositionalism rests which it has set forth too late, because it focuses upon the result. This tardiness is the result of it having been obsessed with the "foundation" of a rationality which only knows the result, and nothing that precedes it counts for anything.

Interrogativity, which affects all of us, reveals itself indirectly in the passion that seems to exclude it. Concern, which comes with weakness and envy, is in fact the very absence of courage, and the problem "what should I do?" is contained as a resolution in the idea of being concerned. It is a way of answering which necessarily pushes to the side what might endanger or what might demand something more. Passion which condemns and consecrates propositional rationality (with its propositions and its certitudes) is a transformation of the answer into that which abolishes it, even though it does not really succeed in doing so. It is, in any event, an interrogative moment. To avoid feeling questioned, or to place oneself in question, are ways of answering the large questions: "How to live?" "What to do?" For instance, desire can be lived through the image of its realization, a kind of petition of principle whereby the problem that is posed is considered resolved: "I want," and it must be so. This shows that there is a passionate moral which exists in the propositionalization of passions. It means living everything in the mode of suppressing the problem, of negating the passionate as such, on account of reason ("I have the right to"). As passion deals with both questions and answers, so it can go more in the direction of questions than answers, and betrays itself by denying the other term of difference for which passions are the *existentialization*.

As for knowing whether there is weakness of the will or ignorance in passion which is unmasked but not suppressed (like in games), we can see that it is the working of a logic of consent, of preference. Propositional reason is based upon intuitions, affected by a passivity which suggests that they must be revealed and presented selectively as though they were evident, as though offering themselves up naturally.

Finally, what remains is to discover whether or not the passive man, who has the passion of non-passion, can escape from his certitudes and establish others, without feeling a sense of unbearable aggression. This is the question we must ask about passion: is life bearable, and, in return, is passion bearable for those who live it as the absolute value of life? Don't we have to deal with its mediocrity as well as its audacity? What choice is left? But we have to do it. Historicity affects all of us. It is manifested in the questioning that obligates us to become aware of the passions of which we were unaware, and which modeled our own sense of the real, if not its very content. How is it possible to face irreducible novelty and unassimilated events when we continue to cling to the old? This tearing of the consciousness shows passion in the most urgent form of the alternative: *guilt*.

What is it to feel guilty? This is an answer to the problem which consists of avoiding the problems, and of not thinking about them, because the questions are there. It is an embarrassment for the consciousness which makes it aware of itself to itself, and forces itself to interrogate itself. It creates anxiety in the face of the renunciation of the certitudes which disintegrate, and the fear of doing so, with all the consequences that follow in train. Anxiety is the result of questions without answers, whereas fear is about answers (Heidegger). Guilt raises a sense of unease, undoes assurance (answers without questions; the inverse of embarrassment, which is the sense of being questioned without being able to answer). It creates oscillation between the old and the new, and the consciousness finds itself divided from itself, contemplating its own division. Guilt gives us the sense of the unacceptable at the very place where we used to accept. Answers can be concern or cowardice for it, just as violence can, which has the effect of projecting upon the Other what is unbearable about our own destiny, and which is rejected through this projection. This can lead right to destruction: this is why human beings are the cruelest of all animals.

Guilt is the passionate of passion in its historical dimension: it is the answer which shows that we can no longer be *irresponsible* in the face of what is happening and repress questions by making them rhetorical. We are beyond guilt that is felt but passive and are now in the domain of responsibility, which is the principle of action. The irresponsible nature of passive individuals has given up its place to the behavior of responsible individuals, the ones who are concerned to ask themselves about what had until then been considered obvious, beyond question. Passion explodes, therefore, to nourish reason, to liberate individuals from their passivity, or to confront them with the *question* of what they are for themselves. The problem remains of what should be done. Can they still believe their own stories, and can they still look themselves in the face? Or do they have to prefer truth, which obliges them to evolve toward other answers?

The fact of being passionate, to which this question is addressed, appears to be questioning itself. It enjoins people to answer, but they are free to the point of being able to refuse questioning, which would be another way of answering, and of unveiling a temperament and some profound passions. And there, it is necessary to separate things, between being able to believe, making others believe, and accepting the need to go beyond ourselves: passion is measured in terms of success, and reason, in terms of truth.

Epilogue

We have arrived at the end of our voyage to the land of the passions, having listened to what most philosophers have had to say to us about human nature.

Aristotle, for example, defined passions as the expression of individual differences. Human beings became aware of what they were by getting in touch with their own passions and those of other persons, all in the hope of extricating a common denominator which would enable them to live together.

This free expression has been eroded through its contact with History. Empires and kingdoms are inauspicious places for the negotiation of individual differences, or even for their simple manifestation.

Hopes withdraw themselves from this world and in the process transform reason into faith, and passion into sin. The body keeps humanity down here: this in itself is already passion, suffering.

The question of passions was no longer the field where the relationship to other persons is dealt with; it became the field of the relationship with God.

But humanity found itself alone, alone with itself, alone with others. Passion asserted itself as human, too human. Comprised of consciousness above all, passion incarnates our interest for the world, its remoteness as well as our implication in it, and our sympathy for others as well as our rejection of their presence.

Passion is the locus of subjectivity, for better or for worse. Since morality can no longer defeat passions through recourse to a Hell defined as "eternal passion," it will be the postulate of a pure and practical reason, situated all at once beyond all possible passion.

This long evolution induces us to rethink historical uniformities which run through all of these theories of the passions.

Some people think that passion blinds its victims, to the point of becoming ignored by them. To discover passion is to break the charm, the enchantment. To render objective a passion is akin to freeing ourselves of it because we become conscious that we have one. Passion is the problem that reason must resolve in order to establish itself. How is it possible if to have passions is to ignore them, and to know them is to have nothing more to combat? Either passion impedes reason, or else reason kills the passions by revealing them for what they really are.

Through passion, I ignore everything, right up to the very trap that it represents, right up to its own existence; I ignore that which I must know. Or, on the contrary, I know that I have nothing else to learn, since the trap unearthed ceases to be one. To know one's passions is to no longer have them, and to have them is to not know them. It is as though passion makes me aware of the obstacle that has to be overcome, and at the same time condemns me to never succeed. Through passion, I know both too much and too little: the problem that it represents becomes insoluble when, under the influence of blinding passion, it is ignored; and the solution that it requires becomes useless when the passion is conscious, and therefore overcome.

What this alternative represents is fundamental for reasons that go beyond historical ones. The inescapable quality of passions has been associated with the existence of a human nature, unavoidable in the way that a destiny can be, although ignored nonetheless existing. The human condition is indivisible; it is experienced, it is passion. There is nothing to be done. Our instincts are there, and with them come desire, sensations, pleasure, and pain.

At the opposite end of the spectrum we find the idea of overcoming, overcoming through reason, which comes from who knows where, but which, by making us conscious of our passions, gives us moral sense and concern for truth in the face of the cult of illusion. At the end of the day, we have History against human nature prior to having History as human nature.

Thus we have passions without hope, and hope against passions: one might as well say that we have an insoluble alternative, lethal for reflection. Passion is natural or historical, mental or physical; so many classic aporias and antinomies.

In reality, what was required was a combination of these two visions into one, in order to produce the impression that passion is both a blinding and a consciousness of this blinding, the latter allowing us to overcome it. From a two-stage model of the passions, we have moved to a model with three levels: passion is ignored, passion is known as a difficulty to be eliminated, and passion is overcome by a triumphant reason, unless reason prefers to be dashed by succumbing to passion. For Kant, the model has two steps: reason is situated above all obstacles, which it overcomes *a priori*. For Catholicism on the other hand, the case is not so clear-cut. To become aware of one's sins is insufficient though indispensable. One must also have the force to combat them, rather than yielding to them.

We have herein a contradictory vision of passions, one which oscillates between pure and affirmed innocence. Between knowing nothing and having nothing further to learn, some authors prefer to uphold a belief that passion is ignorance and knowledge, innocence and guilt, thereby mixing together the very terms of the contradiction into one gigantic paradox. Pascal would have said that to know one's passions is to be no more rid of them than is the fact of discovering in sickness a method of becoming cured. Descartes took the opposite tack, in which reason, conceived of as the passionate which is conscious of itself, is attributed the ability to if not fully eliminate the unmasked passion, at least to dominate it. It is difficult to decide between two conceptions of the passions; passion considered as natural, comprised of instincts and desires, and passion considered as intellectual, comprised of judgments and motives to believe and to act; it is as though the dual nature of passion prohibits all possible resolution that is not paradoxical.

A passion that we recognize as something that must be overcome cannot be ignored. What is the nature of passion if, even unmasked, it still mysteriously continues to act?

To this ambivalent language, let us substitute that of another rationality than the one which places itself in an unstable position with regard to the passion that impedes all reason, while all the while rendering it necessary.

Passion is the proof of our liberty, a problem known as such. It is the knowledge of an ignorance, which passion destroys or annuls; or else, passion confirms this knowledge by demanding resolution of the ignorance.

It is no longer a question of opposing passion and reason, like a strainer which makes of one the blind necessity of the other. Such a rationality, stemming from chance or revelation, makes no sense.

Reason without passion spells the destruction of the soul. Whether passion intoxicates us with comfortable certitudes or awakens us with problems demanding resolution rather than effacement, it brings us face-to-face with existential questions, like so many ways of resolving them and taking them on. The consensual passivity is one way of replying, while active problematization, which makes of us passionate beings, is another.

The articulation of existential problems is passion, and even rational response comes out of this inescapable passion, even if some try to suggest the contrary in order to make people believe that they represent the voice of disincarnated reason.

Human nature, at the end of the day, is the reply that we try to produce in reaction to History, as a means of repulsing it. This denial of History is a constant, which is itself historical. Human nature is in this sense a reality of each era and for each era, aimed at taking on History by condemning it to be repeated, for better or for worse.

Passion is the language of humanity in its variations and its identities, it is a way for humanity to face changes in it and modifications to it, while all the while making it exist.

We exist in response to History, and if this response is itself historical, the fact of looking for it seems to imply that we miss it, while at the same time instituting a transcendence and a liberty that no person should ever give up, beyond all those relativisms which jostle and sometimes sweep us up.

Select Bibliography

Aristotle. *Metaphysics*. Translated by Hippocrates G. Apostle. Bloomington: Indiana University Press, 1966.

———. *The Nicomachean Ethics*. Translated by Hippocrates G. Apostle. Boston: D. Reidel, 1975.

———. *On Rhetoric: A Theory of Civic Discourse*. Translated by George A. Kennedy. Oxford: Oxford University Press, 1991.

———. *On the Soul (De Anima)*. Translated by Hippocrates G. Apostle. Iowa: The Peripatetic Press, 1981.

Augustine, Saint. *The City of God*. Vols. 1 and 2. Translated by John Healey. New York: Aldine, 1973.

Barsky, Robert F. "Marc Angenot." Special issue of *SubStance: A Review of Theory and Criticism*, no. 92 (Fall 2000).

———. "Intellectuals on the Couch: The Sokal Hoax and Other *Impostures intellectuelles*." *SubStance: A Review of Theory and Criticism*, no. 90 (1999): 105–19.

Cicero. *De Finibus Bonorum et Malorum*. Translated by H. Rackham. London: William Heinemann, 1931.

———. *Tusculan Disputations*. Translated by C. D. Yonge. New York: Harper & Brothers, 1894.

Dearin, Ray D. *The New Rhetoric of Chaim Perelman: Statement and Response*. Lanham, Md.: University Press of America, 1989.

Descartes, René. *The Ethics and Selected Letters*. Translated by Samuel Shirley. Edited by Seymour Feldman. Indianapolis: Hackett Publishing, 1982.

———. *Philosophical Letters*. Translated and edited by Anthony Kenny. Oxford: Basil Blackwell, 1970.

———. *The Philosophical Works of Descartes*. Translated by Elizabeth S. Haldane and G. R. Ross. 2 vols. Cambridge: Cambridge University Press, 1912.

———. *The Principles of Philosophy*. Translated by Valentine Rodger Miller and Reese P. Miller. Dordrecht: D. Reidel, 1983.

Diderot, Denis. *Early Philosophical Works*. New York: Burt Franklin, 1972.

Frank, David. "The New Rhetoric, Judaism, and Post-Enlightenment Thought: The Cultural Origins of Perelmanian Philosophy." *Quarterly Journal of Speech* 83 (1997): 311–31.

Freud, Sigmund. *The Ego and the Id*. Translated by Joan Riviere. Edited by James Strachy. New York: Norton, 1962.

Golden, James L., and Joseph Pilotta, eds. *Practical Reasoning in Human Affairs: Studies in Honor of Chaim Perelman.* Dordrecht: D. Reidel, 1986.

Hegel, G.W. F. *Hegel's Lectures on the History of Philosophy.* Translated by E. S. Haldane. London: Routledge & Kegan Paul, 1955.

Hobbes, Thomas. *Leviathan.* Edited by C. P. Macpherson. Harmondsworth, U.K.: Penguin Books, 1985.

Hume, David. *A Treatise of Human Nature.* Oxford: Clarendon Press, 1896.

Kant, Immanuel. *Anthropology from a Pragmatic Point of View.* Translated by Mary J. Gregor. The Hague: Martin Nijhoff, 1974.

_____. *Critique of Judgment.* Translated by Werner S. Phular. Indianapolis: Hackett Publishing, 1987.

_____. *Foundations of the Metaphysics of Morals and What is Enlightenment?* Translated by Lewis White Beck. New York: Bobbs-Merrill, 1959.

_____. *The Metaphysics of Morals.* Translated by Mary Gregor. New York: Cambridge University Press, 1991.

"Le Questionnement." Special issue of *Revue internationale de Philosophie* 3, no.174 (1990).

Locke, John. *An Essay Concerning Human Understanding.* Oxford: Clarendon Press, 1924.

Long, Richard. "The Role of Audience in Chaim Perelman's New Rhetoric." *Journal of Advanced Composition* 6 (1983): 107–16.

Machiavelli, Niccolò. *The Prince.* Translated by George Bull. Harmondsworth, U.K.: Penguin Books, 1980.

Mandeville, Bernard. *The Fable of the Bees and Other Writings.* Abridged and edited with introduction and notes by E. J. Hundert. Indianapolis: Hackett Publishing, 1997.

Meyer, Michel. *From Logic to Rhetoric.* Amsterdam: John Benjamins, 1986.

_____. *Meaning and Reading: A Philosophical Essay on Language and Literature.* Amsterdam: John Benjamins, 1983.

_____. *Of Problematology: Philosophy, Science and Language.* Translated by David Jamison, with the collaboration of Alan Hart. Chicago: University of Chicago Press, 1995.

_____. *Rhetoric, Language, and Reason.* University Park: Pennsylvania State University Press, 1994.

_____, ed. *From Metaphysics to Rhetoric.* Dordrecht: Kluwer Academic, 1989.

_____, ed. *Questions and Questioning.* The Hague: Walter De Gruyter, 1988.

Nietzsche, Friedrich. *The Birth of Tragedy.* Translated by Francis Golffing. New York: Doubleday, 1956.

_____. *Beyond Good and Evil.* Translated by Marion Faber. New York: Oxford University Press, 1998.

_____. *The Gay Science, with a prelude in rhymes and an appendix of songs.* Translated by Walter Kaufmann. New York: Random House, 1974.

_____. *Twilight of the Idols.* Translated by Duncan Large. Oxford: Oxford University Press, 1998.

_____. *The Will to Power.* Translated by Walter Kaufmann and R. J. Hollingdale. Edited by Walter Kaufmann. New York: Vintage, 1967.

Pagels, Elaine. *Adam, Eve and the Serpent*. New York: Random House, 1988.

Perelman, Chaim, with L. Olbrechts-Tyteca. "Act and Person in Argumentation." *Ethics* 61 (July 1951): 251–69.

———. "The Dissociation of Ideas." In *The Realm of Rhetoric*. Notre Dame, Ind.: University of Notre Dame Press, 1982.

———. *Justice, Law and Argument: Essays on Moral and Legal Reasoning*. Dordrecht: D. Reidel, 1980.

———. *The New Rhetoric: A Treatise on Argumentation*. Translated by John Wilkinson and Purcell Weaver. Notre Dame, Ind.: University of Notre Dame Press, 1969.

———. *New Rhetoric and the Humanities: Essays on Rhetoric and Its Applications*. Translated by William Kluback. Dordrecht: Kluwer Academic, 1979.

———. "The New Rhetoric and the Rhetoricians: Remembrances and Comments." *Quarterly Journal of Speech* 70 (1984): 188–96.

———. *The Realm of Rhetoric*. Translated by William Kluback. Notre Dame, Ind.: University of Notre Dame Press, 1982.

———. "Techniques of Argumentation." *The Realm of Rhetoric*. Notre Dame, Ind.: University of Notre Dame Press, 1982.

Plato. *Phaedo*. Translated by R. S. Bluck. New York: Bobbs-Merrill, 1955.

———. *The Republic*. Translated by Robin Waterfield. New York: Oxford University Press, 1993.

Rochefoucauld, the duc de la. *The Maxims of the Duc de la Rochefoucauld*. Translated by Constantine Fitzgibbon. London: Millington, 1974.

Rousseau, Jean-Jacques. *A Discourse on Inequality*. Translated by Maurice Cranston. Harmondsworth, U.K.: Penguin Books, 1984.

———. *Emile; or, On Education*. Translated by Allan Bloom. New York: Basic Books, 1979.

———. *Discourse on Political Economy and The Social Contract*. Translated by Christopher Betts. Oxford: Oxford University Press, 1994.

———. *The Social Contract*. Translated by Christopher Betts. Oxford: Oxford University Press, 1994.

Seneca, Lucius Annaeus. *Works*. Translated by R. L'Estrange. London, 1679.

Spinoza, Benedictus de. *Ethics*. Translated by Andrew Boyle. London: J. M. Dents & Sons, 1989.

Thomas Aquinas, Saint. *Summa theologiae*. Translated by Eric D'Arcy. London: Blackfriars, 1963.

Tocqueville, Alexis de. *Democracy in America, The Henry Reeve Text*. Corrected and edited, and with introduction, notes, and bibliographies by Phillips Bradley. New York: Alfred A. Knopf, 1987.

About the Author and Translator

Michel Meyer is Professor of Philosophy at the Free University of Brussels and the University of Mons, the founder of the journal *Argumentation*, and the editor of the *Revue internationale de philosophie*. He is the author of many books, including *From Logic to Rhetoric*, *From Metaphysics to Rhetoric*, *Meaning and Reading*, *Of Problematology*, *Questions and Questioning*, and in the "Literature and Philosophy" series of the Penn State Press, *Rhetoric, Language and Reason* (1994).

Robert F. Barsky is Professor at l'Université du Québec à Montréal, and Associate Professor at the University of Western Ontario. He is the author of *Constructing a Productive Other: Discourse Theory and the Convention Refugee Hearings*, *Introduction à la théorie littéraire*, *Noam Chomsky: A Life of Dissent*, and *Arguing and Justifying: Assessing the Convention Refugees' Choice of Moment, Motive and Country of Origin*. He is working on an intellectual biography of Zellig Harris.

Index